W9-BNO-189

FAMOUS AMERICAN CRIMES AND TRIALS

**Recent Titles in
Crime, Media, and Popular Culture**

FAMOUS AMERICAN
CRIMES AND TRIALS

Volume 3: 1913–1959

Edited by Frankie Y. Bailey
and Steven Chermak

Praeger Perspectives

Crime, Media, and Popular Culture

Westport, Connecticut
London

Library of Congress Cataloging-in-Publication Data

Bailey, Frankie Y.
    Famous American crimes and trials / Frankie Y. Bailey and Steven Chermak.
      p. cm.—(Crime, media, and popular culture, ISSN 1549-196X)
    Includes bibliographical references and index.
    Contents: Vol. 1. 1607–1859—v. 2. 1860–1912—v. 3. 1913–1959—v. 4. 1960–1980—v. 5. 1981–2000.
      ISBN 0-275-98333-1 (set : alk. paper)—ISBN 0-275-98334-X (vol. 1 : alk. paper)—ISBN 0-275-98335-8 (vol. 2 : alk. paper)—ISBN 0-275-98336-6 (vol. 3 : alk. paper)—ISBN 0-275-98337-4 (vol. 4 : alk. paper)—ISBN 0-275-98338-2 (vol. 5 : alk. paper)
      1. Criminal justice, Administration of—United States—Case studies. 2. Criminal justice, Administration of—United States—History. I. Chermak, Steven M. II. Title. III. Series.
HV9950.B3 2004
364.973—dc22   2004050548

British Library Cataloguing in Publication Data is available.

Library of Congress Catalog Card Number: 2004050548
ISBN: 0-275-98333-1 (set)
      0-275-98334-X (vol. I)
      0-275-98335-8 (vol. II)
      0-275-98336-6 (vol. III)
      0-275-98337-4 (vol. IV)
      0-275-98338-2 (vol. V)
ISSN: 1549-196X

First published in 2004

Praeger Publishers, 88 Post Road West, Westport, CT 06881
An imprint of Greenwood Publishing Group, Inc.
www.praeger.com

Printed in the United States of America

The paper used in this book complies with the
Permanent Paper Standard issued by the National
Information Standards Organization (Z39.48-1984).

10 9 8 7 6 5 4 3 2 1

Contents

Set Foreword

Famous American Crimes and Trials covers over four centuries, from the colonial era to the end of the twentieth century, in five volumes. In each volume, we introduce the social and historical contexts in which the cases appearing in the volume occurred. We discuss the evolution of the criminal justice system and the legal issues that were dominant during that time period. We also provide an overview of the popular culture and mass media, examining in brief the nexus between news/entertainment and the criminal justice system. In each introduction, we also identify the common threads weaving through the cases in the volume.

Many of the cases featured in these five volumes provide examples of what Robert Hariman (1990) describes as "popular trials," or "trials that have provided the impetus and the forum for major public debates" (p. 1). As we note elsewhere, cases generally achieve celebrity status because they somehow encapsulate the tensions and the anxieties present in our society; or, at least, this has been the case until the recent past. In the last half-century, the increasing importance of television (and more recently the internet) in delivering the news to the public, and the voracious appetite of the media for news stories to feed the twenty-four-hour news cycle, has meant that stories—particularly crime stories—move quickly into, and sometimes as quickly out of, the public eye. So, as we address in volume 5, we now have a proliferation of crime stories that vie for the status of "famous." It remains to be seen whether these cases will have true "staying power" in the same sense as the cases that are still remembered today after many decades or centuries.

Oddly enough, some cases that were celebrated, though attracting a great deal of public attention when they occurred, have now disappeared from

American collective memory. Perhaps some of these cases for one reason or another only touched a public nerve at the time because they resonated with some passing interest or concern, or fit some media theme. Occasionally, such forgotten cases are rescued from the dustbins by a journalist, a true-crime writer, or a historian and undergo a new wave of public attention. That has happened with several of the cases that appear in these volumes. Perhaps the rediscovery of such cases reflects their relevance to current social issues; or perhaps these cases are interesting to modern readers because they are not only enthralling stories but because they occurred in the past and are now entertaining "period" pieces.

We think that the reader will agree that the cases included in these volumes are among the most important of each era. Since space was limited, many famous cases had to be excluded, but many of these have been covered in other books or media. The cases that are included cover each crime, the setting, and the participants; the actions taken by law enforcement and the criminal legal system; the actions of the media covering the case; the trial (if there was one); the final resolution of the case; the relevant social, political, and legal issues; and, finally, the significance of the case and its impact on legal and popular culture.

REFERENCE

Hariman, R. (1990). *Popular trials: Rhetoric, mass media, and the law*. Tuscaloosa, AL: University of Alabama Press.

Series Foreword

The pervasiveness of media in our lives and the salience of crime and criminal justice issues make it especially important to provide a home for scholars who are engaged in innovative and thoughtful research on important crime and mass media issues.

This series will focus on process issues (such as the social construction of crime and moral panics), presentation issues (such as images of victims, offenders, and criminal justice figures in news and popular culture), and effects (such as the influence of the media on criminal behavior and criminal justice administration).

With regard to this latter issue—effects of media/popular culture—as this foreword was being written the *Los Angeles Times* and other media outlets reported that two young half-brothers (ages 20 and 15) in Riverside, California, had confessed to strangling their mother and disposing of her body in a ravine. The story was attracting particular attention because the brothers told police they had gotten the idea of cutting off her head and hands to prevent identification from a recent episode of the award-winning HBO series, *The Sopranos*. As the *Los Angeles Times* noted, this again brought into the spotlight the debate about the influence of violent media such as *The Sopranos*, about New Jersey mobsters, on susceptible consumers.

In this series, scholars engaged in research on issues that examine the complex nature of our relationship with media. Peter Berger and Thomas Luckman coined the phrase the "social construction of reality" to describe the process by which we acquire knowledge about our environment. They and others have argued that reality is a mediated experience. We acquire what Emile Durkheim described as "social facts" through a several-prolonged process of personal experience, interaction with others, academic education, and, yes, the mass media. With regard to crime and the criminal justice system, many people acquire much of their information from the news and from entertainment media. The issue raised by the report above and other anecdotal stories of "copy cat" crime is how what we consume—read, watch, see, play, hear—affects us.

What we do know is that we experience this mediated reality as individuals. We are all not affected in the same way by our interactions with mass media. Each of us engages in interactions with mass media/popular culture that are shaped by factors such as social environment, interests, needs, and opportunities for exposure. We do not come to the experience of mass media/popular culture as blank slates waiting to be written upon or voids waiting to be filled. It is the pervasiveness of mass media/popular culture and the varied backgrounds (including differences in age, gender, race/ethnicity, religion, etc.) that we bring to our interactions with media that make this a particularly intriguing area of research.

Moreover, it is the role of mass media in creating the much discussed "global village" of the twenty-first century that is also fertile ground for research. We exist not only in our communities, our cities, and states, but in a world that spreads beyond national boundaries. Technology has made us a part of an ongoing global discourse about issues not only of criminal justice but of social justice. Technology takes us to events around the world "as they happen." It was technology that allowed Americans around the world to witness the collapse of the World Trade Center's Twin Towers on September 11, 2001. In the aftermath of this "crime against humanity," we have been witnesses to and participants in an ongoing discussion about the nature of terrorism and the appropriate response to such violence.

Frankie Y. Bailey and Steven Chermak
Series Editors

Acknowledgments

We would like to thank the contributors who worked so hard on the individual chapters. The contributors are a very diverse group, but they all share a passion for the cases they tackled. We appreciate their hard work and their willingness to quickly respond to our suggestions for revision. Many of the contributors have published frequently about a case, but they took the approach we requested in these chapters to offer fresh insights into their work. Other contributors had not written specifically about a case but answered our solicitation because they were curious about it. Our thanks to all of them for producing very insightful and entertaining accounts of the most important cases and trials that have occurred throughout the history of the United States.

The staff at Greenwood Publishing contributed significantly to bringing this project to publication. We are especially grateful to Suzanne Staszak-Silva, Senior Editor at Greenwood, for encouraging us to work on this five-volume set. We considered several different ways to approach the organization of the five volumes, and we appreciate her insights and suggestions for organizing the work by historical era. We were both skeptical about being able to cover so many different cases in such a short amount of time, but her energy was contagious and she was able to convince us of the great potential for such a large project. Mariah Krok was the Developmental Editor for the volumes, and we would like to thank her for being such an effective liaison between the contributors and us. We were able to avoid the many problems that can arise from a project with so many different contributors because of her ability to keep us organized. Thanks to Dan Harmon for tackling the very arduous task of tracking down illustrations and seeking permissions.

The staff at Capital City Press was terrific to work with: special thanks to Bridget Wiedl.

Steve's wife was incredibly supportive and interested in the work of this project. Alisha and I welcomed Mitchell into our family during this project. Thanks to him for deciding to sleep through the night on occasion—this is when most of the work got done.

Frankie Y. Bailey and Steven Chermak

Introduction

Frankie Y. Bailey and Steven Chermak

The technology for two important new mediums was in place by the end of the nineteenth century. In the twentieth century, movies and radio played key roles in changing American culture. These new mediums did not replace print media but instead allowed the adaptation of print to new forms. Thus, a Southern minister-turned-novelist, Thomas Dixon, could write a book about the Ku Klux Klan that became a stage play and have it adapted by filmmaker D. W. Griffith to become the first blockbuster movie, *Birth of a Nation* (1915). This story of the Civil War and Reconstruction in the South brought protests from a recently formed interracial civil rights group, the NAACP. But President Woodrow Wilson, the first southerner since the Civil War to sit in the White House, described the movie that had been screened for him and for members of the Supreme Court as "like writing history with lightning . . . my only regret is that it is all so terribly true" (Bullard, 1991, p. 19). In truth, in spite of its racial bigotry and stereotypes, the movie was a triumph of filmmaking and drew in audiences who were willing to pay a premium price to see the thrilling battle scenes and the climactic ride of the Ku Klux Klan to the rescue of the besieged white family. But as this blockbuster demonstrated, the new medium had the power not only to entertain, but also to produce and perpetuate distorted information about American culture in a form more vivid than any other medium before (Bailey and Green, 1999, pp. 87–89).

In fact, the impact of the movies on children and young adults was an immediate concern. Some Progressive era reformers were also concerned that the dark and not very clean rooms in which movies were screened also attracted men who preyed upon young women and engaged in other vices. But nickelodeons and later movie theaters were popular with urban working-class men and women seeking entertainment. This increasing patronage of the movies prompted local governments to form committees to view and censor the content of the films that were shown. In 1929, the Payne Foundation underwrote the first major study of the mass media's impact. This research reflected public concern about the effects of movies on juvenile behavior. By the late 1920s, the film industry believed that the only way to avoid federal censorship and to deal with the troublesome problem of local censorship was to self-regulate. The Motion Picture Production Code was created with input from a Catholic priest, to be overseen by Will Hays, a former postmaster general. The Hays Office assumed the role of industry watchdog as producers and directors submitted their films to the Office for a seal of approval. A list of "do's and don'ts" having to do with matters such as sex, violence, profanity, drug use, and race mixing appeared in the Production Code that filmmakers were now expected to observe. One important aspect of the Code for the stories that Hollywood now could tell was that "crime must not pay." A movie gangster could rise to the big time, but he must then pay for his crimes. Before the Production Code, the films about Prohibition gangsters had benefited from sound technology that captured the fast-paced dialogue, the screech of cars rounding curves, and the tat-tat-tat of gunfire. These films now had to be retooled to take the new restrictions into account. Increasingly, the "G-man," a government man in the form of a police officer or one of J. Edgar Hoover's federal agents, was featured as the protagonist (Bailey and Hale, 1998, p. 11; Surrette, 1998, pp. 30–33).

Radio, too, that other medium that was coming into its own in the early twentieth century, featured gang-busting cops both real and fictional in stories going out over the airwaves to listeners. Dick Tracy, the comic strip cop who had gotten his start in the newspapers, now could also be found on the airwaves.

MEDIA COVERAGE OF CRIMES AND TRIALS

Radio also became an important purveyor of the news. In fact, one "trial of the century," the Lindbergh child kidnapping case discussed by Kelly Wolf in chapter 9, was covered not only by newsreel cameras but also by radio commentators. Even earlier in the Scopes "monkey" trial, as Ernest L. Nickels reports in chapter 5, the judge observed that his words would be heard around the world. During World War II, the reports from Edward R.

Murrow in London and the speeches of President Franklin D. Roosevelt and British Prime Minister Winston Churchill cemented the importance of radio in reporting the news—until radio was upstaged in the 1950s by television.

Developments also occurred in print media. Newspapers moved from the "yellow journalism" at the turn of the century to "jazz journalism" during the Roaring Twenties. However, sensational reporting was balanced by the increasing restraint among newspapers that prided themselves on their professionalism. Other print mediums, books, and magazines provided outlets for both fiction and nonfiction writers. Magazines dedicated to crime reporting, such as *True Detective*, had their audience. Pulp fiction magazines and novels were also playing an important role in conveying popular-culture images of crime and crime fighters to readers. The traditional crime story created by Edgar Allan Poe in the 1840s and furthered refined, not to mention popularized, by Arthur Conan Doyle with Sherlock Holmes in the 1880s, had been serialized in newspapers and appeared in magazines. By the early twentieth century, the novels of writers such as Agatha Christie, Dorothy Sayers, and Ellery Queen had strong followings on both sides of the Atlantic. In the postwar period, the dominance of the classic detective writers was challenged by crime fiction writers featuring private detectives and other tough guys who walked the "mean streets of the city." Best known among these writers were authors such as Dashiell Hammett, Raymond Chandler, and James M. Cain. Cain would become famous for his novels *Double Indemnity* and *The Postman Always Rings Twice*, inspired by the 1927 real-life trial and execution of Ruth Snyder and Judd Gray for the murder of Snyder's husband.

By the early twentieth century, Americans lived increasingly in a "mass-mediated" culture, receiving both news and entertainment through media filters. Concern about the impact of Hollywood on the morality of ordinary Americans played a role in the 1921 trials of popular comedian "Fatty" Arbuckle for his alleged rape of a starlet that was said to have resulted in her serious injury and death. In chapter 3, Matthew Pate examines the social context of the trials and the media frenzy that it produced. Pate discusses the injustice suffered by Arbuckle and the destruction of his career.

On the other side of the country, the arrests of two immigrants charged with robbery and murder attracted even more media attention and created more controversy. In chapter 2, Lisa N. Sacco discusses the trials of Nicola Sacco and Bartolomeo Vanzetti, whose involvement in anarchist politics biased the public's response to them. This case occurred in post–World War I America during a period of heightened concern about subversives and anarchists. In fact, the "Red Scare" resulted in federal raids and arrests ordered by Attorney General Mitchell Palmer (Johnson, 1997, pp. 668–670). The executions of Sacco and Vanzetti left unanswered questions about their roles in the crimes they were said to have committed. The case became an international *cause célèbre*.

In a different way, the case of Nathan Leopold and Richard Loeb also attracted public attention and aroused strong feelings. In chapter 4, Diana Proper examines the legal issues raised by the "thrill killing" of twelve-year-old Bobby Franks by two young college men. All three were from upper-class Chicago families. The two men admitted their fascination with the Nietzschian concept of the intellectual "superman" who was above the law. The desire to commit the perfect murder was the motive behind their kidnapping and killing of Bobby Franks. It was up to famed defense attorney Clarence Darrow to convince the judge who presided over the case that Leopold and Loeb did not deserve to die.

Darrow also played a starring role in another famous case, the Scopes "monkey" trial in Tennessee in 1925. Here, as Ernest L. Nickels tells us in chapter 5, the stakes for the defendant were much lower than in the Leopold and Loeb case. In fact, the high school teacher who was on trial had allowed himself to be indicted for teaching evolution to provide a test case of the law. The idea had come from savvy town businesspeople who hoped the resulting attention would fuel the town's economy. Both the prosecutor, William Jennings Bryan, and the defense attorney, Clarence Darrow, were handpicked to try this high-profile case. In the end, the case yielded little in the way of law. However, what the case seemed to represent to those outside the region who heard and read about it was the backwardness of southerners who denied the scientific truth of evolution.

In fact, according to their critics, the backwardness of southerners and the problems with southern justice were on display during several high-profile cases in the early twentieth century. Prior to World War I, the Atlanta trial of Leo Frank attracted national media coverage. Leo Frank, a Jew from New York, had come to the city as the manager of a pencil factory. When a young girl named Mary Phagan was found dead in the factory, Leo Frank was charged with the crime. In chapter 1, Brendan J. Buttimer traces the saga of Leo Frank, including the anti-Semitism and political demagoguery that shaped the outcome.

As James R. Acker, Elizabeth K. Brown, and Christine M. Englebrecht discuss in chapter 8, the arrests of the nine African American youths who became known as "the Scottsboro Boys" for the alleged rapes of two white women also stirred fears of a lynch mob. However, the Scottsboro Boys were prosecuted in a series of trials that resulted in convictions and death sentences. The trials yielded a number of important Supreme Court decisions on appeal about the rights of defendants to adequate counsel and the unconstitutionality of deliberate exclusion of blacks from the juries.

In another controversial case of the early 1930s, Bruno Hauptmann, a German immigrant, was tried and convicted of the kidnap-murder of the infant son of famed navigator Colonel Charles Lindbergh. In this northern case, the media frenzy produced what has been described as a circus-like atmosphere during the trial. Controversy remains about whether Hauptmann received a fair trial, given the anti-immigrant feelings of the era and the biased reporting of the media. Kelly Wolf examines this case in chapter 9.

If the Federal Bureau of Investigation (FBI) came to play a more significant role in the investigation of kidnappings in the aftermath of the Lindbergh case, by the 1930s, the agency was already involved in the apprehension of midwestern gangsters. The Depression era gave rise to rural gangsters such as John Dillinger and Pretty Boy Floyd, who gained much of their fame from media coverage of their exploits and of the efforts of law enforcement—local, state, and federal—to bring them to justice. John Dillinger can still be seen in a famous photograph in which he posed with the female sheriff in whose jail he was being held. He later escaped from the jail and stole the sheriff's car (Bailey and Hale, 1998, p. 156). Such exploits added to the reputations of Dillinger and his comrades. However, even Dillinger was finally killed after being set up by a woman who became known as "the lady in red." Bonnie and Clyde, the subject of chapter 7 by Leana Bouffard, were actually fairly minor criminals who acquired their notoriety because they managed to often elude the police and because Bonnie Parker was fond of sending her poetry to the newspapers, who cooperated by publishing it. Bonnie Parker and Clyde Barrow gained lasting immortality with the 1967 movie *Bonnie and Clyde*, starring Faye Dunaway and Warren Beatty as an undoubtedly more charming and more attractive couple than the real outlaws.

Among the less-charming offenders to appear in these volumes are Albert Fish, the subject of Sean E. Anderson's chapter 6; and Raymond Fernandez and Martha Beck, the "Lonely Hearts Killers" discussed by Mark Gado in chapter 11. Both cases are about serial killers. In 1928, Fish was arrested for the kidnapping and murder of a little girl. The investigators discovered body parts and other gruesome items in his home. He was alleged to have cannibalized the bodies of his victims. He was known to have practiced various forms of self-torture, including sticking pins into his body. In this chapter, Anderson poses the question, one that became central to the trial: was Fish insane?

In the case of the Lonely Hearts Killers, greed seems to have motivated their crimes. As Gado discusses, Beck and Fernandez located their victims through personal ads, or "lonely hearts columns." Pretending to be brother and sister, although they were in fact lovers, they moved in with and eventually killed a number of women. Both Beck and Fernandez were eventually executed for their crimes. The media, however, were particularly unkind in their descriptions of the overweight and lovelorn Martha. How the media cover female defendants is a subject of current interest to criminologists who point to the stereotyping of female offenders so that even in such "killer pairs," the woman is presented as worse than the man, as more "evil."

In the case of Barbara Graham, presented by Sheila O'Hare in chapter 12, Graham's "party girl" lifestyle became an issue when she was placed on trial for participating in the robbery and murder of an elderly woman. As O'Hare discusses, in this case from the 1950s, Graham was portrayed in the media as a violent but glamorous woman. The media gave great attention to her stylish attire—even reporting on what she wore as she walked to the execution chamber. At the same time, as in all of the cases in these volumes, the time period in which the case occurred affected how Graham's alleged crimes were perceived. In the post–World War II era in which home and family were emphasized, and a home in the suburbs was the American dream, Graham by her flamboyance and her lack of "family values" challenged norms about appropriate female behavior.

In another high-profile case of the 1950s, Dr. Sam Sheppard was accused of the murder of his pregnant wife Marilyn. Of the many cases discussed in these volumes, this is one in which we can clearly see the impact of media bias on the criminal proceedings. In chapter 13, Kathy Warnes examines the anti-Sheppard campaign carried on by the local media. On appeal, the court ruled that pretrial publicity and prosecutorial conduct had made it impossible for Sheppard to receive a fair trial. After ten years, Sheppard was released from prison and later acquitted at a second trial. He did not fare well as a free man.

Hank Leyvas, the protagonist in the Sleepy Lagoon Murder case, also experienced prison as a trauma from which he never recovered. In chapter 10, Joe Walker looks at this case, in which the beating death of a young Mexican-American man led to a police round-up of Mexican American teenagers, including Hank Leyvas. This was followed by the largest mass trial in American history, with twenty-two defendants on trial. The time was 1942, and the place was Los Angeles. The arrests and the trials came in the wake of claims by the Los Angeles Police Department and the county sheriff that Mexican American gangs were creating a major crime problem. These gang members were identified as "zoot-suiters." In the second part of this chapter, Walker discusses the social and historical context that gave rise to the several days of riots in 1943, during which off-duty sailors attacked young men wearing "zoot suits." As Walker tells us, these riots threatened to become an international incident and a serious embarrassment to the United States government, which claimed to be fighting for democracy.

With regard to this fight, African American soldiers who were segregated during World War II as they had been during other American wars hoped that by proving themselves in combat, they would gain equal rights at home. African American leaders talked of the battle for democracy on two fronts: at home and abroad. A threatened march on Washington led President Roosevelt to issue an executive order banning segregation in the war industries and opening the way for full employment by African Americans. However, peace did not bring significant change in their status. It did, however, bring increased agitation for change by civil rights organizations, such as the NAACP. The lawyers of the NAACP mounted legal challenges to the segregated education system. In 1954, the Supreme Court reversed the decision it had handed down in *Plessy v. Ferguson* (1896), which had opened the way for segregation in public accommodations. In *Brown v. Board of Education*, the Court ruled that segregated public schools provided an inherently unequal education to African American children (Bailey and Green, 1999, pp. 133–136).

This decision generated outrage from white southerners who began to organize to resist any attempt by the federal government to enforce desegregation. It was the following year, in 1955, that Emmett Till, a fourteen-year-old boy from Chicago, was found dead in a river in Mississippi. He had been murdered. As Marcella Glodek Bush describes in chapter 14, the case produced a public firestorm. When Emmett Till's body was returned to his mother in Chicago, she insisted that the coffin be opened at the funeral so that the world could see what had been done to her son. The photograph of Emmett Till in his coffin in his suit and tie with his battered face became a famous one. Equally famous were the magazine photos and the coverage of the two men who were accused of taking Till from his uncle's house and murdering him. The acquittal of the two men—what would now be described as "jury nullification"—led to assertions by the northern press that this was another example of southern justice.

The Till case occurred as African Americans in the South were preparing to engage in a campaign of civil disobedience against segregation. In a few months, a seamstress named Rosa Parks refused to give up her seat on a bus in Montgomery, Alabama. This sparked a boycott of the bus system and force the bus company and the city government to integrate seating on the buses. This action in Montgomery sparked sit-ins, boycotts, and marches across the country.

By the 1960s, Americans were in the midst of an unprecedented era of civil rights agitation on a number of fronts—from African Americans, Chicanos, Native Americans, women, and migrant farm workers. Later in the decade, students and others would demonstrate against the war in Vietnam. This era of bold activism came in the aftermath of the chill cast in the 1950s by the Cold War espionage trials of Julius and Ethel Rosenberg and the hearings convened by Joseph McCarthy, the junior senator from Wisconsin, to identify members of the Communist Party (Johnson, 1997, pp. 833–837). As we discuss in the introduction to the next volume, this activism by Americans in the 1960s and 1970s would give rise to and be the context for a number of high-profile trials.

REFERENCES

Bailey, F. Y., and Green, A. P. (1999). *"Law never here": A social history of African-American responses to issues of crime and justice*. Westport, CT: Praeger.

Bailey, F. Y., and Hale, D. C. (1998). Popular culture, crime, and justice. In F. Y. Bailey and D. C. Hale (Eds.), *Popular culture, crime, and justice* (pp. 1–20). Belmont, CA: Wadsworth.

Bullard, S. (Ed.). (1991). Box office propaganda. In *The Ku Klux Klan: A history of racism and violence* (4th ed., p. 19). Montgomery, AL: The Southern Poverty Law Center.

Johnson, P. (1997). *A history of the American people*. New York: HarperCollins.

Surrette, R. (1998). *Media, crime, and criminal justice: Images and realities* (2nd ed.). Belmont, CA: Wadsworth.

1

Leo Frank and the Legacy of Southern Lawlessness: A Murder and a Lynching

Brendan J. Buttimer

On April 27, 1913, Atlantans reacted with shock and fury at the news of the discovery of a murdered child at the National Pencil Factory. A watchman found the strangled corpse of Mary Phagan, a thirteen-year-old employee of the factory. The guard, an African American man, had initially been questioned and then arrested, but the case quickly turned toward another, quite surprising, suspect. The manager of the factory, a northern Jewish man named Leo Frank, quickly emerged as a leading suspect. Atlanta's three major newspapers, the *Atlanta Journal*, *Atlanta Constitution*, and William Randolph Hearst's *Atlanta Georgian*—which were already engaged in a fierce struggle for market supremacy—capitalized on the Phagan murder to increase circulation. By the time the grand jury indicted Frank, a majority of the public had decided he was guilty, despite the fact that the prosecuting attorney had relatively little solid evidence.

Nonetheless, Frank stood trial and was ultimately convicted of Mary Phagan's murder. Mobs of curious and angry people gathered outside the courthouse for the duration of the month-long trial. As the jury deliberated, it could hear the crowd, and Frank's attorneys not only felt that this fact intimidated the jury, but they also feared what might happen if the jury acquitted the defendant. In an effort to defuse the potential confrontation,

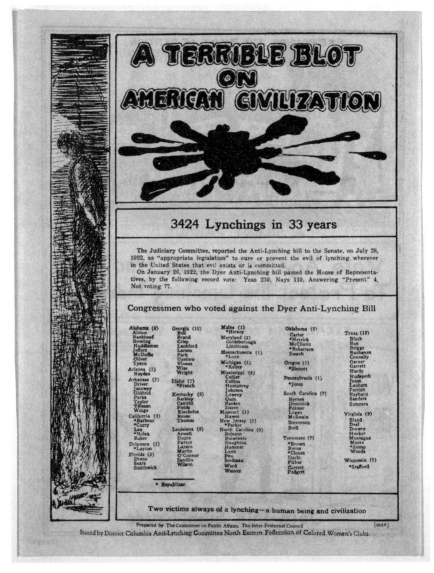

"A Terrible Blot on American Civilization." (Courtesy of Library of Congress)

Judge Leonard Roan, with all parties in agreement, ordered that Frank not be present when the jury announced the verdict. When they returned the conviction, the crowd outside could be heard celebrating.

Leo Frank faced execution for Mary Phagan's murder. Frank's attorneys, however, remained confident that the circus atmosphere of the trial, coupled with the lack of substantial evidence, would win the day for their

Broadside prepared by the Committee on Public Affairs of the inter-fraternal council linking voting to the anti-lynching movement. (Courtesy of Library of Congress)

client. Across the nation, Jewish leaders and gentile sympathizers sought to undo what was perceived as the lawlessness of the Georgia courts. The attempted intervention of "outsiders," particularly northern Jews, infuriated many Georgians who still lived in the long shadow of the Civil War and

Reconstruction. One such person was Thomas E. Watson of Thomson, Georgia.

One of Georgia's most mercurial figures, by 1914 Tom Watson had been a household name in the state, and indeed the nation, for nearly thirty years. At one time a Democratic congressman from the tenth district (east-central Georgia, including Augusta), Watson left the Democratic Party in the 1890s to spearhead the People's Party effort in Georgia. After his old party cheated him out of congressional elections in 1892 and 1894, Watson stood as the vice-presidential nominee for the People's Party in 1896, with William Jennings Bryan at the head of the ticket. In 1908, he served as the final presidential candidate of the virtually dead Populist Party. Then he turned his attention to publishing, launching a successful venture, including his widely distributed *Jeffersonian*.

From about 1908 until 1917, Watson spent much of his energy attacking the Catholic Church. Claiming that the Church sought to rule the United States, Watson unleashed a bitter series of outlandish articles in the *Jeffersonian* that attacked Catholic priests as unpatriotic perverts. In 1914, however, Watson turned his attention to the Frank trial, claiming that the efforts of Frank's friends represented a conspiracy that sought to deny Georgians, and the memory of Mary Phagan, justice. The eventual commutation of Frank's sentence to life in prison seemed to support Watson's claims, and in the face of an armed mob, the outgoing governor of Georgia fled the state after the commutation. Within two months, a well-organized vigilante group lynched Frank, ensuring "justice" had been done.

The murder of Leo Frank did not ease the tensions in Georgia, however. By the end of 1915, in an act that seemed to suggest Frank's lynching was but one step in a growing movement, several prominent Georgians came together to establish the second incarnation of the Ku Klux Klan. Over the next few years, acts of lawlessness—lynchings, beatings, and explicit anti-Semitism and anti-Catholicism—continued across Georgia and swept through the nation.

LEO FRANK AND ATLANTA

Leo Frank came to Atlanta with all the markings of an outsider. Raised in Brooklyn, New York, he received a fine education, eventually gaining a degree in mechanical engineering from Cornell University in 1906. He worked for a time in the North, but eventually ended up in Atlanta as manager and partner in the National Pencil Factory. In 1910, he married into a successful local Jewish family and became fairly prominent in Jewish social circles. Two years later he was elected president of the local B'Nai

B'rith. Thus, although an outsider, Frank quickly found root in the local community.

Atlanta, for its part, often played the role of welcoming hostess. Following the utter devastation of the city and the South in the Civil War, as well as the privation of Reconstruction, Atlanta sought to position itself in the emerging "New South" as its leading city. The term "New South," in fact, came from the Atlanta newspaperman Henry Grady, whose enthusiastic boosterism encouraged Atlanta and the South to reach out to the Northeast for capital and business partnerships. In this regard, men like Leo Frank were not uncommon in the capital of Georgia.

Even more common than the northern capitalist, however, was the poor southerner, both black and white, who came to Atlanta seeking opportunity in the growing industrial economy. The changing landscape of agriculture in the South caused many of these onetime farmers and sharecroppers to try their luck in the city. Consequently, the convergence of industry and rural upheaval swelled Atlanta's population in just a couple of decades to 175,000. The rapid increase in population created many difficulties for its residents.

The city was dirty, sanitation proved difficult to maintain and improve, and Atlantans suffered their share of illnesses as a result. The large number of people coming to Atlanta seeking work meant that there was no shortage of labor. Management exploited the opportunities that this factor presented. Factories could and did demand long hours, and in return employees received only a meager salary. Most factories continued to use child labor, despite the rising tide of public sentiment nationally against it. Conditions in the industrial sector were as bad as anywhere else in Atlanta, further complicating the health problems in the city. The combination of a rapidly growing populace, poor quality of life, and an exploitive labor system created an atmosphere conducive to the growth of vice—drinking and prostitution in particular—with violence and general lawlessness following closely. A city with an unsavory character, Atlanta proved to be a difficult place for working class people; working women especially fared poorly in such an environment.

The incident Atlantans and southerners remembered best in 1913 was the race riot of 1906. Spurred on by a race-baiting gubernatorial election, sensationalistic newspaper accounts, and rumors of black men attacking white women, a group estimated at 10,000 took to the streets of Atlanta intending to restore "order" to the city. For several days in September, parts of Atlanta resembled a war zone, with the police caught between armed black and white factions. When the police finally restored order, at least two dozen people were dead, mostly black, and Atlanta stood as a symbol of prejudice and violence. With the discovery of Mary Phagan's body in 1913, many felt a sense of foreboding.

Thirteen-year-old Mary Phagan was murdered on Saturday, April 26, 1913. A security guard, one Newt Lee, discovered her body early the following morning in the basement of the National Pencil Factory. She had been strangled: a piece of rope and a length of her underwear were around her neck when Lee discovered her. When Frank arrived on the scene, an elevator carried him down to where Lee found her, and when it reached the floor, it crushed human excrement. At the time, investigators ignored this significant clue. Rather, they noted the brutality of the crime. Phagan's body had been covered in dust and was so dirty that police could not tell her race initially. Two curious notes, apparently written by someone with minimal literacy, lay near the body. A relative of one of the police officers, who happened to work at the plant, identified her (Dinnerstein, 1987; Oney, 2003).

As manager of the factory, Leo Frank had been alerted to the situation and was one of the first men on the scene. He told police that he had seen Phagan the day before, as she had come for her pay. This particular Saturday, normally a work day, was Confederate Memorial Day, and thus there had been no one to corroborate Frank's claim that Phagan received her pay with no incident. As it turned out, Frank was the last person to admit seeing Phagan alive. The horror of the scene unnerved Frank. Given his role as superintendent of the plant, and the grisly nature of the murder, his reaction might have been quite normal, but investigators nonetheless found it suspicious. Acting in his business's interest, he contacted both a lawyer and the Pinkerton Detective Agency. While the incident might have upset Frank, initially he acted out of concern for his business, not his personal welfare.

The immediate investigation, conducted by both the police and the Pinkertons, focused on Lee. He had been arrested on April 27, but after three days of intense and, at times, abusive questioning, police could not get Lee to change his story. Although not released, he quickly faded from the spotlight as new evidence emerged. Investigators discovered hair and blood in a room near Frank's office, and allegedly a trail that led to the elevator, indicating that Phagan had been murdered and dragged to the elevator, before being deposited in the basement of the factory. This revelation, coupled with Frank's "suspicious" behavior and his admission that he had seen the victim the day of the murder, prompted police to arrest Frank on April 29.

Frank's arrest might well have come in response to a growing sense of unrest in Atlanta since news of the murder appeared. The three local papers, the *Atlanta Journal, Atlanta Constitution*, and *Atlanta Georgian*, each sought to capitalize on the sensational nature of the story. The *Georgian*, owned by William Randolph Hearst, had infused the local press with yellow journalism. When word surfaced of the murder of little Mary Phagan, Atlantans reacted with rage. Thousands turned out for her viewing and funeral. The papers fed the rage. The *Georgian* responded with a number of extras discussing her life and death. The other papers followed suit; in a business where circulation was king, each paper realized the importance of presenting "the truth" to its readers. In the first days of the investigation, both the *Journal* and the *Georgian* claimed that Newt Lee killed Phagan. They made these proclamations despite the fact that Lee had given the police no substantial evidence, and that six other suspects, including Leo Frank, had been arrested in connection with the case. By the end of the summer, all three papers pronounced a significant rise in circulation, and the *Georgian* could claim to be the top-selling paper in Atlanta.

With the memories of the 1906 race riot still in the minds of public officials, and the newspapers stoking the flames of hysteria, the police were told to keep their evidence and comments out of the press. The governor kept militia units on call in case they were needed to deal with unrest. Despite the arrests of Frank, Lee, and several others, the case seemed to stall, as no further evidence surfaced to sufficiently point out the killer. The *Constitution* collected a fund to bring in an outside investigator to determine who killed Mary Phagan. The police felt immense pressure to find the killer.

Shortly after Frank's arrest, he appeared before the coroner's jury. While Frank repeated his previous statements that he had made to the police as to his actions on the day of the murder, the state began to present witnesses who challenged Frank's character. One young man claimed that Phagan stated to him on the day of her murder that Frank had acted inappropriately toward her; a woman who ran a boardinghouse claimed Frank called her several times the day of the murder, trying to secure a room; a police officer claimed that he had caught Frank months earlier with a young woman (later, the officer admitted he was mistaken). With such circumstantial evidence mounting against Frank, the coroner's jury ordered him held further (Dinnerstein, 1987; Oney, 2003).

People across Atlanta and the state followed the case closely in the papers, thus making the stream of information coming from the press crucial to understanding the sense of frenzy developing in Atlanta. When word of Frank's alleged deviant nature reached the streets, the public quickly began to believe it knew who the guilty party was. Further, the fact that Frank had hired the Pinkerton Agency and a lawyer, in fact to protect the pencil factory, made people presume his guilt. Rapidly, and without any concrete evidence, Frank was quickly becoming the murderer of Mary Phagan.

Just after the coroner's jury's decision to hold Frank (and Lee) for further questioning, Atlanta Solicitor General Hugh Dorsey brought Frank's case before the grand jury. At the same time, the press released an affidavit from one of the other men, Jim Conley, held in connection to the murder. An African American of dubious character who worked at the factory, Conley admitted to having written one of the notes found near Phagan's body. Conley had been arrested after he was discovered with a bloody shirt. Despite the highly suspicious nature of Conley's actions, the police had little interest in him initially. The day the press published his admission of authoring one of the murder notes, the grand jury, unaware of Conley, indicted Leo Frank for Mary Phagan's murder.

THE TRIAL

Frank's trial began in the heat of summer, on July 28. Four months had passed since the discovery of Mary Phagan's corpse, and in that time the press had inflamed the passions of the community. The story remained front-page material throughout the summer, and the papers' scrutiny of the crime had all but convicted Frank in the court of public opinion. Although the dailies had at times cautioned that Frank's guilt remained far from evident, the inflammatory nature of the crime, coupled with Frank's racial background, his northern roots, and his position as a representative of the industrial sector, left him an easy target for a public eager for justice. Frank's actions, and those of his supporters in the days leading up to the trial, also damaged his cause.

The defense team consisted of two of Georgia's most prominent defense attorneys, Luther Z. Rosser and Reuben Arnold. Rosser had initially represented the National Pencil Company when police began their investigation, and then became Frank's personal attorney when the investigation focused on the plant manager. The presence of two eminent defense attorneys on Frank's side fostered a number of prejudices against the defendant. First, it reminded people of his relative wealth; whereas "common people" would have to settle for a court-appointed defense attorney, Frank had two of Georgia's best defenders on his side. Second, their presence at his side gave some people the impression that Frank had something to hide. One defense attorney might have been acceptable, but to hire two must have meant that Frank needed all the help he could get. Third, Rosser and Arnold's reputation as giants in the legal field created enormous expectations among observers. To some degree the two apparently believed much of their own hype, as they frequently conducted themselves in a rather arrogant and careless manner in the courtroom. Public opinion expected that, if Frank were actually innocent, these two men would smash the state's thin case. Thus, any points Dorsey and the state managed to score in the courtroom came across as momentous.

The trial provided Dorsey ample opportunity to score points. Conducted over four weeks in the heat of the Georgia summer, the fate of Leo Frank at times seemed almost secondary to intense personal clashes between Hugh Dorsey and the defense, and even Frank's mother. One of Dorsey's tactics was to portray Frank as a sexual deviant, although the state had made no such criminal charge. At one point during the trial, Dorsey and Arnold nearly came to blows and had to be separated. Frank's mother, having come from New York to support her son, denounced Dorsey in the press and subsequently faced the prosecutor's wrath on the witness stand. While there, Dorsey attempted to humiliate Rae Frank and got her to admit to living on a "modest" savings of $20,000, a sum that must have seemed like a king's ransom to many poor Atlantans. The explosiveness of the trial, the emotional nature of the testimony, and the confrontations between Dorsey and the defense further whetted the appetite of Georgians. Crowds packed the area around the courthouse.

During the month-long event, however, the one witness who most capti-vated observers of the case was Jim Conley. He had been kept out of the defense's reach for most of the pretrial period. Many, including Frank and his legal team, had expected the janitor to discredit himself once he took the witness stand. The prosecution had apparently coached Conley well, as he came off as a credible witness under the prosecution's examination. He stated that Frank had confessed to murdering Mary Phagan and demanded Conley's help in hiding the body. They allegedly took the body downstairs via the elevator. The manager then implored Conley to write the two notes found near the body. Further, he repeated the state's charge about Frank's perversion. He claimed he had stood guard for Frank on several other occasions while Frank entertained other female employees in his office. Conley's salacious account, although well-rehearsed to some ears, also kept the courtroom enthralled. The graphic nature of his tale caused Judge Roan to have women and children removed from the courtroom. Even the papers refused to print all of the janitor's testimony.

Rosser and Arnold spent three days cross-examining Jim Conley. They repeatedly hammered away at his story, and indeed they managed to demon-strate that the prosecution's star witness had exaggerated or lied about a number of key facts. While trying to discredit Conley, the defense team allowed him to assert repeatedly that Frank had female visitors to his office on a number of occasions, thus reiterating the prosecution's attacks on the defendant's character. While they managed to get Conley to amend his testimony on a number of issues, most significantly that he had defecated under the elevator the day of the murder, the main body of his account stood. Thus, the alleged two best defense attorneys in Georgia failed to discredit the prosecution's key witness, and also probably the witness most susceptible to cracking on the stand. Here their formidable reputations served to sink their client's case, for many began to believe—and the prosecution played to this point during their closing argument—that if Conley had indeed been lying, he would have broken under the cross-examination.

The defense team, however, must have felt that they sufficiently ruined Conley's testimony. They proceeded to bolster Frank's damaged moral character and did their best to present him as an upstanding citizen. They submitted a large number of character witnesses, both white and black, and tried to buoy the defense's case as best they could. When several girls from the pencil factory testified on behalf of their employer, the prosecution still repeatedly managed to remind the jury that Frank had allegedly engaged in sexual behavior with a number of other girls at the plant (and perhaps even one male employee). One defense witness, the daughter of a police officer, dealt the defense a serious blow when she turned on Frank, claiming to have witnessed him walking in on girls in the employee dressing room, catching at least one employee with her top removed.

At times, the defense's actions often took contradictory turns. It attempted to cast doubt upon Jim Conley's character, but for the most part the attorneys stayed clear of directly attacking the key parts of his testimony. In fact, the defense repeatedly stumbled when the opportunity presented itself to clear Frank or further discredit Conley. For instance, one employee of the factory testified that the elevator had not been run the day of the murder, yet the defense never paired that information with Conley's testimony about defecating beneath the elevator. Most significantly, the defense never called an insurance agent who purportedly spoke with Conley the day of the murder. This agent had previously claimed the janitor confessed to the crime. The attorneys claimed that they felt Conley's testimony had been injurious enough to the state's case and that the insurance agent's story would be unnecessary. They repeatedly overestimated the strength of their defense and underestimated the effectiveness of Dorsey's plea to "the common man" in the jury box and Atlanta at large. Despite their overconfidence, the defense nonetheless felt it necessary to have their client take the stand in the third week of the trial. In an increasingly explosive climate, with growing numbers turning up outside the courthouse, Leo Frank testified on his own behalf.

Frank's time on the witness stand revealed just how out of synch the defense was with the rest of the courtroom. On trial for murder, Frank spent most of his time dispassionately explaining his duties as manager of the plant. Where Conley came across as sensational, exciting, and ultimately credible, Frank exuded a chilliness that stuck with many who watched him on the stand. Only at the end of his testimony did he begin to exhibit some humanity and passion, and in fact in those few minutes when he did seem to rigorously defend himself, the audience seemed to respond favorably to him. The papers noted that several people wept at this point, but ultimately, what people seemed to remember was a perceived lack of passion. In other words, he struck many as a cold-blooded killer.

Frank's time on the stand all but concluded the third week of the trial. The intensity in the courtroom seemed to grow with each passing day. Spectators both within and outside the courthouse occasionally disrupted the proceedings, and both Judge Roan and the defense became increasingly aware of the hostility Frank generated. In the final days of the trial, Dorsey entered the courthouse to the cheers of the crowd that waited outside, most of whom had been denied admittance to the spectacle. Journalists from across Georgia and the region began to arrive to cover the growing story. As the Frank story grew, so too did the threat of violence. Once again the specter of the 1906 riot came to the forefront of the trial, and with good reason.

With the trial drawing to its conclusion after four long weeks, city leadership, including the newspapers, increasingly viewed the situation with dread. Hugh Dorsey appeared prepared to finish his closing statement on a Saturday, thus opening the possibility of a verdict on a hot Saturday, with a great number of Atlantans on the street with free time and possibly under the influence of alcohol. Dorsey, perhaps out of concern for the situation or in an act of showmanship, claimed he was exhausted and asked the judge for a recess until Monday morning, delaying the inevitable until a workday. Judge Roan complied, but the situation merely grew worse. By Monday, an estimated 5,000 people surrounded the courthouse, ready to cheer a guilty verdict.

Roan realized the predicament he faced. With the wrong verdict, the vocal crowd outside could spark a riot. To make matters worse, the jury room, located on the sixth floor of the courthouse, allowed the jury the opportunity to take note of the situation outside. Roan called both the defense and the prosecution into his office, and both sides agreed that Frank should not appear in the courtroom when the jury rendered its verdict. Although an infringement of their client's right, the defense nonetheless agreed that it was in all the parties' best interest, and Frank remained in detention when the verdict arrived.

Frank did not have to wait long for the jury's decision. It took only two ballots and a few hours before the jury returned a conviction that Monday. The crowd outside erupted into delirium when the news circulated. Dorsey received the adulation of the mob, and Atlantans spent the day celebrating the end of the most infamous trial in the city's and the state's history. The papers printed special editions that sold hundreds of thousands of copies. Frank's legal team, meanwhile, citing the mob atmosphere, immediately called for a mistrial, which Roan denied. Shortly thereafter, Frank was sentenced to die for the murder of Mary Phagan. Unfazed, his defense team began preparing an appeal they were certain they would win.

APPEALS, NATIONAL ATTENTION, AND THE EMERGENCE OF TOM WATSON

Leo Frank did not disappear from view despite his conviction and sentencing. While his story might have receded somewhat from the public's attention, his appeal lay ahead, and the papers kept track of his life in prison. His initial appeal, to be heard again before Judge Roan, would prove to be fairly sensational. Behind the scenes, however, other forces sought relief for Frank, and pushed what had been a prominent regional case into a national issue. When attention moved to the national stage, one prominent Georgian also sought to capitalize on the attention, setting the stage for chaos.

Frank and his lawyers quickly set out to establish their grounds for appeal. They hoped that a well-articulated argument, and the mitigating circumstances of the trial, most notably the influence of those assembled in and outside the courthouse, would win a new trial. Rosser and Arnold drew up a list of over 100 points that they claimed prevented their client from having a fair trial. Most serious of these charges was that two jurors had stated prior to the start of the trial that Frank was guilty. Confident in their appeal, Frank and his lawyers looked forward to their trial in October.

Meanwhile, some southern Jews very quietly began canvassing Jewish leaders in the North for assistance in the case. Proclaiming Frank "an American Dreyfus," southern Jews found little help.[1] Louis Marshall of the American Jewish Committee, an attorney of repute who had spent many years fighting anti-Semitism in the United States, echoed the sentiments of many other prominent northern Jews when he advised Frank's friends that the situation in Atlanta, while prejudicial, was also explosive. For northern Jews to interfere with the law in Georgia would undoubtedly cause Jews in the South further harm. The best course of action would be none, at least in an official capacity. However, Marshall and others in the North might try to bring pressure to bear quietly on Frank's behalf. A similar appeal to Alfred S. Ochs, a southern Jew best known as the man behind the *New York Times*, received little attention from his staff. Ochs, out of the country at the time, typically tried to keep the *Times* from becoming a mouthpiece for Jewish causes. Shortly before Frank's appeal, however, one northern paper, Hearst's *New York Sun*, presented a rather pointed account of Jewish efforts to save the convicted killer.

Frank's appeal before Roan went much like his trial. Dorsey fought diligently on every point, and tempers flared on both sides. The prosecution vehemently denied the charge of juror prejudice, and it enlisted the aid of the foreman and several others in trying to clear the jurors of the allegation. Rosser and Arnold asserted that the mob's presence outside the courthouse presented an unfair burden on the jury and the defense. Dorsey claimed that Frank's legal team assaulted the character of all Georgians with such a claim. Jim Conley's testimony, with its inflammatory attacks on Frank's character, repeatedly arose as a source of contention. By the time Roan rendered his decision, the tension in the courtroom had grown nearly as strong as it had in August. Just as had happened in August, Frank lost. The judge denied his appeal but stated for the record that he had serious reservations about Frank's guilt, leaving the defense optimistic that perhaps Georgia's Supreme Court might reverse the judge's decision and order a retrial.

Roan's doubts buoyed hopes in the Frank camp, but they had to act quickly. The appeal before the Supreme Court came in December, and again the defense made many of the same arguments as they had previously, focusing particularly on Conley's testimony, the presence of a hostile crowd, and then adding Judge Roan's concerns as a final factor making the case worthy of a new trial. The defense pointed out that it was not uncommon for the Supreme Court to issue demands for a new trial when the presiding judge expressed doubt. Despite these arguments, the Supreme Court issued a four to two ruling against Frank the following February, turning much of the argument back at Roan. The court argued that if Roan's doubt had been sufficient to merit a new case, then he, not the Supreme Court, should have overturned the verdict himself. Similarly, if the courtroom had been such a hostile environment, it was up to Judge Roan to deal with that issue then. Georgia's Supreme Court had washed its hands of the matter.

By February 1914, Leo Frank had suffered three major defeats in the court of law. Yet, he and his legal team remained both positive and active. The Supreme Court's handling of the Frank case invigorated northern Jews, who finally decided the time had come to take a stand on Frank's behalf. Alfred Ochs, having returned from Europe and now informed of the situation, devoted the power of the *Times* to Frank's defense. The *New York Times* ran daily articles on the Frank case for months in early 1914. Other papers, such as Hearst's *Georgian*, and eventually the *Atlanta Journal*, *Baltimore Sun*, and *Washington Post*, also sided with Frank. The defense, sometimes in conjunction with the *Times*, began revealing a number of witnesses who recanted their statements. Some claimed that the police had forced them to make false statements. Briefly, it appeared that Frank's team had a fighting chance. After a conviction and two failed appeals, the Frank case should have been closed, but instead it was growing in scope. The national attention of the press, however, embarrassed local officials and the public in Atlanta. What hope the defense might have had with the refutation of a number of incriminating statements quickly disappeared when the police contacted the people who claimed they wanted to recant. Reminded of the harsh penalty for perjury in a capital case, most of the witnesses decided to stick to their original stories.

Besides the emergence of Ochs's *Times* as a mouthpiece for Frank's exoneration, other northern Jews rose to help the cause. Louis Marshall began taking a more active role in Frank's legal defense, advising Rosser and Arnold of the best means to filing an extraordinary appeal. Furthermore, money raised on Frank's behalf helped procure the services of one of the nation's foremost private detectives, William J. Burns. Burns's presence, however, justified many of Marshall's earlier fears and revealed the sensitivity of natives to the meddling of outsiders. Despite making a number of brash statements about the identity of Mary Phagan's killer, Burns did little more than antagonize locals. He soon discovered how little the public appreciated his presence when a mob of several hundred threatened to lynch him in Phagan's hometown of Marietta. While many papers, including a fair number in Georgia, supported Frank's call for a new trial, the people of the Atlanta area had clearly shown that they were intolerant of interlopers and satisfied with the result of the trial.

The Frank case up to this point had already smacked of a circus atmosphere. The various court appearances; the on-again, off-again nature of some of the witnesses; and the general mob presence gave Georgia a much-deserved reputation for volatility and lawlessness. The situation worsened, however, when the state's loudest demagogue, Thomas E. Watson, involved himself in the Frank case. Several years earlier, Watson, a lawyer as well as publisher, defended a Jew in court, claiming at that time that it was impossible for a Jewish person to murder. Watson now used his *Jeffersonian* to attack Frank and those who supported him. Although critics point to Watson's virulent anti-Semitism as an incendiary that eventually let loose a maelstrom, Watson's entrance into the fray might well have come from less-sinister motives.

Tom Watson fancied himself, dating back to his days as a Populist, as a spokesman for "the people." In this role, he often tried to wield his influence to make or break people politically. At one time, he had a fairly close relationship with Hoke Smith, onetime head of the *Atlanta Journal*, former governor of Georgia, and in 1914 a U.S. senator. Smith had long earlier distanced himself from the *Journal*, although it was also well known that the *Journal* was still "his" paper. When the *Journal* began to call for a new trial for Leo Frank, Watson seized an opportunity to attack a political enemy. His initial commentaries in 1914 dealt with the *Journal*'s support for Frank but quickly degenerated into typical Watson demagoguery. The *Jeffersonian*'s circulation spiked accordingly. Watson attacked the outside interests interfering with Georgia's unique brand of justice. He denounced and repeatedly questioned the presence of William J. Burns, suggesting at the end of April 1914 that Burns be run out of Georgia. That was mere days before Burns's automobile broke down in Marietta, and he barely escaped Cobb County with his life. The famous detective's mishap northwest of Atlanta eerily portended events to come in 1915. Meanwhile, the defense team's plea for an appeal based on extraordinary motion failed. Increasingly, Frank's supporters realized that they would have to appeal to the U.S. Supreme Court if they had a chance of obtaining a new trial.

THE "MOB" ATTACKS

By the summer of 1914, the Frank case had taken a back seat to international events unfolding in Europe. Still, the advent of the Great War hardly diminished intense feelings toward Frank, nor dulled his defense team's appeal process. His counsel, now guided directly by Louis Marshall, prepared to appeal to the U.S. Supreme Court (his longtime legal team of Rosser and Arnold gave way to other lawyers in the same firm before the final appeal before the Georgia Supreme Court). They first approached Justice Joseph Lamar, who was responsible for Georgia, asking for a writ of error, based primarily on Frank's absence at the reading of the verdict. However, as the state court refused to grant one to Frank's team, Lamar also refused the request. This allowed the defense to approach the justice of their choice, and thus they sought a similar writ from Justice Oliver Wendell Holmes. He subsequently denied the writ, citing the decision of the Georgia court. Holmes expressed concern, however, that Frank might have been denied due process because of the presence of the mob outside the courthouse. Marshall prepared a writ of *habeas corpus*, asking the court to set aside the verdict in light of the hostile circumstances. In April 1915, the Supreme Court voted seven to two to deny the writ, with Justices Holmes and Charles Evans Hughes dissenting. Leo Frank's legal challenges expired.

Frank now faced doom. His best hope, at this point, was to appeal directly to the governor for clemency. Unfortunately, this approach also meant risking the wrath of "the people," something few politicians in Georgia wanted to do. Tom Watson still loomed, and he wasted no opportunity to score points (and sell his publications) by exploiting the situation. Such had been the case in the autumn of 1914 when Jim Conley's attorney, William Smith, declared publicly that his client had killed Mary Phagan. Smith asserted that the janitor, serving time for aiding Frank, could not be retried for the crime. He claimed he had come forward to help Frank, but Watson quickly denounced the attorney, claiming Frank's people had bribed him. Watson stood ready to assert the public's right to hang Leo Frank.

Smith's announcement, and the various attempts the defense made at the federal level, primed Frank's allies in Georgia to prepare to make an appeal to the governor. While the defense remained confident with each appeal, opportunities were running thin, and this final plan had to be prepared in the eventuality that all appeals failed. Jewish leaders across the country urged Christian political and moral leaders to plead with Governor John M. Slaton for clemency. Indeed, Slaton's office received thousands of requests on behalf of Frank, including thousands from local Georgians. Tom Watson, however, saw the situation in Atlanta and urged "ordinary" people to write Slaton demanding justice. Slaton, scheduled to leave office soon, realized the time was drawing near to make a tumultuous decision: spare Leo Frank's life, or let the death sentence stand.

The date of Frank's execution was set for June 22, 1915, four days prior to Slaton's exit from office. In his place, a man named Nathaniel Harris, a perceived pawn of Tom Watson's, was to take high office. Although Slaton had a professional relationship with Luther Rosser, and thus could claim a conflict of interest, the governor instead chose to consider Frank's plea. A man of conscience, Slaton presumed his position as outgoing governor afforded him the ability to deal with the situation with less political fallout than a new governor. He had no idea of the forces he was about to unleash.

The governor took the plea seriously. He pondered the letters of support for Frank, including a letter from the recently deceased Judge Roan. He then carefully considered the facts of the case. Slaton also went to the pencil factory to observe firsthand the layout of the crime scene. He spent the final days of his term agonizing over Leo Frank, and the state and nation watched intently. The press waited outside the Fulton County prison where Frank was detained, hoping to break the story should the governor decide to act.

Two days prior to Frank's execution, Governor Slaton issued a decree to commute Frank's sentence to life in prison. Mindful of the possibility of trouble, Slaton took precautions to protect the prisoner. The governor had Frank smuggled to the state prison in Milledgeville, more than 100 miles south of Atlanta. Once he was secured there, Slaton released a massive statement detailing his decision. He was personally convinced of Frank's innocence, but decided only to commute his sentence, believing that eventually Frank would be cleared entirely.

For the most part, the press hailed Slaton's courage. Most of the major Georgia papers agreed with the governor's commutation, although all feared the volatility of the situation. Neither Frank nor the state was yet safe.

Indeed, Slaton's act turned out to be even more courageous than anyone realized. Once word circulated of the governor's decision, mobs swarmed the capital, demanding "justice." Tom Watson, of course, added fuel to the fire when he proclaimed that Slaton had raped Georgia. He further contended, as many people who opposed Slaton's decision did, that Frank's men had bought the governor. But before Watson's *Jeffersonian* hit the streets, Atlanta already bore witness to mayhem. In the aftermath of the decision, the mobs that had descended on Atlanta refused to disperse, and for the next week groups of men armed with all manner of weaponry, including shotguns, cudgels, and even dynamite, roamed the streets. At various times these mobs marched on the governor's mansion, and if not for the declaration of martial law and the presence of the state militia protecting the governor, he might well have faced a lynch mob. Slaton, however, remained in Atlanta until June 26, when Nathaniel Harris took office. Once out of office, the former governor hastily fled Georgia for California, where he remained for several years.

Despite the days of anarchy, Frank actually remained safe in Milledgeville for the next few weeks. Local and national papers called for order in Georgia, and although a few troublemakers like Watson persisted in agitating bigotry, the situation seemed to calm down for a short time.

After one month in prison, however, the climate changed. A fellow inmate tried to murder the newcomer, severely wounding him. Frank recovered quickly and still hoped to eventually clear his name. His time, however, had grown very short.

About the time of the attack, Governor Harris learned that a group of men from Marietta and Atlanta sought to lynch Frank. Harris, who also took an active role in dealing with the attack in the prison, took countermeasures to discourage mob justice. A month later, however, on August 16, 1915, a very well-coordinated group of two dozen men succeeded in breaking Frank out of the facility, then drove him approximately 175 miles to Mary Phagan's hometown of Marietta. Very quickly, and without fanfare, the group lynched the beleaguered prisoner. They left Frank's body hanging and dispersed to spread the word around town. Shortly, a large group of locals came to observe the culmination of two years' worth of hatred and injustice.

This final act proved nearly as bizarre as the events that had preceded it. For the most part, those who turned out to view Frank's body did so calmly.

One of the members of the lynching operation, a prominent judge, arranged to have the undertaker remove the body to Atlanta. Once it was there, another crowd gathered and demanded to see the corpse. With a group of fifty police officers present, an orderly crowd estimated at 15,000 viewed the body of Leo Frank.

The papers, with few exceptions (the *Jeffersonian* being one of them), regarded the lynching with horror. The Atlanta papers decried the lawlessness, and national papers regarded Georgia as a state lacking order and honor. The resulting investigation into the lynching, to no one's surprise, failed to turn up anything. While many in Marietta knew who organized the raid, the town guarded the secret fairly closely for decades.

The audacity of Frank's lynching and the apparent lawlessness in Marietta were hardly the work of "the people." Indeed, it appears that most of the participants were among the area's elite. The group included a former governor, a number of prominent lawyers, a judge, a banker, and an official in the prison system. The investigation never yielded results because the county prosecutor was also involved in the lynching. These prominent men, those who later admitted their part, claimed they "merely" carried out Frank's sentence. They also seemed fearful that the mob violence the area witnessed, and the crowds who threatened William J. Burns and Governor Slaton, might resurface and do more damage. Although convoluted, the argument seemed to suggest that murdering Frank would prevent further violence (Dinnerstein, 1987; Oney, 2003).

JUSTICE DELAYED

If these prominent men thought they had carried out justice and prevented further violence, they were wrong. The lynching emboldened the lawless portions of Georgia. Tom Watson, denied the opportunity to continue his rant against Frank, returned to his campaign against Catholics. Although the federal government eventually shut down Watson's *Jeffersonian*, he ultimately had the last laugh, spending the last days of his life in Washington as one of Georgia's senators.[2] The impunity with which Frank's killers operated, Watson's ability to create such an inhospitable atmosphere in Georgia, and the obvious willingness of a number of Georgians to embrace lawlessness, contributed to the November 1915 rebirth of the Ku Klux Klan at Stone Mountain, a few miles east of Atlanta. For the next several years, Jews, Catholics, and African Americans in Georgia (and well beyond) faced the threat of Klan violence.

Leo Frank went to his death calmly proclaiming his innocence. While definitive proof has never surfaced that would have exonerated Frank, the State of Georgia did admit in the 1980s that Frank had been denied due process in the case. The pardon came because an aging former employee of the pencil factory, just fifteen years old at the time of Phagan's murder, admitted that he had seen Conley dragging Phagan's body through the factory. Conley threatened the teenager, and consequently the young man never came forward to clear his employer. That late revelation, coupled with all the other facts in the case, certainly makes the possibility of Frank's role in the crime negligible. Yet at the time, with the press in a frenzy, people quickly accepted Frank's guilt. When the trial ended in conviction, the locals felt that justice would be done, and when the local press raised doubts, the public resisted. When northern Jews and friends of Frank urged the national media to get involved, Georgians reacted defensively. Led by Ochs's *Times*, the national press hammered away at the miscarriage of justice, causing the people of Atlanta and the region to entrench their position, unwilling to listen to "outsiders."

The Leo Frank story continued to resurface in the years that followed. In 1937, Claude Rains played Hugh Dorsey in the movie *They Won't Forget*. A number of other versions of the story surfaced: a television movie (*The Murder of Mary Phagan*), a number of books, a novel (David Mamet's 1997 *The Old Religion*), and a musical (Alfred Uhry's 1998 *Parade*). Over the years, a list of Frank's executioners surfaced, but it was not until 2003, ninety years after Phagan's murder, that a comprehensive list appeared in Steve Oney's massive *And the Dead Shall Rise: The Murder of Mary Phagan and the Lynching of Leo Frank*. Frank's murder, and the complicity of men like Tom Watson, still remain a matter of fierce debate. In 2000, a Marietta rabbi asked the National Football League to investigate and censure a minority owner of the Atlanta Falcons, Tom Watson Brown, the great-grandson of the demagogue, for claiming that Frank's people had bribed Governor Slaton in order to gain the commutation. Brown mimicked the very sentiments of his namesake, and this confrontation showed that despite the passage of nearly a century, and the admission of the State of Georgia, Frank had been denied due process. The legacy of Leo Frank and the lawlessness of his killers remained a profoundly controversial subject.

NOTES

1. The French military court-martialed Captain Alfred Dreyfus on charges of treason in 1894, sentencing him to life imprisonment on Devil's Island. Dreyfus had been wrongly accused and prosecuted on forged evidence. Many of Dreyfus's supporters felt he had been singled out because he was a Jew. The French President, Emile Loubet, pardoned Dreyfus in 1899. In general, however, the "Dreyfus Affair" revealed the depth of anti-Semitic sentiment in France.

2. The federal government shut down Watson's *Jeffersonian* in 1917, claiming that his opposition to the Wilson administration and World War I violated the Espionage Act.

REFERENCES

Bartley, N. V. (1990). *The creation of modern Georgia*. Athens, GA: The University of Georgia Press.

Coleman, K. (Ed.). (1991). *A history of Georgia*. Athens, GA: The University of Georgia Press.

Daniel, P. (1986). *Standing at the crossroads: Southern life since 1900*. New York: Hill and Wang.

Dinnerstein, L. (1987). *The Leo Frank case*. Athens, GA: The University of Georgia Press.

Oney, S. (2003). *And the dead shall rise: The murder of Mary Phagan and the lynching of Leo Frank*. New York: Pantheon Books.

Woodward, C. V. (1967). *Tom Watson: Agrarian rebel*. New York: Macmillan.

Woodward, C. V. (1999). *Origins of the new South, 1877–1913*. Baton Rouge, LA: Louisiana State University Press.

2

The Sacco-Vanzetti Trial: Judging Anarchy

Lisa N. Sacco

On April 15, 1920, a paymaster and his guard were carrying payroll boxes from one building to another when they were shot dead by two men. The two murderers picked up the payroll boxes and fled the scene with a third man to a getaway car, where an additional two men were waiting for them. Five men were involved in this shocking crime, but ultimately only two men would be executed for it—Nicola Sacco and Bartolomeo Vanzetti. The incident took place in South Braintree, a small suburb south of Boston, Massachusetts, but the entire world would come to know the story of Sacco and Vanzetti. History would remember the case as a gross miscarriage of justice and a tragic example of prejudice and intolerance, and the state of Massachusetts would continue to make amends for this apparent injustice even seventy years after Sacco and Vanzetti were electrocuted under its authority.

THE POLITICAL CLIMATE OF THE EARLY 1920s

At the time the South Braintree murders took place, America was recovering from the aftermath of World War I, which had officially ended in 1918. Patriotism was strongly emphasized throughout the war period, and

The front page of Carlo Tresca's Italian language newspaper *Il Martello* (The Hammer) published in New York City four days after the execution of Nicola Sacco and Bartolomeo Vanzetti. (The Granger Collection, New York)

most of the world seemed to be in political turmoil as communist, fascist, socialist, and anarchist movements were spreading quickly, especially in Europe. The Russian Revolution of the Bolsheviks, a socialist party, occurred in 1917, and the subsequent civil war in Russia between the Bolsheviks and the anti-Bolsheviks did not end until 1920 (Karpovich, 1930). This political unrest did not go unnoticed by the United States, and President Woodrow Wilson, a leading pioneer for worldwide democracy, was keenly aware of what was transpiring in the rest of the world.

Wilson's resolve to create democracy throughout the world was not supported by all Americans and, importantly, not by all foreign immigrants who were entering the United States in record numbers at the time. Those who had views that were alternative to democracy were labeled radical, unpatriotic, and dangerous. This generated fear among the American public and in many cases resulted in the display of hatred and bigotry. The Sacco-Vanzetti case fell during a hostile period for those in America who did not believe in democracy. This period would later be termed the "Red Scare."

After World War I, the United States experienced an economic depression. Many workers joined unions, and as working conditions worsened with the poor economy, workers went on strike. Strikers were immediately labeled "Reds," and many were arrested and denied their civil liberties. These strikes were viewed as conspiracies against the government. The Bureau of Investigation (later the Federal Bureau of Investigation), under the direction of William J. Flynn, compiled over 200,000 files on radicals living in the United States. Thousands were arrested or deported, and on just one day, January 20, 1920,[1] 4,000 alleged radicals were arrested all over the United States. Many state and local governments, including Massachusetts, passed laws against radical activity (Burnett, 2000b). The Red Scare lost momentum by the summer of 1920, but Sacco and Vanzetti had been arrested in May of that year, and their case would forever be tainted by the fear and hatred that plagued the justice system during this time period.

THE ACCUSED

Nicola Sacco[2] was born in a small village in southern Italy; and Vanzetti, also from a remote village, was from the northern part of Italy. Both men came from large conservative Catholic families. While living in Italy, neither strayed from his family's traditional republican political views at a time when many of their fellow countrymen turned to radical politics and religion. Although one day Sacco and Vanzetti would both call themselves atheists and anarchists, they left Italy as traditional conservative men with no controversy surrounding their soon-to-be famous names (Avrich, 1991).

Sacco and Vanzetti both left Italy in 1908 but did not meet until 1917. Like many at that time, they were drawn to America by promises of freedom and opportunity. Sacco was the lesser educated but more excited of the two. He was later quoted while in prison as saying he was "crazy to come to this country," because it was a free country—"the country that was always in my dreams" (Sacco and Vanzetti, 1997, p. 10). This notion of freedom is ironically what attracted them to anarchism.

Italian anarchist groups had existed in the United States for nearly thirty years when Sacco and Vanzetti arrived in America. They adhered to a branch of anarchism that was the most radical of all, and they advocated for a violent retaliation against an oppressive government. The use of dynamite and assassination was an approved method of action for this group, justified by its belief that its actions were in response to an even more violent state (Avrich, 1991).

A well-known Italian anarchist, Luigi Galleani, was living in Lynn, Massachusetts, in the early 1900s, and was the publisher of an Italian anarchist newspaper called *Cronaca Sovversiva* (Subversive Chronicle). Galleani was the mentor of many anarchists in the area, and Sacco and Vanzetti were close followers of his ideals and principles. They not only subscribed to his periodical, but also contributed articles and aided in its distribution (Avrich, 1991). Galleani attracted attention from federal investigators when he wrote in a May 1917 issue about whether immigrants should register for the draft for World War I. In this piece he stated that anarchists who did not register would most likely not be sent into the military anyway because they would not be trusted. The Bureau of Investigation launched a serious investigation into Galleani, and this is how the government came to know of Sacco and Vanzetti, who were subscribers to the *Cronaca Sovversiva* (Young and Kaiser, 1985).

In 1917, during the height of the Red Scare, both Sacco and Vanzetti moved to Mexico along with several anarchist friends for a short time to escape the draft for World War I. Sacco had already begun a family with his wife, Rosina, whom he had married in 1912. They had a son, Dante, and Rosina later gave birth to a daughter, Ines, only months after Sacco's arrest. Vanzetti never married. When they left for Mexico, they both assumed different names. Vanzetti did not keep his pseudonym upon returning to the United States, but Sacco would forever be known as Nicola, rather than his true name, Ferdinando Sacco. After living in Mexico for several months, Sacco returned to his family in Stoughton, Massachusetts. Vanzetti moved around the United States and eventually settled in Plymouth, Massachusetts, where he became a fish peddler (Burnett, 2000a). During the three-year period preceding their arrest in 1920, many of their friends, who also subscribed to Galleani's periodical, were arrested and deported back to Italy. The clear message from the government was that radicalism would not be tolerated.

However, Sacco and Vanzetti held steadfastly to their radical beliefs until their deaths in 1927. From Dedham Prison they continued to write for anarchist newspapers and sent hundreds of anarchist-themed letters and pamphlets to those outside the prison. In one letter to Sarah Adams, Vanzetti wrote this of Sacco and himself:

Both Nick and I are anarchists—the radical of the radical—the black cats, the terrors of many, of all the bigots, exploitators, charlatans, and oppressors. Consequently, we are also the more slandered, misrepresented, misunderstood, and persecuted of all. After all we are socialists as the social-democrats, the socialists, the communists. . . . The difference . . . between us and all the other is that they are authoritarian while we are libertarian; they believe in a State or Government of their own; we believe in no State or Government. (Sacco and Vanzetti, 1997, pp. 274–275)

Further on in this letter, Vanzetti stated that he and Sacco did not believe in religion. He told Adams that he and Sacco could have stayed in Italy and grown rich off the poor but they chose freedom instead and denounced that other way of life. Many scholars feel that because they chose anarchism, they were targeted by the government and subsequently eliminated for a horrible crime that they may or may not have committed.

THE CRIME

The robbery and murders took place at the Slater and Morrill shoe factory in South Braintree, Massachusetts, at approximately 3 p.m. on April 15, 1920. Several people witnessed the crime, and these people later provided the crucial testimony that helped to convict Sacco and Vanzetti. The shoe factory had two buildings, and between the two buildings was a railway station. At around 9:30 in the morning, a train arrived at the station and an employee of the American Railway Express delivered money from the train to the factory. This money was intended for distribution to the Slater and Morrill workers. The railway employee later testified that he had seen two strangers in a car, and he claimed that this was the car the murderers used that day. Other people around town had seen the car in various places that day as well and were able to give general descriptions of the men in the car. The railway employee described one of the men as thin and blonde. Other witnesses gave this description, and later in court the prosecution claimed that this description fit Sacco. Just prior to the shooting, these same two men from the car were seen standing against a fence on the shoe factory grounds on Pearl Street. What people did not know was that these two men were waiting for a scheduled delivery of the factory's payroll that had just arrived on the morning train (Fraenkel, 1969).

The money had been separated into pay envelopes and was parted into two separate metal boxes, and these boxes were given to the shoe factory's paymaster, Frederick Parmenter, and his guard, Allesandro Berardelli, to bring to the other factory building. They left the building together with the two metal boxes filled with $15,776.51 in cash. As they approached the next factory building on Pearl Street, the two men who had been standing against the fence jumped from their positions and confronted Parmenter and Berardelli. Berardelli struggled with one of the men, who then shot him three times. This same armed man shot Parmenter twice. The other man picked up the cashboxes that had been dropped and waited for the getaway car as it was driven up the hill toward them. Berardelli, still struggling, tried to get up from the ground when a third man sprang from the car and shot him point blank in the chest. The first two robbers were already in the car, the third bandit joined them, and as they drove away they fired several more shots at the factory windows (Russell, 1971).

One witness, Jimmy Bostock, saw Berardelli and Parmenter fall to the ground from a distance and was even shot at when he tried to approach the scene. Witnesses inside the factory buildings had heard the shots even though the windows were closed, and some had peered through a slit in a jammed window to see the final part of the crime take place. As the car drove away, a barrier blocked its path before the train tracks because a train was nearing the station. After being threatened with a pistol by one of the men in the car, Mike Levangie raised the barrier to let them pass. Other witnesses were able to generally describe the bandits, but few could give specific details. The length of the incident was less than a minute from the time the first shots rang out to when the car disappeared from the scene (Russell, 1971).

There were more than fifty witnesses to the crime, and there were many differing accounts of what took place that afternoon as "the actuality faded and the myth took over" (Russell, 1971, p. 41). Many believe that none of the eyewitness accounts can be taken seriously, because there were so many different stories told to the police:

The car was black, it was green, it was shiny, it was mud-streaked. There were two cars. The men who did the shooting were dark, were pale, had blue suits, had brown suits, had gray suits, wore felt hats, wore caps, were bareheaded. Only one had a gun, both had guns. The third man had been behind the brick pile with a shotgun the whole time. Anywhere between eight and thirty shots had been fired. (Russell, 1971, p. 42)

The witnesses agreed upon some details. There had been five men inside the car, which they identified as a touring car, and the driver was fair-skinned. The two bandits who had initiated the shooting were short and clean-shaven. Three witnesses, including Bostock, identified the man who had been hanging outside the getaway car from a picture that police showed them, but as it turned out that man was in jail in western New York state at the time the crime took place (Russell, 1971). The case was primed to become one of the most controversial in history, because despite conflicting eyewitness accounts and lack of evidence, the Massachusetts authorities were, nonetheless, able to arrest, convict, and execute two men for this heinous crime.

EVENTS LEADING TO THEIR ARREST

Sacco and Vanzetti were well known by Massachusetts law enforcement officials by the time of their arrest in 1920 because they were Galleanistis.[3] Galleani had been deported in 1919, but he continued to publish the *Cronaca Sovversiva* from Italy with monetary support from Massachusetts anarchists (Young and Kaiser, 1985). All Galleanistis were under heavy scrutiny because of a series of bombings that had occurred in the Massachusetts area in 1919 and 1920. This group was suspected of having set off these bombs. Andrea Salsedo, a Galleanisti and close friend of Sacco and Vanzetti, had been arrested by federal authorities in March 1920 on suspicion that he was one of the men behind the explosions. Two months after his arrest and while being detained, Salsedo committed suicide[4] by throwing himself out of a window in New York. The newspapers reported his death and the news that Salsedo had supposedly given the names of all those involved in the bombings before leaping to his death. The *Boston Herald* headline read: "Salsedo Gave Names of All Terrorist Plotters Before Taking a Death Leap" (Avrich, 1991, p. 198). Many Galleanistis fled the country in the two months following his arrest. Sacco was planning to return to Italy but was arrested before he could do so.

In March, Sacco learned of the death of his mother in Italy. When that was coupled with the arrest and deportation of many friends, he decided it was time to move back to Italy with his family. He had made the necessary arrangements with the Italian consulate, quit his job at the 3-K Shoe Factory, and he and his family were to leave the weekend following his arrest. Many suspect that Sacco and Vanzetti believed their names had been given to the authorities by Salsedo before he died, and this is why they were "acting guilty" the night of their arrest. Many also believed that they were plotters of the 1919 and 1920 bombings in Massachusetts. Although police believed that Sacco and Vanzetti were involved in these bombings,[5] this belief is not why they were arrested on May 5, 1920.

On December 24, 1919, several months prior to the shoe factory murders, there had been an attempted robbery at the L. Q. White Shoe Factory in Bridgewater, Massachusetts. In this case, no one was injured, and the four men involved managed to escape but without the $30,000 payroll they were seeking (Avrich, 1991). Chief Michael Stewart of the Bridgewater police believed he knew two men who were guilty of both holdups: Feruccio Coacci, a Galleanisti and a shoe worker who had worked at both the L. Q. White and Slater and Morrill shoe factories; and Mario Buda, a man who was sharing a home with Coacci and his family.

Coacci had been arrested in 1918 and was marked for deportation, but was temporarily released on bond while awaiting a deportation date. He had received notice to report for deportation on April 15, 1920, the day of the South Braintree holdup and murders, but he failed to appear at the immigration station in East Boston. He had telephoned saying that his wife was ill, and as it turned out this alibi was false. When officers arrived at his house, they offered to allow him to postpone his deportation for an additional week, but Coacci refused and left the country on April 18. Stewart heard of this case and immediately suspected Coacci of having committed the South Braintree crime. Stewart also heard an informant's story that a group of Italian anarchists had committed the Bridgewater holdup and believed that both crimes were committed by the same men; Coacci was one of them (Avrich, 1991).

Coacci had already left the country, but Stewart searched his home and found Boda. Stewart questioned him and learned that Boda's car was being repaired at a local shop and that he owned a gun. That Boda owned a car and that he was an associate of Coacci placed him under suspicion (Fraenkel, 1969). Stewart suspected that Boda had hidden the Buick used in the South Braintree crimes in a shack behind the house before it was abandoned. When Stewart returned to question Boda again, he had already escaped through the back door. Stewart located Boda's car at the shop he had specified earlier and told the shop owner, Simon Johnson, to call him if someone came to retrieve Boda's car.

So it came to be that police in southeastern Massachusetts[6] were searching for the perpetrators of both holdups. Since Chief Stewart believed that the perpetrators were the same for both incidents and that they were Italian anarchists, police of the area were on the lookout for Italians who were acting suspiciously and who were looking for a car. Stewart's theory was supported by the Norfolk district attorney's office. However, the Massachusetts state police believed that the South Braintree holdup was the work of professionals. Nevertheless, on the evening of May 5, 1920, when Boda arrived at Johnson's repair shop with three other men—Sacco, Vanzetti, and Riccardo Orciani—to retrieve Boda's car, Johnson's wife called the police. Johnson did not greet them, and because they were unable to retrieve the car, they left. Sacco and Vanzetti boarded a streetcar while Orciani and Boda left separately. Shortly after, Sacco, Vanzetti, and Orciani were arrested by police in Brockton, Massachusetts. Boda was never caught by the police and escaped to Italy later that year (Avrich, 1991).

When they were arrested, Sacco had a loaded Colt automatic with twenty-three extra cartridges in his pocket and Vanzetti had a .38-caliber Harrington & Richardson revolver and shotgun shells in his pocket. Sacco was marked as one of the shooters in the South Braintree robbery, and Vanzetti was pegged as the "shotgun bandit"[7] from the Bridgewater attempted robbery (Avrich, 1991). They were brought to the police station for questioning but were not told why they were being held. Stewart asked Sacco and Vanzetti why they were out on the streets so late at night; they replied that they had been visiting a friend and were on their way home. They both denied knowing Boda or Coacci, and before the guns were found on them they had denied having guns. They were asked whether they were anarchists and whether they supported the government. Vanzetti simply replied that he was different and that he liked things different. When asked why he carried a gun, Vanzetti replied that he needed it for protection because he was in business.[8] Sacco denied being an anarchist and said he needed a gun because there were many bad men around (Russell, 1971). After this questioning, they were locked up at the Brockton police station. The next day Frederick Gunn Katzmann, the district attorney for Norfolk and Plymouth counties, questioned them again, and they repeated the same answers they had given to Chief Stewart. They were brought to Brockton police court, where they pled guilty to carrying concealed weapons, and the judge ordered that they be held without bail.[9]

Over the next several days, many witnesses were brought to Brockton to view the three men. They were not placed in a lineup but rather brought into a viewing room and told to position themselves in various ways. They were told to pretend that they were holding a gun and to crouch in firing position. One witness identified Orciani as one of the men in the South Braintree holdups and another identified him as a gunman in the Bridgewater holdup (Russell, 1971), but the police released him because he had a substantiated alibi for both dates. He had been at work on April 15 and on December 24 and could not have been involved in the crimes (Young and Kaiser, 1985). Sacco and Vanzetti were not so fortunate.

Most of the witnesses could not identify Sacco or Vanzetti as perpetrators in the South Braintree incident. Bostock, one of the witnesses who had been closest in distance to the crime, could not identify either man. One witness thought Sacco resembled the man he saw shoot the guard, Berardelli, and two other witnesses thought Sacco resembled a man they had seen in the getaway car. One witness identified Vanzetti as the driver of the getaway car, but the most common reply from the South Braintree witnesses was that they did not recognize either Sacco or Vanzetti. One of the three eyewitnesses from the Bridgewater holdup who came to the station believed Vanzetti was the man carrying the shotgun, although he had previously given a description different from that of Vanzetti. Of the other two witnesses, one was not sure that Vanzetti was the "shotgun bandit," and the other did not believe Vanzetti was the one he had seen (Russell, 1971). Vanzetti was first prosecuted for the Bridgewater holdup in Plymouth but would forever be known because of the trial held in Dedham a year later.

THE PLYMOUTH TRIAL

On June 11, 1920, Vanzetti was indicted for assault with intent to rob and assault with intent to murder for the attempted holdup in Bridgewater. The trial commenced in Plymouth on June 23 with Katzmann and Assistant District Attorney William Kane representing the Commonwealth of Massachusetts (Joughin and Morgan, 1948). Sacco and Vanzetti's comrades aided the two men by locating lawyers for them. Vanzetti's friends chose Judge John Vahey of the local district court, and Sacco's associates selected James Graham, who was known for getting along well with politicians and helping to exonerate Italians in trouble with the law (Russell, 1971). Both men defended Vanzetti in Plymouth. The presiding judge was Judge Webster Thayer, who had a reputation for disliking foreigners but nonetheless was considered a fair judge (Russell, 1971).

The prosecution built a case around the eyewitnesses to the crime, and they succeeded in discrediting Vanzetti's alibi. Several witnesses testified in court that they believed Vanzetti was involved in the attempted holdup. When Vanzetti was arrested, he was carrying shotgun shells in his pocket, and this was additional circumstantial evidence used against him, since there was a similar exploded shell found at the scene of the crime. Later, in the Dedham trial, Vanzetti stated that he had taken the shells from the Sacco home on May 5 so he could sell them to fund propaganda. In a separate room, the jury opened the shells that were used as evidence against Vanzetti, thereby violating his right to be tried on evidence in an open court. But Judge Thayer never declared the incident, and Vanzetti's lawyers discovered the violation only after the trial was over (Ehrmann, 1969).

The defense had twenty-one witnesses testify on Vanzetti's behalf. Most of these witnesses were Italian, and some of them required an interpreter. Vanzetti was a fish peddler in Plymouth, and the Italian witnesses testified in court that Vanzetti had sold them eels on December 24. The date is important, because in Italian Catholic tradition, eel is the essential part of the feast that is celebrated to end fasting on December 24, Christmas Eve.

The prosecution attacked these testimonies as substantial alibis for Vanzetti, asserting that they could not possibly remember specific times from so long ago. Other witnesses for Vanzetti testified that he never kept his mustache short and "cropped" as the prosecution witnesses had described the "shotgun bandit" (Joughin and Morgan, 1948).

Vanzetti did not testify on his own behalf, and he later harshly criticized his Plymouth lawyers for not having allowed him to do so. Some believe this influenced the jury in convicting Vanzetti. He was found guilty on July 1, 1920, and Judge Thayer sentenced him to twelve to fifteen years in prison. This trial did not receive much publicity. There was only brief mention of it in the newspapers, and very few people attended the trial itself. The case seemed inconsequential to the public, but it was a significant strike against Vanzetti in his upcoming trial with Sacco. In 1927, the year of the executions, Governor Alvan Fuller was presented with new evidence that substantiated Vanzetti's alibi for December 24. A record of an eel delivery for Vanzetti surfaced from an old box of American Express delivery receipts, thus proving that Vanzetti was selling eels that day as witnesses had testified. Fuller did not exonerate Vanzetti, however. He said it was possible that Vanzetti could have sold eels in Plymouth and committed the crime in Bridgewater that same morning, since Bridgewater and Plymouth were only twenty miles apart (Ehrmann, 1969). Vanzetti's lawyers thought the governor's theory was ludicrous. Many people believe that Vanzetti was wrongly convicted of both crimes and that the only conclusion that can be drawn today is that both trials proceeded in a biased and prejudicial manner.

THE TRIAL IN DEDHAM

Sacco and Vanzetti were indicted for the South Braintree murders on September 14, 1920. Their trial began on May 21, 1921, at the Norfolk County Courthouse in Dedham, Massachusetts. The presiding judge was once again Webster Thayer. Defense counsel had changed since Sacco and Vanzetti were arrested. The lawyers representing Sacco were Fred H. Moore and William J. Callahan. Moore was from California and was well known for his defense of radicals and workers. Callahan had represented Sacco at a preliminary hearing in Quincy. Jeremiah and Thomas McAnarney, two brothers and well-known lawyers from Norfolk County, represented Vanzetti. Prosecuting for the Commonwealth again was District Attorney Frederick Gunn Katzmann.

The prosecution went forward with Chief Stewart's theory that the same group of men committed the crimes in both Bridgewater and South Braintree. Holes in the theory were ignored, and this is partly why the case became extremely controversial. The money taken from the Slater and Morrill shoe factory was never recovered. Stewart assumed that Coacci had taken it back to Italy with him, but it was learned that the Italian police had stopped Coacci upon his return to Italy, searched his belongings, and found nothing. Sacco was able to prove that he had been at work on December 24 and therefore could not have been involved in the Bridgewater crime. However, records showed that he was not at work on April 15, which bolstered the prosecution's argument that he was in South Braintree that day committing robbery and murder with four other men (Avrich, 1991).

This theory was not supported by all officials involved in the case. The state police never backed down from their theory that professionals had committed the South Braintree crime. Nevertheless, the prosecution continued with Stewart's theory and brought evidence before the court against Sacco and Vanzetti. The jurors were brought to the scene of the crime, and on the sixth day of the trial they began to hear evidence against the defendants. The state presented sixteen witnesses to identify Sacco. Three of the witnesses placed him at the shoe factory before the crime took place. Of these three witnesses, the defense, upon cross-examination, discovered that one of them had previously failed to identify Sacco's photograph. Another witness put it this way: "While I wouldn't be positive, I would say that to the best of my recollection, that was the man" (W. S. Tracy as quoted in Joughin and Morgan, 1948). The third witness was "pretty sure" that Sacco was the man he saw. Of those who witnessed the shooting, none could positively say that Sacco was the man they saw. Bostock was unable to identify either man at the police station or at the trial. Lewis Wade, who had positively identified Sacco at the police station, expressed his doubts at the trial. Most of the witnesses could only generally describe the men they saw. Some called them short, stout, or dark-skinned, and some said that two of the men were wearing dark hats (Joughin and Morgan, 1948).

A cap found near Berardelli's body was used as additional evidence against Sacco. Sacco's employer and friend George Kelley was asked in court if the cap was Sacco's. He could not say either way. Kelley knew that Sacco's cap was dark and that he hung it on a nail at work every day (Russell, 1971). The cap that had been admitted into evidence was torn in the back, and Judge Thayer concluded that this was a result of Sacco hanging it on a nail. However, it was later learned after the trial's conclusion that a police officer had torn the hat while searching for an identifying mark. When Sacco tried the cap on in court, it appeared to be too small, and this aspect of the case was made famous by cartoonists from the *Boston Post* and the *Boston Herald* (Ehrmann, 1969). Some newspapers mocked the lack of evidence against Sacco and Vanzetti, and cartoons were a popular way to do so.

A bullet found in Berardelli's body was further evidence provided by the prosecution to prove Sacco's guilt. Captain William H. Proctor of the state police was unsure but said it was possible that the fatal shot could have originated from a gun such as the one Sacco carried (Joughin and Morgan, 1948). The defense presented expert witnesses who claimed that the fatal bullet found in Berardelli could not have been fired from Sacco's gun. The ballistics evidence became one of the most controversial issues surrounding the Sacco and Vanzetti case.

The final evidence used against Sacco and Vanzetti involved their actions on the night of their arrest. Evidence of lies and apparent guilty manner on that night was presented to the jury. Katzmann and Chief Stewart had questioned them and were witness to their deliberate deceit. Later, author Paul Avrich argued that this elusive behavior was logical, considering that Sacco and Vanzetti most likely believed that they were being arrested for anarchy. Only two days before their arrest, they learned that Andrea Salsedo had given up the names of his anarchist comrades who were part of the 1919 and 1920 bomb plots in Massachusetts. Fear that their names had been given to officials may have caused them to lie about their political beliefs and their weapons (Avrich, 1991).

Overall, there was less evidence presented against Vanzetti. The prosecution connected Vanzetti to the crime by stressing his association with Sacco, presenting eyewitnesses who believed that one of the men in the car looked like Vanzetti, and claiming that the gun found on Vanzetti the night of his arrest had originally belonged to Berardelli. Those witnesses who identified Vanzetti were unable to describe anyone else with Vanzetti. The testimony of one of the witnesses, Mike Levangie, was impeached because he had previously given different testimony. He had claimed in court that Vanzetti was the driver of the getaway car, but had previously said that he was a passenger. The prosecution then admitted that Vanzetti was not driving the car but perhaps Levangie was confused as to Vanzetti's location in the car. The eyewitness testimony against Vanzetti was not strong (Joughin and Morgan, 1948).

The defense and prosecution presented conflicting testimony as to whether Berardelli had been armed at the time of the robbery. It was known that he had left his gun at a shop a few weeks prior to the incident so that the broken hammer could be replaced. Testimony was given that Berardelli's gun was similar to Vanzetti's gun, which had been presented as evidence. Vanzetti was, however, able to show when and where he had purchased his gun, and expert testimony showed that Vanzetti's gun did not have a new hammer (Joughin and Morgan, 1948). The final evidence presented against Vanzetti was his display of guilt on the night of his arrest.

Vanzetti's alibi was deemed "overwhelming" by Felix Frankfurter, a lawyer and future Supreme Court justice who had been following and assisting with the case. Thirty-one eyewitnesses testified in court that Vanzetti was not one of the men they saw in the getaway car. There were thirteen witnesses who testified that they had seen Vanzetti selling fish in Plymouth on the day in question (Frankfurter, 1954). Sacco claimed to have been in Boston. Several witnesses supported this claim and remembered the day because it was the day of an Italian feast in the predominantly Italian north end of Boston. Sacco had met with an Italian consulate to discuss the paperwork necessary for his upcoming return trip to Italy with his family. The consulate also testified on Sacco's behalf. Katzmann, as he had done with previous defense witnesses, asked the alibi witnesses to recall other events and people from that day and they could not (Ehrmann, 1969). The trial, which lasted nearly seven weeks, did not go well for Sacco and Vanzetti. On July 21, 1921, they were convicted of murder in the first degree.

THE APPEALS PROCESS AND THE WORLD'S REACTION

Two men who came to America to realize a dream unintentionally divided a nation and mobilized the world around them. While many spoke out against Sacco and Vanzetti, millions rallied to their side. After their conviction in 1921, most of the country still had not heard of Sacco and Vanzetti. The *New York Times* only briefly mentioned the conviction in a small piece several pages into the newspaper (Trasciatti, 2003). It was only after six years of appeals and extraordinary defense strategy that international fame came upon these two men. Their plight attracted widespread media attention and their names appeared in headlines all over the world. But newspapers were not the only venue through which their story was told. One of the chief defense attorneys to serve for Sacco and Vanzetti, Fred H. Moore, transformed the traditional means of defending murder suspects by not solely disputing the facts surrounding the crime. Moore heavily politicized the case by openly discussing Sacco and Vanzetti's anarchist beliefs in court, and he tried to establish that his clients were prosecuted solely because of their radical beliefs. The prosecution, of course, denied these accusations, but Moore went further and claimed that this was all part of a government plan to halt the anarchist movement in the United States (D'Attilio, 1999).

Moore's efforts involved contacting unions around the world, distributing many thousands of defense pamphlets throughout several countries, and organizing public meetings. Moore also managed to gain the aid of the

Italian government despite the defendants' anarchist background. Italian dictator Benito Mussolini had taken office in 1922 and was well known for his repression of anarchists in Italy. Surprisingly, he was more than eager to defend Sacco and Vanzetti. He recognized the importance of Sacco and Vanzetti's case and witnessed the insurrections among the Italian people after they had read about the fate of their comrades in the Italian newspapers (Cannistraro, 1996).

Moore had sent a young liberal journalist, Eugene Lyons, to Italy hoping to stir up emotions in favor of Sacco and Vanzetti. Lyons helped set up organizations to gather support and sent countless numbers of articles to leftist newspapers in Italy. The Sacco-Vanzetti Defense Committee, which had been formed in Boston shortly after their arrest, coordinated efforts with those of Lyons in Italy and sent letters and leaflets to Italy declaring that Sacco and Vanzetti had been arrested as a result of their political beliefs. Lyons was later expelled by Mussolini after anarchists, in an unrelated matter, detonated a bomb that killed twenty-one people. The Italian protests nevertheless continued, as did the Italian government's support for Sacco and Vanzetti, even after their executions in 1927 (Cannistraro, 1996).

The Italian government's involvement did not please many anarchist comrades, but it became very apparent that the cause was backed by more than just radical left-wing groups such as socialists and anarchists. Moore's tactics had transformed a small-town case into an international affair, gathering support from every corner of the world. This outreach did not come without costs, however, and Moore's unprecedented methods of defending this case eventually led to his dismissal:

His manner of utilizing mass media was quite modern and effective, but it required enormous sums of money, which he spent too freely in the eyes of many of the anarchist comrades of Sacco and Vanzetti, who had to raise most of it painstakingly from working people, twenty-five and fifty cents at a time. Moore's efforts came to be questioned even by the two defendants, when he, contrary to anarchist ideals, offered a large reward to find the real criminals. (D'Attilio, 1999, p. 11)

By the time of his dismissal, however, his goal had been accomplished, and Sacco and Vanzetti were international celebrities.

William Thompson and Herbert Ehrmann succeeded Moore and continued the attempts to receive a new trial. During the six years after the conviction, many new issues came to light and were raised in appeals. These issues further enraged the public and reinforced the notion that these men had not received a fair trial. Judge Thayer was undoubtedly a prejudiced man, although he did not reveal this prejudice in court records. Before the trial commenced, Thayer, while in the company of several newspaper reporters, learned of the leaflets being distributed in support of Sacco and Vanzetti. In his anger over this public support, he declared before several witnesses, "You wait till I give my charge to the jury. I'll show 'em!" (as cited in Ehrmann, 1969, p. 462). The foreman of the jury, Walter Ripley, had spoken candidly with a friend who had expressed his belief in their innocence, and to this Ripley replied, "Damn them, they ought to hang anyway!" (as cited in Feuerlicht, 1977, p. 202). While Governor Fuller was considering the clemency appeal, he received a letter from a conservative Dartmouth professor, James Richardson, who had spoken with Thayer after the trial ended. Richardson revealed Thayer's comment: "Did you see what I did to those anarchistic bastards the other day? . . . They wouldn't get very far in my court" (as cited in Feuerlicht, 1977, p. 349).

The most intriguing new evidence that was brought before Judge Thayer, and later before an advisory committee, was the confession of a prisoner by the name of Celestino Madeiros. In 1925, while in Dedham Jail with Sacco, he confessed in a note to Sacco that he had taken part in the South Braintree robbery and murders with the four other members of the Morelli Gang. The Morelli Gang was a well-known professional group of robbers from the area. It is important to note that the state police believed that the crime had been committed by professionals. This gang was known for stealing shoes and textiles from freight trains, and many of these crimes had occurred in South Braintree. They spoke English without accents because they were American-born Italians. Some of the witnesses had testified in court that the bandits had spoken perfect English without a trace of an Italian accent. Both Sacco and Vanzetti spoke broken English. Joseph Morelli, the leader of the gang, bore a striking facial resemblance to Sacco. All of the gang members were out of jail at the time of the crime, and two of them had just been released a few weeks before April 15, 1920 (Ehrmann, 1969).

Thompson and Ehrmann spent a great deal of time interviewing Madeiros. One startling discovery they made was that Madeiros's account of the incident differed from the trial account in that he spoke of two separate getaway cars. He claimed they switched cars after the robbery, but the trial record shows that there was only one car. It was discovered a few months later that Madeiros was correct in his version of what happened, and the trial record was wrong (Ehrmann, 1969). Finally, Thompson and Ehrmann learned that Madeiros had $2,800 after he was released from jail in 1921. This was just under one fifth of the money stolen from the shoe factory. In Thompson and Ehrmann's view, the case seemed very strong against the Morelli Gang. They presented this evidence on appeal for a new trial, but Thayer denied the motion (Ehrmann, 1969).

Six appeals for a new trial were made to Thayer, and he denied all of them. This system in which the trial judge ruled on appeals seemed absurd to many people at the time. Judge Thayer ruled on accusations of prejudice made against him. It was because of the Sacco-Vanzetti case that the appeals system was changed following their executions. However, on April 5, 1927, the Supreme Judicial Court of Massachusetts overruled all objections to Thayer's denials. On April 9, Thayer condemned Sacco and Vanzetti to death by electrocution.

An application for clemency was filed with Governor Alvan Fuller on May 4, 1927. In response to this and growing social pressure, Fuller appointed an advisory committee to review the case. The committee consisted of Abbott Lawrence Lowell, the president of Harvard University; Robert Grant, a former judge; and Samuel Stratton, president of the Massachusetts Institute of Technology. This committee became known as the Lowell Committee. Ehrmann and Thompson were dismayed at the Lowell Committee's reaction to evidence of prejudice by Judge Thayer. The committee condemned Thayer's prejudicial conduct, calling it a "grave breech of official decorum" (Lowell as quoted in Ehrmann, 1969, p. 501). However, they did not judge that it justified an order for a new trial. The Lowell Committee dismissed all issues raised before them, and they advised Governor Fuller that Sacco and Vanzetti were guilty. Upon this advice, Fuller denied the appeal for clemency.

After the Lowell report was made public, many newspapers, including the *New York Times*, applauded the decision, while many writers did not agree. Heywood Broun, a reporter for the *New York World*, referred to Harvard University as "Hangman's House" in criticism of its president and added, "What more can these immigrants from Italy expect? It is not every prisoner who has the president of Harvard University throw on the switch for him" (as quoted in Feuerlicht, 1977, p. 381).

THE EXECUTIONS

Many last-minute attempts were made to save Sacco and Vanzetti. An appeal made to the Supreme Judicial Court of Massachusetts was denied, and August 1927 became a tense month for most of the world. Newspapers reported their surprise at the growing international concern for the two anarchists. The Sacco-Vanzetti Defense Committee made a plea to liberals and intellectuals for support. Dorothy Parker, Jane Addams, John Dewey, Edna St. Vincent Millay, and Katherine Porter were among the hundreds of well-known figures of the time to rally to the cause. Letters were sent, petitions were signed and sent to the newspapers, thousands picketed the streets of Boston and other cities, and there were countless strikes and demonstrations for Sacco and Vanzetti (Feuerlicht, 1977). Governor Fuller granted a stay of execution for twelve days while final deliberations were made, but ultimately Sacco and Vanzetti were executed just after midnight on August 23, 1927. The streets of Boston were empty at the time due to strict city orders, but thousands turned out in New York City to protest their executions. After the executions, thousands rioted on the streets of cities all over the world, including Boston, Paris, New York, and Buenos Aires (Selmi, 2001). Thousands of supporters also marched with the funeral procession in Boston, and as the coffins passed, they strew flowers in the coffins' direction. In Massachusetts, however, the population seemed divided. The lower class was sympathetic to Sacco and Vanzetti, but the upper and middle classes were hostile toward them (Feuerlicht, 1977). To the dismay of millions all over the world, Sacco and Vanzetti were not saved, but this is not the end of their story.

THE AFTERMATH AND THE LEGACY OF SACCO AND VANZETTI

Many famous people at the time were convinced that Sacco and Vanzetti were two innocent men who were wrongly executed. Upton Sinclair was one such famous person. Four years after the executions, Sinclair traveled to Boston to gather facts surrounding Sacco and Vanzetti. He came to Boston under the impression that these were peaceful men, and that they were merely "philosophical anarchists" (Sinclair as quoted in Avrich, 1991, p. 161). After learning a great deal from those who worked closely on the case, he concluded just the opposite: they were militant anarchists who believed in and preached the use of violence. Paul Avrich, author of *Sacco and Vanzetti: The Anarchist Background*, concluded that Sacco and Vanzetti were undoubtedly involved in the 1919 bombings in Massachusetts. He was uncertain of their roles in the crime, but their involvement was a "virtual certainty" (Avrich, 1991, p. 162).

Many books were written about the Sacco-Vanzetti case. Some authors believed they were guilty, but most firmly believed in their innocence. In 1969, Herbert Ehrmann published *The Case That Will Not Die*, and he shed new light on the ballistics evidence used against Sacco. He included photos of the bullets admitted into evidence, and he showed that bullets had been tampered with and possibly replaced before the trial began. Many academics and intellectuals have gathered at conferences to discuss the Sacco-Vanzetti case. The injustice that occurred has even stirred much discussion about the fairness and validity of the death penalty in the United States.

The media world has continued to cover the story even as it grows more distant in history. This is partly because of the lasting political and legal effects of the case. The Massachusetts appeals laws were rewritten so that trial judges could not rule on appeals. In 1977, fifty years after the executions, Governor Michael S. Dukakis declared August 23 "Nicola Sacco and Bartolomeo Vanzetti Memorial Day" in Massachusetts. He did not officially pardon them, but he declared that they had received an unfair trial and stated that any stigma attached to their names was removed that day (Young and Kaiser, 1985). In 1997, the first Italian American mayor of Boston, Thomas Menino, dedicated a bronze sculpture of Sacco and Vanzetti and ordered it placed in a public area of Boston. Gutzon Borglum, the creator of Mount Rushmore, had created this sculpture many years ago, but previous Massachusetts governors and Boston mayors had refused to display it (Gelastopoulos, 1997).

In the arts, many writers and directors have honored the memory of Sacco and Vanzetti. There were numerous plays written and acted out on television and in the theater. An opera, *The Passion of Sacco and Vanzetti*, was performed in New York City and other major venues. Several songs were inspired by their story. Documentaries, speeches, and newspaper articles have appeared in the media every year since their death. It is likely that the majority of Americans are still somewhat familiar with the story of the two men due to the attention it has received from the media.

The Sacco and Vanzetti saga will continue to be told in books, plays, periodicals, and television productions. No one can ever be truly positive about whether these men were guilty or innocent, but the majority support the latter. It is undeniable that Sacco and Vanzetti received an unfair trial, and this injustice stirred universal emotions and caused many to criticize the American criminal justice system. They could not possibly have realized in 1927 what their legacy would be, but perhaps Vanzetti had some hint. He found solace in knowing that their deaths would not be in vain, and three months before his execution, he declared in a letter to the *New York World*:

If it had not been for these thing, I might have live out my life talking at street corners to scorning men. I might have die, unmarked, unknown, a failure. This is our career and our triumph. Never in our full life could we hope to do such work for tolerance, for joostice [*sic*], for man's understanding of man as now we do by accident. Our words—our lives—our pains—nothing! The taking of our lives— lives of a good shoemaker and a poor fish peddler—all! That last moment belongs to us—that agony is our triumph. (Vanzetti in Sacco and Vanzetti, 1997, p. lvi)

Their triumph was realized even before their deaths. The power and influence of these two men have been far greater than those of many other foreigners who moved to America to realize a dream.

NOTES

1. Three months prior to the arrest of Sacco and Vanzetti.

2. His name given at birth and as he was known to his family is Ferdinando Sacco, but later while living in Mexico, he assumed the name of his older brother, Nicola, who was then deceased (Avrich, 1991).

3. A Galleanisti is a follower of Galleani's anarchist belief system.

4. Salsedo's death while being detained was considered highly suspicious, but was labeled a suicide by authorities.

5. After the deportation of Galleani, the police recovered a list that contained all subscribers to the *Cronaca Sovversiva*, and Sacco and Vanzetti were among the names they found.

6. Both South Braintree and Bridgewater are located in southeastern Massachusetts.

7. In the Bridgewater robbery attempt, one of the four men involved in the crime had been firing a shotgun at the truck carrying the $30,000 payroll.

8. Vanzetti was a fish peddler but worked for himself.

9. The Brockton judge had the power to do this because of a wartime act still in place. This act stated that men who were suspected of major crimes could be held in jail without bail (Russell, 1971).

REFERENCES

Avrich, P. (1991). *Sacco and Vanzetti: The anarchist background*. Princeton, NJ: Princeton University Press.

Burnett, P. (2000a). The Sacco and Vanzetti trial: Key figures. Retrieved February 10, 2004, from http://www.law.umkc.edu/faculty/projects/ftrials/SaccoV/SaccoV.html

Burnett, P. (2000b). The red scare. Retrieved February 10, 2004, from http://www.law.umkc.edu/faculty/projects/ftrials/SaccoV/redscare.html

Cannistraro, P. V. (1996). Mussolini, Sacco-Vanzetti, and the anarchists: The transatlantic context. *The Journal of Modern History, 68*, 31–62.

D'Attilio, R. (1999). Sacco-Vanzetti case. Retrieved February 11, 2004, from http://www.english.upenn.edu/~afilreis/88/sacvan.html

Ehrmann, H. B. (1969). *The case that will not die: Commonwealth v. Sacco and Vanzetti*. Boston: Little, Brown and Company.

Feuerlicht, R. S. (1977). *Justice crucified: The story of Sacco and Vanzetti*. New York: McGraw-Hill.

Fraenkel, O. (1969). *The Sacco-Vanzetti case*. New York: Russell and Russell.

Frankfurter, F. (1954). *The case of Sacco and Vanzetti: A critical analysis for lawyers and laymen*. Stanford, CA: Academic reprints.

Gelastopoulos, E. (1997, August 24). Sacco, Vanzetti memorial unveiled. *Boston Herald*. Retrieved February 20, 2004, from http://web.lexis-nexis.com/

Joughin, L., and Morgan, E. M. (1948). *The legacy of Sacco and Vanzetti*. Chicago: Quadrangle Books.

Karpovich, M. (1930). The Russian Revolution of 1917. *The Journal of Modern History, 2*(2), 258–280.

Russell, F. (1971). *Tragedy in Dedham: The story of the Sacco-Vanzetti case.* New York: McGraw-Hill.

Sacco, N., and Vanzetti, B. (1997). In M. D. Frankfurter and G. Jackson (Eds.), *The letters of Sacco and Vanzetti.* New York: Penguin Books.

Selmi, P. (2001). Social work and the campaign to save Sacco and Vanzetti. *Social Science Review, 75*(1), 115–134.

Trasciatti, M. A. (2003). Framing the Sacco-Vanzetti executions in the Italian American press. *Critical Studies in Media Communication, 20*(4), 407–430.

Young, W., and Kaiser, D. E. (1985). *Postmortem: New evidence in the case of Sacco and Vanzetti.* Amherst, MA: The University of Massachusetts Press.

3

Roscoe "Fatty" Arbuckle: Cleared by the Court, Convicted by Conspiracy

Matthew Pate

By the time Roscoe "Fatty" Arbuckle was acquitted for the manslaughter of Virginia Rappé in 1922, his movie idol status had been supplanted by that of a pariah. In the early days of American movie-making, Roscoe Arbuckle had a meteoric rise. His stage and film comedies brought delight to millions of fans, but this amusement proved insufficient in the wake of a young starlet's untimely death.

Arbuckle's early years were marked by rejection and tragedy. Born on March 24, 1887, in Smith Center, Kansas, by his first birthday Arbuckle had moved with his family to Santa Ana, California. The boy's father, William G. Arbuckle, left the family soon thereafter to open a business in Watsonville, California. Around the time of Arbuckle's twelfth birthday, his mother, Mary Arbuckle, died, leaving him to fend for himself.

While in Santa Ana, Arbuckle began performing at local theater amateur nights. He quickly showed himself to possess many marketable talents. The minor celebrity he gained as a traveling vaudevillian translated into terrific fame as the star, director, and writer of numerous silent films. Despite his portly form, Arbuckle was an expert tumbler and adept dancer. These skills evolved into now-legendary physical comedy alongside the likes of

Roscoe (Fatty) Arbuckle, movie actor, standing with his hands in coat pockets on sidewalk. (Chicago Historical Society)

Buster Keaton and Charlie Chaplin. Arbuckle also holds the notable distinction of garnering the first million-dollar-a-year contract in cinema history (Yallop, 1976, p. 62). Yet, by the end of 1921 he had been vilified in the press and his films were banned in theaters across the country.

The scandal and trials surrounding the suspicious death of Virginia Rappé, a twenty-five-year-old aspiring actress, might not have been so sensational had the accused been other than Roscoe "Fatty" Arbuckle. Arbuckle was one of America's first "mass [media] celebrities" (Henry, 1995). The novelty of the expanding film industry made possible the spread of performers' images in ways that live shows could not. Just as Arbuckle had benefited by innovations in entertainment technology, he fell victim to another, more traditional information medium. When he stood accused of rape and manslaughter, Arbuckle unwittingly faced three parallel sets of trials: one in the California court system, one carefully managed in newspapers owned by William Randolph Hearst, and a third at the hands of Will Hays and the motion picture standards office.

The set of events leading to the death of Virginia Rappé was in many respects tailor-made for exploitation in the press. The principals were all Hollywood notables. In the middle of Prohibition, the alleged crime took place at a drunken party set in a San Francisco luxury hotel. Sexual promiscuity, predatory guile, and unscrupulous motives enveloped and obscured many of the details. Wealthy newspaper publisher Hearst recognized the unique opportunity before him and crafted a version of Arbuckle's predicament engineered more to sell newspapers than to present balanced accounting of the facts at hand. After weathering two mistrials in the winter of 1921–1922, Arbuckle was acquitted by a third jury with only a few minutes of deliberation, but by that point the damage to his reputation and career was largely insurmountable.

THE LABOR DAY PARTY

By mid-August 1921, Arbuckle was at the top of his career. He had been given a contract by Paramount Studios that included the formation of the Comique Film Corporation for his productions and complete artistic control over his films. He had a deal from Paramount that only one other filmmaker has ever garnered, and then only once: Orson Wells for *Citizen Kane* (Yallop, 1976, pp. 61–62). Arbuckle had finished simultaneous filming of three features: *Gasoline Gus*; *Crazy to Marry*; and *Freight Prepaid* (Oderman, 1994, p. 43). This was a cap to a year in which he had filmed a total of nine seven-reel feature films. As a respite from the hectic schedule, Arbuckle, along with director Fred Fischbach and actor Lowell Sherman, took his Pierce-Arrow automobile to San Francisco to spend the Labor Day weekend (Young, 1994, p. 64). The trio checked into a twelfth-floor luxury suite at the St. Francis Hotel. The hotel was one of Arbuckle's favorites and listed him along with General John Pershing and Billy Sunday as honored guests.

By many accounts, Arbuckle was a man who partied as hard as he worked (Oderman, 1994, p. 152). He allegedly arranged to have a Victrola, several phonograph records, and a quantity of illegal gin and whiskey delivered to his suite at the St. Francis. As this was 1921, the latter delivery was in violation of Prohibition and the Volstead Act.

Almost every detail of the weekend in San Francisco has since fallen under dispute. To begin with, sources differ on exactly how Virginia Rappé came to be in Arbuckle's suite at the St. Francis. One account (Young, 1994, p. 65) suggests that on Monday, September 5, Fischbach met Ira Fortlouis, a friend and clothing salesman, at the Palace Hotel. At the Palace he also chanced to meet struggling actress Virginia Rappé; her manager, Al Semnacher; and another of Rappé's friend's, Bambina Maude Delmont. Fischbach invited Fortlouis, Rappé, and Delmont to join Arbuckle, Sherman, and him back at the St. Francis. According to this version, that afternoon Rappé and Delmont went to the St. Francis. Shortly thereafter, Alice Blake, a showgirl friend of Sherman's, also joined the party along with her friend Zey Prevon.

Another account has Arbuckle calling Rappé (or possibly calling Semnacher or Delmont in order to reach Rappé) out of a long-held infatuation with her. Arbuckle had come to know Rappé through her fiancé, director Henry "Pathé" Lehrman, when he and Lehrman worked at Keystone Studios together (Oderman, 1994, p. 153). Some have also advanced the less probable theory that Rappé, Delmont, and Fortlouis traveled to San Francisco with Arbuckle and company in his automobile (Anger, 1975, p. 33).

The various versions of subsequent events are no less divided. Henry (1995) contends that a parade of guests came and went from the Arbuckle suite and that Arbuckle received his guests while wearing only a pair of pajama bottoms. Henry also states that the many guests consumed large amounts of alcohol and that this detail later complicated the prosecution's case against Arbuckle. The vigorous consumption of alcohol appears consistent across all descriptions of the party.

In an account somewhat more sympathetic to Arbuckle (Young, 1994, p. 65), the actor received Rappé with a surprised "My God! Virginia! Long time, no see!" Young's version also has Arbuckle quickly cornered by Rappé, who proceeded to tell him that she was pregnant and that Lehrman would leave her if he found out about it. There also appears some unanimity about the fact that Rappé was quickly drunk and may have passed out.

At some point, possibly Monday afternoon, a drunk Rappé stumbled into the bathroom of Room 1221. It is at this point that the prosecution alleged Arbuckle to have said, "I've been trying to get you for five years" (Oderman, 1994, p. 153). The prosecution further alleged that Arbuckle followed Rappé into the bathroom, shut the door, and raped her.

Arbuckle's version of events contends that he went into the bathroom only to discover Rappé draped over the toilet, vomiting, and in pain. He helped her over to his bed, thinking that she was just suffering the ill effects of too much alcohol. He then changed out of his pajama pants and rejoined the party (Oderman, p. 154; Yallop, pp. 113–114).

Not long afterward, a crowd gathered around Rappé as she lay on Arbuckle's bed. Her condition was not improving, and at some point, she became hysterical. She tore off her clothes and began screaming that she was hurt or dying (Yallop, 1976, p. 114). According to Young (1994, p. 114), this scene was reminiscent of a 1917 party hosted by Keystone head Max Sennett in which Rappé had also gotten drunk and passed out. There is some consensus that an argument broke out among the inebriated guests as to the best way to treat Rappé (Yallop, 1976, pp. 113–115; Oderman, 1994, p. 154). Allegedly a number of bizarre things were tried, including submersion of the girl in a bath of ice water. One version also has Arbuckle placing a piece of ice on the girl's thigh (or vulva). It is generally thought that this detail is the origin of a rumor that Arbuckle tried to rape Rappé with a shard of ice.[1]

Eventually Arbuckle summoned the hotel management and had Rappé taken to another room where she could recuperate. Her condition persisted even after visits from multiple physicians, who apparently took her malaise as merely an acute hangover (Oderman, pp. 154–155; Yallop, p. 116). Though unimproved, Rappé was not taken to a hospital until approximately three days after her illness began. When she was finally admitted to the Wakefield Sanatorium, her situation did not improve. Wakefield was not a hospital in the conventional sense. Rather, it was "a maternity hospital and a well-known haven for well-to-do women seeking semi-legal abortions" (Henry, 1995). Oderman (1994, p. 175) suggests that Rappé's injuries resulted from a botched abortion that Rappé had undergone not long before the Arbuckle party. A contrasting account (Young, 1994, p. 65; Yallop, 1976, p. 124) states that Wakefield doctors confirmed the pregnancy. These accounts also report the existence of a venereal disease and "a running abscess in her vagina for upwards of six weeks" (Young, 1994, p. 65).

Virginia Rappé died at Wakefield Sanatorium on Friday, September 9, 1921. According to Oderman (1994, p. 175), the cause of death was listed as peritonitis brought on by a rupture of the bladder—caused by an extreme amount of external force. Again, this detail of the "external force" fueled rumors of rape at Arbuckle's hand.

Ironically, by the time Rappé died, Arbuckle and his companions, Fischbach and Sherman, had long since departed San Francisco. Having loaded Arbuckle's Pierce-Arrow automobile aboard a ship named *Harvard*, the trio set sail back to Los Angeles. As they journeyed south, Rappé's condition worsened, but according to Young (1994, p. 66), "At no time during her illness did [Rappé] accuse Arbuckle of any misconduct, and she loudly denied he had injured her in any way when others tried to get her to do so." Whether this accurately reflects Rappé's perspective is unclear. What is certain is that the version of events told by Bambina Maude Delmont was entirely different.

Delmont told police and the press that Arbuckle had taken Rappé into his room, where he beat and raped her. She demanded that he be arrested and prosecuted for murder (Young, 1994, p. 66). According to Delmont, Rappé's last words were, "Maude, Roscoe should be at my side every minute and see how I am suffering from what he did to me" (Yallop, 1976, p. 123). As Young (1994, p. 66) points out, Delmont was not actually present at the time of Rappé's death. Nonetheless, the tide of public curiosity rolled forward.

Instead of a jubilant homecoming to celebrate the hit *Gasoline Gus* had become, Arbuckle was greeted in Los Angeles by a throng of hungry reporters. The headline of the *San Francisco Call*, a Hearst newspaper, read "GRILL FOR ARBUCKLE: ACTRESS DEATH QUIZ" (Young, 1994). By the end of the day on Monday, September 10, Arbuckle had returned to San Francisco, where he was arrested and, after a coroner's inquest, charged with manslaughter in the death of Rappé. Bail was denied. Back in Hollywood, *Gasoline Gus* was removed from theaters.

THE THREE TRIALS

It appears immutably certain that Roscoe Arbuckle liked to drink, that he enjoyed the trappings of a Hollywood movie star's lifestyle, and that he condoned a certain amount of excessive behavior by his associates. What is less certain, however, is that he had any causal part in the death of Virginia Rappé. In the course of establishing this point, Roscoe Arbuckle lost his career, his reputation, and almost everything he owned.

There were a number of individuals who stood to gain from Arbuckle's misfortune. San Francisco District Attorney Matthew Brady clearly saw the groundswell of public attention as an opportunity to advance his political fortunes. Brady, a former judge, wanted to be governor of California. The lure of publicity attached to prosecution of a famous film star was apparent in his zealousness (Young, 1994, p. 68).

Some have also made the case that Brady had direct financial motives for an aggressive treatment of Arbuckle (Edmonds, 1991). In a twist reading more like a Hollywood script than reality, Adolph Zukor, founder of Paramount Pictures, gave Brady a check for $10,000 on at least two occasions (Edmonds, 1991, p. 215). While a clear intent has never been established for these payments, Edmonds tentatively contends that Zukor, long angered over Arbuckle's cost to the studio and his rebelliousness as well, possibly used the trial either to get back at Arbuckle or to cover his own involvement in Arbuckle's predicament. In particular, Edmonds (1991, pp. 252–253) asserts that Fred Fischbach may have had a hand in setting up Arbuckle at the behest of Zukor.

Zukor allegedly had a number of reasons to want the proverbial pound of Arbuckle's flesh. He had been forced into a bidding war over Arbuckle that resulted in Arbuckle's salary quadrupling. Arbuckle refused to make public appearances as Zukor had instructed. Arbuckle purportedly engaged in pranks that irritated Zukor. As testament to this position, Zukor is quoted as having stated that Arbuckle needed "knocking down a few pegs" (Edmonds, 1991, p. 253).

As the theory goes, Fischbach was to orchestrate a wild weekend of drinking, loose women, and tawdry behavior in which Arbuckle could be swept up and then extorted into a more manageable position for the studio. As Edmonds (1991, p. 253) states, "There also needed to be someone who was Zukor's eyes and ears at the party but who would not be implicated.

Fischbach seems the likely candidate." Unfortunately for all involved, Virginia Rappé not only brought her soiled reputation with her, but also a life-threatening health condition and bad timing.

As for Rappé's motives or intent in the scheme, no source has offered much in the way of definitive explanation. It is reasonable to assume that she hoped the affair might stimulate her unremarkable acting career, but this is admittedly just informed speculation. However, the motives of her counter-part, Bambina Maude Delmont, have been widely explored and are substan-tially clearer. Without dissent, all accounts of the Arbuckle trials and scandal paint Maude Delmont as an inveterate liar and con artist. Young (1994, p. 65) states that she was "a woman of few scruples whose sordid past included prostitution, swindling and blackmail." Fussel (1982, p. 65) documents a Delmont telegram to associates in Los Angeles and San Diego that read, "We have Roscoe Arbuckle in a hole here. Chance to make some money out of him."

Immediately upon Rappé's death, Delmont set off telling the press and authorities that Arbuckle was behind it. To the chagrin of District Attorney Brady, the essential facts of Delmont's story changed with each telling (Edmonds, 1991, pp. 185–186). Even though she was the most vocal Arbuckle accuser and poised to be the state's star witness, the prosecutors were so dubious of her veracity that she was never allowed to testify in any of the three trials. Brady knew that her testimony would not stand under defense scrutiny. As a matter of convenience and preservation of his own reputation, he had Delmont locked up on a charge of bigamy and in so doing made her unavailable to testify.

Just as many individuals had a stake in Arbuckle's undoing, there were many others who remained steadfast on his innocence. Arbuckle's wife, Minta Durfee, stated, "The only thing he's guilty of is being too good-natured to throw out a lot of those no-goods who come hanging around a movie star and cage free drinks" (St. Johns, 1978, p. 61). Former boss Mack Sennett told the press, "Fatty wouldn't hurt a fly. . . . He was a good-natured fat man and a good comic" (St. Johns, 1978, p. 61). Buster Keaton and several other Hollywood associates eventually loaned Arbuckle money to pay his legal bills.

Even Zukor, in what was probably a move of obligation (or hedging his bets) more than loyalty, retained attorney Frank Dominguez to represent Arbuckle. Zukor initially opposed assisting in Arbuckle's defense, but Joe Schenck, a Paramount executive, convinced Zukor that it was in the studio's financial interest to do so. Zukor had originally hoped to enlist the aide of Clarence Darrow, but Darrow, in the midst of his own legal problems, had to decline. Paramount also tried to retain famed defense attorney

Earl Rogers, but Rogers's ill health precluded his service. As such, Zukor settled on Paramount's third choice: Dominguez. Dominguez was an able attorney from an old and respected California family (Young, 1994, p. 67). Zukor pressed Dominguez to get the charges against Arbuckle dismissed. When the grand jury instead returned a manslaughter indictment against Arbuckle, an angry Zukor had Dominguez dismissed (Young, 1994, p. 69).

Zukor replaced Dominguez with a team of five attorneys headed by Gavin McNab. McNab was a prominent San Francisco attorney whose familiarity with the local court was thought to be advantageous. McNab proved to be a formidable adversary for District Attorney Brady. McNab's first action as Arbuckle's attorney was to order a background investigation of Rappé (Edmonds, 1991, pp. 213–214).

This investigation turned up numerous licentious details about the woman whom Brady and others portrayed as "sweet and innocent." McNab's Chicago investigators produced reports that Rappé had been in ill health for a number of years. She had undergone several abortions, had possibly borne a child out of wedlock, and had received repeated treatment for venereal disease, all by the time she was sixteen. A physician, Maurice Rosenberg, said that Rappé had been treated for chronic cystitis, a condition that could have started the infection and inflammation that ultimately led to her death (Edmonds, 1991, p. 214).

While the news about Rappé's past proved helpful, the defense team's joy was short-lived. Before jury selection had begun in Arbuckle's manslaughter trial, federal agents filed charges against the actor for violating the Volstead Act, stemming from the liquor present at the Labor Day party. While the case was eventually dropped, its timing was distracting for the defense.

Meanwhile, the prosecution was dealing with problems of its own. Fellow party guests Zey Prevon and Alice Blake were kept "in protective custody" by the prosecution to make certain that their testimony would hold up under cross-examination (Edmonds, 1991, p. 214). Nevertheless, Blake managed to slip away to Alameda County and the home of a friend. Once located, Brady placed her under a subpoena to ensure further compliance.

The First Trial

Jury selection in what would be the first of three trials began on Monday, November 14, 1921. Superior Court Judge Howard Louderback presided. A list of 207 potential jurors had been drawn. The process was almost instantly heated and volatile. Much of the drama stemmed from McNab's accusation that the prosecution had intimidated witnesses, Blake and Prevon in particular. At one point, McNab promised to prove his accusation with the help of seven witnesses, stating, "This is more than an allegation, this a charge. You have tampered with, threatened and intimidated witnesses into lying. You know this is true and I know this is true" (Edmonds, 1991, p. 218).[2] This typified the scene that continued for five days.

Finally, both sides agreed upon seven men and five women as jurors. Fatefully for Arbuckle, one of the women was Helen Hubbard, the wife of a prominent San Francisco attorney and self-admitted fan of Brady, who while stating that she was a movie fan (Edmonds, 1991, pp. 219–220) later confessed that she had made up her mind that Arbuckle was guilty the "moment [she] heard he was arrested" (Young, 1994, p. 69).

The prosecution's first witness was a nurse from the Wakefield Sanatorium named Grace Halston (Edmonds, 1991, pp. 220–221). Halston glared at the defendant and, through her tone, showed an obvious contempt for Arbuckle. She testified that Rappé's body was badly bruised and that several of the victim's organs had ruptured. She concluded "[t]hat both had most likely been caused by force—from a man." Under cross-examination, McNab got Halston to admit that the ruptured bladder could have been caused by cancer and that the bruises might have been caused by Rappé's heavy jewelry. McNab also called Halston's credibility into question, saying, "I would like to know what qualified you to examine the body because you are neither a physician nor a graduate nurse" (Edmonds, 1991, p. 221).

Brady's next witness, Dr. Arthur Beardslee, testified that the bladder seemed to be injured from external force. On cross-examination, he admitted that Rappé had said nothing to him indicating that she had been assaulted by the accused. Inadvertently opening himself up to criticism, Beardslee also stated that Rappé might have benefited from surgery. "It was evident that I was dealing with an operative case" (Edmonds, 1991, p. 222).

McNab attacked. He pressed Dr. Beardslee vigorously on his reasons for not performing surgery that might have benefited the victim, but Beardslee was unable to answer. McNab wondered aloud whether the victim might have survived had she received better medical care. On Monday, November 21, Brady called model and party guest Betty Campbell to the stand. Campbell testified that she arrived about an hour after the alleged rape to find Arbuckle, Sherman, Fischbach, Semnacher, and Prevon sitting around the hotel room relaxed. Edmonds (1991, p. 222) contends, "Brady tried to use this in an attempt to show Arbuckle had neither remorse nor concern for the condition of Virginia Rappé." Under cross-examination, Campbell said the comedian showed "no signs of intoxication."

Under cross-examination, McNab elicited a bombshell from Campbell. She testified that the prosecutor had threatened to have her imprisoned if she did not testify against Arbuckle. Predictably, this sent Brady into a storm of objections.

McNab presented the judge with affidavits from Alice Blake and Zey Prevon reasserting the defense's claim of intimidation by the prosecution. Prevon testified that she had been under duress when she signed the statement in which Rappé had claimed, "He killed me." Alice Blake provided similar testimony. According to Edmonds (1991, p. 224), Blake was "visibly frightened" while under prosecution questioning and "obviously relieved when McNab stepped in."

The prosecution's next witness was a security guard who had worked at Lehrman's studios in Culver City. Jesse Norgard testified that Arbuckle had once approached him with an offer of cash in exchange for the key to Rappé's dressing room. According to Norgard's testimony, Arbuckle wanted it so he could play a joke on the actress. Norgard said he had refused to give Arbuckle the key.

Dr. Edward Heinrich, a criminologist who was especially expert at fingerprints, testified that partial prints of Rappé had been found on the inside of the door to room 1219 with Arbuckle's superimposed over them. To Heinrich this indicated that Arbuckle and Rappé had struggled over the door with Arbuckle preventing her exit. Heinrich also testified that he had sealed the Arbuckle suite eleven days after the party took place.

In rebuttal, McNab called former federal investigator Ignatius McCarthy. McCarthy said he could prove the fingerprints had been faked and strongly implied that Brady was behind the act. McNab also summoned the testimony of a hotel maid who stated she had dusted the door "with a feather duster" several times before it was sealed by Heinrich.

After making an opening statement that drew heated objection from Assistant District Attorney Friedman, the defense began by calling several witnesses with information about Rappé's medical and personal history. The first of these was Dr. Melville Rumwell, who had been one of the attending physicians at Wakefield.

Among Rumwell's testimony were observations that Rappé had gonorrhea and that she was not a virgin. Rumwell's position in the course of events is also suspect because he performed what the coroner's office termed "an illegal autopsy" (Edmonds, 1991, p. 170). It is widely suspected that Rumwell's primary motivation to perform a hasty post-mortem examination was an effort to conceal that he had also performed an illegal abortion on Rappé. Most importantly for the defense, however, was Rumwell's testimony that Rappé never accused Arbuckle of injuring her.

Nurse/masseuse Irene Morgan testified that she had treated Rappé at the home of Henry Lehrman in Hollywood. Morgan said that Rappé suffered from abdominal cramps and had been catheterized on several occasions due to trouble urinating (Edmonds, 1991, p. 227). Morgan also testified that Rappé was known to tear off her clothes and run through the streets naked after a few drinks. Perhaps coincidentally, Morgan was found poisoned in her hotel two days after she testified. She had previously claimed that she was threatened by anonymous phone calls saying that she would be killed if she testified (Edmonds, 1991, pp. 227–228).

Fred Fischbach also took the stand for the defense. He admitted that he had invited Rappé to the party. He also stated that he had heard Rappé "moaning or screaming" and that he had been the one to dunk her into a cold bath to calm her. He also disavowed any knowledge of why Rappé was hysterical in the first place, because he had been "gone for a few hours in the automobile . . . out of the room" (Edmonds, 1991, p. 228).

In a telling moment of character, Arbuckle asked McNab to deliberately stay away from the issue of the alcohol and the Victrola with Fischbach. Arbuckle knew that Fischbach was responsible for bringing the items as well as the party guests to the room. "I'm on trial here, not Freddy" (Edmonds, 1991, p. 228).

After a recess for Thanksgiving on Monday, November 28, Roscoe Arbuckle took the stand (Edmonds, 1991, pp. 230–233). He stood accused of horrible crimes and was apparently relieved at the opportunity to refute the charges. Arbuckle's testimony lasted for a little over four hours.

When asked of his whereabouts, he replied that he was at the St. Francis Hotel and provided the room numbers. He admitted to seeing Virginia Rappé that day at noon. Arbuckle described many details about the party, but he carefully avoided mentioning the excessive drinking. He told how he had planned to take a friend, Mae Taub, riding in the Pierce-Arrow and that he was going into the bathroom to get dressed when he discovered Virginia in pain and vomiting. He described how he accidentally struck her with the door upon entering the bathroom, and how he held her under her waist and at her forehead. He explained how he pulled her hair out of her face as she retched.

Continuing, he stated, "When she finished, I put the seat down, then I sat her down on it. 'Can I do anything for you?' I asked her. She said she wanted to lie down. I carried her into 1219 and put her on the bed. I lifted her feet off the floor. I went to the bathroom again and came back in two or three minutes. I found her rolling on the floor between two beds holding her stomach. I tried to pick her up but I couldn't. I immediately went out of 1219 to 1220 and asked Mrs. Delmont and Miss Prevon to come in. I told them Miss Rappé was sick" (Edmonds, 1991, p. 230).

Arbuckle vehemently disputed Heinrich's conclusions about the door. He also described how Rappé had torn at her clothes, including an instance where he helped her remove her shredded dress when Fischbach came into the room. Arbuckle also corroborated Fischbach's version of having put Rappé into a tub of cold water. When Rappé was carried back to the bed, Maude Delmont rubbed her nude body with ice. Arbuckle stated that he tried to cover the girl with the bedspread and an outraged Delmont rebuked him. Arbuckle replied to Delmont, "If you don't shut up, I'll throw you out the window" (Edmonds, 1991, p. 232).

Assistant District Attorney Leo Friedman conducted the state's cross-examination, asking, "What time did you say Miss Rappé entered your rooms?" Arbuckle reiterated that she arrived at noon. When asked how long he had known her before, he indicated five or six years. Friedman returned to individual details several times. He tried to shake inconsistencies out of Arbuckle, but the comic remained focused.

Just after a recess in the middle of Arbuckle's testimony, the prosecution did a curious thing. In an act that McNab characterized as "disgusting and obscene," prosecutors brought Rappé's ruptured bladder into the courtroom. Other than for the presumed shock value, the utility of the introduction at that particular point is unknown.

In a continuing series of questions, Friedman tried to get Arbuckle to admit that he had deliberately followed Rappé into room 1219. This failing, Friedman tried to depict Arbuckle as indifferent to Rappé's condition.

LF: Did you tell the hotel manager what had caused Miss Rappé's sickness?
RA: No. How should I know what caused her sickness?
LF: You didn't tell anybody you found her in the bathroom?
RA: Nobody asked me.
LF: You didn't tell anyone you found her between the beds?
RA: Nobody asked me. I'm telling you.
LF: You never said anything to anybody except that Miss Rappé was sick?
RA: Nope.
LF: Not even the doctor?
RA: Nope. (Edmonds, 1991, p. 235)

By the time Arbuckle was finished on the stand, most accounts contend he had done well in defending himself and maintaining composure despite the prosecution's best efforts to break him. What followed next was an odd set of rebuttal witnesses, whose testimony focused on the aforementioned bladder.

Dr. William Ophuls (who had attended Rappé with Dr. Rumwell) was called by the prosecution and Dr. G. Rusk by the defense. Edmonds (1991, p. 236) summarized the findings, indicating that experts agreed "that the bladder was ruptured, that there was evidence of chronic inflammation, that there were signs of acute peritonitis, and that the examination failed to reveal any pathological change in the vicinity of the tear preceding the rupture." They concluded that the rupture had not been caused by external force.

Going into summation, both sides felt confident in the cases they had made. District Attorney Friedman's summation continued to portray Arbuckle as a callous villain: "This big, kindhearted comedian who has made the whole world laugh; did he say 'Get a doctor for this suffering girl?' No. He said, 'Shut up or I'll throw you out the window.'"

"He was not content to stop at throwing her out the window. He attempted to make a sport with her by placing ice on her body. This man then and there proved himself guilty of this offense. This act shows you the mental makeup of Roscoe Arbuckle" (Edmonds, 1991, p. 237). As Arbuckle later clarified, his threat to throw someone 'out of the window' was directed toward Maude Delmont, not Rappé. Arbuckle further stated that he did not actually intend to throw anyone out of a window. Nonetheless, the district attorney used the statement to portray Arbuckle as volatile.

In his closing, McNab forcefully argued that Arbuckle was the victim of overzealous prosecution. "It was a deliberate conspiracy against Arbuckle! It was the shame of San Francisco. Perjured wretches tried, from the stand, to deprive this defendant, this stranger within our gates, of his liberty" (Edmonds, 1991, p. 238).[3]

McNab also cast aspersions against the prosecution's case and its tactics, particularly where Blake, Prevon, and Delmont were concerned. Finally, he made a final dig at Rappé, insisting that she was not in good health, would be considered sickly and broken down, and suggesting that a woman in such a state as she was on the day in question would hardly arouse "the passions of the lowest beast that was ever called man" (Edmonds, 1991, p. 238).

The first trial ended on December 4, 1921. After forty-three hours of deliberation and twenty-two ballots, the jury sent word that it was hopelessly deadlocked. The final count was ten to two in favor of acquittal. One of the two holdouts was Helen Hubbard, the self-admitted fan of District Attorney Brady.

The Second and Third Trials

The state decided to retry Arbuckle on the manslaughter charges and set a date of January 11, 1922, in San Francisco Superior Court. Jury selection took six days, nearly twice as long as before (Edmonds, 1991, p. 245). Eighty people were interviewed, and there was some difficulty in finding prospective jurors who had not heard details of the previous trial and scandal.

The trial went poorly for both sides. Both Prevon and Blake were recalled for the second trial. Neither produced compelling testimony, and again

McNab alleged witness tampering. Heinrich reversed his position from the first trial, stating that it was possible that the doorway fingerprints had been forged.

The defense took a different strategy regarding Rappé's virtue. It became a centerpiece of their case. McNab portrayed her as a woman of loose morals who drank to excess and slept her way around town (Edmonds, 1991, p. 246). The defense called numerous witnesses who each told of Rappé's questionable behavior.

Again, the prosecution failed to bring Maude Delmont to the stand, eschewing her for the testimony of Dr. Beardslee. Beardslee relayed to the court various stories about Rappé that Delmont had told him.

The defense made two critical errors in the second trial: they did not put Arbuckle himself on the stand, and they did not offer a closing argument. McNab later admitted that both decisions were mistakes.

On February 2, the jury retired to consider Arbuckle's fate. The jurors deliberated for forty-four hours, held thirteen ballots, and again returned with a deadlock. This time the jury voted ten to two for conviction. One juror later admitted that he was wavering in his decision to acquit Arbuckle and that if the other holdout had voted for conviction, so would he (Edmonds, 1991, p. 246).

The third trial commenced on March 6. It was very different from either of the other two. McNab would not make the same mistakes as before. He provided a very explicit description of Virginia Rappé: her life, lovers, and faults. Whatever delicacy or euphemistic treatment given the matter in the first two trials was set aside in trial three. As Edmonds (1991, p. 247) observes, "Though women in the courtroom gasped, fainted and stamped their feet to drown out the 'vulgarity,' McNab got his point across." McNab also let Arbuckle testify.

The trial was by comparison very brief. The prosecution presented only six witnesses. The jury began deliberations on April 12. The jurors were out for less than five minutes. During that time the jury prepared the following note for the court:

Acquittal is not enough for Roscoe Arbuckle. We feel that a great injustice has been done him. We feel also that it was only our plain duty to give him this exoneration, under the evidence, for there was not the slightest proof adduced to connect him in any way with the commission of a crime.

He was manly throughout the case, and told a straightforward story on the witness stand, which we all believed.

The happening at the hotel was an unfortunate affair for which Arbuckle, so the evidence shows, was in no way responsible.

We wish him success, and hope that the American people will take the judgment of fourteen men and woman who have sat listening for thirty-one days to evidence, that Roscoe Arbuckle is entirely innocent and free from all blame. (Sellers, 1924, p. 139; Young, 1994, p. 71; Edmonds, 1991, pp. 247–248)

Arbuckle was finally free from the clutches of Brady and the Superior Court of California, but his ordeal had scarcely begun. The trial cost nearly $750,000, which left him almost bankrupt, and no one in Hollywood would touch an Arbuckle picture. As if this were not enough, Arbuckle was soon contacted by the Internal Revenue Service. The IRS found that he owed nearly $100,000 in back taxes (Edmonds, 1991, p. 248). The IRS attached what was left of his estate and garnered a court order for any earnings until the debt was settled. Ironically, the worst was yet to come.

A PUBLIC SACRIFICE

In the days following the death of Virginia Rappé, the press besieged Arbuckle. It clamored around him upon his return to Los Angeles and continued to dog him throughout the trials. Most of the scholarship on Arbuckle indicates that the coverage was generally balanced, except in the newspapers owned by William Randolph Hearst. The Hearst newspapers vilified Arbuckle with exaggerated headlines. The *San Francisco Examiner* reported that Arbuckle had been stoned by the crowd when he returned from San Francisco (Edmonds, 1991, p. 208). If anything, the reception was mixed.

Shortly after his arrest, theaters nationwide began pulling Arbuckle films. On September 12, 1921, the Theater Owners Chamber of Commerce in New York banned exposition of Arbuckle films in all of its 300 member venues (Young, 1994, p. 111). Theater owners in Philadelphia, Chicago, Memphis, Buffalo, and several other large cities enacted similar bans. By December 1922, even New York's Sing Sing Prison had banned Arbuckle films (Young, 1994, p. 114). This left Arbuckle and the production studios in a tight spot. Famous Players-Lasky studio had three completed Arbuckle films in the can and no place to show them (Edmonds, 1991, p. 209).

Arbuckle was also the victim of unlucky timing. On the same day that the jury retired during Arbuckle's second trial, Paramount film director William Desmond Taylor was found murdered in his home. Among the prime suspects were Arbuckle's co-star Mabel Normand; Paramount star Mary Miles Minter; and her mother, Charlotte Shelby. The murder generated nasty rumors of homosexuality, a love triangle, and even a drug deal gone bad (Edmonds, 1991; Young, 1994).

As if this were not enough, by March another scandal, this time focused on the drug addiction of actor Wallace Reid, was made public. Reid's hasty withdrawal from his narcotics habit nearly drove the actor insane, forcing him into a sanitarium where he died the following year (Edmonds, 1991; Young, 1994).

The three scandals taken together were enough of a warning signal that the Hollywood establishment felt it had to act. Former United States Postmaster General Will Hays was brought in by studio executives (Zukor, Joseph Schenck, and Jesse Lasky among them) to head the newly formed Motion Picture Producers and Distributors Association (MPPDA), an organization designed to regulate film morals and self-censorship (Young, 1991, p. 71). The Hays Office, as it became known, spent the next twenty-three years enforcing a very tight code of behavior for individuals both on and off screen. So-called "morals clauses" were written into studio contracts, and as Young (1991, p. 71) reports, "[M]inisters nationwide, the powerful Federation of Women's Clubs and bigoted moralists who had deplored films since their beginnings, felt their day had finally arrived."

For whatever reason, Hollywood's blanket self-censure was deemed insufficient. The movement against the perceived debauchery of the film community needed an obvious sacrifice. Arbuckle provided an easy target. On April 18, 1922, the Hays Office issued the following statement:

After consulting at length with Mr. Nicholas Schenck, representing Mr. Joseph Schenck, the producers, and Mr. Adolph Zukor and Mr. Jessy Lasky of the Famous Players-Lasky Corporation, the distributors, I will state that at my request they have cancelled all showings and all bookings of the Arbuckle films. They do this that the whole matter may have the consideration that its importance warrants, and the action is taken notwithstanding the fact that they had nearly ten thousand contracts in force for the Arbuckle pictures. (Blesh, 1966, p. 188)

Arbuckle, whose film career boasted many "firsts" for the industry, now added the mantle of being the first performer ever blacklisted by Hollywood. While the formal ban was lifted only nine months later, the damage to Arbuckle's career had been solidified.

The year 1923 brought a mixed bag of circumstances for Arbuckle. The MPPDA ban was lifted on January 20, but public opposition was still pervasive. On January 30, papers of incorporation were filed for Reel Comedies in Trenton, New Jersey (Young, 1994, p. 115). Nicholas and Joseph Schenck formed the company to give Arbuckle employment and income. Six of Hollywood's largest studios secretly funded $200,000 for the new company. A day later Arbuckle issued a statement in which he said he was "through with acting" and that he was joining Reel Comedies to produce and direct. During the next three years, Arbuckle went on to make thirteen two-reel comedies, but received no screen credit for the work. Throughout the rest of 1923, Arbuckle gave numerous live performances in Chicago and Atlantic City.

While his star was on apparent re-ascension, Arbuckle's personal life again found trouble. In October, Minta Durfee Arbuckle sued for divorce. The pair briefly reconciled, but Arbuckle began a romance with Doris Deane, whom he married shortly after divorcing Durfee.

By August 1925, a poll of *Photoplay Magazine* readers indicated that the majority of the public was still against Arbuckle's full return to the screen (Young, 1991, p. 117). Nonetheless, Arbuckle continued to work with old friends like Buster Keaton and Lew Cody. Oddly enough, in the summer of 1925, Arbuckle and new wife Deane vacationed at the San Simeon home of William Randolph Hearst. Hearst's girlfriend, actress Marion Davies, was set to star in a new film, and Hearst hired Arbuckle[4] to direct it. Of his involvement in the smear of Arbuckle's reputation, Hearst purportedly told Arbuckle, "I never knew anything more about your case, Roscoe, than I read in the newspapers" (Yallop, 1976, p. 285). Arbuckle is said to have not replied.

Arbuckle continued to work in the entertainment industry over the next few years. He was involved in several film projects, a number of stage productions, and various side investments. His marriage to Doris Deane ended in 1928 over allegations of desertion. By late 1931, a readers' poll in *Motion Picture Magazine* indicated that the public was ready for a return of Arbuckle to the screen (Young, 1991, p. 119). In January 1932, Jack Warner, head of Warner Brothers Studios, offered Arbuckle a contract for a two-reel comedy at the company's Vitaphone studios in New York.

While in New York, Arbuckle began a romance with Addie McPhail. The couple married in June 1932. She was twenty-six; he was forty-five. Not long after the marriage, filming completed on *Hey, Pop* at Vitaphone. The trade publication *Film Daily* touted the comedy as an overwhelming success. Arbuckle was immediately signed to make five more films for Warner Brothers.

On June 21, 1933, Arbuckle and McPhail celebrated their first wedding anniversary. A week later, Arbuckle finished filming *In the Dough*, the second of his "comeback" films for Warner Brothers. On June 28, the couple held a party (a belated anniversary celebration) at Billy LaHiff's Tavern in Manhattan. After the party the couple returned to their suite in the Park Central Hotel on Manhattan's west side. Tired from the party and a tough film schedule, Arbuckle retired for the evening. At approximately 2:30 a.m., the comedian's heart gave out. Arbuckle died in his sleep. Long-time friend Buster Keaton would often remark that Arbuckle had "died of a broken heart."

While most newspapers made a gentle report of Arbuckle's demise, Hearst's newspaper, *New York American*, ran the headline "Fatty Arbuckle Lies Dead in the Chapel, But No Eager Crowd Comes to Look" (Young, 1994, p. 85). Even in death, Arbuckle made for scandalous Hearst copy. In truth, a crowd of 800 to 1,000 mourners had come to see Arbuckle, and more than 250 of his friends and associates attended his funeral. At the actor's request, his body was cremated. On September 6, 1934, Addie McPhail Arbuckle spread the ashes out over the Pacific Ocean (Young, 1994, p. 85).

ARBUCKLE'S LEGACY IN CINEMA AND TRIALS

Roscoe Arbuckle was an important force in determining the shape of early American comedic cinema. He was one of Mack Sennett's Keystone Kops. He was a mentor to Buster Keaton and a peer of Charlie Chaplin. He was among the first, if not the first person, on film to throw a pie in someone's face. He was the first performer to be given complete creative control over his movies. Yet, for all his impact as a pioneering filmmaker, "Fatty" Arbuckle became instead a synonym for disrepute and reputations destroyed.

As the first film star to be blacklisted by Hollywood, Arbuckle fell victim to a reactionary climate of oppression that typified studios of the era. In so doing, he became something of an iconic reference point, a touchstone, for almost every celebrity who has since stood accused of foul crimes. Popular culture references to Arbuckle have even surfaced in current film. In *Death to Smoochy* (2000) actor Robin Williams, as the disgraced children's character "Rainbow Randolph," utters the line "Welcome to Fatty Arbuckle-land," while plotting the ruination of another character.

It is arguable that Arbuckle's trials were perhaps the most important celebrity trials of the twentieth century at least until the murder trial of football star–turned actor O. J. Simpson. Even in the shadow of the more recent Simpson trials, the media perennially invoke the Arbuckle case as a point of historical context.

That Arbuckle's predicament became fodder for the yellow journalism of the Hearst newspaper empire was also a harbinger of things to come. While fan magazines such as *Photoplay, Motography,* and *Movie Weekly* were popular during Arbuckle's career, their circulation did not reflect the same magnitude of apparent public interest evidenced by current television programs such as *Celebrity Justice* or tabloids like the *Star* or the *National Enquirer.*

Apart from the media-driven frenzy, the Arbuckle trials and associated scandals were the locus of a broad reconsideration of Hollywood, its products, and its personalities. When Hollywood studios sought the aid of Will Hays and the MPPDA in fear of government-mandated censorship, Roscoe Arbuckle's fate was essentially sealed. Even though his formal blacklisting lasted only about nine months, the damage was done. Images of Arbuckle's cherubic slapstick were forever replaced in the public memory by unsubstantiated acts of drunken excess, rape, and murder. Whether he had actually done the things of which he was accused (and acquitted) was largely irrelevant. Regrettably for the waning star, the popular press along with the film industry had reached an equally damning verdict: Roscoe Arbuckle was no longer wanted. That he had begun to regain public favor just before his death was meager compensation for the needless hardship.

NOTES

1. The rumor that Arbuckle used a shard of ice to violate Rappé is one of several stories popularized by the Hearst newspapers (Edmonds, 1991, p. 243). Equally violent is the rumor that Arbuckle, frustrated by having been made impotent from too much liquor, may have used either a Coca-Cola or champagne bottle against Rappé. Neither story has ever been substantiated.

2. It should be noted that the vast majority of courtroom dialog presented in this account of the Arbuckle trials comes from the work of Andy Edmonds. Edmonds notes in his forward to *Frame Up!* that "someone connected to the case" provided him with "fairly complete" court transcripts (which had been presumed destroyed), and for this reason, his accounts should be credited as the most authoritative source on the matter of the trials. If there are points that to more critical readers appear to need additional documentation with regard to who said what to whom, let this note serve as a blanket acknowledgment that Edmonds is, unless otherwise noted, the source for exact courtroom dialogue.

Young (1994, p. 247) takes issue with some of the dialog in the Edmonds work. Specifically, Young states, "It [Edmonds] contains considerable invented dialog." However, Young gives no indication of which instances in particular are of concern. Whether the courtroom dialog fits that category is unknown.

3. By referring to Arbuckle as "a stranger in our gates," McNab was recalling Deuteronomy 14:21, which contains a prohibition against Israelites eating anything that died of itself, while giving rather interesting direction as to the disposal of such animals: *"Ye shall not eat of any thing that dieth of itself: thou shalt give it to the stranger that is in thy gates, that he may eat it; or thou mayest sell it to an alien: for thou art an holy people to the LORD thy God"* (King James Version). What McNab was rhetorically asking was whether the jury should accord less justice to Arbuckle simply because he was a Hollywood outsider. Additionally, this reference to "a stranger in our gates" is a commentary on the antagonistic relationship between certain sections of San Francisco and the more rowdy Hollywood crowd. Individuals involved in the film industry would often take trips to relatively more sedate San Francisco. Their presence was arguably viewed by some as unwholesome and intrusive.

4. Arbuckle began working under the name William B. Goodrich (*sic* "Will B. Good"), and it was under this name that he was to direct Davies in the MGM

adaptation of *The Red Mill*. The film had a number of other directors and was a failure at the box office.

REFERENCES

A note on the references: Just as the Arbuckle trials produced myriad versions of what "really" took place in the St. Francis Hotel on Labor Day 1921, so too are there many subsequent historical accounts, some quite scholarly and well prepared, and some not. That being said, there appears little consensus on many details, conversations, and other aspects of Arbuckle's life, career, and role in the Labor Day party.

Anger, K. (1975). *Hollywood Babylon*. San Francisco: Straight Arrow Books.

Blesh, R. (1966). *Keaton*. New York: Macmillan.

Edmonds, A. (1991). *Frame Up! The untold story of Roscoe "Fatty" Arbuckle*. New York: William Morrow and Company.

Fussell, B. H. (1982). *Mabel: Hollywood's first I don't care girl*. New York: Ticknor and Fields.

Henry, P. H. (1995, April 4). Roscoe "Fatty" Arbuckle: Profile of an American scandal. Retrieved September 9, 2003, from http://www.phenry.org/text/arbuckle.txt

Oderman, S. (1994). *Roscoe "Fatty" Arbuckle: A biography of the silent film comedian, 1887–1933*. Jefferson, NC: McFarland and Company.

Sellers, A. V. (1924). *Classics of the bar* (vol. 13). Boxley, GA: Classic Publishing Company.

St. Johns, A. R. (1978). *Love, laughter and tears: My Hollywood story*. Garden City, NY: Doubleday.

Yallop, D. A. (1976). *The day the laughter stopped: The true story of Fatty Arbuckle*. New York: St. Martin's.

Young, R., Jr. (1994). *Roscoe "Fatty" Arbuckle: A bio-bibliography*. Westport, CT: Greenwood Press.

4

The Incomprehensible Crime of Leopold and Loeb: "Just an Experiment"

Diana Proper

On May 21, 1924, two young men, nineteen-year-old Nathan Leopold and eighteen-year-old Richard Loeb, set out to commit the "perfect crime." Partially inspired by an inaccurate, self-absorbed reading of the philosophy of Friedrich Nietzsche (Higdon, 1975), the two teens wanted to prove that they were Nietzschean "Supermen" by committing and getting away with the perfect crime. The teens were obsessed with the Superman theory, which states, in part, that there exists in society some super men (the "übermensch") whose talents and intellectual superiority mean that they are above human-made law, and therefore not subject to punishment for violation of such laws. For Leopold and Loeb (and the very embodiment of evil, Adolf Hitler), the theory allowed them to play with the idea that, as Supermen, they should be able to commit the perfect crime and get away with it. However, if caught, they felt that their superior status should exempt them from legal punishment (Higdon, 1975, p. 210). Many scholars of Nietzsche argue that the boys misread the Superman theory. These experts maintain that Nietzsche's Superman is a person so superior that (s)he would never consider committing evil acts, and therefore would never be subject to punishment. In this reading, the Superman is not above the law but rather is so superior

Richard Loeb, Nathan Leopold Jr., and Clarence Darrow, sitting in a crowded courtroom during the Leopold and Loeb murder trial. (Chicago Historical Society)

in nature that violation of any form of human or natural law would simply never occur.[1]

Both Leopold and Loeb were from prominent Jewish families in Chicago, well educated, and considered brilliant. Loeb's IQ was measured at 160, Leopold's at 210 (Higdon, p. 200). However, Leopold and Loeb would quickly learn that they were not their idea of Nietzschean "Supermen" who were above the law. They were flawed and ultimately "abnormal" boys, subject to law in the same way as the "ordinary people" around them.

FORCES UNITING LEOPOLD AND LOEB IN CRIME

Earlier in 1924, Leopold and Loeb had burglarized two fraternity houses at the University of Michigan. Their most successful burglary was of Zeta Beta Tau. There they stole many items, including a portable Underwood typewriter (Higdon, 1975). But this was small-time crime. For months after the burglaries, the teens planned to commit a perfect crime. Their goal was to commit this crime, then end their criminal careers altogether.

Why were Leopold and Loeb interested in committing such a crime? While both were from very wealthy families, and were provided generous allowances, both teens also considered themselves intellectually superior to others. Their feelings of superiority were reinforced by the philosophy of Nietzsche and his concept of the Superman. To Leopold, Loeb represented the Superman. He was handsome, well built, and charming (Leopold, 1958). Each saw the other as superior to himself. However, each was often frustrated by the other. Both, at times, contemplated killing the other, and both had considered committing suicide (Hulbert-Bowman report, in Higdon, 1975). Their relationship was intense and intertwined. Thus, unable to successfully commit a perfect crime alone, they believed it must be planned and carried out together.

THE KILLERS' MASTER PLAN

Leopold and Loeb planned to kidnap and murder the child of a wealthy family. Neither boy relished the idea of killing, but both thought murder a necessary ingredient of the perfect crime (Higdon, 1975, p. 97). Their obsession was with the successful completion of a masterful crime and subsequent escape from detection. After the murder, they would dispose of the child in a culvert by the Wolf Lake area south of Chicago, an area with which Leopold was familiar, since that was the desolate area where he often conducted his ornithological studies. Leopold was well known in the ornithological community. At age nineteen, he published a paper and lectured locally on the subject (Linder, 1999).

After hiding the body, the two men would call the murder victim's family and send them a letter with precise instructions detailing the method by which a ransom should be delivered in exchange for the safe return of their child. The family would then be told to await a telephone call that would direct the father to wait for a Yellow Cab that would be sent to the family home (*New York Times*, May 23, 1924). The father was to take the cab to a nearby drugstore and wait for further instructions. Leopold and Loeb would call the father at this phone and direct him to go to a nearby railway station and purchase a ticket to Michigan City, Indiana (*New York Times*, June 1, 1924). They chose this train because, by the time the father arrived at the station, he would have little time to purchase a ticket and make the train. Therefore, he would be unable to contact police.

On the train, the father was to proceed to the last Pullman car and open the telegraph box (*New York Times*, June 1, 1924). There, he would find a letter from the kidnappers explaining exactly how the money was to be delivered. The father was to wait until he passed a brick building, the Champion Manufacturing Company, then to quickly count *one, two, three*, and throw the package containing the money from the end of the train (Linder, 2003).

After retrieving the money, Leopold and Loeb would go back to their normal lives, attending law school in the fall. Once they had proven to themselves that they could commit the perfect crime, they would have confirmed their superior Supermen status. But as the saying goes, the best-laid plans of Supermen often go awry, as Leopold and Loeb soon discovered.

Criminal Mistakes

Several weeks prior to the kidnapping, Leopold and Loeb set their plan in motion, acquiring items needed to commit their crime. Most were easily purchased: rope, a chisel, and tape to wrap around it (Higdon, 1975). But the matter of transportation to use during the crime proved more challenging. They could not use Leopold's car because its bright red color was too noticeable. Loeb's car needed repair. Furthermore, neither wanted his own car traced back to him. So they devised an elaborate scheme to rent a car without revealing their identities (Rackliffe, 2000–2003).

First, Loeb established a temporary address by renting a room at the Morrison Hotel under an assumed name, Morton D. Ballard (Rackliffe, 2000–2003). He brought a suitcase (which he had filled with library books) with him to the room, and then met Leopold outside. The two then went to a local bank where Leopold opened an account as Ballard and deposited $100, which Loeb had taken from his own account earlier that day (Rackliffe, 2000–2003). Leopold used the Morrison Hotel as his address.

Armed with the hotel address, the bank account, and a list of phony references, Leopold posed as the fictitious Mr. Ballard, a traveling salesperson, in order to secure a rental car from the Rent-a-Car Company. His main reference was a "Mr. Louis Mason," who was actually Loeb, waiting across the street, ready for a possible reference call. Apparently suspicious of Ballard, the company boss called the reference, "Mason," who vouched for Ballard's authenticity. As Ballard, Leopold rented a gray Willys-Knight automobile. The teens kept the car for several hours and then returned it to the car company. Leopold (Ballard) asked the company to send an identification card to his hotel address. This was to ensure that he would have no problem renting a car on the day of the crime.

The next day, Loeb went to the Morrison Hotel to collect the car rental identification (Rackliffe, 2000–2003). When he arrived, he found no mail awaiting Ballard, and his suitcase was missing. He fled the hotel. Now in need of a new address for the rental identification, the teens drove to the Trenier Hotel, where Leopold explained that he, Ballard, planned to stay at the hotel, but had a change of plans (Rackliffe, 2000–2003). He asked the hotel to hold his mail; the staff agreed. "Ballard" then called Rent-a-Car and asked that the identification card be sent to the new Trenier Hotel address (Leopold confession). Finally, the plan for the car was ready.

Prior to committing the crime, Leopold and Loeb wrote two ransom letters to be addressed once they decided upon a victim. The first letter read:

Dear Sir:

As you no doubt know by this time, your son has been kidnapped. Allow us to assure you that he is at present well and safe. You need fear no physical harm for him, provided you live up carefully to the following instructions and to such others as you will receive by future communications. Should you, however, disobey any of our instructions, even slightly, his death will be the penalty.

1. For obvious reasons make absolutely no attempt to communicate with either police authorities or any private agency. Should you already have communicated with the police, allow them to continue their investigations, but do not mention this letter.

2. Secure before noon today $10,000. This money must be composed entirely of old bills of the following denominations: $2,000 in $20 bills, $8,000 in $50 bills. The money must be old. Any attempt to include new or marked bills will render the entire venture futile.

3. The money should be placed in a large cigar box, or if this is impossible, in a heavy cardboard box, securely closed and wrapped in white paper. The wrapping paper should be sealed at all openings with sealing wax.

4. Have the money with you, prepared as directed above, and remain at home after one o'clock. See that the telephone is not in use.

You will receive a further communication instructing you as to your final course.

As a final word of warning, this is an extremely commercial proposition and we are prepared to put our threat into execution should we have reasonable grounds to believe that you have committed an infraction of the above instructions.

However, should you carefully follow out our instructions to the letter, we can assure you that your son will be safely returned to you within six hours of our receipt of the money.

Yours truly,

George Johnson

(Ransom letter, reprinted in Higdon, 1975, pp. 41–42)

The kidnappers collectively called themselves George Johnson.

The next note supplied the instructions for the victim's family to be placed in the Pullman car. The notes and the plan were ready. All they needed was a victim.

May 21, 1924

On May 21, the day of the planned kidnapping, Leopold and Loeb went to the Rent-a-Car Company and rented a Willys-Knight. They drove until approximately 5 p.m. before they found a suitable victim. He was a young boy from a wealthy family who was walking alone.

Bobby Franks, age fourteen, lived near both kidnappers' homes and often played tennis at the Loeb family's tennis court (Higdon, 1975). Since he knew Loeb, he was not afraid to approach the kidnappers. Loeb called to the boy and, as a pretense, asked him about a tennis racket. Loeb asked Bobby if he would ride around the block (Higdon, 1975). Bobby agreed. One kidnapper was driving; the other was in the backseat. The driver (whether Leopold or Loeb remains unknown) opened the front passenger door so that Bobby would sit in the car's front passenger seat with one kidnapper sitting behind him (Higdon, 1975).

As the car turned the corner, the kidnapper in the back seat began to bludgeon Bobby Franks over the head with the chisel. Franks was severely injured and bleeding heavily from the attack, but he was not dead. The kidnapper in back pulled Franks into the car's backseat and stuffed a gag into his mouth. Franks suffocated to death, while Leopold and Loeb continued to drive (Loeb confession, in Higdon, 1975).

The brutal murder was complete. Leopold and Loeb drove through Chicago toward Indiana. In Indiana, they deliberately discarded the items of Franks's clothing that they did not think would burn, including the boy's shoes, class pin, and belt. The pair went back to Chicago and waited until dark. With Bobby's dead body still in the car, the kidnappers stopped for food (Higdon, 1975).

When night fell, the two drove to remote Wolf Lake (*New York Times*, May 24, 1924). As planned, they took Franks's body to the culvert underneath the railroad tracks, where they placed him in an automobile robe, stripped him of the rest of his clothes, and poured hydrochloric acid on his face, body, and genitals to prevent identification. They pushed the body into the culvert. Unwittingly, Leopold dropped his eyeglasses near the culvert. The kidnappers collected Franks's clothes and wrapped them in the robe. On the way to the car, one of the boy's socks fell from the robe (Leopold confession). Neither kidnapper noticed.

Upon returning from Wolf Lake, the young kidnappers made two phone calls. The first was to Leopold's parents. He explained that he would be late returning home and that, yes, he would drive his aunt and uncle home when he returned to the house (Leopold confession). They then stopped at a drugstore to call the Franks home, but became nervous when the operator took a while to connect. They left the store, addressed the previously written kidnap letter, marked it "special delivery," and deposited it into a nearby mailbox (Higdon, 1975, p. 106). They stopped again to call the Franks home. This time the phone was answered, and Mrs. Flora Franks was told that her son had been kidnapped and to await further instructions that would ensure the safe return of her son. She hung up and fainted (Testimony Flora Franks, July 23, 1924, in Higdon, 1975).

The teens then went to Loeb's house, where they burned most of Franks's clothes. Since they feared the smell of the much heavier automobile robe, they hid it behind some bushes. Then they went to Leopold's home. Leopold drove his aunt and uncle home, then returned home, where he and Loeb had a drink with Leopold's father, and then played cards (Leopold confession). Leopold and Loeb then left the house in the rental car. While driving, one kidnapper threw the chisel from the car. A passing police officer saw this, retrieved the chisel, and brought it to the police station (Testimony Officer Hunt, July 24, 1924, in Higdon, 1975). (According to some accounts, the teens met later that evening with two dates and a friend for a meal. They then dropped off the group and returned home.) The next day, the two met on the street where they had parked the rental car and drove it to Leopold's driveway, where they attempted to clean bloodstains from the backseat (Leopold confession). The Leopold family chauffeur, Sven Englund, offered to help, but the boys said that they had merely spilled some red wine in the backseat and could clean it themselves (Higdon, 1975, p. 109).

The Franks Family

Meanwhile, the Franks, also a wealthy family of Jewish descent, had been worried for some time about their missing son. Prior to receiving the call from the kidnappers, Bobby's father called the boy's friends and teachers, as well as a family friend, Attorney Samuel Ettelson (Higdon, 1975, p. 109). Franks, Ettelson, and a teacher searched the school, but Bobby was not there. When they returned to the Franks home, they found Flora, delirious from the call she received while the men were at the school. Franks and Ettelson went to the police that night, briefly explained to officers on duty what had happened, and decided to wait until the next day to speak to lead officers with whom they were acquaintances (*New York Times*, May 23, 1924).

The Immigrant

Early on May 22, Polish immigrant Tony Mankowski (Manke) was walking near Wolf Lake on his way to work when he noticed something odd protruding from a culvert under the Pennsylvania Railroad. It was a human foot. He looked further and found a dead young boy. He flagged down several railroad workers riding toward the scene on a handcar (Higdon, 1975, pp. 39–40). Manke spoke little English, but communicated that there was a body in the culvert. Immediately, the men removed the body to bring it to the police. One railroad worker noticed a pair of eyeglasses near the culvert. He decided to keep them (Higdon, pp. 40–41).

The men placed the body on the handcar, rode to a nearby train station, and called Chicago police. The police asked if the men had noticed anything at the crime scene. One railroad worker mentioned the eyeglasses. The body and the eyeglasses were confiscated and taken to a nearby funeral home (Higdon, 1975, p. 43).

The Investigating Journalists

Meanwhile, the *Chicago Daily News* received an anonymous tip that Attorney Ettelson could provide information on a young male kidnapping victim (*The Chicago Daily News*, 1924, May 31). Reporter James Mulroy located Ettelson at the Franks home, where Ettelson explained what had occurred and asked Mulroy to remain silent for the time being (Higdon, 1975, p. 44). Back at the newspaper, the city editor discovered that police had brought the body of a young boy to a local funeral home. The paper's editors became suspicious that the two cases were related: was the body at the funeral home that of the kidnapped boy? The editor sent reporter Alvin Goldstein to the funeral home; an *Evening American* reporter had also been sent (Higdon, p. 44). Back at the Franks home, Mulroy told the family that a boy's body had been recovered from a nearby culvert. He suggested that someone go to the funeral home where the body was being held so as to ensure it was not that of young Bobby. Jacob Franks's brother-in-law went to identify the body (*The Chicago Daily News*, 1924, May 23).

By now, the Franks had received the kidnap letter promised the night before by "George Johnson." Jacob Franks secured the money requested and awaited the phone call promised in the kidnap letter for further instructions. In mid-afternoon, the phone rang. The caller identified himself as Johnson, and he told Franks to expect a Yellow Cab at his house soon (*New York Times*, May 24, 1924). The caller then provided a drugstore address where Franks was to direct the driver. There, Franks was to wait by the phone for further instructions. Ettelson took the phone and was also given the address. The phone rang again. It was the brother-in-law. The body at the morgue was that of Bobby Franks (*New York Times*, June 1, 1924).

Soon, the Yellow Cab driver appeared at the Franks' door. He explained that a man identifying himself as "Mr. Franks" called for a cab at their address, but provided no destination address (Higdon, 1975). Franks and Ettelson immediately phoned the police.

Meanwhile, Leopold and Loeb called the drugstore where they had instructed Mr. Franks to go. A store employee informed them that no such person was there. The teens hung up, left the first drugstore, and drove one block to another drugstore, where they again called the drugstore to which they had directed Mr. Franks. Again, no one matching Mr. Franks' description was at the store. The teens hung up the phone and then saw the afternoon newspaper's headlines. The body of Bobby Franks, kidnapping victim, had been found and identified. The young men aborted their plans, knowing that if they continued to try to contact Franks, they would be caught. Leopold and Loeb had failed in their attempt to commit the perfect crime.

THE CRIMINAL JUSTICE PROCESS

The Investigation

The police were called after the Franks family learned that the body at the funeral home belonged to Bobby Franks. Police had little information, so they first directed their attention to three teachers at the Harvard School, where Bobby was a student, but there was no evidence to link any of the schoolteachers to the crime (Higdon, 1975).

The main evidence was the eyeglasses found near the dead boy by the railroad workers (Higdon, 1975). The glasses were a common frame and prescription. However, investigators learned that a specific company made the hinges on the glasses, and these were sold only at Albert Coe & Company. A store salesman examined approximately 54,000 records before compiling a list of three possible owners. One pair belonged to a woman, another to an attorney, and the third to Nathan Leopold (Higdon, 1975). At this point, the state's attorney, Robert E. Crowe, called police to bring Leopold in for questioning. When they arrived at the Leopold home, they asked Leopold if he wore glasses. He replied that he did, but only for reading. When asked if the glasses were in the house, Leopold was evasive (Higdon, 1975).

The Polite Interrogation

The police asked Leopold to go with them for questioning by State's Attorney Crowe. To avoid publicity, Crowe met the teen at a hotel rather than at his offices (Higdon, 1975, p. 78). Crowe showed Leopold the glasses and asked whether they looked like the ones he owned. Nathan said they did, but his were at home. After a second fruitless search of the Leopold home for the glasses, Leopold was brought back to the hotel, where he eventually admitted that the glasses belonged to him (Leopold confession). He suggested that the glasses must have fallen from his pocket while he was birding that prior weekend. Leopold attempted to demonstrate this possibility to investigators by placing the glasses into his coat pocket and falling to the floor. The glasses did not fall out (Linder, 2003). Investigators continued to question Leopold, during which time he acknowledged his friendship with Richard Loeb (Higdon, 1975).

Later that day, Loeb was brought to the hotel for questioning (Higdon, 1975, p. 86). The teens told conflicting stories of their whereabouts on the evening of May 21. Both admitted driving in Nathan's car that day, but then their stories diverged. Nathan said the two remained together; Loeb said they parted in the afternoon (*New York Times*, June 1, 1924).

While state officials questioned the teens, the *Chicago Daily News'* Mulroy and Goldstein continued their own investigation into the Franks murder. They learned that Leopold was part of a law school study group. Each week, he typed the session's notes. Goldstein visited a group member and asked to see his notes. Some looked different from others (Higdon, 1975). Goldstein took some sample notes back to the newspaper (*The Chicago Daily News*, 1924, May 31), where a typewriter expert examined the notes and compared them with the kidnap letter. The expert concluded that the notes and the letter were typed using the same machine.

The *Chicago Daily News* handed the evidence to the state's attorney. Although all members of the study group remembered Leopold using a portable typewriter, he denied owning one. No portable was found at his home (Higdon, 1975, p. 90). Leopold and Loeb both maintained their innocence.

State's Attorney Crowe knew he could not hold the teens very long without further evidence. Eventually, an assistant decided that before releasing the youths, he wanted to speak with the Leopold family chauffeur (Higdon, 1975, p. 91). Sven Englund was brought to the hotel and asked about Nathan's use of his car on the night of the murder. Thinking he was helping the boy (Linder, 2003), Englund stated that Leopold drove home that afternoon and asked Englund to fix the car's brakes. According to Englund, the car remained there all day. This directly conflicted with Leopold and Loeb's statements, in which they both now agreed that they had used Leopold's car to pick up two girls (*New York Times*, June 1, 1924).

The Confessions

Armed with this new evidence, questioning became more intense. Investigators told Loeb that they knew the teens were lying about their use of Leopold's car. Their alibi had been broken. Loeb confessed at 1:40 a.m. on May 31 (Higdon, 1975, p. 93).

Crowe then went to see Leopold. He told Leopold that Loeb had confessed, and bombarded him with evidence provided by Loeb, including information about the rented car and the false identities. He then said that Loeb testified that Leopold alone planned the crime and struck the blow that killed Franks (Higdon, 1975, p. 93). Provided this information, Leopold knew Loeb had confessed. Only Loeb knew these details, and Leopold was angry that Loeb had identified him as the killer. At 4:20 a.m., Leopold also confessed (Higdon, p. 94).

The kidnappers were eventually questioned together. They confessed to everything, agreeing on most points regarding commission of the crime. However, there were some points of contention, the most important one being who struck the deathblow. Both pointed the finger at the other (*New York Times*, June 6, 1924).

After confessing, the teens took an odd pride in parading investigators and the press on a two-day hunt to the areas where they had hidden physical evidence. Loeb fainted from stress early in the process, but Leopold continued to take investigators on a step-by-step trip to retrieve evidence. He provided rubber boots used to wade in the mud when disposing of Franks's body. He identified the chisel, found by the police officer when it was thrown from the rental car, as the murder weapon. At the culvert, they found Bobby's stocking. Later, Leopold took the group to a bridge. There, he showed police where to find remnants of the typewriter used to write the kidnap notes (*New York Times*, June 1, 1924).

At the end of the day, Leopold was taken to the hotel where Loeb had been resting (*New York Times*, June 1, 1924). As long as they were providing information, Leopold and Loeb were treated well. They were taken for a lavish dinner and provided changes of clothing from home.

The next day, the macabre evidence-gathering field trip continued. At one point, talking proudly of their research into and commission of the crime, Leopold made his famous statement about killing Franks: "It was just an experiment. It is as easy for us to justify as an entomologist in impaling a beetle on a pin" (*The Chicago Daily Tribune*, 1924, June 2). The teens showed no remorse.

The Defense

Throughout this period, Mike Leopold desperately tried to see his brother. During the first day of evidence-gathering, Mike, Loeb's uncle Jacob, and family cousin/attorney Benjamin C. Bachrach, went to see Crowe. They asked to see the teens, but were denied access.

Frantic, Jacob Loeb knew there was one person who could save his nephew from death. He went to attorney Clarence Darrow, begging him to take the case (*The Chicago Daily Tribune*, 1924, June 3). By the 1920s, Clarence Darrow had become well known as the "champion of the poor and the oppressed" (Higdon, 1975, p. 123). He had defended everyone from murder suspects to union leaders. Though in poor health, he was still a great orator and speechwriter and was known for excellent cross-examinations and an ability to remember facts without use of written notes (Higdon, p. 123). Darrow took the case because he saw in it the perfect opportunity to speak out against capital punishment, a practice he had fought throughout his life (Linder, 2003).

Following the second day of evidence-gathering, Leopold and Loeb were taken back to Crowe's office. During that Sunday morning, Crowe assembled the area's best-known alienists (as psychiatrists were then known) so the defense would be unable to use them in an attempted insanity plea. Prior to the teens' individual examinations, defense attorneys Bachrach and Darrow, along with Jacob Loeb, requested to see their clients. Crowe again denied their request (Higdon, 1975, p. 128). The attorneys would have to wait until Monday to bring the matter before a judge.

Crowe had Leopold and Loeb examined by his expert psychiatrists. All were "traditionalists," who were concerned with elements of the conscious mind. The teens were tested and retested. Afterward, Crowe took them to identify the Willys-Knight they had rented on the night of the murder. That night, Crowe took the teens for another lavish meal (Higdon, 1975, p. 128).

On June 2, Darrow and Bachrach returned to Crowe's office, demanding to see their clients. Again, Crowe denied them access by refusing to send the teens to the county jail (Higdon, 1975, p. 130). In response, the defense brought a writ of *habeas corpus* against Crowe, and was granted a hearing in front of Judge John R. Caverly, then chief justice of the criminal court. Eventually agreeing that the minors were being denied their constitutional rights, Caverly ordered Crowe to move the teens to the county jail, where they could meet with their attorneys. Upon seeing his clients, Darrow told them to stop providing evidence, since by doing so, they were helping the state to make its case (Higdon, p. 131). After their meeting, the teens took the Fifth Amendment when asked further questions. In response, Crowe held them in jail (p. 132).

The Defense Strategy

With the most famous alienists in the region already employed by Crowe, Darrow and Bachrach sent Bachrach's younger brother, attorney Walter

Bachrach, to the annual American Psychiatric Association meeting to find the era's top alienists to analyze Leopold and Loeb (Higdon, 1975, p. 137). Unlike Crowe's alienists, Bachrach chose doctors who were part of the new school of psychiatry, which was more concerned with subconscious rather than conscious motives. Sigmund Freud heavily influenced this new school. In addition to the alienists brought to Chicago, Darrow hired two local doctors, Harold Hulbert and Carl Bowman, to conduct extensive evaluations of the teens. Their 300-page report would be entered into evidence and play a huge role in the youths' defense.

Crowe was prepared to go to trial. He was convinced that Darrow was going to plead Leopold and Loeb not guilty by reason of insanity (*The Chicago Daily News*, 1924, June 7). However, Crowe was armed with his alienists' evidence that the teens knew that their actions were wrong.[2] With all of the physical evidence provided by the teens, Crowe announced that he had a "hanging case" (*New York Times*, June 1, 1924).

Darrow also knew the prosecution had a strong case. He had to rethink the insanity plea strategy. In a move that shocked the state's attorney, Darrow had Leopold and Loeb plead guilty to the kidnap and murder. Darrow explained to the defendants and their families that the plea would do two things: first, it would prevent the defense from being able to seek death on two separate charges: murder and kidnapping. As it stood, the state could ask a jury to seek death on one charge, and if it lost, it could impanel another jury to seek death on the other charge. The only way to prevent Crowe from getting two bites at the apple was to have the teens plead guilty to both charges (Higdon, 1975, p. 64).

Second, and perhaps more importantly, Darrow knew that a not-guilty-by-reason-of-insanity plea meant that a jury would decide the teens' ultimate fate, but a guilty plea would require a judge to make the death decision. It seemed much easier for a jury of twelve persons to sentence the teens to death since they could always argue that it was not themselves, but others on the jury, who pushed for the ultimate sentence. By pleading guilty, the decision whether to take the teens' lives would rest with one person, the judge. Thus, what was to be the trial of the century became a sentencing hearing during which the judge would hear mitigating and aggravating circumstances that he would then weigh in deciding whether the teens should live or die.

The Sentencing Hearing

State's Attorney Crowe was outraged that there would be no trial. Although the young men pled guilty, making moot the need to provide evidence of guilt, Crowe was determined to put all evidence before the court to prove their utter guilt and lack of remorse. During his evidence presentation, he portrayed Leopold and Loeb as evil monsters, suggesting that the boys had sexually molested Franks before killing him, a charge that was unfounded (*New York Times*, May 24, 1924). However, he was careful to maintain that, while their deeds were evil, the teens were not insane.

Darrow and Bachrach's strategy was to show that due to their mental condition and youth, the boys' lives should be spared. Darrow used psychiatric testimony as the primary mitigating factor. Crowe objected. If the defense were to argue that the boys were mentally unbalanced and therefore insane, the hearing should be concluded and a jury impaneled to hear a not-guilty-by-reason-of-insanity case (Higdon, 1975). In response, Darrow maintained that he would prove that the boys were not insane, but instead were mentally "abnormal," and that he would show the distinction between the two and the number of ways in which the teens' abnormalities were shaped and intertwined to produce the crime (Higdon, 1975).

There had been psychiatric testimony in previous trials (Fass, 1993), but there was no real precedent about the use of psychiatric testimony as mitigation in a death sentencing hearing. According to Higdon (1975), the Franks case set this precedent (p. 190). Judge Caverly agreed to hear defense testimony about the psychiatric state of Leopold and Loeb to determine whether such testimony should be allowed in court as official mitigation.

The defense turned to the findings in the Hulbert-Bowman report. In the report, and in all testimony by defense alienists, Darrow insisted that they refer to the teens by their nicknames, "Babe" (Leopold) and "Dickie" (Loeb). He believed that reference to their childlike nicknames would reiterate the boys' youth (Higdon, 1975, p. 206). The Hulbert-Bowman report stated that Babe had been an outcast youth who turned to education and his superior intellect for solace. Babe's life philosophy had been altered by two events. The first was the loss of his mother at age fourteen (Fass, 1993, p. 934). Babe reasoned that if a good person could be taken away at an early age, there must be no God. He decided to avoid emotions and to follow only "cold-blooded intellect" (Higdon, 1975, p. 201). The second experience involved Leopold's sex life. Though never really sexually attracted to women, he was sexually attracted to his friend, Dickie Loeb.

The report next turned to the boys' childhood and fantasies. During his youth, Dickie was provided an extremely strict governess who refused to allow Dickie to play with friends or to read books for fun (Higdon, 1975, p. 201). He was only to study. She wanted to mold him into a great man. In response to this pushing, Dickie began reading his favorite books, detective novels, in secret. He read them whenever he got the chance. Eventually, he became obsessed with, and fantasized about, crime (Hulbert-Bowman report, 1924, in Higdon, 1975).

The alienists reported that Babe's governess had sexually abused him (Higdon, 1975, p. 198). Perhaps as a result, he maintained a rich fantasy life, which usually involved himself as a slave to a king. In this fantasy, he, the slave, saved the king's life and was offered his freedom. But he refused and remained an anointed slave to the king (Higdon, p. 198).

The boys' fantasies merged when they met. According to the report, in Babe's mind, he became the slave to what he considered to be the superior Dickie (Higdon, 1975, p. 205). He wanted to please Dickie, whom he believed to be a Nietzschean Superman. Dickie wanted a partner in crime and believed Babe was superior in intelligence and capable of committing crimes. Through the intertwining of these fantasies, the forces united to result in the death of Bobby Franks.

After hearing this preliminary testimony, Judge Caverly decided that the defense's psychiatric evidence was not the same as evidence of insanity, and therefore, could be used as mitigating evidence of abnormality (Fass, 1993).

Once allowed to testify, defense alienists reiterated much of what they had previously stated. Babe had fears of inferiority. Alienists testified about his obsession with Nietzsche's Superman theory. On the subject of homosexuality, Dickie admitted to allowing Babe some sexual interactions, but solely in exchange for Babe's help in committing crimes (Fass, 1993).

At points during the hearing, Babe was labeled a "paranoid personality" (Higdon, 1975, p. 216), while Dickie was considered to be "abnormal mentally" and to have a "split personality" (Higdon, p. 217). Alienists suggested that Loeb suffered from disorders of the endocrine glands and the sympathetic nervous system, which could partially account for his abnormal behavior (Fass, 1993, p. 933). In effect, he was both mentally and physically abnormal. All of the alienists agreed that the crime never could have happened but for the intertwining of the disordered needs and personalities of the pair (Higdon, 1975).

In response to recasting the boys as victims of their abnormalities, Crowe offered rebuttal evidence. He called a prosecution alienist who testified that he could find in the teens "no evidence of any mental disease" (Testimony, Dr. Church, August 13, 1924, in Higdon, 1975).

The state rested.

Closing Arguments

Darrow was the first to close. This was his opportunity not only to convince the judge to spare the boys' lives, but also to convince the nation of the evils of capital punishment. It would become his most widely renowned speech and considered one of history's most impassioned and moving pleas against the death penalty.

First, however, he began his closing argument by denouncing the continual publicity surrounding the case and the unfairness of newspapers' widespread calls for death. Darrow believed public opinion was the greatest enemy to justice (Higdon, 1975, p. 124). He maintained that since the press had devoted such unprecedented time to the case, everyone in Chicago must have already decided whether the defendants should be put to death (Darrow summation).

Darrow next argued that the state would be out of touch with prior cases if it put to death youth of ages eighteen and nineteen. No one in Illinois under age twenty-three at that time had ever been put to death. He argued that boys of such ages were still children in need of direction. The very act of snatching and killing a child for no reason, and ultimately sacrificing their own lives, could only be the work of "a couple of immature lads" (Darrow summation). Darrow also argued that the defense alienists' testimony proved that the boys were abnormal. The boys lacked the ability to reason. They killed for the experience of it. Clearly, this was not the behavior of normal boys.

Darrow then tried to persuade the court to understand and accept his theory of determinism. He believed a person's life was set at birth, that there was really no free will, but that actions were predetermined by heredity, upbringing, and mental capacity (see Shattuck, 1999). Therefore, these boys should not be held responsible for traits they displayed that had been passed down to them by distant relatives. It was the hand they had been dealt (Darrow summation).

Finally, Darrow turned to his famous argument against the death penalty. He argued that justice should be tempered with mercy, and reiterated that the boys would be imprisoned for life if allowed to live. This case was horrible, he agreed, but not as serious as some others that had previously been before the court. Yet, because the boys came from wealth, they were treated with severe public scrutiny and outcries for death (Darrow summation).

Darrow acknowledged laying the death decision at Judge Caverly's feet, arguing that the judge must live forever with his ultimate decision. It would be easy to sentence the boys to death, thereby caving to "popular" desire. But Darrow pled with the judge to recognize that such a sentence would be looking to the past:

I know your Honor stands between the future and the past. I know the future is with me, and what I stand for here; . . . I am pleading for life, understanding, charity, kindness, and the infinite mercy that considers all . . . that we overcome cruelty with kindness and hatred with love. . . . You may hang these boys . . . by the neck until they are dead. But in doing it you will turn your face toward the past. . . . I am pleading for the future; I am pleading for a time when hatred and cruelty will not control the hearts of men. When we can learn by reason and judgement and understanding and faith that all life is worth saving, and that mercy is the highest attribute of man. (Darrow summation)

By the end of the twelve-hour closing, Judge Caverly was in tears (Linder, 2003).

Next, it was Crowe's turn to convince Judge Caverly to sentence the boys to death. He asked Leopold whether he now believed in God—had it been an accident by the Nietzsche disciple that led to his capture, or "an act of Divine Providence to visit upon your miserable carcasses the wrath of God in the enforcement of the laws of the State of Illinois" (Crowe summation). Crowe implied that the youths' capture was an act of God.

Crowe attacked Darrow's emotional closing. He suggested that Darrow relied too heavily on oratory and ignored facts, the only material the court should consider (Crowe summation). He criticized the determinism defense. Heredity could not be blamed for the boys' behavior. Even the defense's alienists admitted that there was no evidence of hereditary imbalance in the boys known to pass from one generation to another. Crowe called the teens "two perverts" and maintained that they should pay the ultimate penalty.

Crowe further claimed that the wealthy "spoiled" killers could not rely on the age defense, since the Illinois statute under which the case was being tried held that when an individual reached age fourteen, "the law presumes that he has the capacity to commit a crime and is entirely and thoroughly responsible for it" (Crowe summation). In addition, he argued, if American boys were old enough at age eighteen to die to protect the laws of their country in WWI, then these boys, now both nineteen, were old enough to die when they violated such laws.

Finally, Crowe attacked Darrow's blame of Nietzsche for the crime. Students had been reading the philosopher for years, and yet no one had used it as a defense in committing a crime (Crowe summation).

Crowe concluded by reiterating that the case facts proved Leopold and Loeb's guilt, that the young men represented evil incarnate, and that they should be put to death for their actions (Crowe summation).

The fate of Leopold and Loeb now lay with Judge Caverly.

Sentencing

On September 10, in a packed courtroom, Caverly announced his long-awaited ruling (Higdon, 1975). He stated that, although the defense testimony about mental abnormality was strong, it was more important to the study of criminology than to this case. Indeed, Caverly maintained that he was not swayed at all by the defense's psychiatric evidence in making his decision. The crime, he held, was one of "singular atrocity" (Caverly decision).

Caverly sentenced the youths to life for the murder, plus ninety-nine years for the kidnapping and ransom of Bobby Franks. Caverly chose life over death based solely on the teens' youth. This decision, he proclaimed, was in keeping with enlightened changes in criminal law occurring around the world, and with Illinois' own precedents (Caverly decision). Caverly stressed that life imprisonment seemed the worse punishment, as the teens would suffer years of confinement, unable to use the intellectual talents with which they had been so gifted and, ultimately, cursed.

Prison and Beyond

Leopold and Loeb were eventually placed in Stateville Prison after a period of separation (Higdon, 1975, p. 288). There, they began a correspondence school so that inmates could advance their educations, and they reorganized the prison library (Leopold, 1958).

On January 28, 1936, a former cellmate murdered Loeb in the shower. Though the death was ruled self-defense, state prison officials believed that Loeb had been murdered over a dispute about money (Higdon, 1975).

Leopold maintained the correspondence school after Loeb's death (Leopold, 1958). During World War II, he volunteered with other inmates as a test subject for a new malaria vaccine (Higdon, 1975, p. 304). In 1947, the governor decided to review the cases of all men who had volunteered for the malaria project. In 1949, Leopold's sentence was commuted from life plus ninety-nine years to eighty-five years, thus reducing the period he would have to serve before being eligible for parole (Higdon, p. 311).

When parole became a possibility, Leopold spoke with Meyer Levin, a journalist who had originally been assigned to cover the case when it was heard in 1924. They discussed collaboration on a book about Leopold's life. But Leopold wanted to concentrate on his prison years and refused to discuss the crime (except to maintain that he was led by Loeb). This was unacceptable to Levin, who wanted to write about the crime itself (Levin, 1956). The men went their separate ways, each deciding to write a book. Levin went on to write *Compulsion* (1956), a fact-and-fiction account of the crime. Leopold wrote *Life Plus 99 Years* (1958), in which he focused on his accomplishments in prison. He also discussed his relationship with Loeb. He claimed that he loved Loeb, but also hated him for involving him in the crime that had forever changed his life.

In 1957, after turning down his first request, the parole board again reviewed Leopold's case. This time the board had read Leopold's book, and Leopold had retained Elmer Gertz, a famous civil rights attorney, to represent him (Gertz, 1965). Gertz also represented Leopold in a lawsuit against Levin's *Compulsion* and became his lifelong friend (Gertz, 1965). Gertz stressed that Leopold must provide a reason for his crime to be paroled (Higdon, 1978, p. 318). In his prior hearing, Leopold would give no reason. Finally, in 1957, he gave the parole board what they wanted to hear. He stated that he had committed the crime to please Richard Loeb (Leopold, 1958).

Leopold was granted parole in 1958. He moved to Puerto Rico, where he wrote about ornithology. He married and taught mathematics at the University of Puerto Rico. He died in 1971.

THE PRESS: HELPING READERS TO RE-IMAGINE THE CRIME

Chicago in the 1920s witnessed two simultaneous conflicts: the first concerned Prohibition, and the second involved the city's newspapers (Higdon, 1975, p. 28). The latter provided much space for the former. By 1923, there were over 400 deaths per year in Chicago. Most were gangland murders. Life seemed cheap (Higdon, p. 20). In contrast stood the death of Bobby Franks. He was an innocent young victim, and his murder had no connection with the criminal underworld. If Bobby Franks could be murdered, so could any child. Newspapers pounced on this different murder, spreading the word quickly and vying for readers (p. 20).

Though *Chicago Daily News* journalists Mulroy and Goldstein were responsible for some important case breaks, these were overshadowed by the sensationalism surrounding the crime. Editorials demanded Leopold and Loeb be hanged, asserting that mothers were afraid to let their children out for fear that strangers would murder them. William Randolph Hearst, who owned two Chicago newspapers, offered Sigmund Freud any amount of money to come to Chicago and comment on the hearing. (Freud declined due to ill health and his concern that all he knew of the case was what was printed in newspapers, and he was unprepared to comment on evidence related by them [Higdon, 1975].) The *Chicago Daily Tribune* (1924, July 17) argued that courtroom events should be broadcast on its affiliate radio station WGN and hosted an opinion poll to determine whether the public would support such a broadcast. Readers voted against it.

News of each day's court events could be found in each newspaper's next edition. The press published the boys' confessions (for example, *New York Times*, June 6, 1924), conducted interviews with families and friends of the victim and the accused boys, "and speculated about the nature of the 'million-dollar defense' to be mounted by Clarence Darrow and his expensive psychiatric witnesses" (Fass, 1993, p. 923). In his turn, Darrow maintained that newspapers were purveyors of lies and misrepresentations that ultimately shaped public opinion (Darrow summation).

Along with the victim's family and police, two newspapers had each offered a $5,000 reward for information relating to the crime. But at the same time, newspapers published inaccurate stories, including one from the *New York Times* (July 19, 1924) stating that Loeb confessed to striking the fatal blow after learning that the crime's penalty would be the same regardless of who actually committed the physical murder. This was untrue; Loeb never confessed to carrying out the killing.

Press stories covered every sensational case detail (Fass, 1993). Rumors that Franks had been sexually abused intensified when the press became aware of the implied homosexual liaisons between Leopold and Loeb. However, there was no evidence to suggest that such abuse occurred (*The Chicago Daily Tribune*, 1924, May 24).

The press also dissected the teens' behavior by examining their facial features using the now-debunked science of phrenology (*The Chicago Daily Tribune*, 1924, June 1; *The Chicago Herald and Examiner*, 1924, June 1). Leopold was portrayed as a cold-hearted scientist who brutally took part in the murder as an experiment. In contrast, Loeb was seen as popular, and he was at first, and friendly with the press.

Prior to Leopold and Loeb's guilty plea, newspapers provided intensive tutorials for readers on the insanity defense (Fass, 1993, p. 931). But once the case became a sentencing hearing, coverage of psychiatry changed. As the hearing progressed, the public became familiar with new ideas, specifically those coming from the new school of psychiatry called psychoanalysis. The term "abnormal" became part of the social understanding of the apparently senseless crime that had been committed (Fass, p. 931). As the alienists described, the press reconstructed Leopold from a cold-hearted killer to an abnormal, insecure boy.

As defense testimony about the teens' lives was given, some newspapers' sympathy toward the youths increased. The *Chicago Daily News* (1924, June 3) wrote that Loeb, while in jail, was seen teaching a young African American inmate to read. The same article detailed the harsh conditions the wealthy teens faced in jail. One column asked Chicago families to think about how they would feel if one of their children were on trial for murder (Fass, 1993, pp. 928–929). By the end of the hearing, the perception of the boys would change completely, mainly due to the defense's psychiatric testimony. The wealthy monsters became mere boys who had committed a heinous crime (Fass, p. 929). These boys were now written about as abnormal in the psychiatric sense, and this abnormality helped to explain the seemingly random and horrific nature of their crime.

The press reconstruction of the boys from monsters to misguided youth helped the public to re-imagine the crime in understandable terms—it was the work of severely "abnormal" and "disordered" boys (Fass, 1993, p. 938). In the process, understanding of psychological concepts, though both criticized and accepted, became more widespread.

THE LEGACY

The Leopold and Loeb case forever altered perceptions of youth, public knowledge of psychiatry, and problems involved with the interaction between psychiatry and law. In addition, it framed the debate over capital punishment for the rest of the century.

One of the many concerns after the hearing was the fear that the crime represented changes occurring among youth. Young people were becoming uncontrollable, a result of the new parenting culture that allowed too much freedom. While this was not the first time that writers disparaged the way-wardness of youth, the reconstruction of Leopold and Loeb as abnormal boys struck fear in the hearts of many Chicagoans (Higdon, 1975; Fass, 1993). Crime and juvenile delinquency became not just the realm of the poor, but of the wealthy as well (Fass, p. 939). The public was concerned, not only that their children might be victims of "abnormal" others, but that their children might actually *be* "abnormal" (p. 939).

In the realm of criminal justice, appropriate use of expert psychiatric testimony became an issue. While psychiatric testimony had been introduced in trials long before the Leopold and Loeb case, Darrow was the first to use it as mitigating evidence to a crime, and the case brought expert testimony problems into public discourse (Fass, 1993, p. 930). Darrow used it to prevent an ultimate death sentence. But in doing so, he raised troubling questions concerning the appropriate scope and utility of psychiatric testimony that continue to persist.

Even before the expert psychiatric testimony was introduced, a battle waged over its appropriate use in the courtroom. Defense psychiatrists were concerned that the hearing would result in a war between opposing psychiatrists (Fass, 1993, p. 930). The judge would be left with two opposing points of view given by doctors paid by each side to support their positions. But, psychiatry was regarded as a science, and though reasonable doctors could disagree about diagnosis, defense psychiatrists suggested that doctors for both sides meet and agree to an ultimate diagnosis of the boys

(Higdon, 1975, p. 166). But Crowe rejected this idea. He planned for a trial in which insanity would be the question. A consensus among psychiatrists about the teens' states of mind would not help his case, and might very well hurt it.

Years later, one defense alienist who had been involved in the case wrote about the problem of retaining experts to provide findings sympathetic to a client (Fass, 1993). He maintained that the only way to fairly analyze a state of mind in a court setting required that the court itself appoint experts to make diagnoses independent of those argued by prosecutors or by defense attorneys.

Such ideas have been repeatedly voiced as the criminal justice system continues to struggle with often-confusing evidence by dueling experts, but reforms have not been implemented. Perhaps this lack of implementation reflects both the realities of the adversarial setting of the courtroom and the court's unwillingness to take on the additional responsibility of providing oversight of experts.

Continuing Fascination

Publicity played a huge role in shaping public opinion about Leopold and Loeb. They started as Nietzsche-trained monsters and ended up as victims of determinism, self-doubt, and each other's fantasies. But unlike many other trials in American history, the question of Leopold and Loeb's guilt was never at issue (*The Chicago Sun Times*, 1999, May 16). The primary concern was always, why would two wealthy boys of strong intelligence commit such an atrocious act? The teens' response, that they killed Bobby Franks to see if they could get away with the perfect crime, was never accepted as sufficient. Where did ultimate responsibility rest?

No answer to the boys' behavior has been deemed adequate, and so fascination with the case continues. No current theories of criminal behavior appear to be able to explain the apparent thrill killing (Entin, 1999). At the time, most psychiatric experts who examined the boys thought that Loeb was a psychopath (Higdon, 1975, p. 217) and Leopold a paranoid schizophrenic (Higdon, p. 339).

Scholarly publications still dissect the case, and it continues to be the subject of plays, books, and films. Although the film adaptation of Meyer Levin's novel *Compulsion* (1958) confuses the actual nature of events, blending fact and fiction, both the book and the film remain popular accounts of the pair's crime and sentencing. Inspired by the pair's alleged motivation, Alfred Hitchcock's *Rope* (1948) examines the cold Nietzschean philosophy that led two young men to kill a college-age peer—and then entertain dinner guests over his dead body. More recently, *Swoon* (1992) explores the nature of the homosexual and intertwined relationship between Leopold and Loeb. A decade later, *Murder by Numbers* (2002) provided another loosely based account of the Leopold and Loeb case.

Such long-lasting media attention reflects continued interest in the nature of "good" and "evil," and in the intense shades of gray represented by the Leopold and Loeb case. Perhaps more interesting today is Darrow's plea for the future and humanity. He believed himself on the side of history—that state-approved death sentences would soon be abolished. Darrow envisioned a moral society capable of learning from past mistakes. Perhaps mercifully, Darrow died only one year before his faith in a world moving toward a more moral path would be shattered: in 1939, the world was dragged down into the bloodiest war in history, and any hope for a more tolerant and peaceful civilization was eclipsed by one of the darkest eras of humankind.

But in 1924 Chicago, Darrow's beliefs in the future seemed possible, even as society struggled to understand his clients. Leopold and Loeb killed young Bobby Franks and left the world with their disturbing and incomprehensible vision of "the perfect crime." It is this incomprehensibility that has led to fascination with the strange and frightening behavior of the two young men and ensures their immortality in the annals of American crime.

NOTES

1. For Nietzsche's "übermensch" theory, see *Thus Spake Zarathustra* (Nietzsche, 1891/1966).

2. Illinois used the M'Naghten Test at that time, which required that, in order to prove insanity, the perpetrator not have known the difference between right and wrong at the time of the crime (Fass, 1993).

REFERENCES

The Chicago Daily News. (1924, May 31; 1924, June 3; 1924, June 7).

The Chicago Daily Tribune. (1924, June 2; 1924, June 3).

The Chicago Herald and Examiner. (1924, June 1).

The Chicago Sun Times. (1999, May 16).

Clarence Darrow: A plea for mercy. (1924). Retrieved July 1, 2004, from http://www.americanrhetoric.com/speeches/cdarrowpleaformercy.htm

Crowe summation for the state. (1924). Retrieved September 30, 2003, from http://www.law.umkc.edu/faculty/projects/ftrials/leoploeb/LEO_SUMP.HTM

Entin, J. (1999). Using great cases to think about the criminal justice system [Book review]. *The Journal of Criminal Law and Criminology, 89*(3), 1141–1156.

Fass, P. S. (1993). Making and remaking an event: The Leopold and Loeb case in American culture. *The Journal of American History, 80*(3), 919–951.

Gertz, E. (1965). *A handful of clients.* New York: Follett.

Higdon, H. (1975). *The crime of the century: The Leopold and Loeb case.* New York: G. P. Putnam's Sons.

Judge Caverly's decision. (1924). 29 Dick. L. Rev. 1. Retrieved September 30, 2003, from http://www.law.umkc.edu/faculty/projects/ftrials/leoploeb/LEO_DEC. HTM

Leopold, N. (1958). *Life plus 99 years.* New York: Doubleday.

Leopold, N. (2003). Full confession as found at Linder, D., Famous American trials: *Illinois v. Nathan Leopold and Richard Loeb.* Retrieved September 30, 2003, from http://www.law.umkc.edu/faculty/projects/ftrials/ leoploeb/leopold.htm

Leopold confession. (1924). Retrieved September 30, 2003, from http://www.law. umkc.edu/faculty/projects/ftrials/leoploeb/LEO_CONF.HTM

Levin, M. (1956). *The obsession.* New York: Simon and Schuster.

Linder, D. (2003). Famous American trials: *Illinois v. Nathan Leopold and Richard Loeb.* Retrieved September 30, 2003, from http://www.law.umkc.edu/ faculty/projects/ftrials/leoploeb/leopold.htm

New York Times. (1924, May 23; 1924, May 24; 1924, June 1; 1924, June 6; 1924, July 19).

Nietzsche, F. (1966). *Thus spoke Zarathustra: A book for none and all* (W. Kaufmann, Trans.). New York: Viking Penguin, Inc. (Original work published 1891)

Rackliffe, M. (2000–2003). I teach you the overman. Retrieved September 30, 2003, from http://www.leopoldandloeb.com

Shattuck, R. (1999, January). When evil is "cool." *The Atlantic Monthly, 283*(1), 73–78.

Steinberg, N. (1999, May 16). Leopold and Loeb case still haunts after 75 years. *The Chicago Sun Times.*

5

The Scopes "Monkey Trial": A Debate about Evolution

Ernest L. Nickels

The trial of John T. Scopes was brought to session on the morning of July 10, 1925, in the Rhea County Courthouse of Dayton, Tennessee. On its face, the case is hardly noteworthy. It was a misdemeanor criminal trial of a small-town schoolteacher on charges he readily admitted to and—surprising no one—would ultimately be convicted of. As a question of law, however, the case probed the profound frictions in the history of American jurisprudence among academic freedom of public educators, protections against state establishment of religion, and the right of the people to legislative control of the form and operation of public agencies. Further, the case of *Tennessee v. Scopes* served as a spectacular finale to the end of an era, one marked by rapid change in the social, cultural, and intellectual institutions of American life—transformations to which a single trial could no more than bear witness. As narrated by an attentive press, these mere eight days of trial, squaring off the towering figures of William Jennings Bryan and Clarence Darrow, reflected back to a transfixed public all the aspirations and anxieties of a people finding themselves at the dawn of a new age. These were a people diversely, if uneasily, invested in both progress and tradition, in reason and in faith, in science and religion.

POLARIZED VIEWS OF EVOLUTION

Evolution had the attention of philosophers and scientists alike well before Charles Darwin's *Origin of Species* in 1859. It was Darwin's thoroughly naturalistic rendering of an evolutionary account, his contribution of such concepts as "natural selection," and his 1871 attempt in *The Descent of Man* to place the human species within this framework that placed him (if belatedly) at the forefront of a scientific revolution.

Religious antagonism to Darwinism fluctuated in proportion to its acceptance in the field. Mildly condemned for contradicting Biblical teachings on the special creation[1] of life and allowing no explicit role for God in its development, initial scientific resistance to Darwin calmed critics in the religious community temporarily. Until advancements in genetics breathed new and certain life into the Darwinian paradigm after the turn of the century, his works held an uncertain place in the budding sciences. Special creationism (particularly in the United States) and pre-Darwinian evolutionary theories continued to thrive in the meantime. Only with the onslaught of a younger generation of post-*Origin* researchers, rapidly filling the expanding institutions of professional science, were such views eventually displaced.

Dissemination of this growing scientific consensus into the public sphere through high school science curricula lagged behind the field for some time.[2] Revisions of established textbooks, then dominated by creationist views, were not affected by the sweeping changes in the field at the close of the nineteenth century. Newer texts began to appear in the 1880s. However, only after the exponential growth of the public education system at the turn of the century, and the merging of zoology and botany into a single course called biology, did the intellectual monopoly held by older texts loosen. These forces required that the industry produce more, as well as original, materials to meet novel institutional demands—an opportunity for younger scientists. Over the next thirty years, these texts adopted an increasingly evolutionist and explicitly Darwinian stance, one progressively hostile to creationist concepts. In 1914, George Hunter published the hugely successful *Civic Biology*. It included a section on evolution as well as a biographical sketch of Darwin himself. It was Scopes's use of this text that led to his arrest and trial.

It is difficult to discern how the public initially received such ideas. Evidence suggests, however, that Americans today are generally more inclined to view science and religion as competitive realms of knowledge and to be antagonistic toward evolutionary ideas than at the turn of the century. Current views on evolution in the classroom are certainly more defined and polarized now. Far from predetermined, anti-evolutionism in the United States emerged from specific forces at work in religion in Progressive America. One man, a force in himself, was particularly instrumental in how history would unfold: William Jennings Bryan.

THE GREAT COMMONER

A gifted orator, scholar, lawyer, and journalist for popular and religious publications, the Great Commoner (as Bryan was known) had served as secretary of state under President Wilson, and three times ran as the Democratic candidate for the presidency. Committed to populist reform, world peace, welfare, and organized labor, Bryan's politics were emblematic of the Progressive Era. Like many progressives, he was an evangelical[3] dedicated to social reformation through institutional reform and personal salvation—and, failing that, state intervention. Socially progressive and religiously conservative, Bryan and his fellow travelers constituted an enigmatic but effective force of change.

Darwinism initially commanded little attention from evangelicals. It would, however, become the incidental enemy to some within the movement. At the dawn of the twentieth century, substantial numbers came to staunchly oppose "modernism" in the church—a trend toward liberal, nonliteral interpretations of Scripture informed by (among other things) scientific discovery. This offshoot, called fundamentalism, was more socially pessimistic and religiously conservative than the evangelicalism before it. Fundamentalists yearned for a return to "old time religion" premised on unchanging, universal principles (fundamentals) derived from Scriptural literalism. As the movement grew, absorbing the energies and political clout of its forbearers, fundamentalism became a powerful force in the interwar political landscape. Unsettled by the expanding influence science held in shaping the minds of the nation's youth through the public education system, fundamentalists particularly resented indoctrination to evolutionary ideas in the classroom. Bryan's activism helped galvanize these vague sentiments into a full-scale cause.

Though a self-professed "fundamentalist," Bryan's relationship to the anti-evolutionist movement was complex. Not sharing fundamentalism's cornerstone doctrine of Scriptural literalism, Bryan's own motivations were varied. Aware of early scientific criticism of Darwin, Bryan had been initially dismissive of Darwin's theory and continued to insist it was simply flawed science. However, while publicly categorical in rejecting evolution, privately he recognized that future science might demonstrate its factuality (De Camp, 1968, p. 45). Bryan's open objections to teaching human evolution were limited to its presentation as *fact* (rather than hypothesis) and pertained only to public (rather than private) schools. A progressive reformer, Darwinism troubled Bryan more in its application than its idea.

He viewed concepts like "survival of the fittest" as legitimating a *social* Darwinism. An ethic of might-makes-right, he believed, alienated people from their moral obligations. Further inflaming these apprehensions was the popularization of eugenic social policy in interwar America—a movement pioneered by Sir Francis Galton (Darwin's cousin) to apply hereditary knowledge to the cultivation of a genetically "fitter" population through methods perceived un-Christian to many. Likewise, Bryan recognized Darwin's influence on the work of nineteenth-century German moral philosopher Friedrich Nietzsche,[4] a self-proclaimed immoralist many blamed for inspiring German militancy that resulted in World War I. Furthermore, though helping to define the movement, Bryan clearly believed that his activism merely gave voice to the people's will. Dedicated to the populist creed that the people are the ultimate authority on all things public, including public science and its instruction, Bryan believed it was within their rights to banish Darwin from their schools. Likewise an advocate of free speech and an opponent of state establishment of religion, Bryan differed intellectually with measures sought by some fundamentalists to criminalize the teaching of evolution and institutionalize creationism. However, he was not one to highlight such ideological differences. His activism did much to produce anti-evolutionist legislation he could not fully endorse, but would defend nonetheless on principle.

THE MAKING OF A TRIAL

With the backing of groups including the World's Christian Fundamentals Association (WCFA), anti-evolutionism bills found their way first into the legislatures of Kentucky and South Carolina in 1922. Each bill met narrow defeat. Much to Bryan's credit, 1923 brought success in Oklahoma, with the passage of an anti-evolutionist textbook bill. Shortly thereafter, Florida approved a resolution he authored that prohibited the teaching of evolution as fact. Tennessee went further, in 1925, with the passage of the Butler Act, which read,

Chapter 17, House Bill 185 (By Mr. Butler) Public Acts of Tennessee for 1925.

AN ACT prohibiting the teaching of the Evolutionary Theory in all the Universities, Normals and all other public schools of Tennessee, which are supported in whole or in part by the public school funds of the State, and to provide penalties for the violations thereof.

Section 1. BE IT ENACTED BY THE GENERAL ASSEMBLY OF THE STATE OF TENNESSEE, That it shall be unlawful for any teacher in any of the Universities, Normals and all other public schools of the State which are supported in whole or in part by the public school funds of the State, to teach any theory that denies the story of the Divine Creation of man as taught in the Bible, and to teach instead that man has descended from a lower order of animals.

Section 2: BE IT FURTHER ENACTED, That any teacher found guilty of the violation of this Act, shall be guilty of a misdemeanor and upon conviction, shall be fined not less than One Hundred ($100.00) Dollars nor more than Five Hundred ($500.00) Dollars for each offense.

Section 3: BE IT FURTHER ENACTED, That this Act take effect from and after its passage, the public welfare requiring it.

After it passed both state houses, Governor Austin Peay signed the bill into law in March of that year. Many, Peay included, saw the Butler Act as merely symbolic legislation. Plans for enforcement were never publicly entertained (Ginger, 1958, p. 7). Nevertheless, it quickly found application in the arrest of John Scopes.

The American Civil Liberties Union (ACLU),[5] having watched anti-evolutionist initiatives grow bolder, responded decisively to the Butler Act. It issued a press release, quoted in the May 4 edition of the *Chattanooga Daily Times*, announcing that the organization was "looking for a Tennessee teacher who is willing to accept our services in testing this law in the courts" ("Plan," 1925). In Dayton, a small mountain town outside Chattanooga boasting a population of less than 3,000, the ACLU's volunteer was found.

George Rappelyea, an employee of the Tennessee Coal and Iron Company who managed mining properties around Dayton (Scopes and Presley, 1967, p. 36), apparently saw in the ACLU release an opportunity for civic promotion—an event that could put Dayton on the map and bring in new sources of revenue, even if only through tourism during the event. Together with area locals and business leaders, Rappelyea set about enlisting John Scopes, a Rhea County Central High School science teacher and sports coach, in bringing a test case of the Butler Act.

At a local drugstore, the pitch was made. Initially reluctant, Scopes was unsure whether he had even broken the law.[6] Although Scopes did not normally teach biology, the drugstore meeting did uncover that he had substituted for the regular instructor and had used *Civic Biology* to help students review for the final exam. Eventually, Scopes was talked into volunteering for his own arrest. Once agreeable, Rappelyea swore out a warrant against Scopes and sent word to the ACLU, who responded promptly with a promise of *pro bono* representation, financial help, and publicity for his cause. The arrest came May 7, with formal charges three days later accusing Scopes of having taught evolution in April of that year.

Speaking before the annual convention of the WCFA in Memphis on May 11, where the impending Dayton trial was much discussed, Bryan noted in his address his hope that the statute would be upheld. Promptly, the WCFA leadership approached him for assistance in the prosecution. Sue Hicks, a Dayton merchant who helped instigate the case, had also been attempting (without luck) to contact Bryan to elicit aid with the prosecution (Ginger, 1958, p. 21). Two days later, in Pittsburgh, Bryan announced his willingness to aid the state, and he was appointed shortly thereafter as special prosecutor— an unusual occurrence for a misdemeanor trial (Larson, 2003, p. 61). Bryan and his son joined District Attorney General Thomas Stewart and District Attorney Ben McKenzie and his son, Judge J. G. McKenzie, on the prosecution.

On defense, Scopes's Dayton attorney, John Neal, was joined by ACLU trial lawyer Arthur Hays. On learning that Bryan would aid the prosecution, Clarence Darrow and Dudley Malone jointly volunteered their services directly to Neal.

Darrow was a prominent defense attorney and, like Bryan, a social progressive, a friend of labor, and a Democrat. Originally friendly acquaintances, Darrow had even supported Bryan's early political careers. However, Darrow did not share Bryan's populism, tending instead toward libertarian values with pronounced intellectualist overtones. A skeptic, rationalist, and fervent individualist, Darrow was viewed by many as a radical for aiding in the defense of clients who were anarchists, socialists, and communists (De Camp, 1968, pp. 74–79). The Federal Bureau of Investigation (FBI) even maintained a file on him.[7] Particularly on matters of religion and evolution, the two men stood in stark opposition. Their relationship grew publicly antagonistic as a result. In 1923, Darrow challenged Bryan in an open letter to the *Chicago Tribune* to answer fifty questions about human history, attacking Bryan's (inferred) Scriptural literalism. Bryan indignantly declined (De Camp, pp. 74–79).

For his zealous agnosticism[8] and personal antipathies toward Bryan, Darrow rightfully anticipated that the ACLU would wish to avoid his involvement for fear of "transform[ing] the trial from a narrow appeal for academic freedom to a broad assault on religion" (Larson, 1997, p. 100). John Neal had no such reservations. Renowned and experienced in high-profile cases, Darrow had a reputation for winning seemingly unwinnable cases. In the previous year, he had successfully defended Richard Loeb and Nathan Leopold, two wealthy teenagers accused in a thrill-kill murder of a fourteen-year-old boy, against a death penalty verdict by arguing that the defendants were pitiable victims of (among other things) exposure to Nietzschean philosophy. Ironically, Bryan later drew upon Darrow's defense in Leopold and Loeb to illustrate the need to prohibit evolutionism in schools (Larson, p. 100).

All involved in the making of the trial had aspirations for a show of sensational proportions, with various hopes for personal, economic, and ideological gains. The ACLU sought to rigorously defend Scopes. However, expecting defeat, they aimed to win on appeal at the state supreme court and have the law ruled unconstitutional—and, if not there, at the U.S. Supreme Court, where the impact would be national. Further, they hoped to use the trial's publicity to demystify evolution to a national audience, and then rouse popular disfavor for the Butler Act to put the anti-evolutionist movement in check, if not reverse it. Rappelyea and the business interests of Dayton were eager to attract attention and visitors to their town in the hope of spurring the community's economic growth. The WCFA sought a symbolic victory over the forces of modernism, as did Bryan, who further believed that the American public simply lacked understanding of the true fallacies and imminent dangers Darwinism posed for the moral fabric of the nation. Darrow aimed to take a well-publicized shot at fundamentalism by publicly defeating its most visible proponent, and his personal antagonist, Bryan. As these interests converged piece by piece, the stage was set for an event with far greater cultural than legal significance. With Darrow and Bryan now commanding the spotlight, the spectacle was set to begin. Arriving in Dayton, Bryan set the tone:

The contest between evolution and Christianity is a duel to the death. . . . If evolution wins in Dayton, Christianity goes—not suddenly of course, but gradually—for the two cannot stand together. They are as antagonistic as light and darkness, as good and evil. ("Bryan," 1925, p. 6)

THE MONKEY TRIAL

The defense's trial strategy was simple enough: challenge the law on constitutional grounds. Failing that, attack the substance of the statute as incoherent and an unreasonable restriction on public educators by demonstrating the factuality of evolution and its compatibility with (modernist) Biblical interpretation. Waiting in the wing were a number of scientific and religious authorities to provide expert testimony to that effect. A victory at Dayton was unlikely, so they would seek to produce a record of the trial favorable to a case for appeal (Scopes and Presley, 1967, p. 158). The prosecution would move to exclude such testimony and would likely succeed. Any opportunity to enter even a sample of that testimony into the record, however, would be a partial victory.

The prosecution's strategy was simpler: fend off constitutional challenges and argue the case purely on the factual question of whether or not Scopes had taught human descent in violation of the law's letter and intent. Try to suppress expert testimony to avoid debate on evolution's scientific merits and compatibility with Scripture—they simply would not win a contest of credentials with the expert witnesses available to the prosecution (Larson, 2003, p. 66).

John Raulston, an elected circuit court judge for east-central Tennessee and lay minister, presided. Sharing the town's enthusiasm for its newfound fame, he likewise enjoyed his own. Aside from the throngs of journalists from the national media, Scopes is also a landmark trial in criminal justice history in the media for its pioneering use of live radio broadcasts and its continuous feed by cable of the unfolding events to Europe and Australia. Raulston himself was heard to remark, "[m]y gavel will be heard around the world" (Ginger, 1958, p. 103). He was, no doubt, correct.

When proceedings[9] opened on Friday morning of July 10, the first issue was the securing of a new grand jury indictment. The original had been invalidated by a procedural error. Jury selection dominated the afternoon. Darrow was known to engage this process meticulously. So convinced of its importance in determining the outcome of a trial, he had once spent six months in selecting whom to seat. Regional custom in misdemeanor cases, however, was rather informal. A small, initial pool of potential jury members, if insufficient, could be enlarged by having the sheriff round up willing bodies from the available bystanders. Although concessions were made, Darrow was further dismayed to find himself limited to only three preemptory challenges (the ability to dismiss a potential juror without stating cause). Further, these challenges had to be exercised while the person was under questioning or not at all, meaning that he was prohibited to question them all before selecting out those he predicted to be least sympathetic to the defense (Ginger, 1958, pp. 96–97). In short order, then, the twelve jurors were settled upon.

Mostly farmers and primarily Baptists and Methodists, the jury displayed a diversity of viewpoints on faith and evolution largely unappreciated by a national media that lumped the lot of them as "fundamentalists" (Conkin, 1998, p. 87). It mattered little, however, as the jury would spend the vast majority of the trial excused from the courtroom as the prosecution and defense wrangled over legal questions of statutory interpretation and the relevance of expert testimony—matters to which the jury was not permitted to be audience. Instead, the jury followed events as many in the town did, listening to the broadcast of the proceedings over a pair of large speakers on the courthouse lawn. At the close of the day, the defense requested that the jury be sworn before the weekend, to limit their permission to discuss the substance of the case. Local custom held that jurors not be sworn until the first day of trial, in case one should fall ill in the meantime. In keeping with that, Raulston ordered the swearing-in postponed until after opening statements on Monday.

Monday morning, then, with the jury excused, the defense raised its motions to quash the indictment. The law, they argued, was unreasonable in its limitations, it violated protections of due process and free speech as articulated in the state and federal constitutions, and it ran afoul of the state's own constitutional guarantees of the separation of church and state and its expressed mandate in support of the sciences. Attorney General Stewart, for the prosecution, countered. The language of the statute was clear enough. It in no way infringed upon religious freedom to limit the subjects public educators were permitted to speak on in the course of their duties. Further, as the state supreme court had ruled, control of the public schools fell to the discretion of the legislature.

The day concluded with Darrow's first speech to the court, arguing to quash. The speech oscillated between a folksy, good-natured appeal to reason and a terse rebuff of religiously inspired bigotry. On one hand, Darrow attempted to shame the religious sentiments of those in the audience for zealous persecutory practices of the Christian past (alluding to sixteenth-century witch hunts targeting intellectuals). On the other, he largely absolved his audience of responsibility for the Butler Act, casting blame instead onto out-of-state fundamentalist demagogues—those such as Bryan—and appealed to the jury's higher-mindedness to put this bad law to rest. By most accounts, it was a brilliant speech, lionized by those in attendance and the press alike. H. L. Mencken, a widely read and influential syndicated editorialist for the *Baltimore Sun* who, as a friend, had encouraged Darrow to take the case (Larson, 1997, p. 100), was particularly generous in his praise. Likewise, as would be typical of his coverage, he was generously contemptuous of the fundamentalist "yokels" and "morons" in the audience.

Tuesday morning found the court in conflict, once more, over customary procedure. With the jury excused, Darrow objected to the practice of opening prayer at the start of each day. Raulston was unmoved. Noting his own reliance on divine guidance on the bench, he hardly saw impropriety in encouraging the same of jurors. He would concede only to allowing the local ministerial association to provide representatives of other faiths to lead opening prayer. The out-of-town press, believing Dayton was exclusively fundamentalist, interpreted Raulston's attempt at compromise as sarcasm. Of the remaining days of trial, prayer was conducted once by a Jewish rabbi and once by a Unitarian preacher. This also largely escaped the notice of a press selectively attending to its misperceptions of Dayton's residents (Conkin, 1998, p. 89).

After a recess, and a photo opportunity for the press (Ginger, 1958, p. 131), Raulston spent the remainder of the morning dictating his decision on the constitutional issues raised by the defense in private to a court stenographer. Somehow the ruling was leaked to the press. Raulston deferred his ruling until morning, until the culprit was identified and publicly scolded in court. Summarily, then, Raulston dismissed the defense's arguments as without merit. The trial continued. With the jurors now in attendance, the defense entered its plea: not guilty.

The prosecution succinctly stated the charge. Attempting to strengthen its case on appeal, the defense moved for dismissal. Overruled, the defense then stated what would be its two-pronged theory of the case. By the wording of the statute, it argued, the state must first prove that Scopes had taught evolution. The defense conceded Scopes had. Second, however, the state must prove that in so doing he had contradicted the Biblical account of creation. The defense contended that there was nothing inherent to evolution that contradicted anything other than a literalist interpretation of Genesis, and they were prepared to offer expert testimony to that effect.

With the jury finally sworn, the state called its witnesses. First came the superintendent of the Rhea County schools, who had signed the complaint against Scopes. Following that, the state called two students from Scopes's class to testify to Scopes use of *Civic Biology*, and concluded with F. E. Robinson, a party to the drugstore conspiracy. The defense again moved for dismissal and, again overruled, called its own first witness—Maynard Metcalf, an eminent zoologist from Johns Hopkins University.

The prosecution interjected. If Scopes was to testify, he must, under the rules of Tennessee process, be called as first witness. The defense responded that Scopes could provide nothing useful to his defense, as the use of the text was already conceded. Darrow returned to his examination of Metcalf, who had testified to being both an evolutionist and a Congregationalist. When Darrow asked whether he was aware of any scientist who was not an evolutionist, Stewart objected. Raulston concurred. Under the rules of hearsay, one cannot testify on the content of opinions held by anyone other than one's own self. Raulston would, however, allow Darrow to proceed with his examination as a matter of record while deferring judgment on the admissibility of testimony overall. Though clearly predisposed to exclude the testimony, Raulston was reluctant to rule so early on the matter, perhaps thinking of interests at stake for the community (Conkin, 1998, p. 90) and perhaps out of sheer egoism. In any case, the ruling surely would have brought the trial to a premature close. After instructing court reporters that the testimony to follow was not to be released to the press, the judge permitted examination to resume. Metcalf testified that, familiar with the leading authorities in the zoological, geological, and botanical sciences, he was confident that each took evolution to be a fact. They might, however, differ on the particulars of its theory.

Stewart now raised the first of repeated objections insisting that, whatever the factuality of evolution, the sovereign people of Tennessee had decided that the teaching of human descent was inconsistent with Biblical scripture. Therefore, the jury, as the people's representatives, needed no further interpretation by experts of any sort on either the wording or intent of the legislature in putting the act to law. The only pertinent questions were those of the factual circumstances surrounding Scopes's use of the offending text. All other testimony was irrelevant.

Raulston, again excusing the jury, allowed Darrow to proceed. Metcalf testified to his belief that all life began as unicellular plants in the sea, and offered his estimation of this Cambrian period to have occurred more than 600 million years ago—a stark contrast to literalists' estimations that placed the earth's age at a mere 6,000 years. At the close of session, Raulston announced that the question of admissibility would be settled the following day.

When the trial resumed Thursday, and before Metcalf was allowed to continue, the prosecution called for Raulston's ruling on the testimony. Darrow insisted that "evolution" and "creation," key terms in the statute under which their defendant was charged, were not adequately clear and that expert testimony was necessary to demonstrate that Scopes taught the former and contradicted the latter. Raulston ruled that formal arguments on admissibility would be opened by the state, though Darrow argued that that privilege fell to the defense.

Bryan's son presented the prosecution's initial points. A rigorous, if dry, account of the case precedent bearing upon the use of expert testimony, he argued that any experts presented by the defense could only testify to their own opinions on whether they *personally* saw conflict between the account of evolution and the story of creation as they understood it. Further, as a question of fact, it fell upon the jury alone to determine whether Scopes's use of the materials in question had violated the law. Hays responded for the defense. Interpretation of the statute was necessary, and the *factuality* of evolution—which only expert testimony could establish—was certainly relevant to the case before them. The debate carried on fruitlessly for some time, and Darrow moved for its immediate resolution, out of consideration for the witnesses left waiting in the wing. Showing hesitancy once more, Raulston postponed his decision until after the noon recess.

When the trial resumed, William Jennings Bryan took the floor. Up to this point, he had scarcely said a word, passively observing the proceedings. The expectant audience awaited the Commoner's speech. Though evaluations varied, he was mostly in classic form. Animated, he directed his impassioned speech directly to the attentive crowd, rather than the bench—which should have elicited a reprimand from Raulston, but did not. He was, however, an older man now and in declining health, and largely drew upon an arsenal of rhetorical arrows crafted for anti-evolutionist lectures he delivered on circuits around the country. Nonetheless, he ruthlessly lampooned evolutionary thought and strung together Darwin with Nietzsche and German aggression. He attacked a diagram of speciation included in *Civic Biology* that placed the human race indistinguishably amid branches representing other life forms in the animal kingdom, all sharing a single genealogical trunk. "Talk about putting Daniel in the lion's den?" he exclaimed (*World's Most Famous*, 1997, p. 175).

He mocked the notion of reconciling evolution with Genesis, and stressed the caustic effects of Darwinism on a social morality. He accused science of fostering atheism, and proclaimed the jury better qualified for Biblical interpretation than any supposed expert the defense could produce. He attacked Darrow personally, quoting from the record of the Loeb-Leopold case to accuse him of propagating an amoral worldview. Darrow objected, reproaching Bryan for misrepresenting the context of his statements. Bryan concluded by reiterating the prosecution's contention that it was for Tennesseans alone to decide what belonged in their own public classrooms. The jury, as their representatives, should alone determine whether Scopes stood in violation of their law, in its wording and its intent. When he finished, the courtroom burst into applause. Raulston simply looked on.

Malone, who had served under Bryan in the state department and harbored no small amount of resentment toward his old boss, responded for the defense. He reiterated its two-pronged interpretation of the Butler Act and its contention that the state had yet to satisfy both standards. Only the inclusion of expert testimony, he argued, could establish that evolution did not contradict Biblical teachings on divine origin. He appealed to a sense of fairness. To exclude such testimony would leave Scopes without defense, and the prosecution alone would be free to define the issues of the case such that his guilt was predetermined. The defense, he insisted, had a right to use the means necessary to establish its theory of the case. To limit the interpretation of Genesis to fundamentalist viewpoints held by the prosecution, and to use that interpretation as the standard of reasonableness in evaluating the law and its application in this case, was to establish an uneven playing field. To punctuate his appeal, Malone summoned a shameful portrait of zealous dogmatism, analogizing Scopes's prosecution under such conditions to the Roman Catholic Church's persecution of Galileo. He criticized the state team for seeking to exclude knowledge that would enable the jury to reach a fair and informed judgment on the merits of the case.

The crowd again responded favorably—but more so than with Bryan. Malone had won the match. Raulston called for order, but unsuccessfully, as even the bailiff himself pounded the table with his club in cheer. After the crowd calmed, Raulston inquisitively prompted the defense to elaborate its views on compatibility between Scripture and evolution, particularly regarding the ultimate origin of humankind and the immortality of the soul. Darrow skillfully replied that such matters lay beyond the scope of material science, which dealt only with physical processes. As distinct realms of knowledge, science and religion could never be in contradiction. Stewart, concluding for the state, called for a "purely legal discussion" of the principles of construing statutory law, attempting to stymie the defense's two-pronged interpretation. Quickly, however, discussion disintegrated into contentious bickering. Little else more was accomplished that day. The courtroom cleared. Bryan himself gave the starkest evidence that the defense team had taken the day. He complimented Malone on what he claimed to be the greatest speech he had ever heard (Scopes and Presley, 1967, pp. 154–155).

Friday morning, Raulston ruled that expert testimony would be inadmissible. Defense experts could, however, enter their testimony into the record: a small victory, but nonetheless the most profound blow the defense had sustained thus far. Stewart sought tight constraints on the testimony, suggesting a limitation to written affidavits. Bryan rose to inquire about the prosecution's right to cross-examine. Raulston consented, should those witnesses take the stand. Darrow, facing yet another unfavorable ruling, objected. Witnesses served only to state what the defense intended to prove—and at a higher court, to boot. Cross-examination would do nothing to inform this court's decision.

Failing to move Raulston on the point, Darrow's frustration turned to hostility. "We want to make statements here of what we expect to prove. I do not understand why every request of the state and every suggestion of the prosecution should meet with an endless amount of time and a bare suggestion of anything that is perfectly competent on our part should be immediately overruled," Darrow complained.

"I hope you do not mean to reflect upon the court," Raulston replied.

"Well," Darrow quipped, his back to the bench, "your Honor has the right to hope!" The laughter of the audience turned to a quiet tension. Raulston ominously suggested that he had the "right to do something else, perhaps" (World's Most Famous, 1997, p. 207).

Darrow desisted, and court was adjourned early to allow the defense to prepare its statements over the weekend. With expert testimony excluded, popular opinion believed the case was over. As rapidly as they had descended on Dayton in anticipation of the trial, the swarm of reporters seemingly evaporated—including Mencken. Over the weekend, the conflict spilled out of the courtroom and into the press, with Darrow and Bryan each issuing statements, baiting one another on the issues of constitutionality and the integrity of evolutionary theory (Scopes and Presley, 1967, p. 161).

In belated response to Darrow's outburst on Friday, Raulston opened Monday's proceeding by citing him in contempt of court, to be held on $5,000 bail. After another brief spat on their relevance, Hays proceeded to read the defense affidavits into the record. Just prior, the defense had outlined the purpose with which the testimonies were submitted. Scientific experts, the majority of the witnesses, would speak regarding the factuality of evolution. Biblical scholars, then, would lend support to the defense's two-realms-of-knowledge claim outlined earlier. Evolutionary science could not contradict divine creation, they contended, because the teaching that God made man in His own image refers to man's *soul* rather than his body. The soul is the domain of religious knowledge, whereas the body is properly known through material science. The court recessed at noon.

After reconvening, Darrow publicly apologized to Raulston and was relieved of the contempt charge. Nothing seemingly remained but a few affidavits, finding Scopes guilty, and his sentencing. Citing a fear that the large crowds from the prior week had threatened the architectural integrity of the building, but perhaps moved instead by the relentless heat of the courtroom, Raulston adjourned proceedings to the courthouse lawn (Scopes and Presley, 1967, p. 164). Court resumed under the shade of the maple trees.

Hays finished reading the statements into the record. Raulston was prepared to call the jury to return when Darrow demanded the removal of a sign stating, "Read Your Bible," affixed to the wall of the courthouse, in plain view of the makeshift jury box.

Unsympathetic, but sensing that everything was winding down, Raulston consented. Hays unceremoniously entered two versions of the Bible, Roman Catholic and Jewish, as evidence that, contrary to the wording of the statute, more than one Bible existed. Though surprising to many onlookers, the fact that all texts in question told the same creation story escaped the notice of all involved. The court again prepared to summon the jury when the defense played its last, and most famous, hand. Hays requested to call one final witness—Bryan himself. Though recognizing that his testimony could be given no more weight than those entered thus far into the record, the defense wished to have Bryan testify on "other questions involved" (*World's Most Famous*, 1997, p. 284).

"Other Questions Involved"—Bryan Testifies

Expectedly, the prosecution objected. Bryan, unexpectedly, did not. A bewitched Raulston indicated no resistance to this wildly unorthodox request. Whether welcoming the opportunity or not, Bryan could scarcely refuse. As one who, time and again, proffered himself as a Biblical authority, refusing to testify as an expert student of Scripture was unthinkable. After requesting an equal opportunity to question the defense, Bryan took the stand. Darrow directed.

"You have given considerable study to the Bible, haven't you, Mr. Bryan?" Bryan responded that he had tried, more so now than when he was younger. Over Stewart's repeated objections and pleas to the bench to end this examination, Darrow proceeded to interrogate Bryan on issue after issue regarding internal inconsistencies in Biblical accounts and problems for literal interpretation in the face of modern scientific knowledge. In 1923, Bryan had dismissed Darrow's challenge in the *Chicago Tribune*. Now, as Darrow resurrected much of that list in serial fashion under the scrutiny of the crowd and remaining reporters, Bryan was forced to engage Darrow's assault.

The questions themselves were scarcely profound and were rather unoriginal observations. Clearly provoked and frustrated, Bryan responded tersely (if not evasively) to Darrow's questions. At times displaying the subtle wit of his earlier years as an orator, Bryan's answers were largely guarded, murky, and often meandering. Darrow sprinkled the strained façade of an offhanded demeanor with bitter tirade, revealing his own frustration with the exchange.

Was it a fish or a whale that swallowed Jonah? Bryan recalled no mention of a whale. *What of the story of Joshua commanding the sun to stand still, in order to lengthen the day—is it not the Sun, which is fixed, and the earth that revolves?* "Well, it is relatively so, as Mr. Einstein would say," Bryan retorted, before conceding the point that if Joshua lengthened the day, he did so by halting the earth, rather than the sun. *What would happen if the earth were to suddenly come to a standstill in its orbital path?* Bryan said he had not considered the question before. *Isn't it true the earth would have converted into a molten mass of matter?* "You testify to that when you get on the stand, I will give you a chance." *Is the Noachian flood to be taken as a literal event?* "Yes," Bryan replied, though he would not testify to the accuracy of the date of 2348 B.C., as calculated by Bishop James Ussher and included in the marginalia of some Bibles. *How exactly was that estimate arrived at?* "I do not think about things I don't think about," Bryan replied. *Do you think about things you do think about?* Darrow shot back in frustration. "Well," Bryan responded slyly, "sometimes" (*World's Most Famous*, 1997, p. 287).

Darrow moved to questions that were focused squarely on Biblical chronology and genealogy. How could Bryan defend literalist calculations of the age of humankind in the face of modern anthropological knowledge of ancient religions and civilizations, including those of the Chinese and Egyptians? How could he believe that the Tower of Babel was the origin of language types in the face of discoveries in philology? Bryan confessed to having neither an awareness of modern scholarship nor an interest in these questions. Shocking, however, was Bryan's admission that he believed the earth to be "much older" than the 6,000-year estimate offered by literalists, followed by his stated rejection of the idea that the earth was created in six days of twenty-four hours.

To those who failed to appreciate Bryan's ideological differences between himself and the fundamentalist movement with which he had aligned (and Bryan, of course, was loathe to call attention to such disagreements), his answers were a shocking revelation (Conkin, 1998, p. 97). To his fundamentalist supporters, it was a disgraceful concession to modernism and evolutionist heresy. To the prosecution, it was a symbolic regicide of the anti-evolutionist movement. As reported in the press, it was the *coup de grace* in Darrow's thorough and crushing defeat of Bryan on the stand. It was this account of a humiliated and demoralized Bryan having been dressed down by the coolly rational Darrow, hastening Bryan's death, that would dominate headlines and work its way into mythology of the "monkey trial," memorialized in the 1950 stage production and its film adaptation (1955) of *Inherit the Wind*.[10]

Bryan died shortly after the trial, but from years of poor diet and diabetes. Hardly a broken spirit, Bryan had planned to mount a full-scale campaign to reverse the tide, recover face, and renew his anti-evolutionist efforts. Bryan was well aware that Darrow had bested him, but the victory was less than complete and, in the views of many, dishonorably won. Many found Bryan the sympathetic figure and perceived Darrow's attacks as cruel taunts of a respected man of the people and his faith—and, by proxy, their own. The ACLU itself attempted to drop Darrow from the appellate team in light of his conduct (Conkin, 1998, p. 96).

Amid the fray, Bryan was able to carve out a minor martyrdom. To Stewart's demand that Raulston explain the purpose of the examination, Bryan responded, "The purpose is to cast ridicule on everyone who believes in the Bible." Darrow unwittingly took the bait, putting his own intolerance on bold display, retorting, "We have the purpose of preventing bigots and ignoramuses from controlling the education of the United States and you know it, and that is all." This was just the opening the Commoner required to recover some lost ground: "I am simply trying to protect the word of God against the greatest atheist or agnostic in the United States. I want the papers to know that I am not afraid to get on the stand in front of him and let him do his worst. I want the world to know" (*World's Most Famous*, 1997, p. 299). The crowd erupted in cheer.

Darrow did not have the opportunity to finish his examination of Bryan, nor did Bryan have the opportunity to turn the tables. Neither had the chance for closing arguments. Reminiscent of Darrow's 1923 challenge to Bryan in the *Chicago Tribune*, Bryan would, however, issue a release to the press posing nine questions for Darrow. Darrow, in turn, issued his response to each—usually with the agnostic creed, "I don't know" ("Evolution," 1925). Following his death, Bryan's widow released a copy of his closing speech to the press.

When court reconvened on Tuesday, Bryan's testimony and the entire account of the exchange were stricken from the record at Raulston's direction. Dismissing the defense's two-pronged theory, at last, the judge stated that the only thing left to be decided was whether or not Scopes had in fact taught the evolutionary descent of humans. With that, little else remained but to find Scopes guilty and close the trial. The defense agreed that the jury should be instructed to reach a finding of guilt. After arrangements to file the appeal were made, Raulston called the jury and charged them. Raulston informed them that if they found Scopes guilty, and were content with the minimum penalty, the bench could set the fine. Stewart interjected to note that under the state constitution, the *jury* must formally set any fine in excess of fifty dollars. Here, once more, customary norms prevailed. Defense stated that it had no objection. After nine minutes deliberating, the jury returned a verdict of guilty.

At last, Scopes rose to address the court on his own behalf, to explain why the penalty should not be imposed. Denouncing the law as unjust, Scopes swore he would continue to oppose it however he could. "Any other action would be in violation of my ideal of academic freedom—that is, to teach the truth as guaranteed in our constitution, of personal and religious freedom. I think the fine is unjust" (*World's Most Famous*, 1997, p. 313). Scopes was then fined $100. Defense filed notice of appeal to the state supreme court, and bond was set at $500, a cost assumed by Mencken's paper, the *Baltimore Sun*, which had provided material support for the defense.

The various parties all made their final addresses to the court. Bryan struck an optimistic tone. He claimed faith that the case would ultimately be decided correctly, whatever the outcome, by the people. Darrow concurred, but once more expressed his apprehension with what he feared to be a return to the days of pious witch-hunts. Raulston thanked the visiting attorneys. With that, the "monkey trial" closed.

THE EVOLVING AFTERMATH

As circulated popularly and in the press, the term "monkey trial" cut both ways. For anti-evolutionists, it lampooned the absurd (though misunderstood) proposition that humans evolved from primates. Conversely, modernists used it as a rebuke of a proceeding (wrongly) attributed to religious bigotry run amok in the "backward" culture and institutions of the South. Generally, it suggested the surreal, circus-like atmosphere surrounding the trial as chronicled by swarms of (mainly northern) reporters who had infested Dayton for the event. Packaged as a showdown of religion versus science, Bryan versus Darrow, the subtext of these accounts revealed the deeper cultural tension between an urban and progressive North and the rural and traditional South—another chapter in an age-old conflict between populism and elitism in the contest for Truth. Who won or lost are matters of perspective, as well as timeframe.

Scopes was found guilty, but none expected otherwise. Dayton enjoyed notoriety, if not infamy, for its moment in the spotlight, much to the chagrin of Tennesseans who wished that the embarrassing affair had never occurred. Far less economic gain resulted than anticipated, perhaps even resulting in net loss. The ACLU claimed victory in having both stirred a national backlash against anti-evolutionism and in securing the appeal as a steppingstone to the U.S. Supreme Court. National press coverage of the trial, at all stages, would support the first claim (Larson, 2003, p. 72). Scopes lost his appeal before the Tennessee Supreme Court, but few followed the story. In ruling against Scopes, the Court also saw fit to overturn his conviction on a technical error. Stewart was correct to insist that the jury, not the bench, set Scopes's fine (*Scopes v. State*, 1927). The Court instructed that the case should not be retried, in the interest of preserving the dignity of the state. It was clearly a dead end and, as Malone charged, a well-crafted "subterfuge" ("Malone," 1927).

"Fundamentalism" was previously only a pejorative mainly within elite intellectual circles, occupied by the likes of Mencken and Darrow. Now it held strong negative connotations for large swaths of the American public, particularly in the North. Press coverage indelibly linked "anti-evolutionism" with "bigotry" and "ignorance." Its adherents were termed "cranks" and "freaks" ("Cranks," 1925). In Bryan's purported defeat, punctuated by his subsequent death, the movement organized behind the Commoner lost substantial momentum nationally. Mississippi passed an anti-evolutionist bill in 1927, as did Arkansas in 1928, but these statutes remained inactive—as had the Butler Act before and after Scopes. A year after the repeal of the Butler Act in 1967, in *Epperson v. Arkansas*, the U.S. Supreme Court finally ruled such laws an unconstitutional endorsement of religion.

Disenfranchised in the North and significantly marginalized in the South, fundamentalism and its anti-evolutionist cause were down, but not out. As the nation moved on to the tribulations of the Depression and World War II, and oppositional voices diminished under the illusion of an end-all victory at Dayton, fundamentalism faded from the public conscience. However, closed off behind institutional structures tailored to their own specifications, buffered from trends in the broader culture (Larson, 2003, p. 233), fundamentalists thrived. Their numbers swelled, convictions polarized, and influence grew; and their tactics changed.

Through localized efforts, fundamentalists sought district-by-district democratic control over public education administration in their communities. They also targeted state agencies responsible for approving classroom texts. Both strategies were unlikely to be met with judicial review, cutting out the problem at its source. It was wildly successful. In order to stay viable, the textbook industry was forced to produce editions marketable in all regions. This meant vetting evolutionary content, and even explicitly catering to creationist demands. Teachers were left to their own resources (and, in fundamentalist-controlled districts, their own peril) to introduce evolution in the classroom. In the end, subtle political pressures and the logic of markets did what even a vigorously enforced Butler Act could never have achieved. In subsequent decades, upwards of 70 percent of public high schools dropped evolution from their curriculum. It was all but eclipsed in portions of the South and West (Larson, 2003, p. 231). Effectively stifling the main conduit of scientific knowledge of evolution to the public consciousness, for three decades anti-evolutionist ideas ran largely unopposed. Their influence expanded even to mainstream sectarians. While the agents of science pushed back beginning in the 1960s (Larson, 2003, p. 86), recovering lost ground in public school curricula, the intellectual commitments and ideological trenches had, by then, grown unfathomably deep.[11] By this point, the conflict of "science versus religion," a conflict few Americans even perceived at the dawn of the twentieth century, had gathered a lengthy and profound history—one complete with heroes and villains, insurgents and martyrs, battles won and battles lost. Always and unerringly, this folklore draws us back to the day Darrow met Bryan in Dayton.

NOTES

1. The belief that God created all species uniquely, and that their forms exist unchanged to this day. Some adherents accept evolution among nonhuman animals.

2. See, generally, Larson (2003).

3. "Evangelicals" are a loosely defined group of largely mainstream denominational Protestants who dedicated themselves to social reform by living and proselytizing their faith through what they called the "social gospel." They were instrumental in the abolitionist, suffragist, and prohibitionist movements as well as in bringing about labor reform, welfare programs, and universal public education.

4. Bryan (1924) noted, "Nietzsche carried Darwinism to its logical conclusion and denied the existence of God, denounced Christianity as the doctrine of the degenerate, and democracy as the refuge of the weakling; he overthrew all standards of morality and eulogized war as necessary to man's development" (p. 146).

5. Originally, the Civil Liberties Bureau—a collection of activists and lawyers who organized during World War I to protect the rights of conscientious objectors. Afterward, the ACLU adopted a broader mission of defending civil rights, particularly those of organized labor, minorities, free speech, and academic freedom.

6. Under Tennessee's declaratory judgment act, the mere fact that Scopes was a state-employed teacher with a vested interest in the law gave him standing to challenge its constitutionality—a criminal indictment was unnecessary (Larson, 2003, p. 60).

7. Surviving documents are now available through the Freedom of Information Act, and online from the FBI's Freedom of Information Act website at http://foia.fbi.gov/darrow.htm

8. Agnosticism is a position of principled skepticism on questions of theology, such as the existence of divine entities, a creed captured as "I don't know." Darrow's agnosticism was rather militant, closer to "I don't know, *and neither do you!*"

9. The account to the proceedings, unless otherwise specified, is taken from the stenographic record of the case trial, as published in *The World's Most Famous Court Trial* (1997).

10. Which were, in fact, fictionalized accounts written as commentaries on the politics of McCarthyism.

11. Gallup polls conducted during the 1980s and 1990s on attitudes toward creationism and evolutionism show a remarkable stability in responses. Consistently, 35–40 percent believe humans developed over millions of years from less-advanced forms of life with God guiding the process. Approximately 45 percent believe God created humans essentially as they exist today within the last 10,000 years. About 10 percent of respondents reliably respond that human evolution occurred with God having no part in the process.

REFERENCES

Bryan in Dayton, calls Scopes trial duel to the death. (1925, July 8). *New York Times*, p. 6.

Bryan, W. J. (1924). *Seven questions in dispute.* New York: Flemming H. Revell.

Cranks and freaks flock to Dayton. (1925, July 11). *New York Times*, p. 1.

Conkin, P. K. (1998). *When all the gods trembled: Darwinism, Scopes, and American intellectuals*. New York: Rowman and Littlefield Publishers, Inc.

De Camp, L. S. (1968). *The great monkey trial*. Garden City, NY: Doubleday and Company, Inc.

Evolution battle rages out of court. (1925, July 22). *New York Times*, p. 2.

Ginger, R. (1958). *Six days or forever? Tennessee v. John Thomas Scopes*. Boston: Beacon Press.

Larson, E. J. (1997). *Summer of the gods: The Scopes trial and America's continuing debate over science and religion*. New York: BasicBooks.

Larson, E. J. (2003). *Trial and error: The American controversy over creation and evolution* (3rd ed.). Oxford: Oxford University Press.

Malone criticizes decision. (1927, January 16). *New York Times*, p. 28.

Plan assault on state law on evolution. (1925, May 4). *The Chattanooga Times*, p. 5.

Scopes v. State, 154 Tenn. 105, 289 SW 363 (1927).

Scopes, J. T., and Presley, J. (1967). *Center of the storm: Memoirs of John T. Scopes*. New York: Holt, Reinhart and Winston.

The world's most famous court trial: Tennessee evolution case, a complete stenographic report of the famous court test of the Tennessee anti-evolution act, at Dayton, July 10 to 21, 1925, including speeches and arguments of attorneys. (1997). Union, NJ: The Lawbook Exchange, Ltd.

6

The Crime and Trial of Albert H. Fish: Divine Hunger

Sean E. Anderson

On March 6, 1932, the *New York Times* published an article titled "Kidnapping: A Rising Menace to the Nation" by R. L. Duffus. Duffus wrote, "No conceivable event, unless it were an invasion of the White House itself, could have so dramatized the crime of kidnapping as the carrying off last Tuesday night of the infant son of Colonel Charles A. Lindbergh. None could so have focused public attention on a species of felony that is centuries old, yet which has recently shown signs of being organized on an unprecedented scale and with unheard of extremes of cruelty and audacity" (p. 21). To the dismay of the family and the nation, the Lindbergh baby was not only kidnapped but also murdered.

The abduction and murder of the cultural icon's son prompted dramatic reactions in the public media and in public policy. President Franklin Roosevelt declared war on kidnapping (Schechter, 1990, p. 97), and J. Edgar Hoover and his agents from the Federal Bureau of Investigation would be hailed for stopping an epidemic of kidnappings (Evans, 1998, p. 252). While not as infamous as the kidnapping and murder of the Lindbergh baby, the abduction of Grace Budd would foreshadow a different menace facing America. When Grace's mysterious disappearance was finally solved,

America was introduced to a new villain: Albert H. Fish. His abduction, murder, and cannibalism of the child, and allegedly many other children, became part of America's fascination with the serial killer.[1]

THE ABDUCTION AND MURDER OF GRACE BUDD

Albert and Delia Budd and their five children lived in a cramped apartment in Manhattan. Their eldest son, eighteen-year-old Edward, had placed a classified ad seeking employment in the country. On May 28, 1928, there was a knock at the door. Delia answered the door and saw a slight, elderly man in a suit standing there. He introduced himself as Frank Howard and explained that he was a farmer from Long Island and might have an opportunity for employment for Edward. Delia invited him in. Edward and his friend Willie Howard arrived shortly and were introduced to Frank. He explained that one of his farmhands was moving on, and he needed a replacement. Edward claimed that he was a hard worker and Frank offered him the job, which he gladly accepted. Edward then asked if his friend Willie could also have a job. Frank said yes, before leaving for an appointment, promising to pick them up the next weekend.

Though Frank was to arrive on June 2, instead he delivered a handwritten Western Union message saying that he had been detained by business and would come the next day. The next day Frank arrived with a pail full of cheese and fresh strawberries, which he gave to Delia. Delia offered him lunch. Edward's father, Albert, finally met his son's new employer. Albert asked whether the cheese and strawberries were from his farm, and Frank said yes. Albert was a bit surprised when Frank asked if his son still had the Western Union message. Albert said yes and pointed to it on the mantle. Frank picked it up and put it into his coat pocket. Albert thought that it was odd to do such a thing, but he did not attach great significance to it at the time.

As they sat down to eat lunch, the door opened and Grace Budd appeared. Grace was a pretty ten-year-old girl still wearing her dress from church. Frank said that he would pick up the two boys later that evening, but that first he had to go to his niece's birthday party. He gave the boys money for the movies and set out to leave, then stopped. He asked whether Grace wanted to go to his niece's birthday party. He promised Delia and Albert that he would take good care of her and have her back by nine that night. Delia asked him where his sister lived, and he told her. The parents consented and Frank left with little Grace in hand.

What the Budds did not know until later was that Frank Howard was a fraud. There was no farm in Long Island. There was no niece's birthday party. The man who claimed to be Frank Howard was actually Albert H. Fish.

Fish would later explain during numerous police interrogations and psychiatric interviews that he had been feeling a blood thirst—a need to sacrifice a child. When he came across Edward's situation (job) wanted ad, he decided that this was an opportunity to satisfy that thirst. His plan was to dupe Edward out into the country. Once there he was going to tie him up, cut off his penis, let him bleed to death, and quickly leave town. His plan changed, however, when he saw little Grace. He decided that she would be his sacrifice instead of Edward.

After they left the Budd home, Fish and Grace took a series of trains out of Manhattan into Westchester County near the town of Worthington. They walked to an abandoned cottage from the train station. He told her to play in the field of wildflowers and he went into the house. Inside he took off his clothes and unpacked a canvas-wrapped bundle that contained a butcher knife, meat cleaver, and small handsaw. He called Grace in. When she entered the house and saw him naked she started screaming. Fish grabbed her and choked her to death as she desperately flailed at him. He became aroused, ejaculating as he killed her. He then proceeded to decapitate and dismember her. Fish carved out flesh from her torso and sliced off her ears and nose. He wrapped these up in some newspaper, went to the train, and rode it home with the bundle on his lap. At home he proceeded to cut up her flesh into smaller chunks, mixing them with carrots, onions, and bacon to make a stew. He spent the next nine days in a state of extreme arousal, masturbating and eating the stew.

The Budd family spent a sleepless night waiting for Grace to come home. The next morning Edward was sent to the police station to report his sister's disappearance. Lieutenant Samuel Dribben and three other officers arrived at the Budd home and questioned Delia and Albert about Frank Howard. Dribben told them the address for the niece's party was fictitious ("Hunt," 1928).

The next day, Grace's abduction hit the newspapers. The publicity of the case generated many tips. Several witnesses to Grace's departure with the elderly man claimed to have seen them meet up with others, leading the police to think that perhaps this had been a professional abduction. Although the Budds' poverty made such an explanation unlikely, the police had to treat this information as if it had merit ("Tips," 1928).

A massive search ensued. Officers were assigned to search the neighborhood as well as Long Island in search of Frank's farm. They printed up and distributed flyers with the particulars of the case and a picture of Grace to a thousand precincts in the United States and Canada. Thousands more were posted throughout New York City. This led to a rash of sightings, all of which turned out to be false.

As in any case that generates publicity, the Budds received letters from people claiming responsibility for the abduction. The police tried to trace the sources of the letters, but none of these, at the time, panned out ("Letter Gives Clue," 1928).

It soon became clear that none of the information the police had was factual. There were few solid clues for them to go on. They found where Frank had sent the Western Union telegram from and had a copy of the handwritten message. They also uncovered where he had bought the pail to carry the cheese. Otherwise, Frank and Grace had disappeared. Two weeks into the investigation, the police were baffled. It was as if Frank and Grace had vanished into thin air.

It appeared as if they had a break when Albert Corthell was identified as a suspect. Corthell, who vaguely resembled Fish, was a con man who had served time in Florida. He was identified as a possible suspect by Warden J. S. Blitch when Blitch analyzed the flyer that had been sent across the nation. An indictment and bench warrant were issued for his arrest. District Attorney Harold Hastings announced that Albert's arrest and Grace's recovery were days away. However, the days turned into years before he was arrested. Meanwhile, acting on another lead, Charles Pope was arrested. Pope, an elderly janitor, was the victim of a vindictive wife who claimed that he was the abductor of Grace. Eventually, Corthell was also arrested. The police now had two suspects for the abduction of Grace in their custody ("Case of Budd Girl," 1928).

During Pope's trial, it became clear that he was not the man they were looking for, and the judge directed the jury to return a verdict of not guilty, and the jury complied with the judge's direction, allowing Pope to go free. It had also become obvious that there was no evidence to link Corthell to the crime, and he was discharged without trial. The police had spent two years chasing down the wrong men ("Janitor Acquitted," 1930).

Fish had a long arrest history dating back to 1903, and had even spent time in Sing Sing Prison for larceny. Fish was also a compulsive writer of obscene letters to women. He found some of these women in the classified ads and described his sadomasochistic desires to them. He was arrested three times for writing obscene letters. Twice he was sent to Bellevue Hospital, and once to Kings County Hospital, for psychological observation. Each time he was declared sexually perverted but sane, and charges were either dropped or he was put on probation. Later the police would realize that he had been arrested and released six times since the abduction.

William F. King, a detective with the Missing Persons Bureau, was eventually assigned as the lead investigator, working on the case to the very end. One of his unique strategies included planting phony stories about the case from time to time in the New York City newspapers, thus ensuring that the public did not forget. After every article, a new wave of tips came in for the police to investigate. One journalist who was open to helping the police was the famous gossip columnist Walter Winchell. On November 2, 1934, Winchell wrote in his column for the *Daily Mirror* that the case was about to be broken wide open. So far this strategy had not worked.

Fish had followed Grace's abduction through the newspapers and had clipped and saved each story. Since June he had felt an urge to tell Delia Budd what had happened to Grace.

THE GRISLY LETTERS

On November 12, 1934, a letter addressed to Delia Budd arrived. It had been over six years since Grace's abduction. Delia was illiterate, so she was spared the details as Edward silently read it. When he finished reading it, he immediately ran to the police. The letter described how a friend of the author's had sailed to China, which was suffering from a great famine at the time. He explained that meat had become scarce and that children were being sold to butchers. As a result, his friend acquired a taste for human flesh. To satisfy his hunger once he returned to New York, the friend abducted two young boys, tying them up and putting them into a closet where he periodically whipped and tortured the boys. In the end, the friend consumed the boys. The author of the letter explained: "He told me so often how good Human flesh was that I made up my mind to taste it. On June the 3—1928 I called on you. . . . Brought you pot cheese—strawberries. We had lunch. Grace sat in my lap and kissed me. I made up my mind to eat her" (Schechter, 1990, p. 118). He then described taking her to the abandoned cottage and preparing to murder her.

When she saw me all naked she began to cry and tried to run down stairs. I grabbed her and she said she would tell mamma. First I stripped her naked. How did she kick—bite and scratch. I choked her to death, then cut her in small pieces so I could take my meat to my rooms, Cook and eat it. How sweet and tender her little ass was roasted in the oven. It took me 9 days to eat her entire body. I did not fuck her tho I could have had I wished. She died a virgin. (Schechter, 1990, p. 118)

The Budd family had received many depraved, crank letters after Grace's abduction. Yet, this one was worse than any of the others. Detective King decided to see whether the handwriting matched the copy of the Western Union message. Finally he had his first real break. They seemed to match. Even more important, the envelope had a strange marking. Detective King was able to track down the origin of the marking to a boardinghouse. The landlady was given one of the old flyers that described Frank. She said that the description resembled that of a tenant who had just moved out. King compared the boardinghouse register against the letter. It matched, only the name in the register was Albert Fish. The landlady revealed that Fish would return to pick up a check that his son would soon send to him. She said that Fish had asked her to hold it for him until he got a chance to pick it up. The landlady agreed to notify King when Fish returned. On December 13, 1934, he received the call that Fish was there to pick up his check. Detective King arrived, arrested him, and hauled him off to the police precinct.

Fish confessed to the abduction and murder of Grace Budd to King. He claimed that he was feeling a blood thirst, a need for a sacrificial victim. When he arrived at the Budd house the first time, Fish explained, he was disappointed that Edward looked too much like an adult, but that was not going to change his plans. But his first look at Grace did change his plans. Fish described the murder in great detail, except for the claims that he had cannibalized Grace. Neither Fish nor King mentioned it. Instead Fish claimed that he returned four days later to dispose of the body ("Budd Girl's Body Found," 1934).

Taken by the police to the cottage where he had murdered Grace, he led them in a re-creation of the crime. They found a small skull and eventually recovered the complete skeleton. Fish made several more confessions to other law enforcement personnel. One of the interrogations took place in front of a crowd of police officers, reporters, and even local celebrities. There are two significant features that arise from these multiple interrogations, both of which played a significant role in his trial. First, no one ever questioned Fish about the alleged cannibalism. Second, each of Fish's several confessions, while virtually identical, did have slight discrepancies. In each confession were various hints that he felt remorse for the crime and that he knew what he was doing was wrong. As an example, District Attorney Frank Coyne asked Fish if he knew what he had done was wrong, to which he replied, "Oh, yes" ("Police Try to Link Budd," 1934, p. 3).

Detective King brought Albert and Edward Budd into the police precinct, where they identified Fish as the man who had taken Grace away. Dental records helped to identify the body as Grace's. In Westchester, a team of officers had recovered more bones in a different location on the property. The police began to suspect that there were more bodies buried. Dr. Amos Squire, the Westchester medical examiner, claimed that Fish was the type of person who "would be apt to commit other murders." A large crowd of onlookers observed the goings-on at the cottage, and the police had to prevent some from taking away souvenirs ("Budd Murder

Site," 1934). In no time at all, public officials swarmed Fish and tried to connect him with every unsolved child abduction in the Northeast. Fish denied his involvement with any of the other cases ("Police Try to Link Budd," 1934).

The punishment for first-degree murder was execution. Frank Coyne, the outgoing Westchester district attorney, anticipated a plea of not guilty by reason of insanity and engaged two psychiatrists, Dr. Charles Lambert and Dr. James Vavasour, to examine Fish. After their examination, they reported to the new district attorney that Fish was legally sane. Fish's attorney, James Dempsey, had hired his own psychiatrists to examine him. In an unusual move, Dempsey approached new Westchester District Attorney Walter Ferris about a deal. Dempsey proposed that Fish could be used as a subject for scientists to examine in exchange for a life sentence. Ferris rejected the deal. He claimed that it was illegal and that "[a]s long as Fish is alive he will be a menace" (Schechter, 1990, p. 226; "Fish Held Sane," 1934).

Fish wrote a letter to Detective King in which he revealed some of his unique methods of inflicting pain upon himself. He wrote, "A few months after I done that deed I shoved five needles into my belly—legs—hip. At times I suffer awful pains. An Ex Ray will show them. Three weeks ago I spilled Alcohol on my behind and then lit a match. I can hardly sit still now" (Schechter, 1990, p. 183). Fish also admitted these actions to the psychiatrists who examined him, prompting them to x-ray his abdomen. He claimed that he inserted the needles into his body as penance for his sins. The x-rays confirmed that he had inserted the needles ("Fish's Body," 1935).

CAN A CANNIBAL BE SANE? THE TRIAL OF ALBERT FISH

The insanity defense is a controversial and often misunderstood criminal defense (for an overview of the insanity defense, see Slovenko, 1995). In the case of an insanity defense, the fact that a crime was committed is not disputed; rather, the central question revolves around whether the defendant had the necessary mental intent, *mens rea*, to hold him or her legally responsible for the crime. The crux of such a defense is that the defendant, being under some mental defect or disease, did not have the capacity to know right from wrong, or could not control his or her behavior, all of which repudiates his or her responsibility for the crime. A person found not guilty by reason of insanity is typically committed to a mental institution until he or she is deemed recovered.

The M'Naghten Test was the legal standard that Fish needed to meet in order to receive a verdict of not guilty by reason of insanity. The thrust of the standard was that "it must be clearly proved that, at the time of the committing of the act, the party accused was laboring under such a defect of reason, from the disease of mind, as not to know the nature and quality of the act he was doing; or, if he did know it, that he did not know he was doing what was wrong" (as cited in Cohen, 1991, p. 489).

It is important to emphasize that insanity is a legal, not a medical, concept. That is, a psychiatrist cannot make a diagnosis of insanity. Psychiatric testimony is entered on behalf of the prosecution and the defense; the jury then weighs in its consideration of whether or not the defendant was insane while committing the criminal act. Not everyone who is mentally ill would be considered insane.

On March 11, 1935, the trial started. The court was packed. Justice Frederick Close presided over the trial. He made it clear that on the heels of the media circus surrounding the Bruno Hauptmann trial (the Lindbergh baby kidnapping case), he would have an orderly trial. Jury selection was the first order of business. The lead prosecutor was Elbert Gallagher, who was chief assistant district attorney for Westchester County. Dempsey queried the potential jurors by asking them whether the gruesome story they must hear would bother them so much that they would not properly weigh the evidence. He also asked whether they had been, or knew anyone who had ever been, treated at Bellevue Hospital. Dempsey's strategy was to scapegoat Bellevue, whose psychiatrists had found Fish to be sane, resulting in his subsequent release from the institution. Gallagher asked the prospective jurors whether they would vote guilty if they found out that the defendant knew right from wrong. He also asked whether they had any prejudice against the death penalty.

On March 12, twelve jurors and one alternate were impaneled, and the attorneys made their opening statements. Gallagher's opening statement focused on detailing the criminal act while also proclaiming that Fish was sane, that he knew right from wrong, and that he was guilty of Grace's murder. Dempsey, on the other hand, emphasized that Fish was not a monster; rather, he was a victim of psychosis when he committed the crime. Since the criminal act was not in question, Dempsey focused on describing Fish's life and the role Bellevue had played. He also stressed the fact that the prosecution was charged with proving that Fish was sane.

The three Budd family members and Willie Howard testified that Fish was the man who had taken Grace. Detective King finished the first day of the trial and all of the second recounting the investigation of the crime and Fish's confession ("Fish 'Confession,'" 1935).

On the third day of the trial, a box was brought into the courtroom. In the box were the bones of Grace Budd. Close overruled Dempsey when

Dempsey objected that it was damaging to the defense due to its inflammatory nature. Dempsey made several objections, even calling for a mistrial, all to no avail. Close saw the macabre box of evidence as having value in establishing *corpus delicti* (literally, a dead body). However, Dempsey may have been right, because when Gallagher picked up the skull and held it aloft before handing it to Detective King, the courtroom spectators were audibly shaken.

The key to Dempsey's cross-examination of King was to demonstrate the fact of cannibalism. His logic was that no sane person would ever consume the flesh of another human. He showed that every statement in the letter Fish wrote to Delia was corroborated; then, by extension, logic would dictate that the cannibalism was also true, even though Fish had never been questioned directly about it. However, King declared that he did not believe that Fish had committed cannibalism with the body.

Gallagher presented three more confessions from Fish. Dempsey objected to each confession and made a motion for a mistrial because this was prejudicial to Fish. Its only value, he claimed, was to turn the jury against his client. His motion was denied. These confessions were crucial. Each version revealed different elements that indicated that Fish felt remorse for the crime and tried to avoid detection by the police, all of which seemed to show that he did know right from wrong.

The state rested its case on Friday, March 15. Dempsey asked for a directed verdict of insanity. He argued that the prosecution had presented evidence that negated the presumption of sanity. In short, Dempsey claimed that the prosecution had proved the defense's claim that Fish was insane. His motion was again denied ("Fish's Weird Acts," 1935).

Dempsey called his first witness to the stand: Albert Jr., the defendant's son. He described an occasion when he unexpectedly showed up at the apartment they were sharing to see his father beating himself with a nail-studded paddle. He told of finding blood-covered paddles on other occasions. He also told of a time when he had come across several needles. He asked his father about them. His father told him that he shoved the needles into his body when he had certain feelings and that when he could not do it to himself, he shoved the needles into other people. Albert Jr. also provided a new moniker for the tabloid press when he revealed that his father seemed to have a craving for raw meat when there was a full moon. The "Moon Maniac" was born.

The next defense witness was Dr. Roy Duckworth, who had supervised the x-rays of Fish's pelvic region. He testified to the precise location of the various needles, claiming that some were so eroded that they had to have been in his body for a long period of time.

Dr. Duckworth was followed by the testimony of Fish's daughter Gertrude Demarco. Gertrude testified to how well Fish took care of his children after his wife ran away with another man, and how he never spanked or physically harmed them. In her eyes, he was a good father with some odd quirks. One of those quirks was shoving needles into his body.

On Monday, March 18, Justice Close banned female spectators from the courtroom because of the unsavory testimony that the court would hear that day. Grace Shaw and Helen Karlson testified to the obscene correspondence Fish had with them.

Mary Nicholas, Fish's stepdaughter, was the next to testify. She explained the various games that Fish liked to play with his children. One game, "Buck Buck How Many Hands Up," involved Fish stripping into a little pair of trunks, giving a child a large paint stick, and getting down on his hands and knees. Each child would take a turn sitting on his back, the child would hold up any number of fingers, and Fish was to guess the number of fingers. If he was wrong, they were to strike him with the paint stick. She testified that he never guessed right.

Several of Fish's other children testified. His oldest daughter, Anna Collins, revealed other odd behaviors, as well as catching him spanking himself. His son Eugene testified to having witnessed his father sticking needles into himself. When he asked his father why he was doing that, his father's reply was that "he had a message from Christ" (Schechter, 1990, p. 266).

The next day the defense brought in its experts to testify to Fish's sanity. The first psychiatrist to take the stand was Dr. Fredrick Wertham. Dr. Wertham was a prominent psychiatrist who is probably best known for his attack on comic books as a cause of juvenile delinquency, resulting in the creation of a comic books code to regulate the industry. Justice Close once again cleared the courtroom of women. Dr. Wertham testified that in his investigations he had found at least seven immediate relatives of Fish's parents who suffered from mental illness. Dr. Wertham then proceeded to chronicle the abnormal development of Fish. Dr. Wertham, of all the psychiatrists to testify, had spent the most amount of time interviewing Fish. He claimed that Fish had made a connection between pain and sex at an early age during his time in an orphanage. He was aroused when he saw other boys being whipped, including when he himself was whipped for mis-behavior. Fish's sexual desires were not limited to sex and pain; Dr. Wertham argued that he manifested every known sexual perversion, including being aroused by consuming feces and urine. In fact, Dr. Wertham noted that Fish engaged in behavior that was not contained in any medical case histories ("Fish Now Insane," 1935).

Dr. Wertham claimed that Fish had raped over one hundred children during his lifetime. According to his analysis, it was not sexual relations that he desired from these children; rather, it was the infliction of pain that aroused him. He used candy or change to seduce the child to come with him. He then, typically, took them to a remote location, where he would tie them up, rape them, and beat them, or even mutilate and kill them. He often chose poor children of color because he thought that the authorities did not care as much when they were missing.

Dr. Wertham proclaimed that in his fifties, Fish developed a psychosis with delusions and hallucinations revolving around the central theme of redemption through pain, suffering, and sacrifice. It was this obsession of purgation through pain that compelled him to expand upon his past transgressions and to develop a fascination with castrating and killing young boys as penance for his own sins. Fish had always been aroused by particular passages in the Bible; now he was consumed with the story of Abraham, and God's command for him to sacrifice his son Isaac. Fish thought that when he set out to sacrifice Grace, Dr. Wertham explained, "an angel would stop him if he did the wrong thing" ("Fish Now Insane," 1935).

Dr. Henry Riley testified next and revealed that Fish claimed that he had had several visitations from Christ and that he felt compelled to sacrifice a virgin before she became a harlot. Dr. Smith Ely Jelliffe, a famous neurologist, Freudian proponent, and an experienced expert who had testified at a number of other sensational trials, testified last. Dr. Jelliffe testified to the religious nature of the murder: "The psychosis of a divine command justified the act in his mind" ("Fish Held Insane," 1935). All three defense experts concluded that Fish was insane ("Fish Held Insane," 1935).

Gallagher's expert witnesses were brought in next to rebut the testimony of the defense experts. Dr. Wertham would later write that these expert witnesses shamed the profession of psychiatry with their testimony.

Dr. Menas Gregory, the former head of Bellevue Hospital's psychiatric department, was the first to testify for the prosecution. Dr. Gregory had examined Fish on one of his prior commitments there. He claimed that while Fish was abnormal, he was sane. Under cross-examination, Dr. Gregory claimed that Fish was no different from millions of other people. When asked whether the consumption of urine and feces was unusual, he responded that it was not, and that many people did it. Dempsey also attacked him on his handling of the case, to which Dr. Gregory responded that he had done the best that could be done.

Next to testify was Dr. Perry Lichtenstein, physician for the Tombs Prison. Dempsey attacked his psychiatric credentials based on the fact that the physician had no formal training. Dr. Lichtenstein claimed that his expertise was derived from twenty years of studies of inmates. Judge Close denied Dempsey's challenge of Lichtenstein's credentials. Dempsey asked Lichtenstein, "[T]hat a person takes alcohol and puts it on cotton and puts that into his person and sets fire to it, does that indicate an aggravated mental condition?" Lichtenstein stated, "That is not masochistic. He is only punishing himself and getting sex gratification that way" (Schechter, 1990, p. 282). Clearly, the doctor had not read a psychiatric textbook, because that is the definition of masochism.

Dr. Charles Lambert was called to the stand next. He testified that Fish had sexually preyed upon hundreds of children, but was sane. When posed with the hypothetical question of whether a cannibal such as Fish could be sane, his flippant response was "Well, there is no accounting for taste" (Schechter, 1990, p. 282). When probed by Dempsey as to whether consuming feces was normal, he replied that it was and that several prominent people he knew did it.

The last expert witness to testify was Dr. James Vavasour. Dempsey questioned the doctor's objectivity when Vavasour brought up the fact that in his five years of working with the Westchester district attorney's office, he had never found a person insane. Like the other experts, Dr. Vavasour testified that consuming feces was not unusual. Not surprisingly, Dr. Vavasour claimed that Fish was sane. The state rested its case.

On the tenth and final day of the trial, closing arguments were heard. Dempsey focused on how a father could do what Fish did unless he was insane. He also questioned why the police did not probe the issue of cannibalism and how Bellevue could have released such a man.

Gallagher's summation was straightforward. He claimed that the case was clear, that it had been demonstrated beyond a reasonable doubt, and that the defense had tried to divert the jury from the truth with its psychiatric experts. The truth, he claimed, was that Fish, while sexually abnormal, was sane when he killed Grace.

Justice Close charged the jury in a simple, succinct manner. He read the relevant sections of the penal code, emphasizing that a compulsion to perversion is not an adequate defense to the crime, and outlined the six possible verdicts. He then sent the jury away to deliberate.

The alternate juror, Thomas Madden, was dismissed. When asked by reporters what his verdict would have been, he said that while he found the expert testimony confusing, he would have said that Fish was insane. Reporters conducted a poll among themselves and came to a similar verdict.

THE VERDICT

After three and a half hours of deliberation, the jury returned a guilty verdict. Most felt that he was insane but deserved to die. Fish was sentenced to be executed. Upon hearing his sentence, Fish waved to the court and said, "Thank you, Judge" ("Fish Is Sentenced," 1935; "Fish Found Guilty," 1935).

After the conviction, Fish confessed to the abduction and murder of four-year-old Billy Gaffney and seven-year-old Francis McDonnell. He also claimed to have tortured at least two others, but did not know whether they had died ("Fish Is Sentenced," 1935, March 26, 1935; "Fish Says," 1935).

Dempsey appealed the sentence, and the execution was stayed. The appeal was based on three elements. Dempsey claimed that Gallagher's bone-rattling theatrics prejudiced the jury against his client, and that Justice Close was hostile to the defense. Finally, Dempsey noted that there was reasonable doubt about Fish's sanity. The Court of Appeals upheld the sentencing and rescheduled Fish's execution ("Fish Death Sentence," 1935).

Dempsey was not done. Along with Dr. Wertham, Dempsey had scheduled a meeting with New York Governor Herbert Lehman to hear a plea for commutation. The two pleaded for the governor to commute the sentence to life in prison so that scientists could study their client. Dr. Wertham claimed that by studying Fish, it might be possible to prevent future acts of this nature. Lehman took no action.

Fish was executed on January 16, 1936. He was sixty-five, the oldest man ever executed at Sing Sing. Part of the folklore surrounding his execution is that the needles in his body either caused the electric chair to short out or that a burst of blue sparks was produced when the electricity was activated ("Slayer Dies," 1936).

CONSUMING CRIME IN THE MASS MEDIA AND POPULAR CULTURE

Fish was an avid reader of newspapers. He used newspaper ads to find women to whom he could write in the hope that he might find a partner for his perverted fantasies. It was also a newspaper ad that led him to Grace. Moreover, after his arrest when the police searched his apartment, they found a bundle of clipped articles about sensational stories that had tickled his fancy. Included in his collection were all the newspaper articles about the abduction of Grace in which he had a starring role.

Once the grisly details of Grace's murder were known, the *Daily News* claimed that Fish was a mass murderer of historic proportions, trying to connect him to sensational criminals like Jack the Ripper and Fritz Haarmann. The connection between Haarmann and Fish is an interesting one. Haarmann abducted young male refugees during World War I in Hanover, Germany. He and his partner Hans Grans murdered them, butchered the bodies, and sold the meat on the black market. Fish had cut out and saved every news story on Haarmann's crimes.

In a search of his residence, the police found sewing needles with his collection of newspaper clippings as well as more needles stored in a copy of *The Narrative of Arthur Gordon Pym* by Edgar Allan Poe (1930). Poe's story is revealing, since a pivotal sequence of the novel deals with cannibalism. The narrator and three other men survive a mutinous attack on their ship. They are starving, slowly dying, and at their wits' end when the suggestion is made that one should die so that three could live. They draw straws to see who shall die, and the loser is killed and consumed. This not only indicated Fish's obsession with cannibalism, but it is also illuminating because Poe's literary art has had a major impact on our contemporary fascination with serial killers (Elmer, 1995).

Aside from the macabre and sensational stories that attracted Fish, it is important to point out how large a role the Bible, the most popular cultural text ever produced, played in Fish's life. Fish was drawn to those lurid scenes of pain, punishment, and sacrifice that shape the larger message of the Bible. His imaginative interaction with the Bible was certainly influential in his violent acts toward himself and others.

The public's consumption of the mass media also contributes to police work. From the news media's coverage of the case, a series of tips on the crime came to the attention of the police. Of course, this attention also produced a large number of crank letters that were sent to the Budd family. The fierce attention to the abduction may also have produced a furor in the public bordering on panic: any stranger near a child was in danger of being mobbed by a crowd. In addition, the attention drew a large crowd of sightseers to the murder scene.

While the police tried to tie Fish to Gaffney's abduction, the *Daily Mirror* printed photos of Fish and pleaded with its readers to notify them if they recognized his face. This brought in several people, some of whom identified him as being the suspect seen with Billy Gaffney on the day of his disappearance.

As a final note, Fish's downfall can, at least partially, be traced to the mass media. The coverage of the story led him to send his confession to the Budds. And, of course, the *Daily Mirror* took credit for Fish's capture because of Winchell's column proclaiming that a break in the case was near.

The complexity of the mass media's relation to crime is starkly seen here. Fish was fascinated by mass media accounts of depravity, which may in part have fueled his behavior. But at the same time, in the end, the coverage of the case generated his downfall.

Producing Media

What are covered in the mass media are the atypical cases like the abduction and murder of Grace. There is bias toward coverage of sensational, emotionally engaging acts of crime. Media portrayals will be geared toward coverage of the rare, unusual crimes rather than real everyday criminal activities that exemplify the reality of crime and the criminal justice system. There were several elements that contributed to the widespread coverage. The victim was a young, pretty girl. One could speculate that the media coverage would not have been as dramatic if she were not Caucasian. The offender was a seemingly nice, elderly man. Here in a nutshell we have the common Gothic picture. We have a picture of deep evil hidden behind a mask of innocence, an evil that may be anywhere, and may erupt at anytime, and is uncontrollable (Edmundson, 1997). As a background, there was national interest in kidnapping. Then, later, the outrageous acts of murder, dismemberment, decapitation, and consumption of her flesh fueled even more attention to the case. In other words, we had the most heinous crime and the most innocent victim.

To report on crime, the news media need access to experts on crime, the victims and offenders, and their families and friends. The Budd and Fish families played prominent roles in the construction of the story. Reporters tracked down family members to gather every sordid detail and relied upon the criminal justice officials involved in the case to paint the picture of this crime. Fish's autobiography was serialized in the papers, as were as his confessions of other crimes. When it was evident that the insanity defense would be utilized, the *Daily Mirror* sought out two experts to assess his sanity and printed their judgment.

The two major New York tabloids, the *Daily Mirror* and *Daily News*, constructed sensational morality plays about the crime. The *Daily Mirror* spiced up the story with the many lurid labels they had for Fish. They called him at various times the "Vampire Man," "Werewolf of Wisteria," and the "New Jack the Ripper" (Schechter, 1990, p. 168). This demonization of Fish painted him as an animalistic, incorrigible killer. He was a monstrous predator who was held in check only by the equally supernatural efforts of the police. This highlights the mythical nature of much that we know about serial killers. A real killer is aligned with fictional figures or situated in the hall of fame of murderers. To come to grips with acts of this nature, we construct them in the familiar fictional forms. The result is that the boundaries between fact and fiction are erased (Grixti, 1995).

The *Daily Mirror* even reconstructed the murder, step by step, through an artist's graphic reconstruction. It also printed a series of photographs that traced the route Fish and Grace took that fateful day, with captions that tried to place the readers as witnesses to the crime. For instance, a photograph of the elevated train station was accompanied by the caption "Perhaps you used the station that day, rubbed shoulders with them" (Schechter, 1990, p. 169).

Monsters and Heroes: Repercussions of Coverage

Fish has not generated the same attention in the realm of popular culture that other serial killers like Jack the Ripper, Theodore Bundy, or Jeffrey Dahmer have. He has no fan club, as does Ed Gein (Schechter and Everitt, 1996, p. 85). While there are no extant films rendering his life in celluloid, the heavy metal band Macabre includes him among the pantheon of serial killers it sings about in the audio CD *Sinister Slaughter/Behind the Walls of Sleep* (2000). His image graced *Film Threat*'s 1990 "Mass Murderer" calendar (Schechter and Everitt, 1996, p. 38) and a set of serial killer trading cards. The artist Michael Rose has painted several scenes from Fish's life, including one where he is flagellating himself with a nail-studded board (Schechter and Everitt, 1996, p. 218).

The news stories of crime often produce not just "monsters" like Fish, but also heroes like Detective King. King received a medal and promotion for his patience in solving the Budd case. His public prestige also made him a crucial expert who testified before a New York legislative committee. He used the Budd case to emphasize the need for the police to receive fingerprints of all mental inmates and probationers and parolees. He argued that access to these records could greatly reduce sex crimes ("Seek Fingerprints," 1937). Of course, it is debatable whether such access would have foretold or led to a quicker apprehension of Fish. This does, however, illustrate how sensational cases tend to draw focus to the criminal justice system and its perceived shortcomings. Often the attention is on how the police are handcuffed by the monstrous bureaucratic machine called the criminal justice system.

NOTE

1. For America's fascination with serial killers, see Simpson, 2000; Seltzer, 1998; and Caputi, 1990.

REFERENCES

Budd girl's body found; killed by painter in 1928. (1934, December 14). *New York Times*, pp. 1, 3.

Budd murder site yields more bones. (1934, December 16). *New York Times*, p. 2.

Caputi, J. (1990, Fall). The new founding fathers: The lore and lure of the serial killer in contemporary culture. *Journal of American Culture, 13*(3), 1–12.

Case of Budd girl solved, police say. (1928, August 2). *New York Times*, p. 23.

Cohen, F. (1991). *The law of deprivation of liberty: Cases and materials.* Durham, NC: Carolina Academic Press.

Duffus, R. L. (1932, March 6). Kidnapping: A rising menace to the nation. *New York Times*, p. 21.

Edmundson, M. (1997). *Nightmare on main street: Angels, sadomasochism, and the culture of the Gothic.* Cambridge, MA: Harvard University Press.

Elmer, J. (1995). *Reading at the social limit: Affect, mass culture, and Edgar Allan Poe.* Stanford, CA: Stanford University Press.

Evans, H. (1998). *The American century.* New York: Alfred A. Knopf.

Fish "confession" is read to jurors. (1935, March 14). *New York Times*, p. 44.

Fish death sentence is upheld on appeal. (1935, November 27). *New York Times*, p. 44.

Fish found guilty of first-degree murder; slayer of Budd girl is calm at verdict. (1935, March 23). *New York Times*, p. 1.

Fish held insane by three experts. (1935, March 21). *New York Times*, p. 46.

Fish held legally sane. (1934, December 28). *New York Times*, p. 6.

Fish is sentenced; admits new crimes. (1935, March 26). *New York Times*, p. 3.

Fish now insane, expert testifies. (1935, March 20). *New York Times*, p. 44.

Fish says he slew the Gaffney boy. (1935, March 25). *New York Times*, p. 3.

Fish's body holds 27 pieces of metal. (1935, January 1). *New York Times*, p. 5.

Fish's weird acts told by children. (1935, March 16). *New York Times*, p. 4.

Grixti, J. (Spring 1995). Consuming cannibals: Psychopathic killers as archetypes and cultural icons. *Journal of American Culture, 18*(1), 87–96.

Hunt man and child he took to party. (1928, June 5). *New York Times*, p. 12.

Janitor acquitted in Budd kidnapping. (1930, December 24). *New York Times*, p. 34.

Letter gives clue in Budd girl hunt. (1928, June 15). *New York Times*, p. 52.

Macabre. (2000). Albert was worse than any fish in the sea. *Sinister slaughter/Behind the walls of sleep.* Nuclear Blast America.

Poe, E. A. (1930). *The narrative of Arthur Gordon Pym.* New York: The Heritage Press. (Original work published 1838)

Police try to link Budd girl's slayer to 3 other crimes. (1934, December 15). *New York Times*, pp. 1, 3.

Schechter, H. (1990). *Deranged: The shocking true story of America's most fiendish killer!* New York: Pocket Books.

Schechter, H., and Everitt, D. (1996). *The A to Z encyclopedia of serial killers.* New York: Pocket Books.

Seek fingerprints of mental inmates. (1937, November 18). *New York Times*, p. 48.

Seltzer, M. (1998). *Serial killers: Death and life in America's wound culture.* New York: Routledge.

Simpson, P. (2000). *Psycho paths: Tracking the serial killer through contemporary American film and fiction*. Carbondale, IL: Southern Illinois University Press.

Slayer of Budd girl dies in electric chair. (1936, January 17). *New York Times*, p. 20.

Slovenko, R. (1995). *Psychiatry and criminal culpability*. New York: John Wiley and Sons.

Tips fail to trace kidnapped girl of 10. (1928, June 6). *New York Times*, p. 13.

Wertham, F. (1949). *The show of violence*. Garden City, NY: Doubleday and Co.

7

Bonnie and Clyde: A "Mad, Dizzy Whirl"

Leana Allen Bouffard

You've read the story of Jesse James
Of how he lived and died
If you're still in need for something to read
Here's the story of Bonnie and Clyde.
—"The Story of Bonnie and Clyde," by Bonnie Parker (Milner, 1996)

In January 1930, to help out with housework, Bonnie Parker agreed to temporarily move in with a neighbor who had broken her arm in a fall. During her stay, another friend of the neighbor, convicted car thief Clyde Barrow, also paid a visit. Clyde's mother claims that over a shared pot of hot chocolate, he instantly fell in love with Bonnie. For Bonnie, it was also love at first sight. This chance encounter set off a two-year violent crime spree and an enduring nationwide fascination with the gangster couple Bonnie and Clyde.

Clyde Chestnut Barrow was born in March 1909 to Henry and Cumie Barrow, tenant farmers in Texas. Clyde was the fifth of eight children, and his parents often had trouble with money. The children were frequently shuffled among the homes of various relatives. Finally, they gave up farming and moved to a poor part of Dallas. Clyde was a fan of Western outlaw movies, idolizing Jesse James. He often skipped school, and he dropped out

Bonnie Parker and Clyde Barrow, American criminals.
(The Granger Collection, New York)

at sixteen to begin working. Clyde's earliest criminal activity involved stealing a flock of chickens with his older brother, Buck. After that, he continued getting into trouble with the law.

Bonnie Parker was born in October 1910 to Charles and Emma Parker. She was the middle child, with an older brother and younger sister. Bonnie's family was somewhat better off than the Barrow family. Her father was a brick mason, and the family lived a quiet and comfortable life in a small town near Dallas. When Bonnie was five years old, her father died suddenly, and her mother was forced to move to one of the toughest parts of Dallas to live with her parents (Bonnie's grandparents). Bonnie was described as a good student in school, high-spirited and tender-hearted. She won awards for her essays and poetry. At fifteen, Bonnie began spending time with a classmate, Roy Thornton. By the next year, they were married, and eventually the couple moved in with Bonnie's mother. Bonnie was deeply infatuated with Thornton and had their names tattooed above her right knee. Despite this infatuation, Thornton was not the most loyal and attentive of husbands. He frequently left. In January 1929, he reappeared after an absence of nearly a year, and Bonnie refused to take him back. Thornton was later arrested during a robbery and sentenced to five years in prison. Bonnie stayed married to him, believing that it would be inappropriate to divorce him while he was in prison, but that did not prevent her from seeing Clyde.

BONNIE'S FIRST CRIME

> Then I left my old home for the city
> To play in its mad dizzy whirl,
> Not knowing how little of pity
> It holds for a country girl.
> —"The Story of Suicide Sal," by Bonnie Parker (Milner, 1996)

During the first few weeks that Bonnie and Clyde were seeing each other, police found him at the Parker home and arrested him on suspicion of burglary. While he was in jail, Bonnie sent him letters urging him to go straight and get a job when he got out. In March 1930, Bonnie traveled with Clyde's mother to Waco, Texas, to see him. She stayed with her cousin and visited Clyde in jail. During one visit, Clyde and one of his cellmates, William Turner, convinced Bonnie that she could help them escape by smuggling a gun into the jail. Turner drew a map of his parent's home and told her where she could find the key and the gun. Taking her cousin with her, Bonnie went to the Turner home, found the key, and began looking for the gun. It was not where Turner said it would be, and the two girls left the house in considerable disarray. But they had found the gun, and Bonnie smuggled it into the jail. This was Bonnie's first foray into criminal activity.

The next night, Turner pretended to be sick. When the jailer opened the cell door, another inmate, Emery Abernathy, pulled the gun and placed the jailer in the cell. Clyde, Abernathy, Turner, and another inmate strong-armed the keys away from the jailer and escaped into the night, stealing a car and driving through Texas, Missouri, and into Illinois. When they reached Illinois, Clyde sent Bonnie a telegram to let her know that he was safe. With Clyde on the run, Bonnie returned home to wait for him. However, Mrs. Parker suspected Bonnie's involvement in the escape. She believed that Bonnie enjoyed being the center of attention and viewed the whole incident as exciting and romantic.

Meanwhile, Clyde and the other escapees committed several robberies, burglaries, and car thefts. During one of their burglaries, a witness noted their license plate number, and police caught up with the group. Though Clyde used an alias, police eventually learned that the three were the Waco escapees. In April 1930, Clyde was transferred to Huntsville Prison. On intake, he claimed that his middle name was "Champion" and that Bonnie was his wife. From Huntsville, Clyde was assigned to the Eastham Prison Farm. During his imprisonment, Bonnie went back to work, started dating, and for a while stopped corresponding with Clyde.

Clyde's mother lobbied authorities to shorten his sentence from fourteen years to only two years. But Clyde, depressed by the slow progress of the appeal, persuaded another inmate to cut off two of his toes so that he would be transferred back to the prison hospital at Huntsville. Soon after, the governor agreed to parole Clyde. He returned to Dallas and immediately went to see Bonnie. Reunited with Clyde, she dropped her current boyfriend and the two resumed their relationship. When Clyde's sister arranged for him to have a construction job in Massachusetts, Bonnie was pleased that he seemed to be going straight. Two weeks after starting the job, Clyde returned to Dallas because he was homesick. Soon Bonnie told her mother she was moving to Houston for a job selling cosmetics. In reality, she was joining Clyde and his new associates.

THE BARROW GANG

> Now Bonnie and Clyde are the Barrow gang,
> I'm sure you all have read
> How they rob and steal
> And those who squeal are usually found dying or dead.
> —"The Story of Bonnie and Clyde," by Bonnie Parker (Milner, 1996)

Upon his return to Dallas, Clyde hooked up with Raymond Hamilton and Ralph Fults, two petty criminals. In March 1932, the three attempted to rob a hardware store, with Bonnie acting as lookout. A night watchman spotted them and alerted police, who gave chase. The gang's car got stuck in the mud, and the four tried to escape by running through nearby fields. Fults was captured, Hamilton and Clyde escaped, and Bonnie hid in the field until the next day. She began hitchhiking home but was stopped and taken in for questioning. While in jail waiting for the grand jury to convene, Bonnie wrote a poem, "Suicide Sal," about a woman who fell for a criminal and eventually took the blame for his crimes. This appears to have been a period of disenchantment with Clyde.

While Bonnie languished in jail, Clyde and Hamilton met up with Frank Clause, who had recently been released from prison. The group committed several crimes, but the most serious occurred in April 1932 when they robbed a small service station owned by John and Martha Bucher in Hillsboro, Texas. The three scoped out the store and returned at midnight, requesting entry to purchase guitar strings. As the Buchers opened the safe, Hamilton fired his gun, killing John Bucher. He later claimed that the shooting was an accident. Martha called the police after the three robbers left, and a few days later, she identified Clyde and Hamilton from police photographs. Clyde hid out temporarily at his family's home, and a few days later, he joined Clause in another robbery. This time they held up two service stations, kidnapping the attendants at gunpoint. Both men were later released unharmed.

After Bonnie's grand jury hearing in June 1932, she was released due to lack of evidence. She returned home to her mother, claiming she would have nothing more to do with Clyde. Toward the end of June, Bonnie went to Wichita Falls, telling her mother she would be applying for a job. In reality, she, Clyde, and Hamilton had rented a house there. In August 1932, the group returned to Dallas and picked up another gangster, Everett Milligan. With Milligan serving as the getaway driver, Clyde and Hamilton robbed a packing company at gunpoint. The police gave chase, but Clyde's speedy and reckless driving left them in the dust. Leaving Bonnie at her mother's, the men headed out of state to Oklahoma.

In Oklahoma, Hamilton wanted to stop at an open-air dance floor. Despite feeling that it was too dangerous, Clyde stopped. They danced and tried to relax, drinking whiskey from fruit jars, which caught the notice of a local sheriff, C. G. Maxwell, and deputy, E. C. Moore. The Prohibition laws were strictly enforced in Oklahoma, and the officers told the men that they were under arrest. Clyde and Hamilton both began firing their pistols, shooting Moore in the head and wounding Maxwell. The two men then sped away, heading back to Texas along back roads. Milligan, who had been dancing at the time of the shooting, tried to blend into the crowd. He asked a new friend for a ride into town, where he left for Texas by bus. Hearing from witnesses about a third member of the group, police tracked Milligan to Texas and captured him there. Between Milligan's confession and Clyde's fingerprints on one of the abandoned vehicles, police were able to put names to the suspects.

Hamilton retrieved Bonnie from her mother's house, and they met up with Clyde. With search parties looking for them, the gang decided they should move to a place where they were not known. They decided to go to New Mexico. A sheriff's deputy in New Mexico became suspicious of their out-of-state license plates. Upon learning that their car was stolen, Deputy Joe Johns followed the gang to their hideout and asked to speak to the car's owner. With a shotgun, Clyde confronted the deputy, taking him hostage, and the three began another flight from the law. Police throughout New Mexico and Texas began an intense manhunt. Deputy Johns was released unharmed several hours and several hundred miles later. On their flight, the gang continued to steal various cars. One of the victims reported the theft immediately, giving police the information they needed to set up an ambush. Clyde, however, noticed the trap and quickly turned the car around, firing his pistol and wounding one officer in the process. Despite a large posse with heavy firepower, the gang was again able to evade police.

Until September, the gang robbed various businesses in Texas—but did not kill or kidnap any of their victims. Hamilton left the gang, and in October, Clyde met up with two other men, Frank Hardy and Hollis Hale, to rob a small grocery store. As Clyde held the salesclerk at gunpoint and collected the money, the meat market manager, Howard Hall, appeared and offered some resistance. Clyde punched the man once, and Hall grabbed at his arm to prevent a second blow. In a rage, Clyde fatally shot Hall. He attempted to shoot the clerk as well, but the gun misfired. Police broadcast a description of the gunmen to agencies in the surrounding area. Another manhunt ensued, but Clyde evaded capture, picking up Bonnie around midnight, then driving into Oklahoma. Two individuals later positively identified Clyde Barrow as the person who committed the robbery and murder.

Throughout November, Clyde, Hardy, and Hale committed various robberies in Missouri. At the end of the month, they decided to rob a bank. Bonnie scoped out the bank but was not allowed to participate in the actual robbery. When the men entered the bank with guns drawn, the guards began firing. Hardy grabbed as much money as he could while Clyde fired back, and they ran to the getaway car. Hardy and Hale took all of the money, hitchhiked into town, and disappeared. Short on cash, Clyde decided to rob another bank using Bonnie as a lookout. Unfortunately, it had gone bankrupt, and there was nothing to steal. After those failures, the couple decided to return to Texas. During December, Bonnie and Clyde stayed with family and added another member to their gang, sixteen-year-old W. D. Jones, who had known the Barrow family for nearly ten years.

On Christmas day, 1932, Clyde decided to steal another car. Jones found a car with the keys inside and attempted to start it. Neighbors noticed the attempted theft and ran out to stop him. With three people standing on the sidewalk yelling, Clyde became agitated, and he and Jones began pushing the car to get it started. After it got rolling, Clyde jumped into the driver's seat, and Jones stood on the running board waving his gun. Doyle Johnson, the owner, ran after the car and jumped on the driver's side running board, grabbing Clyde's arm to prevent him from getting away. Clyde fired his gun, hitting the front fender of the car, and Jones reacted to the shot by firing his own pistol. Johnson was hit in the neck, and he fell to the street and later died. The two men fled in the stolen car. Meanwhile, Bonnie slid behind the wheel of Clyde's car and left the scene, unnoticed. Also in December, Raymond Hamilton was captured by police and awaited trial for his part in the Bucher murder.

In January, the Barrow gang returned to Dallas. Bonnie spent a few minutes with her mother while Clyde visited Hamilton's sister, Lillie McBride. He gave her a radio with a hidden saw blade to deliver to Hamilton in prison so that he could escape. The group reconvened and hurried to an abandoned farmhouse to hide. Police, meanwhile, had been tipped off about McBride's relationship to Hamilton and went to her home. She had gone to the prison to see Hamilton, so they decided to wait. Noticing a car circling the block, the police turned off all of the lights in the house. The gang returned, and Clyde approached the front door with a sawed-off shotgun. He noticed the shadow of a policeman in the front window and fired a shot into the house. The police returned fire, and Jones began firing as well. Other officers converged on the front lawn, and Clyde shot one of them at close range, killing him. He made it back to the car, and the group sped away, ending up in Oklahoma. At the end of January, the gang kidnapped and released another police officer.

THE GANG'S NEW MEMBERS

> The road gets dimmer and dimmer
> Sometimes you can hardly see
> But it's fight man to man, and do all you can
> For they know they can never be free.
> —"The Story of Bonnie and Clyde," by Bonnie Parker (Milner, 1996)

In March 1933, Clyde's brother, Buck Barrow, was released from prison. He planned to take his wife, Blanche, to visit her parents in Missouri and hoped to settle on their farm. Along the way to Missouri, Buck decided, against his wife's wishes, that he would visit his brother. They met up in Arkansas and drove together to Joplin, Missouri, where they rented a garage apartment. Within a few days, neighbors and police became suspicious of this group with guns and out-of-state license plates. Eventually, police decided to confront them. In April 1933, police pulled up outside the garage, parking their cars in the driveway to block escape routes. Clyde noticed the officers approaching, alerted the group, and grabbed his rifle. Clyde, Jones, and Buck began shooting from the windows. Bonnie started packing, but Blanche was terrified and ran into the street, screaming. The rest of the gang jumped into their car and raced out of the garage, side-swiping a police car on the way. They followed Blanche into the street and pulled her into the car.

In the shootout, two police officers were killed and two others were wounded. When police searched the apartment, they found Buck and Blanche's marriage license as well as the pardon that Buck had received. Two rolls of film that the gang had taken of their exploits were also left behind. The evidence helped police identify the group as the Barrow gang. The pictures immediately made it into the newspapers, and the public had names and smiling, unremorseful faces to go with the stories of their crimes.

In late April 1933, the gang needed a getaway car for a planned robbery. They located a suitable vehicle, and Jones quickly drove away in it. The owner of the car, H. Dillard Darby, and a friend, Sophia Stone, chased after Jones. They came upon Clyde and the rest of the group, who kidnapped the pair, releasing them the next day unharmed and with some money to get home. Buck and Blanche decided to finally go visit her parents in Missouri. In June, they were to meet back up with Bonnie, Clyde, and Jones. On their way to the rendezvous, Clyde was speeding along the highway and did not notice that a bridge had been washed out ahead of them. The car flew into a ravine, flipping twice. Clyde was thrown from the car, and Bonnie ended up pinned under the wreckage. Clyde pulled Jones out of the car but could not free Bonnie. A farmer who lived nearby arrived to help, and Bonnie was rescued, but not before the car had caught fire and severely burned her legs.

The men carried Bonnie to the farmer's home, where his wife treated the burns. A neighbor had called police, and when they arrived, Clyde and Jones took them hostage. Clyde ordered the two officers into the back of their car and lay Bonnie across their laps. He then drove to meet Buck in Oklahoma. There, they released the two officers, deciding not to kill them since they had been kind to Bonnie. From there, the group drove to Fort Smith, Arkansas, where they rented a tourist cabin. Bonnie's sister, Billie, arrived in Fort Smith to care for her. During their stay in the cabin, Clyde did not leave Bonnie's side. Buck and Jones committed a few robberies to get some cash. In one of those robberies, they shot and killed the town marshal. After that, Clyde knew they would have to move again.

Clyde sent Billie back to Dallas, and the gang drove to the Red Crown Tourist Camp in Platte City, Missouri, committing various robberies along the way. They rented two rooms, and Clyde continued to care for Bonnie and her injuries. The clerk on duty became suspicious of the group with the heavily bandaged woman. He called police, and they realized it was the Barrow gang. Various police agencies pooled their resources and planned their attack. They surrounded the rooms and knocked on the door. Blanche stalled them while the group packed a few belongings and left through a side door into the garage. Police had blocked that exit with an armored car, but Clyde and Jones fired an automatic rifle at it, wounding one of the officers. Meanwhile, Buck fired at the rest of the posse from the cabin window. When they returned fire, he was shot twice in the head. Clyde loaded everyone, including a semiconscious Buck, into their car, and they crashed through the garage, shooting as they went. Police again returned fire, shattering the car windows and sending splinters of glass into Blanche's eyes. They raced out of Platte City.

Clyde drove through that night and the next day, eventually finding a thickly wooded spot near a stream in Iowa. The group rested there and tried to recover from their wounds, but again, local citizens became suspicious. Police in Iowa were alerted and planned an ambush of the group with the help of the Iowa National Guard. Early the next morning, Bonnie noticed the police surrounding their camp. Clyde and Jones grabbed their rifles and began shooting. Bonnie limped to the car, and Blanche struggled to drag Buck in the same direction. On the way, Bonnie was wounded, Buck was shot twice, and Jones was shot in the chest. The group piled into the car but soon realized that they would not be able to avoid the posse's fire. Clyde ordered everyone to hide in the woods. Buck was shot several more times, and Blanche tried to shield him from any more gunfire. Clyde was shot in the arm but carried Bonnie to a nearby farmhouse where they stole a car at gunpoint. Clyde, Bonnie, and Jones escaped, but Buck and Blanche were captured. Several days later, Buck died in the hospital. Blanche was sentenced to fifteen years in the Missouri State Prison. Jones eventually left the group but was captured and convicted of murder.

In late November, Bonnie and Clyde began planning a prison break. Raymond Hamilton had been sentenced for the murder of John Bucher, and he was serving his time at Eastham Prison Farm. Hamilton's brother and a former inmate, James Mullin, were also in on the plan to hide two pistols on the grounds of the prison farm. A trusty in the prison retrieved the pistols and passed them to Hamilton and a friend, Joe Palmer. Hamilton and Palmer took the pistols with them the next day when they began work. Clyde and Mullin waited just off prison grounds, and Bonnie stayed in the getaway car. When Hamilton and Palmer drew their pistols, a gunfight erupted between the inmates and guards. Hearing the shooting, Bonnie began honking the horn. Hamilton, Palmer, Henry Methvin, and two other inmates ran toward the sound of the horn and escaped with Bonnie and Clyde. At the prison, one guard had been killed and another wounded.

THE BEGINNING OF THE END

> They don't think they're tough or desperate
> They know the law always wins

They've been shot at before, but they do not ignore
That death is the wages of sin.
—"The Story of Bonnie and Clyde," by Bonnie Parker (Milner, 1996)

The prison director at Huntsville, Lee Simmons, swore that he would find and punish those responsible for the death and wounding of the guards at Eastham. Research into the history of the escapees led him to Mullin, who confessed to his part and implicated Bonnie and Clyde. Simmons began formulating his plan. He created a new position, special investigator for the Texas prison system, and selected Frank Hamer, a former Texas Ranger known for his fearlessness, to fill the position. Simmons then convinced Governor Miriam Ferguson to offer a pardon to any associate of the gang who would help in their eventual capture.

After the prison break at Eastham, the gang, now composed of Bonnie and Clyde, Raymond Hamilton, Henry Methvin, and Joe Palmer, continued committing robberies and stealing cars throughout Texas. Hamilton contacted Mary O'Dare, the wife of a former gang member, who agreed to join them as his mistress. Near the end of February 1934, the gang, numbering six, converged on Lancaster, Texas. With Methvin as a lookout, Clyde and Hamilton entered a bank with a sawed-off shotgun and a pistol. Clyde ordered the bank's manager to open the safe. Hamilton collected all of the cash from the safe and from the tellers' drawers, and the two men escaped through a side door. As soon as they were gone, the bank official contacted police, who determined that the descriptions fit Clyde Barrow and Raymond Hamilton.

In this robbery, the gang had pulled off one of their biggest hauls, just over $4,000. The three men joined up with the rest of the gang, and they all drove out of state. On this trip, tempers flared. Clyde observed Hamilton pocketing some of the cash before it had been divided. Bonnie did not like Mary O'Dare or her habit of flirting with all of the men in the gang. This conflict reached a breaking point after the Lancaster bank robbery. Clyde and Bonnie left Hamilton and O'Dare in Indiana and returned to Texas with Henry Methvin.

As Easter approached, the couple returned to the Dallas area. On Easter Sunday, April 1934, Bonnie, Clyde, and Methvin napped in their car on a highway near Grapevine, Texas. Police had been assigned to patrol the area for speeders, and three motorcycle officers noticed the parked car. Bonnie woke up and alerted Clyde that the police were approaching. He told Methvin, "Let's take them," implying a kidnapping. Methvin, who had only been with the couple a short time and was not familiar with their habit of kidnapping police, assumed that Clyde meant to begin shooting. He opened fire, killing one officer instantly and severely wounding another, who died on his way to the hospital. The three sped away from the scene, avoiding capture, but this incident further aroused law enforcement.

After the death of the two officers near Grapevine, the captain of the highway patrol also swore that he would find and punish those responsible. He had heard rumors about Hamer's new job and contacted him. He tried to persuade Hamer to include one of his men in the plan. Though he preferred to work alone, Hamer eventually agreed, and highway patrol officer Manny Gault, also a former Texas Ranger, joined up. Hamer and Gault recognized the circular traveling pattern that Bonnie and Clyde favored, from Dallas north through Oklahoma and Kansas, east into Missouri, south to northern Louisiana, and back to Dallas. They concluded that they would have to stop the couple somewhere along that circle.

The tracking party expanded to four when Simmons recognized that Hamer and Gault would not be able to identify Bonnie and Clyde on sight. He contacted Dallas police for assistance, and they assigned two officers, Bob Alcorn, who knew Bonnie and Clyde; and Ted Hinton, who was familiar with the Barrow family. The four men discussed the possibility of gaining help from a gang member in exchange for clemency. They settled on the family of Henry Methvin, who lived in the town of Arcadia in northeastern Louisiana, a spot on the Barrow gang's traveling circle. They contacted the local sheriff, who set up a meeting between Hamer and Henry Methvin's father.

Hamer offered Methvin's father a deal. In exchange for information about where the couple would be at a certain time, the governor would write a letter giving Methvin a full pardon. Over the next few days, the gang was spotted in various towns in Texas and Oklahoma. It had been raining for several days, and outside of Commerce, Oklahoma, the gang's car got stuck in the mud. Unable to wave down a passing car, the group was still struggling to free the car when Chief of Police Percy Boyd and a constable, Cal Campbell, arrived. A gun battle ensued. The officers' shots narrowly missed Clyde, but the gang's gunfire did not miss. Both Boyd and Campbell were seriously wounded, and Campbell died at the scene. Luckily for the gang, a local trucker, Charles Dobson, had heard the shooting and drove toward the scene. Another motorist, Jack Boydston, also appeared. At gunpoint, Clyde ordered the two to use the truck to haul their car out of the mud. Clyde and Methvin forced Chief Boyd, who had suffered a severe head wound, into their car, and they sped away. Boydston and Dobson alerted local police, who determined that the killers were Bonnie and Clyde and began a search involving both police cars and a plane. However, law enforcement lost their trail.

During the chase, Bonnie and Methvin bandaged Chief Boyd's head wound, and Boyd tried to have a friendly conversation with his kidnappers.

Clyde claimed that they had had nothing to do with the murders of the two highway patrolmen near Grapevine, and Bonnie asked Boyd to tell the world that she didn't smoke cigars. She blamed reporters for spreading that lie about her after the joke pictures of the gang had been discovered in Joplin. Eventually, the gang arrived in Fort Scott, Kansas. Outside of town, the gang released Boyd, who walked back to Fort Scott and told his story to local police and reporters.

THE AMBUSH

> Someday they'll go down together
> And they'll bury them side by side
> To few it'll be grief, to the law a relief
> But it's death for Bonnie and Clyde.
> —"The Story of Bonnie and Clyde," by Bonnie Parker (Milner, 1996)

Throughout April, Bonnie and Clyde eluded police. On April 29, 1934, the gang stole a nearly new, tan-colored Ford V-8 sedan belonging to Jesse and Ruth Warren of Topeka, Kansas. The next day, Bonnie, Clyde, Methvin, and Joe Palmer robbed a Kansas bank and got away with nearly $3,000. Palmer again decided to leave the gang, and Bonnie, Clyde, and Methvin returned to Dallas. They set up a meeting with the Barrow and Parker families. At this meeting, Bonnie requested that her family take her home when she died rather than letting her go to a funeral parlor. She also gave her mother a poem she had written called "The Story of Bonnie and Clyde," in which she foretold Clyde's and her deaths together. This was the last time the families would see the couple alive. Bonnie and Clyde headed toward Louisiana.

On May 19, 1934, Hamer's posse arrived in Shreveport, Louisiana, with heavy firepower. Coincidentally, Bonnie, Clyde, and Henry Methvin were also in town. They had been staying at a cabin with Methvin's father and had gone into town for lunch. While Bonnie and Clyde waited in the car, Methvin went in to place their orders. As they were waiting, Clyde noticed a police car making a routine patrol and sped away, leaving Methvin inside the café. Having planned a rendezvous point in case they got separated, Methvin left the café and hitchhiked back to his father's home. He told his father about the meeting, and his father passed the information along to the police, upholding his part of the deal. The next morning, Hamer and his group heard about the strange behavior of the café customers. The waitress identified Methvin as her customer. Hamer also got word that the elder Methvin had passed along important information about a meeting between his son and Bonnie and Clyde that would take place near Arcadia, Louisiana. The four men packed and drove to Arcadia to set up the ambush.

When Hamer's group arrived in Arcadia, they were joined by the sheriff, Henderson Jordan, and his deputy, Prentiss Oakley. The six men drove to the meeting point and staked out their positions overnight. The next morning, May 23, 1934, Methvin's father arrived, parking his truck on the side of the road. He removed the front tire and left the spare lying on the road to make it appear as if he needed assistance. Then, he joined Hamer's group in the trees. Bob Alcorn spotted the tan Ford approaching and identified the couple. Clyde recognized Methvin's truck and slowed. He then saw the officers aiming their rifles and reached for his gun. Hamer's group opened fire. As the car was riddled with bullets, Clyde's foot slid off the brake, and the car rolled off the road. The posse continued to fire until Hamer signaled the men to stop. They approached the car cautiously and observed the slumped, bloodied bodies of Bonnie and Clyde.

After ensuring that his son was not in the car with the couple, Ivan Methvin fixed his truck and left. Hamer instructed members of the posse to arrange for a tow truck and the coroner to respond to the scene. Hinton, another member of the posse, filmed the scene with a sixteen-millimeter movie camera. Hamer began an inventory of the car's contents and found fifteen sets of license plates, three Browning automatic rifles, a shotgun, eleven pistols, a revolver, and more than 2,000 rounds of ammunition (Roth, 1997).

The public heard about the deaths quickly. Local farmers who had heard the gunfire arrived at the scene. In nearby Arcadia, a member of the posse found the coroner, Dr. James L. Wade, and asked him to return to the scene to rule on the cause of death. Dr. Wade called his wife to let her know he would be late for lunch, and the operator, who had stayed on the line and overheard the news, quickly spread the word throughout town. People immediately drove out to the scene. The operator also called the local newspaper, which sent the story out to the rest of the nation. As the word spread, a reporter called Bonnie's mother, asking if she had heard that police had killed Bonnie and Clyde in Louisiana. Other reporters told Clyde's family the news, while still others contacted everyone who had been involved in the crime spree. Some talked with former gang members W. D. Jones and Raymond Hamilton. Others found Bonnie's husband, Roy Thornton. Reporters in Oklahoma talked with Chief Boyd, who had been kidnapped by the gang only weeks earlier.

At the scene, local townspeople began collecting souvenirs, including shell casings, pieces of glass from the car, pieces of bloody clothing, and locks of hair. One man even attempted to cut off Clyde's left ear. The number of people at the scene made Dr. Wade's work extremely difficult. Eventually, the tow truck arrived, and the sedan was towed into town in a procession that included police cars and onlookers. On its way, the caravan passed a high school, and students poured into the streets to look into the sedan.

Eventually, the parade pulled in front of Conger's Furniture Store and Funeral Parlor in Arcadia. The bodies were carried in amid the gaping crowd and taken to a small corner that was the mortuary. Local police wanted to put the bodies on display to give the large and increasingly aggressive crowd what it wanted, and Dr. Wade was hurried through his work. Carroll Rich (1970) published Dr. Wade's autopsy notes, in which he noted three tattoos on Clyde's body and the missing toes on his left foot. Bonnie's autopsy was performed second and was more rushed. He noted Bonnie's tattoo of the name *Roy* and a wedding ring as well as the extensive scars on her legs that had resulted from the car crash a year earlier. Dr. Wade concluded that both Bonnie and Clyde had died as a result of multiple gunshot wounds. A local photographer took pictures of the bodies, selling them to the public for five dollars each and to newspaper reporters for fifty dollars. After a hurried cleaning and embalming, the couple was covered to the neck with white sheets and rolled into the furniture store for public viewing. A line of people filed by the bodies for nearly six hours.

Clyde's father arrived that afternoon with an ambulance to take his son's body back to Dallas. The hearse to transport Bonnie's body arrived later. In Dallas, neither of Bonnie's last wishes, spoken to her mother and immortalized in her poem, was fulfilled. Their bodies were taken to different funeral homes, where thousands lined up to see their caskets, not home as she had asked. The couple was also not buried together. Bonnie's mother said that Clyde had had her in life, but she would have Bonnie now. They were buried in separate services in separate cemeteries, and Clyde was buried beside his brother Buck. At Clyde's funeral, an airplane dropped a wreath of flowers on his grave. In the four days between the ambush and their burial, newspapers flew off the shelves.

THE FOLKLORE OF BONNIE AND CLYDE

"They're young . . . they're in love . . . and they kill people"
—Ad for *Bonnie and Clyde*, 1967 (Hoberman, 1998)

Throughout Bonnie and Clyde's crime spree, the media faithfully reported on their activities, occasionally aided by the writings and poems that Bonnie sent to newspapers for publication. Some refer to Bonnie and Clyde as the world's most-photographed gangsters. After the ambush at Joplin, Missouri, the police found a roll of pictures taken of the gang. These photos soon appeared in the newspapers. The most famous of these photographs includes a picture of Bonnie in a long, dark-colored dress and beret with one foot perched on the bumper of their car, clutching a pistol and smoking a cigar. From this picture, Bonnie was referred to repeatedly in newspaper accounts as Clyde's "cigar-smoking gun moll" (Treherne, 1985, p. 120). Bonnie disliked this reference. She, in fact, hated cigars and only smoked cigarettes. In another picture, Bonnie holds a shotgun on Clyde. In both of these, Bonnie holds weapons, and this contributes to her image as an active participant in the murderous activities. However, members of the Barrow gang interviewed after the deaths of Bonnie and Clyde said that Bonnie never liked guns or fired one.

Cartoonists of the time also weighed in on the events. A cartoon in the April 9, 1934, edition of the *Dallas Journal* depicted law enforcement as a confused sheriff holding a gun and baton, head reeling as he tries to catch Bonnie and Clyde's car jumping in and out of holes in the ground (Treherne, 1985, p. 187). The image clearly demonstrated the gang's knack for escaping very close calls and law enforcement's frustration with trying to capture them. In the May 16, 1934, edition of the *Dallas Journal*, a cartoon appeared foreshadowing a violent end for the couple. The cartoon includes a drawing of an electric chair with a "Reserved" sign hanging on the wall behind it and the inscription "Clyde and Bonnie" (Treherne, 1985, p. 198). Only a week later, the couple would die at the hands of law enforcement.

After the couple's death, the government, particularly the Bureau of Investigation (later the Federal Bureau of Investigation), was determined to portray the pair negatively. A book on gangster crime published in 1936 with a forward by J. Edgar Hoover stated: "not a kind word may truthfully be said of Bonnie Parker or her mate, Clyde Barrow. They were physically unclean. The woman boasted that she never took a bath" (Treherne, 1985, p. 229). Meanwhile, the Barrow and Parker families were equally as determined to tell their side of the story. Published in 1934, a book based on the stories of Bonnie's mother and Clyde's sister describes two attractive and charming individuals driven to a life of crime by the harassment and unfair treatment they received from the law.

Soon, however, public attention turned to more pressing matters: recovery from the Depression, the rise of Hitler, and an impending world war. As Robertson (2002) points out, the couple languished in the "dusty backroom of the national memory." However, some media attention still focused on the story of Bonnie and Clyde. In 1939, the movie *Persons in Hiding*, based on a book written in collaboration with J. Edgar Hoover, was released. The goal was to dispel the public's sympathetic view of 1930s gangsters. The book and the movie are loosely based on the exploits of Bonnie and Clyde, portraying an attractive woman who longs for a glamorous life. She meets and marries a small-time criminal and turns him into a serious gangster. The movie was only moderately successful, and the government's propaganda did little to dispel the romantic image of Bonnie and Clyde.

Gun Crazy, released in 1950, tells the story of two people, Annie and Bart, who are obsessed with guns. They meet and begin their courtship as sharp-shooting acts in a fair sideshow. Then, because of Annie's need for excitement and material possessions, the couple turns to a life of crime, committing bank robberies and murders. The film portrays Annie as dominating the relationship, taking sensual pleasure in shooting and killing, and forcing Bart to participate. This story is among the early versions to link sex and violence, especially in the story of Bonnie and Clyde. The phallic symbolism of the gun and its attractiveness to the female member (Bonnie) appeared in other stories as well. Additionally, the distorted image of Bonnie as the dominant member of the couple continued.

In 1958, *The Bonnie Parker Story* was the first movie to specifically depict the lives of Bonnie and Clyde (called Guy Darrow in the film). Bonnie's story begins as Guy/Clyde shows her his machine gun. She is seduced and excited by their criminal adventures. The couple is joined by Guy/Clyde's brother, Chuck/Buck, and his girlfriend, who are shot by police. After this incident, Bonnie takes charge, organizing a prison break and taking up with a number of different men, including a handsome architect (Paul) who gives Bonnie a glimpse of the life she could have had. In the final scene, Bonnie and Guy/Clyde are killed in an ambush by police. This film further embellishes the image of Bonnie as the dominant partner and Clyde as a nearly impotent sidekick.

The story of Bonnie and Clyde was popularized most by the 1967 movie *Bonnie and Clyde*, directed by Arthur Penn and starring Faye Dunaway and Warren Beatty. Originally criticized as tasteless and grisly, the movie received enormous publicity and became a box office hit, receiving ten Oscar nominations. Hoberman (1998) notes that this movie represented a new style for Hollywood. In 1930, the Motion Picture Association of America's Production Code was revised to eliminate realistic violence in movies, stating that there could be no on-screen bleeding and that a gun and its victim could not appear in the same shot. The major concern of the industry was that viewers should not be seduced into siding with the criminals, so stories should not be told from the criminal's point of view. In 1966, this self-regulation was dismantled, and *Bonnie and Clyde* was among the first movies to take advantage of the change to a rating system.

In the Dunaway-Beatty movie, the title couple was portrayed sympathetically as both victims and offenders, which infuriated critics even as the movie fostered an emotional attachment among audiences to the charming, laughing pair. At the same time, the movie offered a negative depiction of law enforcement, appealing to a strong anti-authoritarian theme in the youth culture of the 1960s. Clyde and Bonnie were portrayed as Robin Hood and Maid Marian, beginning their bank-robbing career after meeting a poor farmer who had lost his farm to the bank. The image in the movie was that of Bonnie and Clyde as champions of the little people who were trapped into a series of violent confrontations. Critics noted that the danger of the movie lay in its claim to historical accuracy. In reality, there are notable inaccuracies in the movie version, from their first meeting to the rumor of Clyde's impotence to the crimes that they committed. However, through the enormous publicity and public support, critics were forced to recant their negative reviews.

Director Arthur Penn commented that the problem with most movies about violence was that they were not violent enough. He viewed the movie as a cautionary tale (Hoberman, 1998). Violence and sexuality are also intimately linked in the movie from the first view of Bonnie, naked in her bedroom, to her first meeting with Clyde, in which she caresses the barrel of his gun and recognizes the thrill and sexual excitement that he offers. Other themes in the movie, including changing positions of women and rebellious youth, also resonated with 1960s movie-goers. After its initial release, and the re-release in 1968, the movie inspired fashion trends around the world, including calf-length skirts and berets for women, and fedoras and wide ties for men.

Since the smash hit of the 1967 movie *Bonnie and Clyde*, the story has continued to inspire musical and theatrical works, further cementing the couple's place in American history. "Foggy Mountain Breakdown," the theme song from the 1967 movie, reached the top ten on the music charts. Musicians from Merle Haggard to Mel Torme have told the story of Bonnie and Clyde in a variety of genres, including country, rock, and rap. British singer Georgia Fame used machine-gun fire as a backdrop to his song "The Ballad of Bonnie and Clyde," which was banned in Norway and France (Hoberman, 1998). Today's musicians, including Tori Amos, Travis Tritt, and Eminem continue to invoke the story of Bonnie and Clyde in modern-day versions. Additional movies influenced by the story include *Thelma and Louise*, *Natural Born Killers*, *Drugstore Cowboy*, and *Teenage Bonnie and Klepto Clyde*.

An unusual development in the legend is a musical version of the story (*Bonnie and Clyde: The Musical*). The musical premiered July 1, 2003, at the Guildhall School of Music and Drama in London. In addition, after touring the country as a carnival attraction, the Bonnie and Clyde death car and the shirt Clyde was wearing when he died remain on display at the Primm Valley Resort near Las Vegas. Over the years, the couple have loaned their names to various things, including the Bonnie and Clyde Trade Days, a monthly flea market held near Arcadia, Louisiana. Gibsland, Louisiana, also holds the annual Bonnie and Clyde Festival, which includes an appearance by the car used in the 1967 movie and re-enactments of a bank robbery and the ambush resulting in the couple's death.

Clyde was just an ordinary criminal, and his crimes were mostly ignored until he met up with Bonnie. She was the unique feature at a time when violent crime was becoming more common, and the combination captured the public's imagination. Throughout their crime spree and in the nearly seventy years since, public perception of the Barrow gang and their crimes has been shaped by the media coverage. Part of the allure of the story of Bonnie and Clyde is the image of the couple as star-crossed lovers. They were the Romeo and Juliet of the 1930s. Their deaths together and Bonnie's self-composed eulogy put a romantic spin on their violence. Later Hollywood productions went even further and linked their violence to sexuality.

Movies and stories of Bonnie and Clyde imply that, like other outlaws, they were fighting a battle for the little people, robbing the banks that had contributed to the Great Depression and murdering law enforcement officers, symbols of the government. In reality, Bonnie and Clyde's crimes were committed primarily against ordinary citizens, such as John Bucher, a store owner; Howard Hall, a meat market manager; and Doyle Johnson, a man in the wrong place at the wrong time. Of the hundreds of robberies committed by the gang, only a few targeted banks. The story of Bonnie and Clyde has become larger than life, due in part to newspaper coverage at the time and in even larger part to Hollywood exaggerations.

REFERENCES

Cartwright, G. (2001, February). The whole shootin' match. *Texas Monthly*, 74–79, 119–124.

Hoberman, J. (1998). "A test for the individual viewer": Bonnie and Clyde's violent reception. In J. H. Goldstein (Ed.), *Why we watch: The attractions of violent entertainment* (pp. 116–43). New York: Oxford University Press.

Kirchner, L. R. (2000). *Robbing banks: An American history, 1831–1999*. Rockville Centre, NY: Sarpedon.

Knight, J. R. (1997). Incident at Alma: The Barrow gang in northwest Arkansas. *Arkansas Historical Quarterly*, 56, 399–426.

Milner, E. R. (1996). *The lives and times of Bonnie and Clyde*. Carbondale, IL: Southern Illinois University Press.

Phillips, J. N. (2000, October). The raid on Eastham. *American History*, 54–64.

Rich, C. Y. (1970). The autopsy of Bonnie and Clyde. *Western Folklore, 29*, 27–33.

Robertson, T. (2002). Bonnie and Clyde. In *St. James encyclopedia of popular culture*. Retrieved July 14, 2003, from http://www.findarticles.com/cf_0/g1epc/tov/2419100158/print.jhtml

Roth, M. (1997). Bonnie and Clyde in Texas: The end of the Texas outlaw tradition. *East Texas Historical Journal, 35*, 30–38.

Simpson, W. M. (2000). A Bienville parish saga: The ambush and killing of Bonnie and Clyde. *Louisiana History, 41*, 5–21.

Steele, P. W., and Scoma, M. (2000). *The family story of Bonnie and Clyde*. Gretna, LA: Pelican Publishing Company.

Treherne, J. E. (1985). *The strange history of Bonnie and Clyde*. New York: Stein and Day Publishers.

8

The Scottsboro Boys Trials: Black Men as "Racial Scapegoats"

James R. Acker, Elizabeth K. Brown, and Christine M. Englebrecht

Scottsboro. The very name of this northern Alabama town evokes images of the racial, regional, and ideological conflicts that smoldered during the Great Depression and then exploded in the trials of nine black youths charged with raping two white women. The trials exposed glaring fault lines in the administration of Alabama justice and represented an indictment against courtrooms and cultural norms throughout the South. The youths' convictions and death sentences produced two landmark U.S. Supreme Court decisions, rulings that were especially noteworthy because of the justices' willingness to measure the fairness of state criminal trials against the demands of the federal Constitution. Through widespread and enduring news and mass media attention, the Scottsboro cases most conspicuously signified the bitter legacy of institutionalized racism and class oppression, and shattered the myth that a nation's entire people could fully participate in the American Dream.

THE ALLEGED CRIMES

In 1931, as the country reeled in the economic crisis ushered in two years earlier by the collapse of the stock market, it was not uncommon for itinerants in search of work to hop the trains that crisscrossed America.

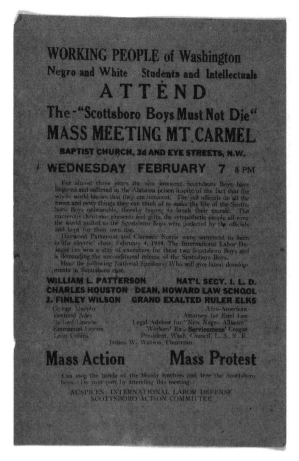

Broadside announcing mass meeting to save the
Scottsboro Boys. (Courtesy of Library of Congress)

A Southern Railroad train left Chattanooga, Tennessee, on March 25 of
that year, headed west for Memphis on a route that snaked through northern
Alabama. Scottsboro, a town of 3,500 people and the Jackson County seat,
lay on the rail line, nearly equidistant from Stevenson to the east and
Paint Rock to the west. Four traveling companions, all young Negroes,[1]
had boarded the train in Chattanooga, hoping to find jobs in Memphis:
Haywood Patterson, eighteen; Eugene Williams, thirteen; Andy Wright,
nineteen; and Andy's younger brother, Roy Wright, thirteen. Many others
had hitched rides on the forty-two-car train as it headed west through
Alabama, including five other black youths who lived in scattered parts of
Georgia: Olen Montgomery, seventeen; Clarence Norris, eighteen; Ozie

Powell, sixteen; Willie Roberson, seventeen; and Charles Weems, nineteen. The Georgia teenagers did not know one another, nor did they know the four Chattanooga youths (Carter, 1969, pp. 3–6; Geis and Bienen, 1998, p. 49; Goodman, 1994, pp. 4–5; Linder, 2004a). The nine would soon be irretrievably linked and thereafter identified collectively as the Scottsboro Boys.

Two young white women, twenty-one-year-old Victoria Price, and seventeen-year-old Ruby Bates had sneaked into a boxcar on the same train. Both women were returning to their homes in Huntsville, Alabama, from Chattanooga, where they had unsuccessfully searched for work. By the time the train pulled out of Stevenson, Alabama, at least some of the black youths crossed paths with several young white men who were also on board. A fight broke out and all of the white youths except one were thrown or jumped from the train. The jettisoned youths made their way by foot to Stevenson and complained to the stationmaster. By this time, the train already had passed through Scottsboro and was approaching Paint Rock, some forty miles west of Stevenson. The Stevenson stationmaster forwarded word that a gang of blacks had assaulted the young white men. A posse of white men were quickly deputized, armed themselves, flagged down the train at Paint Rock, and arrested all of the blacks they could find. The nine Scottsboro Boys were handcuffed, tied together with a rope, and transported in a flatbed truck to the Scottsboro jail.

Not until arriving in Scottsboro did the nine young men learn that Victoria Price and Ruby Bates had accused them of rape. The origins of the charge were somewhat obscure. After the two women were removed from the train in Paint Rock, Price either volunteered that she and Bates had been sexually assaulted by the Negroes, or she assented to a deputy sheriff's inquiry that had made that assumption. Price elaborated that six of the young men had raped her at knifepoint, and that another half-dozen black youths had assaulted Bates. The women were whisked away for a medical examination performed by two local physicians. A frightened Roy Wright accused the other young men of committing the crimes while insisting that he, his brother, and his Chattanooga friends were innocent (Carter, 1969, p. 16). The other arrested youths either maintained silence or denied the charges, which brought immediate retribution from their captors (Norris and Washington, 1979, p. 21). At least some of the Scottsboro Boys were unlikely participants in either a fight or a sexual assault. Olen Montgomery, who claimed to be traveling alone on the train, was blind in one eye and had extremely poor vision in the other. Willie Roberson suffered from both syphilis and gonorrhea, which resulted in swelling and painful lesions about his genitals and caused him to hobble with the aid of a cane (Carter, 1969, p. 6).

As news of the outrageous crimes spread, a threatening mob gathered outside of the Scottsboro jail. Fearing a lynching, Jackson County Sheriff M. L. Wann placed an urgent call to the governor's office. Governor Benjamin Meeks Miller responded by dispatching armed troops to Scottsboro from the nearest National Guard post (Carter, 1969, pp. 7–10). The Alabama Supreme Court later summarized the events of March 25, 1931:

If the two girls, Victoria Price and Ruby Bates, are to be believed, the defendants were guilty of a most foul and revolting crime, the atrocity of which was only equaled by the boldness with which it was perpetrated. . . . [I]n many respects [the details are] too revolting, shocking, to admit of being here repeated. (*Powell v. State*, 1932, p. 204)

IN THE COURTS: THE LEGAL SAGA

The Jackson County grand jury quickly convened. Indictments returned on March 31 charged each of the boys with rape, a crime punishable by ten years' imprisonment to death, at the discretion of the trial jury. The nine defendants appeared in court that same day for arraignment. Acting pursuant to Alabama law, which required the appointment of counsel for indigents accused of capital crimes, Judge Alfred E. Hawkins announced that he was assigning all seven licensed attorneys in Scottsboro to represent the boys (Carter, 1969, p. 17; *Powell v. Alabama*, 1932, p. 49). Not guilty pleas were entered on the boys' behalves, and their trials were scheduled to begin the following week, on April 6. As the trial date approached, however, three of the originally assigned lawyers were assisting in the prosecution of the cases, while others had withdrawn their services.

Stephen Roddy, a Chattanooga attorney hired by concerned citizens from that city, appeared in court on April 6, but insisted that he was unfamiliar with Alabama law, that he had not officially been retained for the case, and that he was unprepared to represent the boys. A Scottsboro lawyer, Milo Moody, volunteered to represent the defendants in conjunction with Roddy. Neither lawyer had investigated the charges, and they had met with the boys for barely half an hour before the trial. Roddy had a drinking problem and already smelled of alcohol when the trial commenced. Moody was approaching seventy years of age and was notoriously forgetful (Carter, 1969, pp. 17–23; Geis and Bienen, 1998, p. 50; Norris and Washington, 1979, p. 22). Judge Hawkins authorized them to proceed on the boys' behalves, "[a]nd in this casual fashion the matter of counsel in a capital case was disposed of" (*Powell v. Alabama*, 1932, p. 56).

The trials progressed in lightning fashion, with predictably disastrous consequences for the defendants. Although Roddy and Moody did not object to the boys' being tried jointly, prosecutors elected to go forward in four separate trials, proceeding first against Clarence Norris and Charles Weems. Victoria Price, the principal prosecution witness, described the fight that had broken out between the black and white youths on the train, culminating with the white boys being thrown from the train. She identified Norris and Weems as among the six Negroes who had raped her in a gondola car filled nearly to the top with chert, or crushed gravel. The two physicians who had examined Price and Bates on their arrival in Scottsboro, shortly after the alleged assault, confirmed the presence of semen in their vaginas.

After the prosecution rested, Weems took the witness stand and admitted participating in the fight with the white boys, but denied seeing any women on the train, let alone having anything to do with Price or Bates. Norris then shocked defense counsel by testifying that Roy White had held a knife on the young women while the other Negroes, including Weems, took turns raping them. Norris maintained that he alone did not assault the women. Following the prosecution's closing argument and demand for the death penalty, the defense counsel elected to waive final arguments before the jury. The twelve white men serving as jurors then retired to deliberate on a verdict as jury selection began for the second trial (Carter, 1969, pp. 24–35).

The remaining trials unfolded with minor variations. All concluded by the end of the day on April 9. The verdicts were reported with chilling regularity as one trial gave way to the next. Eight of the Scottsboro boys were convicted of rape and sentenced to death. Because of his youthful appearance, Roy Wright had been prosecuted separately, in the last of the trials, and the solicitor had asked only for a sentence of life imprisonment. The thirteen-year-old Wright was convicted, but notwithstanding the solicitor's call for mercy, seven members of the jury insisted on sentencing him to death. The resulting lack of unanimity caused a mistrial to be declared in his case. The executions of the remaining defendants were scheduled for July 10, 1931 (Carter, 1969, pp. 35–48).

Shortly after being returned to jail at the conclusion of their trials, the boys were visited by lawyers from the International Labor Defense (ILD), the legal arm of the American Communist Party. Party leaders had seized on the Scottsboro trials as a cause that would help unite black and white workers in the communists' worldwide struggle to achieve political, economic, and social equality. "By publicizing the plight of the boys and defending them in court, the Party saw the chance to educate, add to its ranks, and encourage the mass protest necessary not only to free the boys but also to bring about revolution" (Goodman, 1994, p. 27). Discerning the potential significance of the case too late, the National Association for the Advancement of Colored People (NAACP) engaged in an awkward and eventually losing tug of war with the ILD over the boys' legal representation. To the dismay of the NAACP's leaders, the ILD funded and assumed control over the appeal of the rape convictions (Carter, 1969, pp. 51–102; Goodman, 1994, pp. 32–38; Van West, 1981, pp. 40–43). The scheduled executions were postponed while the eight death-sentenced boys were dispatched to Alabama's death row in Kilby Prison to await the outcome of their appeals (Norris and Washington, 1979, p. 47).

The Alabama Supreme Court wasted little time in affirming the convictions and death sentences (*Patterson v. State*, 1932; *Powell v. State*, 1932; *Weems v. State*, 1932). Only Eugene Williams's conviction was overturned by the state's high court, on the ground that he had not yet turned sixteen at the time of the offense and thus fell within the exclusive jurisdiction of the juvenile court unless formally transferred for criminal trial (*Powell v. State*, 1932, pp. 211–213). Chief Justice John C. Anderson dissented from the decisions upholding the other defendants' convictions. He argued that community passions had been stirred to a "fever heat" by the crimes, which, he opined, were "of such a revolting character as to arouse any Caucasian county or community" (*Powell v. State*, 1932, p. 214). This atmosphere, combined with the "rather pro forma" representation provided by appointed counsel, led the chief justice to conclude that the defendants had not been given a fair trial (*Powell v. State*, 1932, pp. 214–215).

At the Supreme Court

The ILD retained Walter Pollak, a prominent expert in constitutional law, to pursue the cases in the U.S. Supreme Court. The conservative majority of the nation's high court was known during this era for its unwillingness to approve of President Roosevelt's New Deal reforms, and was almost equally reluctant to become involved in matters traditionally reserved for state law. The justices nevertheless were unable to condone the boys' treatment in the Alabama courts. In a seven to two ruling, the Court reversed the convictions and vacated the death sentences in the seven cases joined for decision in *Powell v. Alabama* (1932).

Justice George Sutherland's majority opinion concluded that the late resolution of appointment of counsel, and the consequent deficiencies in investigation and representation in these capital cases, denied the defendants fundamental fairness as guaranteed by the due process clause of the Fourteenth Amendment. *Powell v. Alabama* had ramifications far beyond reprieving the seven condemned Scottsboro boys. The Court's decision emphatically signaled that the U.S. Constitution imposed limits on how state criminal trial courts would be allowed to conduct business. Powell laid the foundation for the Court's landmark ruling three decades later in *Gideon v. Wainwright* (1963), that the Sixth Amendment entitles indigent defendants charged in state courts with serious crimes to representation by court-appointed counsel (Heller, 1951, pp. 121–125; Lewis, 1964; Mello and Perkins, 2003, pp. 348–355).

Retrial

In preparation for the boys' retrial, the ILD contacted Samuel Leibowitz, a New York City attorney widely regarded as the best criminal defense lawyer of his day. Leibowitz agreed to take on the cases, but wary about the Communist Party using the trials for ideological purposes, refused payment for his services and insisted that he be allowed to work independently of the ILD. After a change of venue was secured to Decatur, fifty miles west of Scottsboro in Morgan County, the new trials were slated to begin March 27, 1933. Leibowitz immediately moved to quash the rape indictments returned by the Jackson County grand jury, and also challenged the Morgan County jury venire. Both motions were based on the systematic exclusion of blacks from the respective jury pools, which Leibowitz attempted to demonstrate through detailed presentation of evidence. Judge James E. Horton Jr. denied the motions, and the prosecution elected to proceed against Haywood Patterson in the initial trial (Carter, 1969, pp. 181–202).

As if to affirm the Supreme Court's insistence in *Powell v. Alabama* about the importance of competent trial counsel in safeguarding defendants' rights, Leibowitz's entry into the case shed dramatic new light on the rape allegations. During his pounding cross-examination of Victoria Price, Leibowitz introduced records of her prior convictions for adultery and fornication. He portrayed Price as a prostitute who frequented hobo camps and as having engaged in sexual relations with a companion, Jack Tiller, shortly before her alleged rape on the train. Following up with one of the Scottsboro doctors who had examined Price just an hour and a half after she was removed from the train, Leibowitz established that Price had appeared calm and had experienced no vaginal bleeding or tearing. She had only a few superficial cuts and small bruises on her arms and back, surprising in light of her story that she had been repeatedly assaulted while lying on top of jagged gravel. The doctor also had detected only a small amount of semen in her vagina— consistent with her having had intercourse with Tiller the previous day, and extraordinary in the face of her claim that she had been raped just a few hours before by six men. Moreover, the sperm in the semen sample were immotile, which the doctor testified was unusual because sperm typically remained alive twelve hours to two days following intercourse (Carter, 1969, pp. 204–210).

When the defense opened its case, Leibowitz aggressively attempted to establish Patterson's innocence. Several of Patterson's traveling companions testified that they had neither seen nor had any interactions with Price on the train. Contrary statements that some of the boys had made during the earlier trials were attributed to fear inspired by their predicament and threats leveled by the authorities. Patterson testified and maintained his innocence. Leibowitz then examined Lester Carter, who described how he and Ruby Bates had engaged in sexual intercourse in a hobo camp on March 23, 1931, while Jack Tiller and Victoria Price had similarly had sexual relations. But the defense's most important witness was Ruby Bates, who made a surprise appearance at the trial. In response to Leibowitz's questioning, Bates recanted her story of being raped. She confirmed Carter's account that the two of them had had sexual intercourse on March 23, as did Price and Tiller. Bates then underwent a grueling cross-examination that called attention to her fine clothes and suggested that both her clothes and her testimony had been bought while she had taken refuge in New York City (Carter, 1969, pp. 219–234; Linder, 2004b).

When the attorneys delivered summations to the jury, Morgan County Solicitor Wade Wright vigorously defended the prosecution's case and ripped into Leibowitz's attempt to discredit Victoria Price and her testimony. Solicitor Wright challenged the twelve white jurors from his community: "Show them, show them that Alabama justice cannot be bought and sold with Jew money from New York" (Carter, 1969, p. 235). Leibowitz's furious motion for a mistrial was denied. The jury began its deliberations at one o'clock on a Saturday afternoon. It returned to the courtroom at ten o'clock Sunday morning with a verdict: Haywood Patterson was guilty of rape. His punishment was death.

The verdict was greeted by large demonstrations in New York and other northern cities (Carter, 1969, pp. 243–245). Unable to contain his contempt, Leibowitz explained the trial's outcome to the New York press. Referring to the jurors, he exclaimed, "If you ever saw those creatures, those bigots whose mouths are slits in their faces, whose eyes popped out at you like frogs, whose chins dripped tobacco juice, bewhiskered and filthy, you would not ask how they could do it" (Goodman, 1994, p. 148, quoting the *New York Daily News*, 1933, April 10). In retrospect, Leibowitz's frontal assault on Victoria Price during Patterson's trial appeared to have backfired. "Too late the chief defense attorney realized that Mrs. Price had become a symbol of white Southern womanhood" (Carter, 1969, p. 210). Southern newspapers excoriated Leibowitz for the "brutal manner" in which he had questioned Price (Carter, 1969, p. 210, quoting Sylacauga, Alabama *News*, 1933, April 7).

Conceivably, a local defense without the triple disadvantage of being radical, Jewish, and "northern" could have gained a compromise such as life imprisonment, but the jury's loyalty to its white caste could only be proved unequivocally by a guilty verdict. Whether Haywood Patterson was guilty or innocent was, at most, a peripheral question (Carter, 1969, p. 242).

Judge Horton ordered a delay in the remaining trials to allow the clamor surrounding Haywood Patterson's conviction and sentence to subside and to consider Leibowitz's motion to set aside the verdict. Meanwhile, thousands of marchers supporting the Scottsboro Boys descended on Washington, DC. The NAACP and ILD reached an uneasy truce and agreed to work cooperatively to defend the boys; and even southern papers, including Alabama's *Birmingham Post*, began questioning the charges (Carter, 1969, pp. 243–254). On June 22, 1933, more than two months after the conclusion of Patterson's retrial, Judge Horton stunned prosecutors and defense counsel alike by announcing in a carefully detailed ruling that the evidence failed to support the jury's verdict. He ordered that Patterson be granted a new trial (Norris and Washington, 1979, pp. 63–78; *Street v. National Broadcasting Co.*, 1981, pp. 1237–1246 [reprinting Judge Horton's order]). Hailed by some as a hero in the Scottsboro saga (Van West, 1981, pp. 44–46) but reviled by others, Judge Horton lost his bid for re-election the following year (Carter, 1969, p. 273). Much later, while reflecting on the Scottsboro cases, Horton recited a Latin phrase to explain his decision: *fiat justicia ruat colelum*—"let justice be done though the heavens may fall" (Linder, 2004c).

The next round of trials began November 20, 1933, in Decatur before a new judge, William Washington Callahan. Callahan repeatedly clashed with Leibowitz, interrupted his questioning of witnesses, hurried the cases along, and indicated in his rulings and demeanor his antagonism to the defense efforts. He denied Leibowitz's renewed motions to quash the Jackson County indictments and the Morgan County jury venire. The judge rejected the former motion after inspecting the Jackson County grand juror rolls and disputing Leibowitz's contention, supported by the testimony of a handwriting expert, that the names of several Negroes had fraudulently been entered after the fact to make it appear as if they had been considered by the jury commissioners. Judge Callahan also refused to allow Leibowitz to interrogate Victoria Price about her sexual activity prior to the alleged rapes— which was crucial to support the defense theory regarding the source of the semen detected during her medical examination—or to introduce Lester Carter's related testimony (Carter, 1969, pp. 274–293). Following the presentation of evidence, the judge's instruction to the jurors included the admonition that "[w]here the woman charged to have been raped, as in this case[,] is a white woman there is a very strong presumption under the law that she would not and did not yield voluntarily to intercourse with the defendant, a Negro" (Carter, 1969, p. 297). The validity of this premise notwithstanding, the defense of course had not built its case on consent, but rather disputed that any of the defendants had engaged in sexual relations with Price at all.

The trials of Haywood Patterson, and thereafter Clarence Norris, were conducted before Judge Callahan in this fashion. Following brief deliberations, the separate juries returned guilty verdicts and sentenced each defendant to death. Leibowitz secured a postponement of the remaining defendants' trials to allow the appellate courts to review Patterson's and Norris's convictions and resolve issues that were likely to recur in the ensuing cases. National protests erupted in the wake of these most recent verdicts, while the *Birmingham Post* and many other newspapers assailed Judge Callahan's handling of the trials (Carter, 1969, pp. 300–305).

The Alabama Supreme Court upheld the new convictions and death sentences on appeal. In doing so, it dismissed the argument that blacks had systematically been excluded from the grand jury and jury lists, concluding with dubious logic that their absence "would not, however, show discrimination, but selection only, and the exercise by the [jury] commissioners of their discretion" (*Norris v. State*, 1934, p. 563). The court dismissed Patterson's appeal without even reaching his claims of error, ruling that a filing deadline had been missed in the case (*Patterson v. State*, 1934). The U.S. Supreme Court once again agreed to review the state court holdings. During Liebowitz's oral argument, the justices took the extraordinary step of visually inspecting the juror lists that allegedly had been altered (*Norris v. Alabama*, 1935, p. 593, n. 1) and were visibly dismayed by what they saw (Goodman, 1994, p. 243; Kennedy, 1997, p. 176). In a second important ruling stemming from the Scottsboro proceedings, the justices overturned Norris's conviction because of Alabama's discriminatory jury selection procedures (*Norris v. Alabama*, 1935). The Court also vacated Patterson's conviction and remanded his case with the strong suggestion that the Alabama courts take corrective action notwithstanding the asserted missed filing deadline (*Patterson v. Alabama*, 1935).

Leibowitz continued to represent the boys, although his relations with the ILD had grown increasingly strained, especially after two ILD attorneys were caught offering to bribe Victoria Price to change her testimony (Carter, 1969, pp. 310–318). Following protracted negotiations, the ILD ceded control over the cases to a newly formed coalition, the Scottsboro Defense Committee, while the boys' cases returned to Judge Callahan's courtroom for retrial. A newly formed grand jury in Jackson County, which included a single black member, had returned new indictments against all nine of the Scottsboro Boys in November 1935.

Acknowledging the animosity that many of the locals harbored against him, Leibowitz took a back seat to Alabama attorney Clarence Watts when Haywood Patterson's fourth trial commenced on January 20, 1936. Judge Callahan quickly resumed hectoring the defense and again excluded evidence that the defense lawyers considered essential to cast doubt on Victoria Price's testimony. The new Morgan County solicitor, Melvin Hutson, pointedly reminded the trial jurors that they would have to go home and face their neighbors following their verdict. He requested the death penalty for Patterson as he emphasized that Price "fights for the rights of the womanhood of Alabama" (Carter, 1969, p. 344). The jury once again consisted of twelve white men, as the dozen black venire members called under Morgan County's revised selection procedures either opted out of service or were challenged peremptorily by the prosecutor. The jurors' deliberations lasted the better part of a day. They returned to announce their verdict just as jury selection was being completed for Clarence Norris's trial. To no one's surprise, the jury foreman announced that Patterson had been found guilty. He then shocked the courtroom with the further announcement that the jury had fixed punishment at seventy-five years in prison, sparing Patterson the death penalty (Carter, 1969, pp. 346–347).

Although the conviction hardly represented a victory for the defense, the sentence was another matter. The *Birmingham Age-Herald* speculated that Patterson's case was "probably the first time in the history of the South that a Negro has been convicted of a charge of rape upon a white woman and has been given less than a death sentence" (Carter, 1969, p. 347, quoting *Birmingham Age-Herald*, 1936, January 24). As Norris's trial loomed, Judge Callahan announced an indefinite recess owing to the illness of the physician who had examined Victoria Price the day of the alleged crimes. Norris, Roy Wright, and Ozie Powell were handcuffed together and placed in the back seat of a sheriff's department vehicle to be transported back to the Birmingham jail. An altercation broke out during the drive. The sheriff characterized the affray as an escape attempt (Goodman, 1994, pp. 259–260), while Norris recounted that it had begun with an exchange of words and a deputy slapping Powell in the face (Norris and Washington, 1979, pp. 162–163). It was undisputed, however, that Powell stabbed the deputy in the neck with a knife that he had secreted on his person. In response, the sheriff, who was driving the car, shot Powell in the head. The bullet lodged in Powell's brain. Although he survived following emergency surgery, Powell "was never the same" (Norris and Washington, 1979, p. 166) following the shooting.

The Alabama Supreme Court affirmed Patterson's most recent conviction in June 1937 (*Patterson v. State*, 1937), barely a month before the remaining trials were to resume before Judge Callahan. Clarence Norris's trial began on July 15, with Clarence Watts again serving as primary defense counsel and Leibowitz playing a supporting role. Pursuant to Callahan's hurry-up procedures, the trial concluded the following afternoon, and the all-white jury returned a guilty verdict and fixed punishment of death. A devastated Watts was unable to continue, so Leibowitz took command as Andy Wright's trial commenced. Declaring that they were satisfied that Patterson and Norris had been the "ringleaders" in the rape, prosecutors conceded that they would not seek the death penalty against Wright. The trial resulted in another swift conviction, and Wright was sentenced to ninety-nine years in prison. The prosecution similarly declined to pursue a capital sentence against Weems, whose trial an angry Leibowitz derided as a "travesty of justice." He railed to the jury that "It isn't Charley Weems on trial in this case, it's a Jew lawyer and New York State put on trial here by the [prosecutor's] inflammatory remarks" (Carter, 1969, p. 374). Weems's conviction followed, and the jury fixed his sentence at seventy-five years in prison.

Then, in rapid succession, the cases against the remaining defendants were resolved. Ozie Powell pled guilty to assaulting the deputy whom he had knifed; Judge Callahan imposed a twenty-year prison sentence. He then dismissed the rape charge against Powell. The prosecution thereupon announced that it was dismissing the rape charges against Olen Montgomery, Willie Roberson, Eugene Williams, and Roy Wright. The lead prosecutor explained that the state was convinced that Roberson, crippled by venereal disease, and the nearly blind Montgomery had not been involved in the assault. Moreover, Williams and Roy Wright were juveniles and each already had served well over six years in prison (Carter, 1969, pp. 375–377). Various newspapers interpreted the dismissals as evidence that all nine of the Scottsboro Boys were innocent, a conclusion disputed by Alabama officials (pp. 377–379). Alabama Governor Bibb Graves commuted Clarence Norris's death sentence to life imprisonment in July 1938, just six weeks before Norris's scheduled execution (Norris and Washington, 1979, p. 173).

The Scottsboro Defense Committee then stepped up efforts to secure the release of the five boys who remained incarcerated. Governor Graves appeared to be primed to commute the outstanding prison sentences in November 1938, secure in the belief that Alabama newspapers would support such action. Those plans disintegrated after a disastrous encounter between the governor and the boys, during which Patterson was found in possession of a knife and Norris threatened Patterson's life (Carter, 1969, pp. 386–394;

Goodman, 1994, pp. 352–355).[2] The intensity of news media coverage of the Scottsboro Boys' cases subsided shortly thereafter.

WHAT BECAME OF THE PRINCIPALS

The Scottsboro defendants met various fates. With periods of incarceration ranging from six and a half to nineteen years, the nine young men in combination spent more than 100 years behind bars following their arrests for rape. Haywood Patterson remained in prison until 1948, when he escaped and made his way to Detroit. The governor of Michigan refused to honor Alabama's extradition request after the FBI discovered Patterson's whereabouts. Patterson killed a man in a Detroit bar in 1950, received a fifteen-to-twenty-year prison sentence for manslaughter, and died of cancer two years later while still incarcerated, at age thirty-nine (Carter, 1969, p. 415; Linder, 2004a). Returning from a lengthy stay at sea while employed with the merchant marine in 1959, Roy Wright accused his wife of being unfaithful and then killed her before taking his own life (Carter, 1969, pp. 414–415; Linder, 2004a). Roy's brother Andy was originally paroled in 1944, only to be re-incarcerated for a parole violation. He finally was released from the Alabama prison system in 1950, the last of the group to gain his freedom (Goodman, 1994, pp. 370–375; Linder, 2004a).

Most of the remaining Scottsboro Boys "returned to obscurity" (Carter, 1969, p. 415). In the 1970s, however, news media including the *Washington Post*, the *Atlanta Constitution*, and the *New York Times* brought Clarence Norris, the last surviving Scottsboro Boy, back into the spotlight through their coverage of his efforts to obtain a pardon (Van West, 1981, p. 46; Goodman, 1994, pp. 384–388). Norris, who was released from prison in 1946 and then absconded to New York in violation of his parole, enlisted the assistance of the NAACP to campaign for an official pardon (Linder, 2004a). The Alabama Board of Pardons and Paroles finally issued Norris the sought-after pardon in November 1976. Governor George Wallace congratulated Norris personally in his Montgomery office and made the pardon official (Norris and Washington, 1979, pp. 229–247, 271–283). When Norris died in 1989, his obituary was widely printed in major national and international papers (Clarence Norris; Obituary, 1989; Krebs, 1989, p. 21; Associated Press, 1989).

AN ANALYSIS OF THE NEWS MEDIA PORTRAYAL OF SCOTTSBORO

The Scottsboro Boys case exemplifies a "super primary" news story, one that receives sustained coverage not just for weeks or months, but for decades;

a story that influences public opinion, politics, and has a lasting impact on the fabric of society (Chermak, 1995). Indeed, the story of the Scottsboro Boys could not accurately be told without acknowledging the important role played by the media. Contemporary newspaper accounts, for example, decisively helped shape public perceptions of the boys and directly affected both prosecution and defense efforts to mobilize support. Beyond the immediate news attention ignited on March 25, 1931, the mass media, including literature, film, and the visual arts, have continued to reaffirm and redefine the social and political significance of the Scottsboro Boys case (Murray, 1977).

When the Memphis-bound freight train carrying its ill-fated passengers pulled into Paint Rock, Alabama, on March 25, 1931, a news story of dramatic proportions was in the making. By that evening, the two local weekly papers, the *Jackson County Sentinel* and the *Progressive Age*, had printed stories detailing the gruesome, violent rapes of two young white women by nine black boys. The *Chattanooga Times* initially depicted the boys as common criminals, although none had police records at the time (Maher, 1997, pp. 103–104). While only a handful of national papers covered the case within the initial days of the boys' arrest, the Associated Press released a story focusing on how the National Guard was called out to maintain order in Scottsboro (Pfaff, 1974, p. 73). The local news coverage sparked an enormous uproar that eventually captured the attention of the nation and the world, and in the process significantly shaped the issues at stake as the boys went on trial for their lives.

Racial issues inevitably permeated and helped frame news media depictions of the case over the years. In addition, during the years immediately following the arrest and conviction of the nine young men, the news media tended to depict the case as a struggle pitting the North against the South, and a Jewish New York lawyer against the Alabama attorney general. The story was also framed as a struggle between the ILD and the NAACP, as both organizations sought to represent the boys, motivated in part by the importance of securing publicity to help gain supporters for their causes. Emphasis shifted again when historical accounts of the case, such as *Scottsboro: A Tragedy of the American South* (Carter, 1969), criticized both the ILD and the NAACP for their handling of the case. The made-for-television movie *Judge Horton and the Scottsboro Boys* later reframed the saga to focus on the actions of Judge Horton (Van West, 1981, p. 45). While racial prejudice was at the heart of the events surrounding the arrest and prosecution of the Scottsboro Boys, the news media helped to create and convey the shifting symbolic and socially important themes related to sectional division and political ideology.

Race and Gender

The Scottsboro case involved the presumption of a crime considered to represent the most egregious breach of Southern cultural boundaries in 1931: the raping of white women by black men. The story of the nine boys and their accusers served as a lightning rod for sentiments about interracial affairs and helped focus attention on issues of racism in the criminal justice system (Bailey and Green, 1999, p. 112; Brownmiller, 1975, p. 210). Rape tended to receive relatively modest coverage in the news media at that time, and the few cases inspiring media attention typically involved blacks accused of raping whites (Brownmiller, 1975, p. 213). The media largely ignored accusations of intraracial sex crimes, particularly those involving blacks (Benedict, 1992, p. 26). News coverage thus delineated the crimes meriting public attention and had the effect of putting white women on a pedestal, elevating them to a "separate and unequal sphere" (Lawson, Colburn, and Paulson, 1986, p. 6), while the plight of black women often was overlooked.

The news media have often been criticized for disproportionately portraying blacks as the perpetrators of crimes (Barlow, Barlow, and Chiricos, 1995). Such portrayals have contributed to and helped perpetuate the image of the dangerous black man, tapping into people's fear about crime generally, and black criminality specifically (Russell, 1998, p. 71; Boser, 2002). "The case of the Scottsboro Boys is perhaps the best known example of Black men being used as racial scapegoats" (Russell, 1998, p. 79; see also Kennedy, 1997, p. 100). Historically, the most notorious false accusation against a black man has been the claim of rape made by a white woman, and in this respect the Scottsboro Boys cases resonate with an intensity similar to the trial in Harper Lee's *To Kill a Mockingbird*. During the era of the Scottsboro trials, capital punishment for rape was confined almost exclusively to the South. Moreover, nearly 90 percent (405 of 455) of the executions for this crime between 1930 and the 1964 involved black defendants, a large proportion of whom had been convicted of raping white women (Wolfgang and Riedel, 1973). The Scottsboro Boys came perilously close to being added to those rolls, with the media coverage of their cases alternatively fanning and attempting to quell the flames of racial prejudice.

Regionalism

By the start of the first trial on April 6, 1931, local townspeople and media had converged on the Scottsboro Courthouse, with only a smattering of national media sources represented (Ross, 1999, p. 50). Soon after the trials concluded and the ILD assumed representation of the boys, however, the northern news media descended en masse on Alabama, where they were not warmly received (Van West, 1981, p. 38). Alabama newspapers, including the *Huntsville Daily Times*, the *Birmingham Age-Herald*, and the local Scottsboro papers, recoiled at what they considered to be a gross imposition by northern papers such as the *Daily Worker*, the *New York Times*, and the *Nation*. The published rhetoric of the *Daily Worker*, for example, was often vehemently refuted and criticized in the southern press. The southern news media perceived northern news sources to be latching onto the case to demonize the South and play savior to the boys; actions which, some charged, would compromise justice. On the other hand, many among the northern news media were moved to assume a protective role by calling attention to the plight of the nine defendants and urging the correction of perceived injustices (Van West, 1981; Ross, 1999, p. 53).

The regional media divide remained strong until March 1932, when the Alabama Supreme Court upheld the boys' original convictions. Then, although the *Montgomery Advertiser*, a prominent Alabama newspaper, supported the state court decision, the *Birmingham Age-Herald* and the *Birmingham Post* began to express doubts about the case (Maher, 1997, p. 109). The softening stance of select southern papers may have been linked to broader national and international campaigns in support of the boys. Red Aid, the international arm of the Communist Party, mobilized support for the boys with the help of individuals including Ada Wright (the mother of Roy and Andy Wright), thus focusing international attention on the case (Miller, Pennybacker, and Rosenhaft, 2001).

The temporary lull in regional media antagonism did not endure, however, for upon losing the retrial in March, 1933, defense attorney Leibowitz lashed out at southerners through the *New York Herald Tribune*, claiming that Alabamans were bigoted, dirty, and unintelligent (Maher, 1997, p. 110). Leibowitz's intemperate remarks ignited angry responses from the southern press. In similar fashion, when Ruby Bates spoke out in support of the boys in Washington, DC, Alabama's *Huntsville Times* assailed her character. Likewise, several Alabama newspapers criticized Judge Horton when he publicly expressed doubts about Victoria Price's character. It was the *New York Times'* turn to criticize the judging in the case after Horton was replaced by the conservative Judge Callahan (Maher, 1997, pp. 110–111).

Ideology

In addition to the regional divide observed in news media coverage of the Scottsboro case, the ILD and NAACP battled for control over the legal defense of the Scottsboro Boys. These two ideologically disparate groups claimed that they were best suited to protect the boys from what they both perceived as a biased justice system. The Communist Party, relying on outlets including the *Southern Worker*, the *Daily Worker* and international media, portrayed the case as an example of political subjugation of young blacks by the white, capitalist justice system (Maher, 1997, p. 106). The NAACP decried what that organization perceived as racially motivated injustices in the Scottsboro Boys' prosecution.

It has been argued that both groups saw the case as an opportunity to further their own goals, to promote their ideological messages, and add supporters to their rosters, with the effect of dividing what otherwise might have been unified support for the boys (Maher, 1997, p. 108). Whatever their motivations, both the ILD and NAACP utilized the news media to garner attention and mobilize action surrounding the Scottsboro Boys (Miller et al., 2001). Although the NAACP was somewhat overshadowed by the rhetoric of the ILD in the early years of the case, NAACP leaders continued to work on behalf of the boys throughout the resolution of their cases and, thereafter, to protect their legacies.

Popular Culture

The social and cultural impact of Scottsboro also endures through the visual arts, film, music, and literature. The case has influenced and inspired the creation of a vast body of artistic work, much of which conveys powerful social commentary. Though varied in their interpretations, the bulk of the artistic works that draw on the Scottsboro case are sympathetic to and supportive of the boys. These works include paintings, lithographs, and block prints that focused on the newly invigorated anti-lynching movement (Park, 1993, p. 311). For example, *Christ in Alabama*, a Scottsboro-inspired lithograph, depicts the lynching mentality in the South (Park, 1993, p. 334). Another lithograph shows a young white girl sitting on the lap of an older white man. Underneath the image are the words "Alabama Code—Our Girls Don't Sleep with Niggers (1933)" (Park, 1993, p. 337). A visual history of African American experience is portrayed in *Scottsboro: A Story in Block Prints* (originally called *Scottsboro: A Story in Linoleum Cuts*). The book traces experiences of African Americans, including slavery and subjugation to Jim Crow laws. It features an artistic interpretation of the Scottsboro case in which the Scottsboro Boys were framed and coerced by the white authorities (Williams, 2000, p. 53).

The significance and drama of the Scottsboro case also have been captured in plays and poetry. Originally produced in 1934, John Wexley's *They Shall Not Die* portrayed aspects of the case on the stage. Wexley's production, which depicted lynchings as a sort of "southern holiday," included dialogue from the actual court transcripts, adding to the realism of the piece (Duffy, 2000, p. 31; Williams, 2000, p. 53). *They Shall Not Die* created controversy and stirred antiblack, anticommunist, and anti-Semitic sentiments, as blacks and whites mingled on stage to support the boys and to oppose the Southern oppression of blacks (Hilliard, 2001).

Intermingling themes of both economic and racial oppression, Langston Hughes wrote extensively about the Scottsboro Boys (Duffy, 2000, p. 24). His short poem "Christ in Alabama," which originally was published in a student magazine at the University of North Carolina, encapsulates the racial, social, sexual, and regional conflicts of the case. Hughes voiced frustration during the Scottsboro trials at prominent black leaders, including college administrators, for their silence about the boys' treatment. In an essay titled "Cowards from the Colleges," he blasted southern schools and their leaders for their lack of commitment to the black struggle and, specifically, the injustices associated with the Scottsboro case. Hughes' commitment to the Scottsboro case was evidenced in other work and in his philanthropy. With the help of Carl Van Vechten and Prentiss Taylor, Hughes published a pamphlet, *Scottsboro Limited*, which included a play by the same title, as well as short poems and lithographs (Thurston, 1995). The play attempted to unite the causes of economic and racial justice, evoking references to the "Red Voices" and the "Red Negro." Proceeds from the pamphlet's sales were donated to the ILD fund (Duffy, 2000, p. 29; Thurston, 1995).

The stories of the nine Scottsboro youths can also be seen in films and heard in the lyrics of songs. The Scottsboro case inspired several films, including the 1976 television movie *Judge Horton and the Scottsboro Boys*, which was nominated for Emmy awards for writing and directing. In 1998, a second film, *Crime Stories: The Scottsboro Boys*, was aired on television. Most recently, a 2001 documentary titled *Scottsboro: An American Tragedy* was released to critical acclaim (Internet Movie Database, 2004).

Many songs were written in response to the boys' struggle. For example, a song entitled "The Scottsboro Boys Shall Not Die" was inspired by the words of Samuel Leibowitz, and was composed to help in the effort to free the nine boys (Williams, 2000, p. 52). Additional songs followed, including "Song for the Scottsboro Boys," "Scottsboro Blues," and simply "Scottsboro Boys." Some of the songs dramatically portrayed southern whites as animals, while the boys were lamented as victims of a racist society and justice system (Williams, p. 59).

THE LEGACY: MEDIA INTERPRETATIONS AND JUDICIAL CHANGE

A large memorial plaque was installed in Scottsboro on January 25, 2004, to commemorate the lives of the nine Scottsboro Boys, more than seventy years after the beginning of their plight. The memorial resides on the lawn of the Jackson County courthouse, the site of the original trial. It represents the town's first official acknowledgment of the Scottsboro case. Scottsboro mayor Ron Bailey expressed hope that the plaque would help promote the healing process. "Otherwise, [the case] will be a stumbling block to the future," he said (Associated Press, 2004). Ann Chambliss, past president of the Jackson County Historical Association, declared, "we cannot change the course of human events that began on March 25, 1931, but we can unite to heal the long-standing wounds" (Aldrich, 2004). Similar sentiments were expressed by Reverend R. L. Shanklin, president of the Alabama Conference of the NAACP, who stated at the memorial's dedication that "today is the beginning of the healing process" (Aldrich, 2004, p. 1).

Although no memorial can repair the lives shattered in the Scottsboro Boys case, the trials and their aftermath spawned several profoundly significant living legacies. The two major Supreme Court decisions having roots in Scottsboro embody vital principles of American justice, including the right of poor people to the services of competent legal counsel, and the participation on juries of all qualified citizens, free from invidious racial discrimination. The Scottsboro trials harbingered and undoubtedly helped precipitate the civil rights struggles of the ensuing generation that subsumed yet spilled far beyond correcting inequities in criminal justice. The case threatened to cleave the country along many divides and yet, if the contemporary townspeople are correct, perhaps the healing process has begun. However viewed, the enduring significance of the Scottsboro Boys case, and its multiple symbolic dimensions, are the direct outgrowth of the media interpretations and representations of this epic historical event.

NOTES

1. We use the term *Negroes* because this word was commonly employed in media and other reports when the Scottsboro Boys case arose in the 1930s. The term is intended to be used interchangeably with *blacks*, as frequently occurs elsewhere in this chapter.

2. The meeting between the boys and Governor Graves was arranged in anticipation of the governor issuing a pardon before his term of office expired; before acting, Graves wanted to interview the boys and satisfy himself that it would be appropriate to release them from prison.

REFERENCES

Aldrich, M. (2004, January 27). A sign of change, a chance to heal. *Scottsboro Daily Sentinel*. Retrieved February 10, 2004, from http://www.thedailysentinel. com/story.lasso?wcd=323

Associated Press. (1989, January 26). Clarence Norris, falsely accused in key case. *Toronto Star.* Retrieved February 12, 2004, from LexisNexis Academic Database Guided News Search.

Associated Press. (2004, January 13). Marker is planned for landmark case. *New York Times.* Retrieved February 11, 2004, from LexisNexis Academic Database Guided News Search.

Bailey, F. Y., and Green, A. P. (1999). *"Law never here": A social history of African-American responses to issues of crime and justice.* Westport, CT: Praeger.

Barlow, M. H., Barlow, D. E., and Chiricos, T. G. (1995). Economic conditions and ideologies of crime in the media. *Crime and Delinquency, 41,* 3–19.

Benedict, H. (1992). *Virgin or vamp: How the press covers sex crimes.* New York: Oxford University Press.

Boser, U. (2002, August 26–September 2). The black man's burden. *U. S. News and World Report, 133*(8).

Brownmiller, S. (1975). *Against our will: Men, women, and rape.* New York: Simon and Schuster.

Carter, D. T. (1969). *Scottsboro: A tragedy of the American South.* Baton Rouge, LA: Louisiana State University Press.

Chermak, S. (1995). *Victims in the news: Crime and the American news media.* Boulder, CO: Westview Press.

Clarence Norris [Obituary]. (1989, January 27). *London Times.* Retrieved February 12, 2004, from LexisNexis Academic Database Guided News Search.

Duffy, S. (2000). *The political play of Langston Hughes.* Carbondale, IL: Southern Illinois University Press.

Geis, G., and Bienen, L. B. (1998). *Crimes of the century: From Leopold and Loeb to O. J. Simpson.* Boston: Northeastern University Press.

Gideon v. Wainwright. 372 U.S. 335 (1963).

Goodman, J. (1994). *Stories of Scottsboro.* New York: Pantheon Books.

Heller, F. H. (1951). *The Sixth Amendment to the United States Constitution: A study in constitutional development.* Lawrence, KS: University of Kansas Press.

Hilliard, R. L. (2001). When theatre courage counted. *Theatre History Studies, 21,* 5–9.

Internet Movie Database. (n.d.). Retrieved February 16, 2004, from http://www.imdb.com/find?tt=on;nm=on;mx=20;q=Scottsboro

Kennedy, R. (1997). *Race, crime, and the law.* New York: Vintage Books.

Krebs, A. (1989). Clarence Norris, the last survivor of "Scottsboro Boys," dies at 76. *New York Times,* p. 21. Retrieved February 11, 2004 from http://web.lexis-nexis.com/universe/document?_m=c205eb845c74f8bb3a90835c9659

Lawson, S. F., Colburn, D. R., and Paulson, D. (1986). Groveland: Florida's little Scottsboro. *Florida Historical Quarterly, 65*(1), 1–26.

Lewis, A. (1964). *Gideon's trumpet.* New York: Random House.

Linder, D. O. (2004a). Biographies of key figures in "The Scottsboro Boys" trials. Retrieved February 6, 2004, from http://www.law.umkc.edu/faculty/projects/FTrials/scottsboro/SB_biog.html

Linder, D. O. (2004b). Excerpts from the trial of Alabama v. Patterson, March–April, 1933. Retrieved February 6, 2004, from http://www.law.umkc.edu/faculty/projects/FTrials/scottsboro/SB_tri33tml.html

Linder, D. O. (2004c). Judge James E. Horton. Retrieved February 6, 2004, from http://www.law.umkc.edu/faculty/projects/FTrials/scottsboro/SB_BHort.html

Maher, M. (1997). The case of the Scottsboro Boys (1931). In L. Chiasson Jr. (Ed.), *The press on trial: Crimes trials as media events* (pp. 103–116). Westport, CT: Greenwood Press.

Mello, M., and Perkins, P. J. (2003). Closing the circle: The illusion of lawyers for people litigating for their lives at the fin de siecle. In J. R. Acker, R. M. Bohm, and C. S. Lanier (Eds.), *America's experiment with capital punishment: Reflections on the past, present, and future of the ultimate penal sanction* (2nd ed., pp. 347–384). Durham, NC: Carolina Academic Press.

Miller, J. A., Pennybacker, S. D., and Rosenhaft, E. (2001). Mother Ada Wright and the international campaign to free the Scottsboro Boys. *American Historical Review, 106*(2), 387–430.

Murray, H. T., Jr. (1977). Changing America and the changing image of Scottsboro. *Phylon, 38*(1), 82–92.

Norris, C., and Washington, S. D. (1979). *The last of the Scottsboro Boys*. New York: G. P. Putnam's Sons.

Norris v. Alabama, 294 U.S. 587 (1935).

Norris v. State, 156 So. 556 (Ala., 1934). Reversed in *Norris v. Alabama*, 294 U.S. 587 (1935).

Park, M. (1993). Lynching and antilynching: Art and politics in the 1930s. In Jack Salzman (Ed.), *Prospects: An annual of American cultural studies* (pp. 311–365). New York: Cambridge University Press.

Patterson v. Alabama, 294 U.S. 600 (1935).

Patterson v. State, 141 So. 195 (Ala., 1932). Reversed in *Powell v. Alabama*, 287 U.S. 45 (1932).

Patterson v. State, 159 So. 567 (Ala., 1934). Vacated and remanded, *Patterson v. Alabama*, 294 U.S. 600 (1935).

Patterson v. State, 175 So. 371 (Ala., 1937). Cert. denied, 302 U.S. 733 (1937).

Pfaff, D. W. (1974). The press and the Scottsboro rape cases, 1931–1932. *Journalism History, 1*(3), 72–76.

Powell v. Alabama, 287 U.S. 45 (1932).

Powell v. State, 141 So. 201 (Ala., 1932). Reversed in *Powell v. Alabama*, 287 U.S. 45 (1932).

Ross, F. G. J. (1999). Mobilizing the masses: The *Cleveland Call* and *Post* and the Scottsboro incident. *Journal of Negro History, 84*(1), 48–60.

Russell, K. K. (1998). *The color of crime: Racial hoaxes, white fear, black protectionism, police harassment, and other macroaggressions*. New York: New York University Press.

Street v. National Broadcasting Co., 645 F.2d 1227 (6th Cir. 1981). Cert. granted, 454 U.S. 815 (1981). Cert. dismissed, 454 U.S. 1095 (1981).

Thurston, M. (1995). Black Christ, red flag: Langston Hughes on Scottsboro. *College Literature, 22*(3), 30–49.

Van West, C. (1981). Perpetuating the myth of America: Scottsboro and its interpreters. *The South Atlantic Quarterly, 80*(1), 36–48.

Weems v. State, 141 So. 215 (Ala., 1932). Reversed, *Powell v. Alabama*, 287 U.S. 45 (1932).

Williams, L. B. (2000). Images of Scottsboro. *Southern Cultures, 6*(1), 50–67.

Wolfgang, M. E., and Riedel, M. (1973). Race, judicial discretion, and the death penalty. *The Annals of the American Academy of Political and Social Science, 407*, 119–133.

9

The Lindbergh Baby
Murder Case:
A Crime of the Century

Kelly Wolf

Charles Augustus Lindbergh was an international hero. In May 1927, he became the first person ever to fly across the Atlantic Ocean alone—3,610 miles in a single-engine plane named *The Spirit of St. Louis*. His fame and popularity with the public were enormous. He met and married Ann Morrow, daughter of Dwight D. Morrow, a U.S. ambassador and extremely wealthy man, in May 1929. Their first baby arrived on June 22, 1930. He was named Charles Augustus Lindbergh Jr., after his father, and also became known as the "Eaglet." The birth of the baby was a national sensation. The media allowed the Lindberghs little privacy; pictures of the new family were everywhere, as were pictures of their newly built house, the Hopewell Estate in New Jersey. The house was not yet finished, so the family would only spend weekends there, leaving on Mondays for the Morrow Estate where Ann's mother resided.

THE CRIME

One particular weekend in March, the twenty-month-old baby became ill, and Ann and Charles decided to spend an extra night at the Hopewell Estate. They phoned the baby's nursemaid, Betty Gow, at the Morrow Estate and

Portrait of Mrs. Charles Lindbergh (Anne Morrow
Lindbergh) sitting at the side of an airplane in Chicago,
Illinois. (Chicago Historical Society)

informed her that she would be driven to Hopewell to help tend to the
child. Gow then phoned her boyfriend, Red Johnson, and cancelled her
date with him, telling him about the sick child. The butler drove her
to Hopewell.

On Monday, March 1, 1932, Gow began getting young Charles ready
for bed. Since he had a cold, she gave him some milk of magnesia, which
the baby spit out, soiling his pajamas. Gow decided that since there was a
chill in the air, she would make the child a flannel shirt to wear underneath
his pajamas. Gow rubbed some Vicks VapoRub on the child and dressed him,
once again, for bed. She attached his thumb guards to prevent the baby
from sucking his thumb, and put him into the crib. Pulling the blankets
tightly around the Eaglet, she put two safety pins, one on each side, into the
mattress to secure the blanket. The nursemaid sat in the dark with the baby
until 8 p.m., when she could hear him breathing evenly. All of the shutters
were closed and locked except for the one on the southeast side of the

nursery: it was warped and could not be locked. Gow went downstairs to have dinner with the other Lindbergh staff.

Lindbergh had returned home at around 9 p.m. and was having dinner with Ann when he heard a cracking sound that he later identified as slats of an orange crate falling off a chair. At the time, he dismissed it as an accident in the kitchen. Lindbergh and Ann sat in the living room reading the paper and talking for a few minutes. Lindbergh then went upstairs to draw himself a bath. After his bath he went back to the den to do some more reading. Ann decided it was her turn for a bath. While getting cleaned up, she discovered that she had run out of tooth powder. She entered the nursery, which was connected to the Lindbergh's bathroom, and went straight to the dresser. Not noticing that the baby was missing, she took the powder and returned to the bathroom.

At 10 p.m., Gow returned to the nursery for her final check on the baby before turning in. She discovered that he was gone and quickly ran to Ann's bedroom, asking if she had the child. Ann replied no, and they both went downstairs to see whether Lindbergh had the boy. Lindbergh said that he did not and rushed up the stairs, two at a time, to the nursery. He quickly scanned the room and went directly to his closet to grab his Springfield rifle. He looked at his wife and said "Ann, they've stolen our baby" (Waller, 1961; Fisher, 1987; Behn, 1994, p. 46; Berg, 1998, p. 254; Hixson, 2001). Lindbergh called his personal friend and attorney Colonel Henry Breckinridge, and ordered the butler, Oliver Whately, to call the police.

THE INVESTIGATION

While scanning the nursery, Lindbergh discovered a white envelope lying beneath the open window, which appeared to have been the kidnapper's escape route. He waited for the police to arrive before he opened it. The officer read the ransom letter out loud as the Lindberghs listened intently.

Dear Sir!

Have 50,000$ redy 2500$ in 20$ bills 1 5000$ in 10$ bills and 10000$ in 5$bills. After 2–4 days we will inform you were to deliver the Mony.

We warn you for making anyding public or for the polise the child is in gut care.

Indication for all letters are singnature and 3 holes. (Waller, 1961; Fisher, 1987; Behn, 1994)

There was a symbol at the bottom of the letter. It consisted of two interlocking circles outlined in blue, with a solid red circle where the two other circles connected. There were three holes punched into the paper horizontally, one in the middle of the red circle and the other two in line with the outside two circles. The note was free of fingerprints. In fact, the entire nursery was free of any prints whatsoever—not even Ann's, Lindbergh's, or the nursemaid's prints were found. It was almost as though somebody had wiped down the entire nursery before the police arrived.

Outside, underneath the nursery window, a chisel and a wooden dowel pin were found lying in the mud. It was theorized that the chisel was brought along to pry open the window shutters. When the kidnapper realized that he did not need it, he tossed it to the ground. Footprints were also present; however, police failed to make a mold of the imprints or to take any measurements of their size. A second, smaller print was found near the scene; it was dismissed as being from Ann's earlier walk on the grounds. Fourteen feet away were remnants of a handmade ladder. The ladder could be folded into three parts for easy transportation. It weighed about thirty pounds and could be extended up to eighteen and a half feet. There was a split in the side rails; the position where the ladder would have split sat about five feet from the ground. Later tests with a replication ladder also proved that the ladder was able to hold the weight of the kidnapper on the way up, but unable to support both the kidnapper and the baby upon descent.

By midnight, the entire nation knew of the Lindbergh kidnapping. Radio stations broadcast the story over all the airwaves, and newspaper reporters printed special editions of the story. People began flocking to Hopewell to see the crime scene. Police, reporters, and curious onlookers were unrestrained and most likely destroyed crucial evidence. The footprints and tire impressions had been trampled, and so many people had handled the ladder that the kidnapper's fingerprints could not be singled out, if they had been present at all. The head of the New Jersey state police, Colonel H. Norman Schwarzkopf, was unable to control the mob. Schwarzkopf would be a key figure throughout the investigation and trial, and would be criticized for the investigation in the years to come.

With all of the police and media attention, Lindbergh became concerned that the kidnappers would cut off contact. After all, they had specifically told him not to contact the authorities. Lindbergh made sure the police knew that he was in charge and requested that they not interfere in his dealings with the kidnappers. Lindbergh would maintain control throughout the investigation. He set up a communications center in his garage. Five telephone lines ran from nearby Princeton University to the Hopewell Estate. It was through this setup that he was able to control what information was released to police as well as the media.

Schwarzkopf, Lindbergh, and most of the detectives were under the impression that the kidnapping was the job of an underworld organization. Upon hearing of the kidnapping, mob leader Al Capone, then serving a prison sentence for tax evasion, offered his assistance in return for his freedom. His offer was refused. Against the advice of Breckinridge, Lindbergh hired a respected figure of the underworld, Morris "Mickey" Rosner. Rosner was given a copy of the ransom letter, which he showed several underworld criminals and forgers, in search of information on the kidnappers. Lindbergh also identified two other underworld agents, Salvatore Spitale and Irving Bitz, as go-betweens for the kidnappers. The use of go-betweens was a common practice at a time when mobsters would kidnap the children of wealthy citizens in order to collect large cash sums from them. For the kidnappers, the purpose was to have an intermediary who would later be unable or unwilling to identify them. The use of newspapers to communicate with kidnappers was also common, and was another strategy the Lindberghs employed to reach the person who took their baby.

Three days had passed with no word from the kidnappers. Lindbergh was prepared to fully cooperate with everything they demanded. He publicly pledged to keep their identities a secret. This promise upset the authorities, who came out with a statement that reminded the public that Lindbergh did not have the power to grant immunity and that the kidnappers would be prosecuted for their crime. Finally, on March 4, another ransom note, with the designated symbol, arrived:

Dear Sir. We have warned you note to make anything public also notify the police now you have to take consequences—means we will have to hold the baby until everything is quite. We can note make any appointment just now. We know very well what it means to us. It is realy necessary to make a world affair out of this, or to get your baby back as soon as possible to settle those affair in a quick way will be better for both—don't by afraid about the baby—keeping care of us day and night. We also will feed him according to the diet.

We are interested to send him back in gut health. And ransom was made aus for 50000 $ but now we have to take another person to it and probably have to keep the baby for a longer time as we expected. So the amount will be 70000 20000 in 50$ bills 25000 $ in 20$ bills 15000 $ in 10$ bills and 20000 in 5$ bills Don't mark any bills or take them from one serial nomer. We will form you latter were to deliver the money. But we will note do so until the Police is out of the cace and the pappers are qute. The kidnaping we prepared in years so we are prepared for everyding. (Waller, 1961; Fisher, 1987; Behn, 1994, pp. 87–88)

The letter comforted the Lindberghs that the baby was being taken care of. Ann had published a menu of what the baby ate, hoping that the kidnappers would read it and feed the child accordingly. It appeared that all the kidnappers wanted was money, and they had no intention of hurting the child. They made no threats against the child's life in any of the thirteen ransom notes.

A retired schoolteacher from the Bronx took it upon himself to submit a plea in the *Bronx Home News* to the kidnappers offering his life savings of $1,000 in addition to the ransom for the safe return of the child. He also offered himself as intermediary for all ransom dealings. The following day, this man, named John F. Condon, received a letter from the kidnappers. It contained the secret signature.

dear Sir: If you are willing to act as go-between in the Lindbergh case please follow strictly instruction. Handel incloced letter personaly to Mr. Lindbergh. It will explain everything. don't tell anyone about it as soon we find out the press or Police is notified everything are cancell and it will be a further delay. After you get the money from Mr. Lindbergh put these 3 works in the New-York American

Mony is redy After notise we will give you further instruction. don't be affraid we are not out for your 1000$ keep it. Only act stricly. Be at home every night between 6–12 by this time you will hear from us. (Waller, 1961; Fisher, 1987; Behn, 1994, pp. 96–97)

Condon immediately phoned Lindbergh, who was unimpressed until he heard about the strange symbol. Lindbergh requested that Condon come to the house immediately. When he reached the house, Lindbergh and Breckinridge were waiting. It was decided that they would put the "Mony is redy [*sic*]" message in the newspaper that following day. They would use Condon's initials, J. F. C., or "Jafsie," as a name by which the kidnappers could identify Condon without alerting the public and press.

Condon received the promised phone call from the kidnappers. He was told to be at home between six and twelve o'clock the next evening and he would receive a note giving him further instructions. Toward the end of the phone call, Condon heard a voice in the background yell "Statti citto!" which is Italian for "Shut up!" The caller abruptly hung up. This strange incident served to further encourage the theory that the kidnapper was a part of the underworld and not working alone.

The next evening Condon received a letter from a taxi cab driver. In it were directions to a hot dog stand. He was to come alone and bring the ransom money. On reaching the stand, he found a note hidden under a rock. The note told him to cross the street to Woodlawn Cemetery. Condon went to the cemetery as directed by the kidnappers; however, the ransom money was not yet ready. He had hoped to meet the kidnapper in person and speak with him about his terms. Condon wanted proof that the child was still alive. The man in the cemetery identified himself as John and told Condon that he was one of six people involved in the kidnapping. Condon took note of John's face, which he saw only briefly. It was triangular in shape, with deep-set eyes and a small mouth. He appeared to be about thirty-five years old, five feet ten inches and around 160 pounds. The two talked briefly about John's involvement in the kidnapping. John insisted that his only job was to collect the ransom money, and that he had nothing to do with the actual crime. At one point in the conversation, John became nervous and asked Condon, "What if the baby is dead? Would I burn if the baby is dead?" (Waller, 1961; Fisher, 1987; Behn, 1994, p. 122; Berg, 1998, p. 275; Hixson, 2001). Condon was shocked; what was the point of these negotiations if the child was dead? John quickly recovered and told Condon that the baby was in good health and that there was no need to worry. Condon requested to see the baby before delivering the money. John refused, saying it was too dangerous. He would send proof that the baby was alive. He would send the child's sleeping suit.

On March 16, a package was placed in Condon's mailbox. It contained the Eaglet's sleeping suit and another letter from the kidnappers:

Dear Sir: ouer man faill to collect the mony. There are no more confidential conference after we meeting from March 12. those arrangemts to hazardous for us. We will note allow ouer man to confer in a way like befor. circumstance will note allow us to make transfare like you wish. It is impossibly for us. wy shuld we move the baby and face danger. to take another person to the place is entirely out of question. It seems you are afraid if we are the right party and if the boy is allright. Well you have ouer singnature. It is always the same as the first one specialy them 3 holes.

Now we will send you the sleepingsuit from the baby besides it means 3 $ extra expenses because we have to pay another one. please tell Mrs. Lindbergh note to worry the baby is well. we only have to give him more food as the diet says.

You are willing to pay the 70000 note 50000 $ without seeing the baby first or note. let us know about that in the New York-American. We can't do it other ways because we don't like to give up ouer safty plase or to move the baby. If you are willing to accept this deal put these in paper.

I accept mony is redy

Ouer program is:

After 8 houers we have the mony received we will notify you where to find the baby. If there is any trapp, you will be Responsible what will follows. (Waller, 1961; Fisher, 1987; Behn, 1994, p. 130)

Lindbergh wondered aloud why the child's garment appeared to have been laundered. Dismissing this oddity, Lindbergh and Breckinridge began their preparation of the ransom package. The kidnapper had specified what type of box to place the money in and even gave specific measurements. When it came time to pack the money into the box, only $50,000 of it fit. The rest was wrapped in a sack that would later be easily identifiable to authorities.

Although many wealthy members of society generously offered to put up the ransom for Lindbergh, he insisted on coming up with the money himself. In the midst of the Great Depression, Lindbergh was forced to sell over $350,000 worth of stock to raise the $70,000 ransom. J. P. Morgan and Company delivered $50,000 to the Fordham branch of the Corn Exchange Bank; Condon had access to the special vault in which the money was placed. Against Lindbergh's wishes, the serial number from each ransom bill was recorded. Not a single bill was in sequential order. Most of the ransom bills were gold notes, meaning that they contained a round yellow seal. This was helpful in later identifying the ransom bills, as the United States was going off the gold standard. In a few months, it would be illegal to possess a gold note.

That Saturday, Condon received a letter giving him directions to a greenhouse. On the table outside, under a rock, was another set of instructions. Condon was to go to St. Raymond's Cemetery and bring the money with him. Condon got out of Al Reich's Ford Coupe and walked around the area specified by the kidnappers. Lindbergh waited in the car. He was armed. After a few minutes of waiting, Condon walked back to the truck to see what Lindbergh wanted him to do, as the kidnapper was nowhere in sight. Suddenly, they both heard a heavily accented voice call out, "Hey Doctor! Here Doctor! Over here! Over here!" (Waller, 1961; Fisher, 1987; Behn, 1994, p. 146; Berg, 1998, p. 281). Condon approached the man who had spoken, whom he recognized as John. A few minutes later, the ransom was turned over. Condon had talked John out of $20,000, stating that Lindbergh was suffering from hard times because of the Depression and could not afford to pay such an extra amount. John agreed to settle for the original $50,000, which turned out to be a mistake on Condon's part. What Condon failed to realize was that the $20,000 bag contained several large bills in gold notes that would be very easy to identify when they were spent. John gave Condon an envelope with directions on where he could find the baby. The stipulation was that they had to wait eight hours to open it.

Condon managed to talk Lindbergh into opening the letter as soon as they reached a private property owned by Condon. Breckinridge was also present. The letter told them that the baby could be found on a "boad" named *Nelly*, off the Elizabeth Islands. Lindbergh waited the demanded eight hours and began to search the waters of the Elizabeth Islands in an amphibious aircraft. He dreamed of holding his son in his arms; that moment never came. They searched for two days and did not find anything fitting the description John gave of the boat *Nelly*. They realized that they had been scammed.

Lindbergh, refusing to give up hope, contacted another possible lead. Months earlier, a man named John Hughes Curtis had said that he was in contact with the kidnap gang. He said he knew a man named Sam who had directed him to form a committee of prominent Norfolk, Virginia, citizens to act as intermediaries for the kidnappers. The ransom would be deposited in a bank in Norfolk and would be delivered to the kidnappers only upon the return of the child. Initially, Lindbergh agreed to give merit to the story if Curtis could prove that Sam actually had the child. But now, with limited options, Lindbergh followed Curtis's lead. He spent many days at sea with Curtis, searching various areas of the Elizabeth Islands, but to no avail. It was on one of these boats that Lindbergh was told of the discovery of his child's body somewhere else. He had been the victim of a cruel hoax. There was no Sam or kidnap gang. Curtis had made up the entire story.

THE DISCOVERY

On May 12, truck driver Orville Wilson and his partner, William Allen, were delivering lumber to Hopewell when Allen needed to stop on the side of the road to relieve himself. As he stepped into the brush, he discovered a small, decomposing body. Allen went back to the truck to get Wilson. They both agreed that it was the body of a child. They quickly notified the police.

The baby was found face down in a hollow in the ground. It appeared to have been covered with leaves and branches to make it less noticeable. Although the body was badly decomposed, the baby's face, which had not been exposed to air, had been fairly well preserved and was still recognizable. The signature dimple in the baby's chin and the child's overlapping toes on his left foot were key identifiers of the corpse. The child was missing his right leg from the knee down, and both hands were gone. It appeared that wild animals had been at the body. Some of the child's clothes were intact and could be identified as those that the child was wearing the night he was stolen. In the area surrounding the body, the police found tufts of blonde, curly hair, a burlap sack, a toenail, and six human bones. Then they realized that, only a few feet away, lay the cable from Princeton that Lindbergh had used to set up his communication center.

The cause of death was determined to be a blow to the head. Death was instant or within a few minutes of delivery of this blow. Gow, the nursemaid, was asked to identify the clothing that had been taken from the corpse. She said that they were indeed the same articles she had dressed the baby in the night he was kidnapped. She also went to the morgue and positively identified the body. Ann was notified immediately, and a wire was sent to Lindbergh. By 6:30 p.m., the nation had heard of the death of the Eaglet. Once again the airwaves filled with news of the Lindbergh baby. The nation was stunned. How could anyone do such a thing to a national hero?

Lindbergh had decided to view the body so no doubt was left in his mind that this actually was his baby. After only three minutes, Lindbergh remarked, "I am satisfied that this is my child" (Waller, 1961; Behn, 1994, p. 174; Berg, 1998, p. 290; Hixson, 2001). The Lindberghs planned to have the body cremated in order to avoid scavengers and souvenir hunters who might decide to dig up the grave. Before cremation, two unknown reporters gained access to the morgue and took photographs of the Eaglet's remains. They later sold the photographs for five dollars apiece.

THE SEARCH

Since the baby had been found murdered, the public was angry and wanted those responsible to be punished. The police had been kept in the dark when it came to the dealings with John, and they had no other leads. It was time to turn to the ransom bills for clues. The previous month, a fifty-seven-page pamphlet containing the serial number of each bill had been released to banks across the country. Police now encouraged tellers to keep an eye out for the ransom bills and offered five dollars for each bill coming to the authorities' attention.

On June 22, Congress passed the Cochran Bill, nicknamed the Lindbergh Law, making penalties for kidnapping harsher and allowing the Federal Bureau of Investigation (FBI) jurisdiction if the person who had been abducted was transported across state lines. This law made kidnapping a federal offense, punishable by death. However, this law was not retroactive and, therefore, would not apply to the Lindbergh child's killer.

Gold ransom bills began showing up in various places around the Bronx area, including a movie theater and several banks. A ten-dollar gold bill had been passed at a gas station. Fearing he would get in trouble for possessing a gold certificate, the attendant wrote down the license plate number of the man who gave him the bill. Once the bill reached the bank, it was discovered as a ransom bill. The police looked up the license plate number and found that the car belonged to a Bruno Richard Hauptmann.

In the United States illegally, Hauptmann had been born in Germany in 1899. He had served in the German infantry as a teenager and later studied carpentry and machinery in trade school. He was later arrested for the burglary of three homes and robbing two women pushing young children in carriages on the street. He took their food coupons. He was convicted and served four years of his five-year sentence. He was arrested on another stealing charge, but escaped from prison and fled to the United States. His history would follow him throughout the trial and convict him in the minds of many.

The police found Hauptmann's address and began to stake out his residence. He appeared on the morning of Wednesday, September 19, 1934, and went into his heavily secured garage. He got into his 1930 Dodge sedan and drove away, presumably to report to work. The authorities followed Hauptmann onto a busy street. When they thought they might lose him, he was pulled over and searched. In his possession was a twenty-dollar gold ransom bill. Hauptmann fit Condon's description of the kidnapper and spoke with a heavy German accent. The initial search of Hauptmann's house turned up nothing. The garage was heavily padlocked, and there was even a switch that could be flipped from the bedroom that would illuminate the entire structure. Upon searching the garage, the police made a shocking discovery: they found large sums of ransom money hidden behind some loosely placed boards. It totaled $11,930. Other evidence later found inside the house included notebooks with sketches of a ladder similar to the one found at the Hopewell Estate; Condon's phone number and address written inside a closet; and Hauptmann's tool chest, missing a chisel the same size as the one found below the Lindbergh nursery (Fisher, 1987; Behn, 1994; Berg, 1998; Hixson, 2001).

The police took Bruno to the station to be questioned. Not understanding what he was being arrested for, he simply thought that the police believed he had stolen the money they had found in his garage. Hauptmann told police that a close friend, Isador Fitch, had given him a box of money to keep until he returned from a trip overseas. Fitch died while abroad, and Hauptmann decided to spend some of the money. Hauptmann was interrogated for thirty-two hours and denied food, sleep, and legal counsel. He accused authorities of tying him to a chair and severely beating him. A prison doctor confirmed that he had been struck repeatedly with a blunt object.

Eyewitnesses including Condon, the taxi driver, the gas station attendant, and the woman who sold a movie ticket to someone who paid with a ransom bill gathered for a lineup. Hauptmann, disheveled and unshaven after his interrogation, was placed in the lineup with thirteen well-dressed, clean-cut police officers who were over six feet tall. Every eyewitness identified

Hauptmann as the kidnapper, except for Condon. Condon asked all the men in the lineup to repeat certain phrases and to hold out their hands so he could look at them. He made a big show of this and his expertise as an eyewitness. He then refused to identify anyone in the lineup as John, stating, "I have to be sure; a man's life is at stake" (Fisher, 1987; Behn, 1994, p. 221; Hixson, 2001). Condon later received much public criticism and scrutiny for this.

Some accounts say that the police showed the eyewitnesses photographs of Hauptmann before exposing them to the lineup, telling them he was a prime suspect. At one point in his interrogation, Hauptmann was asked to repeat the phrase "Hey Doctor! Here Doctor! Over here! Over here!" from several angles in the room. Unbeknownst to him, Lindbergh was sitting in the room in a disguise. He positively identified Hauptmann as the voice he had heard in the cemetery, on the night the ransom was paid, over two years before.

THE TRIAL

In New York, Hauptmann was found guilty on the count of extortion and was extradited back to New Jersey to stand trial for the murder of Charles Augustus Lindbergh Jr. James M. Fawcett was appointed Hauptmann's lawyer. In his first criminal trial, David T. Wilentz would act as prosecutor for the case. The trial was set to begin on January 2, 1935.

At the last minute, Mrs. Hauptmann agreed to let the *New Jersey Journal* pay for Hauptmann's defense in exchange for her exclusive story of the events occurring before and during the trial. The *New Jersey Journal* decided to hire the famous Edward J. Reilly to replace Fawcett. Reilly had been known as "Death House" Reilly because he had defended a large number of murder suspects. He began drinking and his career had started to waiver.

On the first day of the trial and thereafter, Flemington, New Jersey, was inundated with reporters and sightseers. Everyone seemed to take advantage of the opportunity to make money. Vendors sold food, miniature replicas of the famous kidnap ladder, and fake locks of the baby's golden blonde hair. The town was packed. People were paying huge sums of money to stay in hotels and local residents' homes. No cost was too high.

The jury consisted of eight men and four women. The seventy-eight-year-old Thomas W. Trenchard, with twenty-eight years' experience on the bench, presided over the trial. Ann Lindbergh took the stand on one of the first days. She described the events of the evening, identified the child's clothing, and was able to provide a picture of the child to the jury. She was not cross-examined by the defense; they felt she had been through enough already.

Charles Lindbergh took the stand and remained poised throughout questioning. He had carried his gun every day of the trial, except for when he took the stand. He knew Reilly would ask him whether he was armed. Rumor had it that Lindbergh would shoot Reilly if the questioning went too far. Betty Gow summoned jurors' sympathy when she described how happy the baby had been the day of the kidnapping. She also described the garment she had sewn for the child the night of his disappearance. She told of how she was able to identify the child at the morgue and described the phone call to her boyfriend, Red Johnson. The questioning had been such a strain on her that she fainted on the way back to her seat. The testimonies of Ann, Charles, and Gow did not add much to the case against Hauptmann, but the prosecution knew that they would be able to stir up the emotions of the jury.

The prosecution's case was well prepared. Prosecution witnesses were poised and appeared credible. They remained calm during cross-examination and told their stories with confidence. Wilentz presented overwhelming evidence and spent thousands of dollars on handwriting experts, wood experts, eyewitness testimony, and autopsy reports. He was organized, well spoken, and polite. In contrast, Reilly was flamboyant, overly dramatic, and disorganized. Instead of attacking holes in the prosecution's case, Reilly came up with far-fetched theories and scenarios of what he thought might have happened that night. He often came back from lunch with alcohol on his breath and appeared to be using the case to gain publicity for himself and his career. Reilly told the press that he believed his client was guilty, and he spent only thirty-six minutes conferring with Hauptmann throughout the entire trial. Reilly's witnesses and experts were sub-par at best. Most of them had inconsistent testimonies, as well as criminal records. He offered money to anyone who would testify on behalf of Hauptmann, and many perjured themselves on the stand in order to make a buck and be a part of the most famous trial of the time. His so-called wood experts were nothing more than lumberyard workers, and his barrage of handwriting experts backed out at the last minute, stating that their testimony would hurt the defense. His cross-examinations often led nowhere and only increased the jury's dislike for the defense. Hauptmann, from another country, did not understand the American legal system but took the stand at the advice of his attorney. It did more harm than good.

The fact that Hauptmann showed very little emotion (and when he did, it was in the form of angry outbursts) did not sit well with the jury. To get some sympathy for the defense, Hauptmann's wife and small child, Manfred, sat in plain view of the jury. However, the fact that the public and media had already tried and convicted Hauptmann may have made the jurors feel that they would be ostracized, if not in danger, if they did not come to the same conclusion.

THE VERDICT

The jury was sent for deliberations at 11:21 a.m., and although the prosecution's case was based entirely on circumstantial evidence, the jury reached a verdict by 10:28 p.m. On February 13, 1935, the thirty-second day of the trial, Bruno Richard Hauptmann was found guilty of first-degree murder. The sentence for murdering the Lindbergh baby was death by electrocution. Hauptmann did not show any emotion when the verdict was read, but upon returning to his cell he broke down, sobbing throughout the night. Hauptmann was transferred to the New Jersey State Prison in Trenton. He was placed in a cell only a few feet from the electric chair. The state of New Jersey had spent a total of $600,000 on the case, the most expensive trial of the time.

All of Hauptmann's appeals were rejected, even his plea for a new trial on the basis of inadequate counsel, which was clearly the case. However, the governor of New Jersey, Harold G. Hoffman, had suspicions that Hauptmann was innocent or at the very least had not received a fair trial. He felt that key evidence had been tampered with or destroyed, and upon reviewing the case he firmly believed that there had to be more than one kidnapper. Knowing very well that his involvement in the case would likely ruin his career, thirty hours before Hauptmann was scheduled to be executed, Hoffman granted him a thirty-day reprieve so that further investigation could be conducted.

Among Hoffman's attempts to find evidence that would cast doubt on Hauptmann's guilt was his request to have him take a lie detector test. Hauptmann eagerly agreed to this, but the judge denied the motion. All attempts to enter evidence that would have possibly proved Hauptmann's innocence were blocked by judges as being inadmissible. Hoffman decided to take another approach to save Hauptmann's life. Prosecuting attorney Wilentz and Hoffman visited Hauptmann in prison and urged him to confess, even if he was innocent, and they would commute his sentence to life in prison instead of the death penalty. Hauptmann refused to confess, and would deny all involvement in the kidnapping and murder of the Eaglet for the rest of his short life.

Four years after the kidnapping and murder of Charles Augustus Lindbergh Jr., Bruno Richard Hauptmann was executed for the crime. On Friday, April 3, at 8:47 p.m., after receiving 2,000 volts of electricity, Hauptmann was pronounced dead. The execution lasted three minutes, and fifty-seven people were present. A quiet ceremony was held for Hauptmann on April 6, in Queens, with thirty people in attendance. He was later cremated.

ALTERNATIVE THEORIES OF THE CRIME

Many people still believe that the wrong man was convicted of the murder of the Lindbergh baby. Several theories have been offered since the kidnap-murder occurred. One theory is that Elisabeth Morrow, Ann's sister, was the murderer. According to this theory, the public believed that Elisabeth would be the one to marry Lindbergh. She became insanely jealous when he chose Ann. One day she went over the edge, lost control, and killed the child. Fearing bad publicity and as a service to the Morrow family, Lindbergh agreed to cover up for Elisabeth; he did so by keeping the police and media at bay during the investigation. Lindbergh counted on the greed of extortionists to direct attention away from family members and toward the underworld. Hauptmann's possession of so much of the ransom money was just a coincidental stroke of luck. As it happened, Elisabeth died of heart disease before Hauptmann's trial began (Behn, 1994).

Another theory is that Lindbergh accidentally killed the child himself while playing one of his infamous practical jokes. He often played jokes on his family and domestic staff. Sometimes they were not so funny. There were reports that he had pretended his son had been kidnapped on a previous occasion after hiding the baby in the closet. Lindbergh might have unintentionally killed his son during one of these games (Behn, 1994; Ahlgren and Monier, 1993).

One popular, but unlikely, theory is that the Lindbergh child was never killed. The child was kidnapped and raised by his abductors, and is still alive today. The body found in the woods was that of a child from an orphanage near the Lindbergh Estate. Many people have come forward claiming to be the Lindbergh heir (Behn, 1994).

THE MEDIA: A CARNIVAL ATMOSPHERE

From the night of the kidnapping to the execution of Bruno Richard Hauptmann, and even thereafter, the media were ever-present in the Lindbergh baby kidnapping case. In many ways, the press hindered the investigation more than it helped. Reporters had arrived at the crime scene shortly after police and tramped through the estate, possibly destroying vital evidence.

However, Lindbergh had a talent for using the media to his advantage. He released only those details of the case that he wanted the press to know. In this way, he had total control of the information that reached the public.

The media were also an important element in the correspondence between Lindbergh and the kidnappers, via the newspapers.

The media and the "carnival" atmosphere they produced were most evident during Hauptmann's trial. New Jersey was inundated with nearly 700 reporters, not to mention curious tourists who hoped to get a spot in the courtroom. Spectators were allowed a seat on a first-come, first-served basis, and every available space was filled. As many as 600 people were reported to have crammed into the tiny courtroom. Even though cameras were not allowed inside, Judge Trenchard ignored the feeble attempt made by newsreel companies to hide them, one inside a clock and another in a box on the balcony. It was quietly agreed upon that the cameras could stay as long as the footage was kept secret until the trial's end (Cohn and Dow, 2002). These clips were played in movie theaters in New York and New Jersey.

Outside the courtroom, the town of Flemington bustled with vendors and tourists. Local restaurants got in on the action by touting food specials named after important figures in the case: Lamb Chops Jafsie; Baked Beans Wilentz; and "Lindys," which were nothing more than ice cream sundaes (Berg, 1998). Crowds on the street could be heard inside the courtroom shouting their beliefs that Hauptmann was guilty and deserved the death penalty.

After news of Hauptmann's conviction and his sentence to the electric chair, the media coverage died down significantly. People slowly filed out of Flemington and returned to their normal lives. Very few people gathered outside the prison on the night Hauptmann was executed.

THE AFTERMATH OF THE MAJOR PLAYERS

The case did not end with the execution of Bruno Richard Hauptmann. The lives of the key players would be affected by the case as long as they lived. Hauptmann's wife, Anna, filed a civil suit against the New Jersey officials involved in the case. She sued for $10 million, claiming that they had framed her husband. The case was dismissed, and the U.S. Supreme Court refused to review it.

Defense attorney Edward Reilly checked himself into a mental hospital following his diagnosis of paresis as a result of syphilis. Fourteen months later at fifty-six, he returned to a meager law practice until his death in 1940. In contrast, prosecuting attorney David Wilentz's practice flourished. He died a successful lawyer in 1988, at the age of ninety-three.

Harold Hoffman's political career was ruined following the Hauptmann trial. He had hoped to run for the presidency, but he did not receive support from his party. He was hired as the administrator of the Division of

Employment Security (DES), but then allegations of money laundering during his term as governor were made public. Authorities found that Hoffman had mismanaged funds to the tune of $450,000 and had sold political favors while in office. He was forced to step down from his position in the DES. Hoffman was found dead in his apartment on June 4, 1954, apparently from a heart attack. However, rumors spread that Hoffman had committed suicide. Attendance at his funeral was reported to be 10,000.

In 1942, during World War II, H. Norman Schwarzkopf spent five years in Iran heading a mission. He continued his military involvement for several years and then returned to work for the state of New Jersey until his death in 1958. His son, General H. Norman Schwarzkopf Jr., following in his father's footsteps, was a war hero in Desert Storm in 1991.

The Lindberghs had enough of all the publicity following the trial and decided to flee to England, saying that they were concerned for the safety of their second son, Jon. After lying low for a while, Lindbergh would soon be back in the limelight. He and Ann flew to Germany in response to an invitation sent by Hermann Goering, a high-ranking officer in Adolf Hitler's regime. Not long after, Lindbergh made his affection for Hitler and Germany's Third Reich publicly known. Nazi leaders told Lindbergh of their vast aeronautical machinery and gave him inflated numbers of the German air force and production rates. Lindbergh reported this back to the chief of the United States Army Air Force, insinuating that Germany was invincible and it would be better that the United States stayed out of the war. As a reward for his allegiance, Lindbergh was presented with the highest honor bestowed on a civilian, the Service Cross of the German Eagle. Ann urged Charles to give it back, but Lindbergh refused. It would be a decision he would later regret. Lindbergh continued to speak publicly about keeping America out of the war, swearing that he was not pro-Nazi, just antiwar. His popularity with American citizens plummeted; they felt he had turned on them.

As time went on, Lindbergh regained some of his lost favor with the American public. His autobiography, released in 1953, immediately became a best-seller. He was appointed to the Air Force Scientific Advisory Board and became an avid animal activist. He was diagnosed with lymphatic cancer in 1974 and died on August 26 of that year.

"THE CRIME OF THE CENTURY"

It is clear that the Lindbergh kidnapping had a tremendous impact on Americans. The baby of a national hero had been stolen from his crib. The public was shocked and wanted justice. The passing of the "Lindbergh Law" increased the penalties for kidnapping and made it a federal offense, allowing for capital punishment. Meanwhile, newspapers sold out and citizens were glued to their radios. With the massive media coverage, the entire affair turned into a three-ring circus. However, when the trial and execution were over and the dust had settled, many Americans believed they had seen justice done in the case that was described as "the crime of the century."

REFERENCES

Ahlgren, G., and Monier, S. R. (1993). *Crime of the century: The Lindbergh kidnapping hoax.* Boston, MA: Branden Publishing Company.

Behn, N. (1994). *Lindbergh: The crime.* New York: Atlantic Monthly Press.

Berg, S. A. (1998). *Lindbergh.* New York: G. P. Putnam's Sons.

Cohn, M., and Dow, D. (2002). *Cameras in the courtroom: Television and the pursuit of justice.* Lanham, MD: Rowman and Littlefield.

Fass, P. S. (1997). Kidnapped: Child abduction in America. In *The Nation's Child . . . is dead* (pp. 95–131). Oxford, NY: Oxford University Press.

Fisher, J. (1987). *The Lindbergh case.* New Brunswick, NJ: Rutgers University Press.

Hixson, W. L. (2001). Murder, culture, and injustice: Four sensational cases in American history. In *Vengeance: Bruno Richard Hauptmann and the Lindbergh baby kidnapping* (pp. 67–128). Akron, OH: The University of Akron Press.

Waller, G. (1961). *Kidnap: The story of the Lindbergh case.* New York: The Dial Press.

10

The Sleepy Lagoon Murder and the "Zoot Suit" Riots: Los Angeles at War

Joe Walker

When the history of Latinos and their role in the development of Los Angeles are discussed, almost all references go to the original pueblo that was built over 200 years ago in what is now downtown Los Angeles. There is much interest in and much written about the Spanish missions that were built in the 1700s and 1800s all throughout California, and the four within Los Angeles County. However, very little is written about how the indigenous Mexican populace adapted to the huge influx of European immigration that began in the middle of the nineteenth century. Two events, the Sleepy Lagoon murder and the subsequent "zoot suit" riots in 1942 and 1943, had much more to do with the way the two cultures mixed—and did not mix.

Nothing remains of the Williams Ranch and the swimming hole that in 1942 were the center of one of the biggest murder mysteries in local history. Located near Slauson Avenue in the city of Bell, the ranch is now an industrial park and warehouse with ominous "no trespassing" signs posted. No wonder. This place had a significant role in Los Angeles history, and the current owners probably do not want sightseers climbing the fence.

In late 1941, with huge world tensions from to the devastating Japanese attack on Pearl Harbor and the frightening Nazi takeover of most of Europe, local newspapers paid more and more attention to the native threat

Alleged leaders of Zoot Suit Gang. (Herald Examiner Collection/Los Angeles Public Library)

to national security. As the U.S. government rounded up hundreds of thousands of Japanese Americans, attention turned to another large minority population—Mexican Americans. Primarily driven by the large newspaper chains, the circulation-hungry local papers gave big play to any and all incidents of Mexican American crime.

Many stories have been told over the years about what triggered the Sleepy Lagoon legend, but some facts are not disputed. The night of August 1, 1942, started like any other, with young people enjoying their independence in the Los Angeles car culture. Some went to an area near the Williams Ranch on the east side of Los Angeles. There was a pond in an abandoned gravel pit that was used for swimming (McWilliams, 1968, p. 228). Hank Leyvas had taken his girlfriend, Dora Barrios, for a drive there. Hank would play a key role in the saga that followed. So would another young man named José Díaz.

THE ACCUSED AND THE VICTIM

Enrique "Henry" (Hank) Leyvas

Enrique "Henry" Leyvas, known to his friends as Hank, was born in Tucson, Arizona, on April 24, 1923, to Guadalupe Reyes and Seferino Leyvas. Hank spent his earliest years in Arizona, but his family soon found a home and a comfortable life in the 38th Street neighborhood of Los Angeles. Early in his life, Hank became known as a guy who was always there when trouble started. He started getting arrested for "suspicion" of various crimes, which was how the local police arrested people they identified as the criminal element without actually having a legitimate reason or charge. Hank attracted so much negative attention from the police that he and his brother once spent three days in jail for car theft, when the car they were driving was actually their father's. Trumped-up charges like this were common for Hank, who was never polite and deferential when stopped by the police. He was someone who spoke up for his rights, a rare thing in the early 1940s for a Mexican American teenager. One time the police stormed his house, saying that he had been seen committing an armed robbery earlier that night, when he was actually in jail at the time of the alleged incident. It was no secret that the Los Angeles police had it in for Hank. According to historian Eduardo Pagán, the Los Angeles police labeled Hank "a delinquent with a chip on his shoulder, largely because he was the kind of kid who would stand up for his rights. . . . He would protest if he were arrested, for example. He would challenge them" (Eduardo Pagán interview, PBS, 2001).

The same could be said of José Díaz, whose murder triggered the Sleepy Lagoon trial and brought Hank so much notoriety. Hank worked hard to earn enough money to assist his family. But he never embraced the migrant farm worker life the way José did. To this day, it is not known whether Hank and José ever knew each other or ever met, but if they had they would have found that they had much in common. Both were quite devoted to their mothers, a trait that has a long, honorable history in the Mexican culture. Both men were very much concerned with their appearances, and Hank also favored the "zoot suit" look, also known as "drapes," that was sweeping the Mexican American community of Los Angeles (McWilliams, 1968, p. 242).

When Hank was not socializing while dressed up in his zoot suit, or being harassed by the police, he was most likely under the hood of a car learning about its workings and fixing some difficult mechanical problem. Hank's skills were of a technical and mechanical nature, and he was well known in his neighborhood as a lover of fast cars and fast driving, and well liked for his ability to fix other people's cars.

However, Hank was widely seen as the leader of the 38th Street Boys, and was both feared and respected by his peers. On the night of August 1, 1942, without warning or provocation, Dora, his girlfriend, and Hank were attacked by a group of boys called the "Downey Boys" from a rival neighborhood. Hank and Dora were badly beaten. The boys and young men from the 38th Street area were not gangs in the sense that is known today. They were more like "cliques," groups of friends bound together by common language and heritage.

After the attack, Hank returned to his neighborhood and notified his friends. Volunteers were easy to find. Beating a rival's girlfriend was a major violation of street rules, and revenge had to be swift and severe. Approximately forty young men and women in eight automobiles headed for the Sleepy Lagoon, located on the Williams Ranch (Pagán, 2003, p. 64).

José Díaz

That same night, José Díaz was at a birthday party on the Williams Ranch where he and other Mexican American families worked and lived. José was also celebrating another milestone in his life. He had recently signed up for the U.S. Army, which had a long tradition of providing immigrants with a stable life with a better chance of success than staying behind at the home front did. Another factor that must have weighed on Díaz's mind was the policy of granting citizenship to foreign nationals who served in the U.S. military. (This policy was in effect before World War II and was even an issue widely discussed during the 2003 Iraq conflict.)

The Díaz family was like many Mexican American families who arrived in California in the first third of the twentieth century. Fleeing famine and the violent aftermath of the Mexican Revolution, they saw the North as an island of calm and political stability. When the stock market crashed in 1929, the Díaz family was living a peaceful existence in ranch bunkhouses. There were many such ranches on the outskirts of Los Angeles. Tight subcultures existed there, and many of the families celebrated holidays together, along with weddings and funerals. Almost all the Mexican American families who lived on the ranch were Roman Catholics. The Catholic Church had a strong presence in this community, going back to the days of the Spanish priests who built the string of twenty-one missions in California in the late 1700s and early 1800s.

That night, the 38th Street Boys carefully approached the place where Hank and Dora had been attacked. Adrenaline was running high as they anticipated a swift and violent retribution. Then they realized no one was there. Disappointed, they searched the area for signs that the assailants still remained in the area. Within moments they heard the sound of the party and assumed that the Downey Boys were the ones throwing the event. Hank and his friends approached the house, and fighting immediately broke out between the men and women. After what could roughly be considered a stalemate, the 38th Streeters returned to their cars and drove away. It is not known if any of the group saw José Díaz lying in the grass nearby.

José Díaz was a twenty-two-year-old farm hand. While the press and police would name José and his attackers as gang members and hoodlums, he was not in any organized gang or club. He simply had people with whom he socialized. Díaz had been born on December 9, 1919, to Teodolo and Panfila Díaz in the Mexican state of Durango. José enjoyed listening to jazz music, which was popular with young people at the time, and he followed the teenage trends when it came to his style of dress (Eduardo Pagán interview, PBS, 2001). Clothes and appearance were important to José. When he went out, he loved wearing white shirt and pegged pants that were a part of what was known as a "zoot suit." Regarding this fashion fad, Josélit writes:

Adopted by African-Americans, Mexican-Americans, and aspiring hepcats, the outfit spoke of freedom and release rather than restraint and control. (The term itself, with its origin in urban jazz culture, connoted exaggeration). Despite its unusual proportions and snug fit—the jacket hugged the knees while the trousers were so tightly pegged at the bottom that a shoehorn was required to help poke the feet through—the zoot suit, according to social worker Fritz Redl, was a "declaration of independence." (2001, p. 192)

On the night that he died, José had told his mother he really didn't want to go to the party to which he was invited. Excited about his upcoming army induction, and so bursting with pride that he had recently had his first professional photograph taken, José was moving away from the culture that marked teenage life and looking forward to a life away from the Williams Ranch and farming. The summer of 1942 had seen constant newspaper and radio reports about the war in the Pacific and the war with Germany. Los Angeles had just completed an evacuation of almost all Japanese American residents, identifying them as security risks. War fever was at an all-time high, and José wanted to be a part of it. The risks of being injured or killed were far in the back of his mind in the way that young people never really believe that a dangerous venture could lead to a fatal outcome. José was a daring young man who had his life ahead of him—until he was killed that night at Sleepy Lagoon (Eduardo Pagán interview, PBS, 2001).

There has never been any mention, or any real proof, that José Díaz had anything to do with the Leyvas attack. There is also no evidence that he even knew about it. About thirty minutes before the 38th Street Boys made their appearance at the party, Díaz left with two other partygoers. The Williams Ranch party was well attended—with plenty of food, drink, loud music, and dancing. Eleanor Delgadillo, the young woman whose birthday party was being held at the house, later testified that José left with two young men named Luís "Cito" Vargas and Andrew Torres. Nothing was ever learned from these men as to what they saw or heard; indeed, they were never considered suspects in the Díaz death (PBS, 2001).

When neighbors found Díaz's badly beaten but still breathing body lying in the grass near the party, they contacted the police. The Los Angeles County Sheriff's Department patrolled this area of the unincorporated county, and sheriff's deputies and detectives began their investigation. They learned about the gathering the night before, the fight, and the key players involved in crashing the party. They quickly arrested Henry Leyvas and dozens of other Latino men and Latina women who were associated with him and his group.

Meanwhile, Lino Díaz, José's brother, was home at the time that his brother was found. He rushed him to the Los Angeles County General Hospital. José died soon after. The death certificate stated that the cause of death was a contusion of the brain and a subdural hemorrhage due to a fracture of his skull. His face was cut and swollen, he had been stabbed twice, and a finger on his left hand was broken. The rest of José's family had been out of town in Central California working on the prune harvest. When Soccorro, José's brother, became ill, the family cut short their employment and returned home on the night of the murder. Little did they know as they returned to the Williams Ranch that they were about to be at the center of the most racially charged murder case in Los Angeles history.

THE ARRESTS

According to Alice McGrath, a young legal assistant who worked tirelessly on behalf of the boys, the Díaz murder was really nothing more than a pretext to round up hundreds of local youth and pacify the increasingly racist media. The local media announced that there was a "Mexican crime wave" taking place, and on the nights of August 10 and 11, over 600 young people were arrested on trumped-up charges ranging from "suspicion of assault" to armed robbery. Of the 600 arrested, all of them Mexican Americans, about 175 were held on the charges (PBS, 2001; Mazòn, 1984, pp. 19–20).

The Los Angeles County Sheriff's Department Foreign Relations Bureau investigated this hysteria about "Mexican crime waves" and "pachuco gangs." The head of the Bureau, E. Duran Ayres, wrote a long report that correctly identified widespread racism and discrimination against Mexican-Americans; but in what was likely a spin designed to win favor with the judge and the racist law enforcement community, Ayres testified before the grand jury that "Mexican-Americans were essentially Indians, and therefore Orientals or Asians." Throughout history, he testified, "Orientals have [had] less regard for human life." Undoubtedly, many accepted this sentiment because Americans at the time were receiving horrible reports from the Far East about Japanese atrocities against American prisoners and Chinese living under brutal

Japanese military rule. In his report, Ayres went on to say that Mexican-Americans had inherited their "naturally violent tendencies" from the "blood-thirsty Aztecs" of Mexico, who practiced human sacrifices. He suggested that Mexicans would forever keep their wild and violent ways no matter how much education or assistance society gave them (Pagán, 2003, p. 183; Mazón, 1984, pp. 21–24).

In this context of racial/ethnic bias, twenty-four men were charged with either being directly involved in Díaz's murder or being indirectly responsible. Out of the twenty-four indicted, two were able to obtain lawyers who managed to get the charges dropped. That left twenty-two defendants for the courts and the public to try.

THE TRIAL

During this precedent-setting trial, none of the defendants were allowed to confer privately with their own private or court-appointed lawyers. None were allowed a change of clothes, and none were allowed to get haircuts. By the time the twenty-two of them went to trial, they were an extremely motley looking group, which is just what the police and prosecution wanted.

Judge Fricke

No examination of the Sleepy Lagoon case can be done without considering the judge in the case, Charles W. Fricke. A native of Milwaukee, Wisconsin, and a graduate of New York University in 1902, Fricke served as a district attorney and a judge in Wisconsin before coming out west for "health reasons." He worked as a prosecutor in the Los Angeles district attorney's office. He soon became chief deputy in the district attorney's office and published numerous textbooks on law and evidence, among them *Manual of Criminal Law and Procedure for Peace Officers* (reprinted five times since 1925), *Outlines of California Criminal Procedure* (1926), and *California Criminal Law* (1927). All this high visibility brought him positive attention from the state capital in Sacramento and soon he was appointed to a position on the superior court bench.

Judge Fricke was part of Anglo-American society. He belonged to all the right clubs and social organizations. He also was part of the growing public opinion in the early war years that young people who were not in the military, mostly Mexican American, were a threat and a danger to the ruling elite. The local media, dominated by the *Los Angeles Times*, had almost daily reports of violent and unruly Mexican American "delinquents" whose dress and music styles were quite different from those of middle-class Los Angeles. The popular conservative press also thought that these young people were ripe for exploitation by the enemy, and possibly vulnerable to recruitment as German or Japanese spies (PBS, 2001).

With this trial, Judge Fricke had his hands full with such a large number of defendants, but legal scholars have had little sympathy for his courtroom procedures. Fricke ordered the defendants to be seated in two rows, facing the jury. Their seven lawyers were not allowed to sit with them, and if they wanted to confer with their clients, they had to wait for the break. Fricke stated that to have the lawyers talk to their clients when court was in session would be a "disruption to the proceedings." Later, this policy would be one of many that not only exposed the huge flaws in the trial, but also changed the way trials were held in the future.

Fricke's bias in favor of the prosecution is legendary. The prosecution introduced as evidence of the defendants' guilt their style of dress and their hairstyles. As noted above, the authorities had refused to allow the boys to have their hair cut or to change into clean clothing. As the trial wore on, the boys wore the clothes they were arrested in, and their hair grew longer and longer. The defense attorneys objected constantly, but Fricke denied their requests. The reason for this was that he wanted the jurors to see what he believed was the "true character" of the accused. Not letting the young men groom themselves was his way of doing this. The defendants, who had taken great pride in their dapper appearances before their arrests, were horrified at this, as were their parents. Fricke summarily denied their many objections (Alice McGrath interview, PBS, 2001).

George Shibley was one of the highly respected and effective attorneys who joined the case midway through the trial. He was shocked to see the bias displayed by the judge. However, Fricke saw Shibley as just one more in a long line of liberal attorneys who were far too passionate about defending clients of whom Fricke did not approve. Fricke perceived Shibley's objections as slowing the case down, and he made a practice of denying the hardworking attorney's objections even before he had finished making them. Many observers felt that Fricke deliberately and maliciously humiliated Shibley in order to prejudice the jury in such a way that they would not seriously consider the possibility that the 38th Street Boys might be innocent.

However, Fricke was not the only officer of the court who had a well-known bias against the defendants. Clem Peoples, chief of the criminal division of the sheriff's office, moonlighted for a national pulp magazine called *Sensation*. He wrote a story featuring a photograph of Hank Leyvas with the words "Ring Leader." Because of Fricke and Peoples, Hank and his supporters knew that there was no way he could get a fair trial.

George Shibley

"He took cases that no one else would," said Eleanor Shibley, George's wife of many years. "When no one else would defend homosexuals, minorities, or political radicals, George would stand up and take the case" (PBS, 2001). Labor organizer and prominent Communist Party official LaRue McCormack knew of Shibley's reputation for always fighting for the underdog even when he was not paid. McCormack thought Shibley would be perfect as a replacement when one of the attorneys dropped out of the Sleepy Lagoon case. Shibley learned quickly that it was one thing to defend a political figure or a homosexual on a weak case, but defending what most people were sure was a gang of cold-blooded killers brought him a lot of negative attention. But he never regretted his involvement in the case.

Shibley was born in New York City to Arab immigrants on May 6, 1910. Like everyone else involved in the Sleepy Lagoon case, and like so many Californians over the years, his family migrated there from somewhere else. He grew up in the middle-class city of Long Beach and attended Stanford University and Stanford Law School, graduating in 1934. Soon Shibley had a bustling private law practice, and he gained a reputation as an aggressive and thorough lawyer. Never forgetting the racism and harassment he received due to his Middle Eastern background, he developed a great sympathy for minorities.

When he was hired to work on the Sleepy Lagoon case, he quickly earned the wrath of Judge Fricke, who was not accustomed to a young, progressive lawyer from Long Beach, a suburb of Los Angeles twenty miles south of the Sleepy Lagoon, challenging him with all his years of experience. Attorney Shibley played what is now called the "race card," knowing full well that the highly conservative all-white jury would not be swayed by liberal rhetoric. Instead, he played to the press and public, who watched the trial carefully, and he related to the jury, "[I]t's always been open season for the police on Mexicans" (PBS, 2001). All along he knew that this case would never win in front of a jury, and that his only hope was on the planned appeal.

Of course, he planned to be a part of that appeal. However, the U.S. government had other plans. He received a draft notice days after the verdicts, which was not such a big coincidence. During World War II, men were selected for the military draft based on lists provided by local draft boards. These boards were highly political and wielded a lot of power. Hence, a politician's son could more easily get a deferment than could the relative of someone who did not have power or influence. Many times the potential draftee would appeal and negotiate with these boards; however, Shibley reported for the draft. In his absence, attorney Ben Margolis did an excellent job.

In the waning years of his life, Shibley gave an interview to his local newspaper, the *Long Beach Press-Telegram*, which explained how important the Sleepy Lagoon case was in legal history:

Its effect on constitutional law was felt throughout the United States. . . . This has got to be one of the most outstanding cases of open police brutality ever recorded in this country. As a result of this case, the court held that a defendant had a right to participate in his own defense. . . . In an action called the Zammora Decision the court said that if the courtroom was not big enough to enable defendants to sit with their attorneys, then some place must be found that is big enough. In short, it has made it almost impossible to hold mass trials. (As quoted in PBS, 2001)

During the Sleepy Lagoon trial, many witnesses were called, but not one testified to seeing Díaz attacked or killed. Several girls at the party were charged with conspiracy, but none of them were convicted. One of the girls at the party, Lorena Encinas, claimed to know who did commit the murder. However, she revealed the truth only on her deathbed, in the early 1990s.

LORENA ENCINAS AND HER REVELATION

Lorena Encinas was born to Lorena Gerlach and Teodoro Encinas on September 4, 1922, in Nogales, Arizona. Her parents had recently come from Mexico. Two years after she was born, her mother gave birth to Lorena's baby brother, Louis Jesus. Lorena protected and cared for him all his life. Mainly because of Lorena's silence, Louis was never one of the original twenty-two defendants.

When the Encinas family arrived in Los Angeles, they settled in the 38th Street neighborhood. Growing up there, Lorena was a typical fun-loving teenager who enjoyed socializing with friends. However, when their father died when she was thirteen years old, leaving a family of five, she had to step in and take care of her little brother. Little Louis Encinas began getting into trouble. This was a lifelong pattern of brushes with the law and time in reform school or jail. Always, Lorena was there to bail him out or help in any way she could.

Many years later, Lorena told her children that, on the night of the Díaz murder, she was present at the Williams Ranch. She saw her brother Louis crash the party along with some of his friends. After being kicked out of the party, they encountered Díaz and beat him up. When police investigated the party the next day, Lorena refused to talk and she was arrested.

Lorena and several other girls were charged as accomplices to the "gang" of boys who were rounded up. The women all refused to testify, although only

Lorena really knew anything. However, as further proof of the extremes that the local officials went to, they managed to arrange for several of the young women to be committed to the Ventura School for Girls. One hundred miles north of Los Angeles, the Ventura School had a reputation for being the worst place to be sentenced. Established in 1913 by the California Youth Authority, the conditions were widely known to be worse than those of any men's correctional facility, and the girls suffered terribly while there. However, the girls had not been sent there by the courts. They were sent there due to pressure from the police and the district attorney, who convinced the girls' parents to have them committed. Lorena was incarcerated for one year, leaving behind a young son to be raised by her family. She was shocked by the conditions at the Ventura School.

Lorena was released from the institution on her twenty-first birthday in September 1943. She joined the millions of women working in the local defense plants, immediately going to work to help support her mother, her son, and her siblings. A year later she got married and soon adopted a baby girl.

Lorena's relationship with her younger brother Louis endured for many years. Soon she became the only person in the family who would help him or lend him money as he went in and out of jail. She even cared for his children when he was incarcerated in the late 1940s and early 1950s. Despite her unconditional love and support, he never got out of his life of crime, and Lorena was devastated when he committed suicide while robbing a Bank of America branch in 1972. Lorena revealed her secret about the Sleepy Lagoon murder to her children shortly before her own death on January 5, 1991.

But it was nearly fifty years before the truth came out, and in 1942, the public and Judge Fricke wanted only one thing—swift "justice." Out of the twenty-two defendants, only five were acquitted. Five were found guilty of assault. Nine were found guilty of second-degree murder, and three were found guilty of first-degree murder. The harshest sentences were life imprisonment.

ALICE McGRATH AND THE SLEEPY LAGOON DEFENSE COMMITTEE

One of the attorneys for the original defendants, George Shibley, introduced Alice McGrath to the twelve who were serving time at San Quentin. At first the twelve were highly suspicious of a Caucasian woman championing their cause, but after many letters back and forth and many visits to the prison, she earned their trust and respect. McGrath had been a secretary to activist Carey McWilliams, and she ended up coordinating the many volunteers who mobilized during the trial and during the time the Sleepy Lagoon twelve served their time.

Alice McGrath was born in Calgary, Canada, in 1917. Her family moved to Southern California in 1922, in search of the same things that the Díaz and Leyvas family sought: jobs, good weather, and better opportunities. McGrath was not a traditional young woman of her era. She was highly political and ran in the liberal progressive circles of the day. At the time, the "Left" was energized by the policies of President Franklin Delano Roosevelt, the first true political liberal to ever sit in the White House. They also were excited by his choice of Henry Wallace as his vice president. Wallace had held other prominent places in the Roosevelt administration and was extremely friendly to liberalism. This was an exciting time to be young and in the Democratic Party, and soon McGrath was championing the cause of the Sleepy Lagoon defendants.

McGrath became executive secretary of the Sleepy Lagoon Defense Committee. Labor activist LaRue McCormick had earlier formed a committee, called the Citizens' Committee for the Defense of Mexican American Youth (CCDMAY) that included many Hollywood celebrities in its ranks. Numerous fundraisers were hosted and attended by celebrities, including actor and director Orson Welles, actress Rita Hayworth, and singer Nat King Cole. Indeed, Rita Hayworth even lent some of her clothes to the sister of Hank Leyvas when they went to a fundraiser for the group. Carey McWilliams eventually reorganized the group into the Sleepy Lagoon Defense Committee (SLDC). This was done to make the group much more specific in its goal and to not lose sight of its ultimate objective, which was the freedom of all the imprisoned young men. The committee achieved great prominence and support, as more and more people became supportive of the defendants, and the fund-raising coffers filled. These funds were raised during a time of great patriotic appeals to the public to buy war bonds and make other sacrifices. It was only natural that appeals for liberal causes would bring in money. These funds were later used with great effectiveness in the legal challenges that lay ahead.

A real talent that Alice McGrath had was the ability to win the trust of the imprisoned young men. She would visit them every two months in San Quentin, keeping them informed of the status of the appeals and letting them know how much the outside world cared about them. They were delighted to read the committee's newsletters and bulletins. At first some of the men were quite suspicious of her; others warmly welcomed her immediately. But eventually they all grew to love her. Even Hank, the tough guy whom all of society saw as a dangerous murderer, eventually grew to trust Alice (PBS, 2001).

Meanwhile, Ben Margolis Jr., a well-known liberal lawyer, was the lead attorney on the appeal. In early 1944, the Second District Court of Appeals heard the case. Accepting the arguments put forth by the defense, Judge Clement Nye threw out the convictions. He agreed that there was insufficient evidence to convict and that Fricke's courtroom policy was a blatant denial of the right to counsel. As soon as the court reached its verdict, Alice raced to the nearest Western Union office, where she sent a telegram to Hank at San Quentin. Soon the Sleepy Lagoon defendants would be free.

THE RISE OF MEXICAN AMERICAN POLITICAL ACTIVISM

Political activism in the Latino community in the 1940s was rare. Mass deportations in the 1920s of Latino workers, both illegal and legal, had made many residents nervous about doing anything that resembled political involvement. Los Angeles would not see a single elected official of Hispanic heritage until after World War II. (Even into the twenty-first century, no city that has a Hispanic majority has ever had more than one-third Hispanic representation on the city council, and Los Angeles has not had a Hispanic mayor since the nineteenth century.)

The deportations of Mexican Americans in the 1920s and 1930s were both a political and a racial issue. The experience of World War I and the changing geopolitical scene alarmed the isolationist federal administration. Known as the "Red Scare raids," they started with deportations of what were termed "political radicals" who supported V. I. Lenin and the Russian Revolution. Because many people thought that Mexican residents were left-leaning and a political and national threat, the government sweeps moved swiftly west.

In the early 1930s, at the height of the Great Depression, the California State legislature voted in a law that made it illegal for any company that had contracts with the state government to employ citizens of another country. After this, many Mexicans and Mexican Americans who had been born in the United States lost their public works jobs on highway building and in construction.

This racism was not limited to California. President Herbert Hoover publicly identified Mexican workers as the cause of most of California's economic ills. U.S. officials quickly turned to deportation and began forcibly returning Mexicans across the border. Authorities justified their actions by saying that they had a right to control the borders and to throw out illegal immigrants. Unfortunately, many of those Mexicans sent south were U.S. citizens.

These actions marked the first time in U.S. history that the American government had removed large numbers of immigrants. In a six-year period, over half a million Mexican workers and Mexican Americans were deported (PBS, 2001). These deportations shocked the Mexican American population. By the beginning of World War II, and right before the Sleepy Lagoon incident, the nation's Mexican-born population was half of what it had been before the Depression. Despite this large-scale persecution, there were leaders and protestors who emerged from the community.

One of these activists was a local radio commentator named Pedro Gonzalez. Gonzalez had fled north from Mexico following the Mexican Revolution, as he was not in agreement with Pancho Villa and his supporters. He had been arrested by Villa's men, who accused him of using his position as a telegraph operator to inform on their troop movements. Threatened with execution, he came north in 1917. Eventually, Gonzalez established himself as a political commentator; and his early morning radio show, broadcast completely in Spanish, was the first show of its kind in Los Angeles. Given the unusual time slot of 4 a.m. to 6 a.m., Gonzalez struck a chord with the thousands of local residents who got up at that time to go to their low-paid factory jobs, cannery jobs, and field jobs.

Gonzalez used his radio show as a platform to protest the unjust deportations and discrimination. His popularity grew so much that in 1934 he was unfairly accused of raping a minor. He was sentenced to six years in San Quentin. Eight months after the trial, the alleged victim signed an affidavit stating that she had been forced into testifying against Gonzalez due to the police threats that she would be sent to the very same Ventura School for Girls as the Sleepy Lagoon women. After Gonzalez had served his six years, he was deported immediately back to Mexico. Like the Sleepy Lagoon defendants, Gonzalez was eventually vindicated, and in 1984 the film *Ballad of an Unsung Hero* was made about his story.

THE RIOTS

While the convicted Sleepy Lagoon defendants served their time in prison, another huge story was developing in Los Angeles and to a limited degree in other parts of America. Soldiers home on leave and waiting to be shipped overseas formed the opinion that "zoot suiters" were in some way draft dodgers, criminals, or disloyal to America, and massive riots broke out in the summer of 1943 in Los Angeles.

Los Angeles was undergoing major transformations in the early war years. White men enlisted in the military, and their wives and other women took the jobs that were needed to fill the huge military-industrial complex.

African American and Mexican American men and women also filled these jobs. Many whites saw two wars going on—one against the Axis powers overseas and another against integration and racial change at home. This was fueled in large part by the government-sanctioned relocation of thousands of Japanese Americans in the first months of 1942. Although it is hard to imagine it in the twenty-first century, there was a real fear on the West Coast of a Japanese attack or invasion at this time. The cities were under strict blackout rules so as to not give possible attackers any advantage. The local beaches had citizen patrols that watched for signs of the enemies, and more than once anti-aircraft guns blazed away at what overzealous but well-meaning civil defense captains thought was certainly a Japanese air raid. Of course, no such attack ever took place. However, Los Angeles was a major military outpost, and up to 50,000 servicemen could be found there at any time.

It was not just new workforce demographics and massive population changes that were affecting Los Angeles and all of the United States at the time. Jazz music was taking hold among young people, and its tone and flavor were extremely different from the very conservative Big Band "hit parade" music that mainstream radio favored. The very popular singers and bands such as Bing Crosby, Ella Fitzgerald, and Benny Goodman gave way to younger, "hipper" jazz musicians who in many cases were African American. Jazz music and jazz dancing were very different from what middle America was accustomed to, and as with the entrance of Elvis Presley fifteen years later and the Beatles twenty years later, young people delighted in shocking their conservative parents with a tiny dose of normal rebellion. Another aspect of the jazz age was the mixing of races both among artists and in dancing.

Out of this musical transition also came a change in dress style, which is where the zoot suit made its appearance. Many minority youths wore this flamboyant style of dress, which not only shocked white Americans, but went against the unwritten but strongly enforced rule that Mexican Americans and African Americans should be largely unseen and in the background in public places. This fashion was also strongly opposed by the parents of the Mexican American youth, who were overwhelmingly conservative, Catholic, and had the belief firmly ingrained in them that the best way to fit into Anglo-American society and "avoid trouble" was to not stand out but to embrace traditional Anglo values and traditions as quickly as possible.

The zoot suit style turned this policy of being unseen on its head. Men in their new zoot suits paraded confidently down the city streets and stood out against the uniformity of the soldiers, who all wore the same uniforms and sported the same short hair cuts. The "zoot-suiters" stood out, and their increasingly heightened profiles as members of the criminal class played right into the hands of the bored and, in many ways, envious servicemen. Tensions had always existed between the citizens and the men serving in uniform. Rowdy soldiers would often drink too much, chase local girls too much, and engage in fights with each other and non-uniformed personnel. The Mexican American community in particular resented the way white servicemen behaved, and there were many instances of drunk sailors and soldiers getting robbed and beaten by groups of local teenagers who met these outsiders in their traditional neighborhoods.

Urban legends began to develop in the Mexican American community about white soldiers coming into Hispanic neighborhoods seeking women, and similar rumors grew of mobs of Latinos attacking soldiers who dated Mexican American women. It was a common belief that Mexican American men would taunt and sexually harass the wives and girlfriends of white servicemen. More and more fights broke out when members of the two groups met, and in June 1943, tensions escalated to the boiling point. These became known as the "zoot suit riots."

On Monday, May 30, 1943, a dozen or so sailors were walking on a downtown street. When they saw some Mexican American women nearby, they approached them. A group of men wearing zoot suits saw this and the two groups met. Sailor Joe Dacy Coleman, thinking a fight was about to start, grabbed the arm of one of the suited men. This was the trigger that both angry groups needed. Sailor Coleman was hit over the head and knocked unconscious. Other civilians joined in on the attack with rocks, bottles, and fists. The sailors escaped, carrying Coleman back to the naval armory. "The Monday night fracas on the last day of May, 1943, lasted little more than a few minutes, but the shock wave reverberated for days," wrote historian Eduardo Pagán in his 2003 book about the riots. "The details of the fight grew larger and more distorted in each re-telling from sailor to soldier" (Pagán, 2003, p. 165). The sailors waited a few days, patiently planning their revenge.

On the night of Thursday, June 3, about fifty sailors went to the nearby neighborhood of Alpine Street (near Chinatown). There were no zoot suiters out that night, so they marched downtown to the Carmen Theater. The sailors turned on the house lights looking for them. All they found were several twelve- and thirteen-year-old boys. But that was close enough for the drunk and angry mob. Despite the moviegoers' protests, the sailors tore the suits off the boys and savagely beat them with their hands and clubs. They then set their clothes on fire.

Later that same night, eleven sailors on shore leave said they were attacked by a group of Mexican American men. Word spread throughout the naval armory, and twenty cabs transported over 200 sailors downtown in search of the attackers. Anyone wearing a zoot suit was a target for the mob, and dozens of Mexican American men were beaten and stripped of their clothes (Pagán, 1996).

As the mob ran amok, news of the events began to reach the armory's watch commander, executive officer Lieutenant Charles Bacon. He responded to the scene of the fights and found the shore patrol (navy police responsible for navy personnel) with a large group of sailors. They had arrested the men and were taking them to the nearby LAPD Central Division Jail. Lieutenant Bacon intervened and made sure that none of the men were arrested or jailed.

The next night was more of the same. Sailors could not find zoot suiters on the street, so they headed to nearby Mexican American neighborhoods, where they assaulted people in bars, cafes, and restaurants. Many of the victims of the sailors' violence had no connection to zoot suits, and were beaten simply because of their ethnicity. For example, the sailors stumbled across a group of Mexican musicians who had just left the Aztec Recording Company after a recording session. Although the musical artists were all adults, and had no connection to zoot suiters, they were also savagely attacked. The major media at the time, which were hugely sympathetic to the white soldiers and sailors, did not report such instances of noncombatants being targeted.

The Los Angeles Police Department and Los Angeles Sheriff's Department were also unwilling to step in and protect innocent civilians. One officer was quoted as saying, "You can say that the cops had a 'hands-off' policy during the riots. Well, we represented public opinion. Many of us were in the first world war, and we're not going to pick on kids in the service." If any arrests occurred at all, they were almost always the beaten Mexican American citizens who were taken into custody, not the men who assaulted them (PBS, 2001).

Mexican American youth fought back. One man, Rudy Leyvas, recalled how his friends set traps for the sailors, using decoys to lure their attackers in. "And they let out a cry: There they are! There they are! And they came in. As they came in, once they got all the way in, we all came out. I, myself, had a bat. And I used it" (PBS, 2001).

The violence peaked on Monday, June 7. By this time, the mob had grown to include soldiers, marines, and sailors from other installations all over Southern California and the Southwest. Everyone wanted in on the violent anti-Mexican attacks.

Al Waxman, editor of the *Eastside Journal*, a small Jewish newspaper, wrote about what he witnessed. He described a "mass of humanity locked in violent struggle, arms swinging, legs kicking, shrieking with anger." The police were arresting dozens of young Mexican Americans. "Why am I being arrested?" one of them asked (Pagán, 2003, p. 179). The response was a savage clubbing with a nightstick. Although the boy fell to the sidewalk unconscious, police kicked him in the face. *LA Opinion*, a Spanish-language daily newspaper, had a similar bleak view of the military and its seeming indifference to the actions of the servicemen. On June 9, it printed a telegram that had been sent to Washington, DC, lamenting the current situation and suggesting that it threatened the stability of American diplomatic relations with other countries. Eduardo Quevedo, president of the Coordinating Council of the Young People of Latin America, wrote,

Despite precautions taken on the part of the military police and local authorities to control the situation, the servicemen continue to walk the streets of Los Angeles armed with clubs and appear to be tacitly supported by many city and local officials in charge of keeping the peace; their attacks have now expanded to include blacks. This situation, which is prompting racial antagonism between the Mexican, Anglo-Saxon and Black communities, will undoubtedly have grave international repercussions, which will inevitably damage the war effort and thwart the gains made by the Good Neighbor policy. We urge immediate intervention by the Office of War Information so that it moderates the local press which has openly approved of these mutinies and which is treating this situation in a manner that is decidedly inflammatory. (as quoted in PBS transcript)

Even the Mexican embassy in Washington intervened. It called for a formal investigation to be launched into the riots. Carey McWilliams, president of the National Lawyers Association in Los Angeles, sent a petition to U.S. Attorney General Francis Biddle calling for an investigation. He stated that the riots were a direct outgrowth of the hysteria and police abuses that reached their most fevered pitch during the Sleepy Lagoon case, and that the two episodes represented a long pattern of police abuse of the Mexican community over the previous eighteen months.

McWilliams, who was also the head of the Sleepy Lagoon Defense Committee, wrote an article for the June 21, 1943, issue of the liberal *New Republic* magazine. In this article, McWilliams denied that there were organized criminal gangs in the Mexican community, and asserted, "98 percent of the Mexican youth in Los Angeles is American-born, American-raised, American-educated" (as quoted in del Castillo, 2000, p. 387).[1]

Finally, military officials declared Los Angeles off limits to all sailors, soldiers, and marines. The shore patrol gave orders to arrest disorderly personnel. The following day the city council adopted a resolution that banned the wearing of zoot suits on Los Angeles streets, punishable by a thirty-day jail term. The zoot suiters disappeared from the streets, and the military personnel stayed on base. Things returned to relative calm. Governor Earl Warren and Los Angeles Mayor Fletcher Bowron implied that the riots and their aftermath were almost entirely the fault of the Mexican American youth, and completely dismissed or greatly minimized the involvement of the military personnel. *Time* magazine was one of the few in the national media that presented a balanced view of the riots. In fact, the U.S. ambassador to Mexico, George S. Messersmith, wrote the U.S. secretary of state to complain that the Mexico City edition of the June 18, 1943, issue of the magazine had an article about the "zoot suit war" that "treats the zoot suit disturbances in such a way as to make it appear as an anti-Mexican movement and blames the police for encouraging attacks on Mexicans and accuses the military authorities of laxity" (as quoted in del Castillo, 2000, p. 378). The ambassador was concerned about the impact of this media coverage on Mexican perception of the riots.

APPEAL GRANTED

Meanwhile, in the era of relative calm following the riots, the appeal for all the Sleepy Lagoon defendants was granted. When the Sleepy Lagoon case reached the Second District Court of Appeal, the court agreed with every point the defense committee made. The justices agreed that Judge Fricke had erred in not allowing the defendants to have access to their attorneys, that the judge was highly biased, and that the jury heard extremely volatile testimony that gave it an unfairly balanced view of the defendants. All the defendants were freed in October 1944. The Court of Appeal did fail to do one thing that had more to do with how judges and lawyers related to each other than anything. It said in its decision that there had been no racism by the judge or prosecution (Pagán interview, PBS, 2001). However, they did find that Fricke's refusal to let the defendants consult with their lawyers denied them due process, and this landmark case effectively ended mass trials of this sort for the future.

The Sleepy Lagoon defendants' records were cleared, but the case was never reopened, and José Díaz's killer was never brought to justice. After the young men were released, they quickly merged into the hustle and bustle of wartime Los Angeles. By the time they were free again, the zoot suit riots that had affected so many of their peers were over—but not forgotten.

THE ZOOT SUIT RIOTS IN POPULAR CULTURE
AND THE ARTS

The night of the riots is the opening scene of the 1992 movie *American Me*. In this scene, a young Chicano couple, who are "zoot suiters, and proud of it" are out for a night with friends when they are attacked by rampaging sailors. Beaten by the sailors and dragged from a tattoo parlor, the young man is stripped of his suit in front of the crowd outside. As this is happening, his girlfriend is raped by two of the sailors in the backroom of a tattoo parlor. This night in the 1940s is recalled as a flashback in the film, narrated by the couple's adult son. In modern Los Angeles, the son is a gang member and drug dealer who is serving time in Folsom Prison.

The playwright Luis Valdez has played an even more important role in presenting the riots to modern audiences with his play *Zoot Suit* (later made into a film). Valdez is a leading artist in El Teatro Campesino (Farmerworkers Theater Company). His play is a controversial musical with a protagonist named Henry Reyna. Reyna's alter ego is the mythical figure El Pachuco, who addresses the audience as the narrator. The media are personified by the allegorical figure "the Press." Valdez has been both praised for his imaginative use of Chicano culture and criticized for his use of violent stereotypes and for his lack of attention to female characters. In the play, Henry Reyna carries a switchblade knife to a dance. Pizzato (1998, p. 2) quotes one of Valdez's "strongest critics" as saying that "[t]his is a glaring misrepresentation of the historical event . . . because the actual 38th Street Gang, led by Henry Leyvas, did not carry switchblades, nor did most pachucos at that time." But in spite of the concerns expressed by his critics, Valdez's play was a hit on the Los Angeles stage in 1978 and the first Chicano play on Broadway (Pizzato, 1998, p. 1). It exposed modern audiences to the story of the zoot suiters and Los Angeles in the 1940s.

But what became of the real Hank Leyvas and the other people who lived through the Sleepy Lagoon murder case?

THE AFTERMATH

Hank Leyvas had a difficult time returning to the life he had left behind when he was sent to prison. He tried to fit, reconciling with his old girlfriend, Dora. However, the beatings and the abusive treatment he had received had a lasting effect, and soon he was running with a far worse crowd than the 38th Street Boys. Soon he was supporting himself by dealing drugs. He eventually served about ten years for narcotics trafficking. In the 1960s, Hank got out of the criminal and drug lifestyles and opened a restaurant called "Hank's" in East Los Angeles. The Brown Berets, a Chicano youth movement born in 1960s Los Angeles, got to know Hank, and he would frequently tell them his story and offer advice about political issues and organizing. Hank had never married and had no children, so the community of young political radicals and the people he met at his family restaurant became the children he never had. Hank's café was right on Whittier Boulevard, where numerous parades and marches were held in the 1960s and 1970s protesting the Vietnam War and the treatment of Chicanos. (It was nearby that in the summer of 1970, Mexican American journalist Ruben Salazar was killed by a projectile fired by Los Angeles County Sheriff's deputies.)

But even though Hank had gotten out of the criminal life, his love for drinking and partying remained. Indeed, the nightlife and party scene that sent his life on such a downward spiral on that warm summer night in 1942 was very similar to another warm night, on July 6, 1971, when he dropped dead of a heart attack after hours of drinking at a nearby bar. He was only forty-eight years old.

George Shibley practiced law for many years afterward, and in his long career not one of his clients ever received the death penalty. He achieved more national attention when he worked on the defense of Sirhan Sirhan, the assassin of Senator Robert Kennedy. He also kept close contact with many of the Sleepy Lagoon defendants. He always referred to them as "the boys." When he died on July 4, 1989, many attended the funeral.

Alice McGrath did not stop her political activism with the end of the Sleepy Lagoon case. She continued into the twenty-first century, always available to writers, researchers, and historians. As of 2003, she was still an activist, involved in humanitarian programs in Mexico and Nicaragua (Pagán, 2003, p. 211). Her passion never subsided, and she has been a role model for liberal activists for nearly sixty years. Through it all, she remained friends with the Leyvas family.

José Díaz's remains rest at Calvary in East Los Angeles, the oldest Catholic cemetery in the city. Louis Encinas, whom many believe and whom Lorena believed was José's killer, rests nearby.

NOTE

1. Later in *North From Mexico,* published in 1948, McWilliams would write, "Thus concurrently with the growth of the gangs there developed a new stereotype of the Mexican as the "*pachuco* gangster[,]" the "zoot suiter" . . . the *pachuco* stereotype was born in Los Angeles" (p. 242).

REFERENCES

del Castillo, R. G. (2000). The Los Angeles "zoot suit riots" revisited: Mexican and Latin American perspectives. *Mexican Studies/Estudios Mexicanos, 16*(2), 367–391.

Josélit, J. W. (2001). *A perfect fit: Clothes, character, and the promise of America.* New York: Henry Holt and Co.

Mazòn, M. (1984). *The zoot-suit riots: The psychology of symbolic annihilation.* Austin, TX: University of Texas Press.

McWilliams, C. (1968). *North from Mexico: The Spanish-speaking people of the United States.* Westport, CT: Greenwood Press.

Pagán, E. O. (1996). *Sleepy Lagoon: The politics of youth and race in wartime Los Angeles, 1940–1945.* Chapel Hill, NC: University of North Carolina Press.

Pagán, E. O. (2003). *Murder at the Sleepy Lagoon: Zoot suits, race, and riots in wartime L. A.* Chapel Hill, NC: University of North Carolina Press.

Pizzato, M. (1998, Summer). Brechtian and Aztec violence in Valdez's "zoot suit" [Electronic version]. *Journal of Popular Film and Television, 26*(2), pp. 1–10.

Public Broadcasting System (PBS). (2001). American Experience series. Transcript of the film *Zoot Suit Riots.* Available at http://www.pbs.org/

11

Martha Beck and Raymond Fernandez: The Lonely Hearts Killers

Mark Gado

"I'm still a human, feeling every blow inside, even though I have the ability to hide my feelings and laugh," she said, "but that doesn't say my heart isn't breaking from the insults and humiliation of being talked about as I am. Oh yes, I wear a cloak of laughter" (Beck letter, 1950, September 28). Such were the words of accused killer Martha Beck, who in the blistering hot summer of 1949 went on trial for murder in New York City. She and her thirty-four-year-old Hawaiian-born lover, Raymond Fernandez, were accused of killing an Albany woman named Janet Fay, who was lured into their clutches by a false promise of marriage. During the previous year, Beck and Fernandez had gone on a fraud and killing spree that victimized single, lonely females. They may have killed as many as seventeen women (Nash, 1995, p. 64). After their arrest for a double murder in Michigan, Beck and Fernandez became known as the "Lonely Hearts Killers."

The daily revelations about this most bizarre couple had New York City's press corps working overtime to keep up with a tale that seemed too sleazy even by tabloid standards. Martha's physical build became the target of never-ending speculation by newspapers, which estimated her weight to be anywhere from 200 to over 300 pounds (and never accurately reported this fact). Public ridicule prompted Martha to write a series of angry, animated letters from Sing Sing's death row to various reporters, including the legendary Walter Winchell, complaining of her shabby treatment. But the Latino Casanova and the chubby, lovesick girlfriend who murdered lonely, sex-deprived women was an irresistible story and one that was more disturbing than anything out of the trashiest pulp magazines of the 1940s.

THE CRIMES AND THE CRIMINALS

Martha Beck

She was born Martha Jule Seabrook on May 6, 1920, in a small town in northwestern Florida. While still a child, she developed a glandular condition that caused her to mature faster than other children. She had a woman's body by the time she was a teenager, which made her target of cruel jokes by school classmates. At her murder trial in 1949, it was suggested that her brother sexually assaulted her when she was very young, although no proof was ever offered. Her mother blamed Martha for the assault and beat her for being the cause of trouble in the family. Afterward, her mother followed Martha wherever she went. If any boy displayed even casual interest in her daughter, her mother chased the boy away with insults and threats. Not surprisingly, Martha became reclusive and developed few friends her own age. She gained a great deal of weight, which further intensified her feelings of isolation and despair.

When she was a young woman, Martha Seabrook went to nursing school in Pensacola, Florida, where she excelled in every category and finished at the head of the class. But upon graduation, she was unable to secure a job because of her overweight appearance. Due to financial pressures, she took a job in a funeral home, where she helped prepare dead bodies for burial. It was probably a surreal experience for a young woman who was already dejected and withdrawn. As she worked into the night, she may have found a strange comfort in the company of those who could not wound her with criticism and ridicule.

However, in 1942, she decided to try for a new life in California. She obtained a job at an army hospital as a nurse. Soon, the twenty-two-year-old became pregnant by a soldier who refused to marry her and later attempted suicide. Unable to convince the father to marry her and ashamed that he would prefer suicide to marrying her, Martha Seabrook returned to Florida, still pregnant. She told neighbors that the father was a navy officer in the South Pacific and he would eventually return from the war. Realizing she could not maintain this sham forever, she concocted a scheme in which the father was allegedly killed in action. For a time, the community mourned for her and she received a great deal of attention (Frasier, 1972, p. 143). In 1944, she gave birth to a daughter, Willa Dean.

Within a few years, Martha Seabrook met and married a local bus driver named Alfred Beck. She had a second child, a son, but the marriage did not work out. She was soon divorced and broke once again. Despondent with her life and convinced nothing good would ever happen to her, Martha immersed herself in romance novels and movie-fan magazines. She dreamed of a storybook romance and yearned for the day when her "knight in shining armor" would rescue her from her own life. She attended afternoon movies religiously and worshipped the contemporary screen actors, especially Charles Boyer. A friend who pitied her placed an advertisement for a man in a magazine. But when Martha Beck read the ad, she felt deep humiliation. "How could I forget that day?" she later wrote. Desperate for attention and male companionship, she placed a second advertisement in a magazine called *Mother Dinene's Family Club for Lonely Hearts* (Frasier, 1972, p. 142). Each day she would check her mailbox anxiously waiting for her Prince Charming to respond. Instead, she received a letter from a Raymondo Martinez Fernandez.

Raymond Fernandez

He was born on the island of Hawaii on December 17, 1914. Raymond's parents were from Spain, a proud couple who worked hard their entire lives to make a better life for their children. But Raymond was not a healthy child. He was sickly, frail, and spurned athletics. His father was ashamed of Raymond for those reasons and wished for a stronger son. He was openly critical of the sensitive teenager, which must have hurt the boy deeply. In 1932, when Raymond was only eighteen years old, he went to Spain to work on an uncle's farm. By the time he was twenty, he had married a local girl named Encarnacion Robles and began to settle down. He matured into a handsome, muscular young man, and in the town of Orgiva, where he lived and worked, Raymond was admired and well liked.

When the war ended in 1945, Fernandez decided to return to America. He would send for Encarnacion and his newborn son when he had enough money. He bought passage on a cargo ship that sailed for the island of Curaçao in the Dutch Antilles. During this journey, in December 1945, Fernandez experienced a life-altering event. One morning, as he attempted to come up to the deck, an open steel hatch cover fell on his head. The impact caused a severe indentation in his skull and he remained unconscious for several days. When the ship arrived in port, Fernandez was placed in a hospital, where he remained until the spring of 1946.

After he was discharged from care, it was evident that Fernandez had undergone a personality transformation. Before the injury, he was outgoing, friendly, and courteous to people. Afterward, Fernandez became moody, distant, and very quick to anger. When he spoke, he would ramble incoherently at times. He suffered from sudden but intense headaches and constantly swallowed aspirin to relieve the pain. There was no doubt that Fernandez was a changed man.

He tried to continue his journey, but when he arrived in the port of Mobile, Alabama, Fernandez was arrested for stealing a large quantity of the ship's linens. At trial, he told the judge he did not know why he did it; he just stole because he thought he could get away with it. He was sentenced to one year in a federal detention center in Florida. There, he became friends with a Haitian prisoner who introduced him to the ancient religion of Vodun. Fernandez immersed himself in the practice of voodoo and plunged into the world of the occult. For months, he fell under the spell of West Indian black magic and studied its ceremonies, charms, and incantations.

He convinced himself that he had a mystical power over women that derived from voodoo. Fernandez believed that his sexual skills were at their peak when enhanced by the energy and blessing of the voodoo gods. He told friends that he could make love with women from vast distances by using sacred powders and brews. He sent letters to women all over the world, obtaining their addresses from magazines and newspapers. When he developed a correspondence with a woman, he requested that she send a lock of her hair, a piece of jewelry, or some other personal item that he could utilize in blessed rituals designed to strengthen his control over them. In his own eyes, Fernandez became a voodoo *hougan*, a holy man, who thought he could seduce unsuspecting women at will. They would fall at his feet, he believed, helpless to resist the holy powers of Raymondo Martinez Fernandez.

By 1947, he was out of prison. He made his way to New York, where he took up residence with his sister in Brooklyn. His relatives were concerned about Raymond's appearance, which had changed drastically since the accident. Before, he had a healthy crop of dark luxurious hair; now, he was nearly bald. The scar from the injury was plainly visible on the top of his skull. His behavior was also strange. Sometimes he would lock himself in his room for long periods of time and later complain of painful headaches. Fernandez was a compulsive letter writer and received mail daily. On occasion, he disappeared for days, and when he returned, he offered no explanation of where he had been or what he had done. Fernandez began to write letters to so-called "lonely hearts" clubs. By promising love and companionship, he learned how to gain the confidence of women who were looking for romance. Once he secured their trust, he stole money, jewels, or bank checks. The victims, who were frequently too embarrassed to report the crimes to the police, would usually accept the loss.

During 1947, he bilked dozens of women out of their money and valuables. That same year, Fernandez met a woman named Jane Thompson through the mail and soon began a romantic relationship with her. They took a trip to Spain that was paid for by Thompson. For weeks they traveled throughout the countryside, dining in the best restaurants and living as man and wife. Fernandez even took her to meet his first wife, Encarnacion. But on the night of November 7, 1947, Thompson was found dead in her hotel room from unknown causes. Fernandez, it seemed, was nowhere to be found.

He made his way back to the United States where, with Thompson's forged will, Fernandez took over her apartment in New York City. Police in New York were unaware that Thompson had died under suspicious circumstances and that Fernandez was wanted for questioning in Spain. From Thompson's apartment, he sent Martha Beck her first letter. She was thrilled to receive the communication, and a flurry of letters was exchanged between them. Fernandez told her he was a successful businessman from Europe who had come to America to seek his fortune. He said he lived alone in New York "here in this apartment much too large for a bachelor but I hope someday to share it with a wife" (Buck, 1970, p. 17). He wrote his letters in a flowery style, very elaborate but always courteous. Fernandez told the starry-eyed Martha that he wrote to her because "I know you have a full heart with a great capacity for comfort and love" (Buck, 1970, p. 17). True to form, Fernandez asked for, and received, a lock of her hair.

In December 1947, Fernandez went to Florida to meet his newest victim. Initially, he must have been surprised at Martha Beck's size, since she never mentioned her overweight condition in her letters. But Martha was thrilled. He was everything that she had ever hoped for. She pictured Fernandez as her own "Charles Boyer." They spent several days together in her home, and when Fernandez pretended to fall in love with his gullible victim, they shared a bed. He studied her home life and tried to determine the extent of her financial assets. But Fernandez was running low on money and was forced to return to New York to continue his career of fraud.

Martha Beck later followed him to his apartment and brought her two young children. Fernandez, however, would have no part of her kids and demanded that she leave. In a decision that would haunt her for the rest of her life, she abandoned her children on the steps of a Salvation Army office in Manhattan on January 25, 1948. For the next three years, she had no contact whatsoever with them. Once the children were out of the way, Fernandez decided to tell his new girlfriend what he did for a living. At first, she was shocked. But later, Beck decided that since she had already given up so much to be with Fernandez, she might as well help him in his work. Together, they planned the future.

The Victims

The nomadic couple first traveled to Pennsylvania, where they met with a Mrs. Henne, a lonely woman who had been corresponding with Fernandez for several weeks. Martha posed as his sister. Within two weeks, Mrs. Henne married Raymond Fernandez in Virginia. They returned to New York, where the unlikely trio lived together in Thompson's old apartment. The situation deteriorated quickly when Fernandez demanded all of Mrs. Henne's money and personal belongings. "For four days, he was very polite to me," she later told police. "Then he gave me tongue lashings when I wouldn't sign over my insurance policies and my pension to him" (Brown, 1952, p. 109). Mrs. Henne later fled the apartment minus her car and thousands of dollars, never to return.

Their next victim was a woman named Myrtle Young of Greene Forest, Arkansas. On August 14, 1948, she and Fernandez were married in Cook County, Illinois. Once again, Martha Beck posed as Raymond's sister. But Myrtle complained about Martha's presence so much that Fernandez decided to drug her. With Martha's help, he dropped her onto a bus headed for Little Rock, Arkansas. She was later found unconscious in a rear seat and taken to a hospital. Myrtle Young died the following day in Little Rock.

In the meantime, Beck and Fernandez fled back to New York, where Raymond had already developed a new victim, sixty-six-year-old Janet Fay of Albany, New York. Mrs. Fay was a religious woman with money in the bank and enjoyed writing letters to lonely-hearts clubs. Fernandez made arrangements to drive up to Albany, and in December 1948, he met with Mrs. Fay. After several dinners, Fernandez then introduced Martha as his sister. They got along well and within a few days, Fernandez asked for Mrs. Fay's hand in marriage. She quickly accepted, and they made plans to move out of Albany. After helping Mrs. Fay clean out her bank accounts, they moved to an apartment in Valley Stream in Long Island.

On the night of January 9, 1949, Martha and Mrs. Fay had some type of disagreement. "I was just burning up with jealousy and anger," Martha later said at her trial ("Alone with Victim," 1949, July 28, p. 44). What exactly transpired between them will never be known, for Martha related several different versions to the police. Martha later said that she blacked out and could remember very little. "The next I knew," she said on the witness stand, "Fernandez had me by the shoulders and was shaking me!" ("Mrs.

Beck Defends," 1949, July 30, p. 28). The body of Janet Fay lay at her feet. She had been bludgeoned to death with a hammer and strangled with a scarf. Beck and Fernandez cleaned up the mess and hid Mrs. Fay in a closet. Later, they dumped the body in a large trunk and brought it to Raymond's sister's house. Eventually, they buried the trunk in the cellar of a rented house. Then, they moved on.

Fernandez already had his next target lined up. She was Delphine Downing, 41, of Grand Rapids, Michigan, recently widowed and the mother of a two-year-old child, Rainelle. Delphine knew Fernandez as "Charles Martin" through his correspondence. In January 1949, Fernandez and his "sister" Martha visited Delphine at her home in a suburb of Grand Rapids called Byron Center. Soon, Fernandez was sharing Delphine's bed, which enraged Martha. One night, the two women became involved in a heated argument. Fernandez suddenly shot Delphine in the head with a gun that had belonged to her husband. They buried Delphine's body in the basement and covered it with fresh cement. Little Rainelle witnessed the event and became hysterical. Despite attempts to keep her quiet, she would not stop crying. In an act of desperation and true depravity, Martha drowned little Rainelle in a tub of dirty water in the cellar. They buried the child next to her mother. Over the next few days, Beck and Fernandez lived in Delphine's house, eating her food and sleeping in her bed. But suspicious neighbors called police after they noticed that Delphine and Rainelle had disappeared.

When police responded, they quickly located the freshly made graves. The murderous couple was finally arrested. They confessed to the Byron Center detectives in an epic seventy-three-page statement that detailed their activities across the country the previous year. Smug, arrogant, and boastful of their crimes, Beck and Fernandez seemed almost proud of what they had done.

The next day, the story of the "Lonely Hearts Killers" was front-page news across America. The *New York Times* headline read, "3 Lonely Hearts Murders Trap Pair; Body Dug Up Here" (Seigel, 1949, March 2). Just as quickly, the dehumanization of Martha Beck began. From the very beginning, newspapers were derogatory to the extreme whenever her name was mentioned. Reports were particularly harsh in her physical description as well. She was called "the fat girlfriend," "simpering," "a weird woman," and the "kill companion." In an obvious intent to demean the defendant, many tabloid stories during that time always included her weight, which was falsely reported in nearly every instance.

After Governor Thomas Dewey made several phone calls to Michigan, a deal was struck with county prosecutors. They would temporarily waive prosecution for the Downing murders pending the outcome of any New

York charges for the Fay murder. Prosecutors wanted Beck and Fernandez to face the death penalty. Michigan had none.

THE TRIAL

Their trial opened on June 28, 1949. A change of venue was granted from Nassau County, Long Island, where the Fay murder had been committed, to the Bronx County courthouse. It was larger and more accessible, and both sides agreed to the change. The prosecutor was Nassau County Assistant District Attorney Edward Robinson Jr., who had participated in the deal to extradite the defendants back from Michigan. The defense attorney was Manhattan lawyer Herbert E. Rosenberg. He was assigned to represent both defendants, an unusual arrangement that surely acted against the interests of the accused. Judge Ferdinand Pecora presided over the trial. He was a jurist who had a fine reputation for fairness.

Raymond Fernandez, dubbed the "mail order gigolo" by the *New York Daily News*, took the stand on July 11, 1949. He freely admitted to killing Delphine Downing but denied any role in the Fay killing. He said that he only confessed to Michigan police because "all my statements were made for the purpose of helping Martha" (Dillon and Lee, 1949, July 12, p. 4). Appealing to the jury's mercy, Fernandez explained that he was just a young man hopelessly in love. "With soft voice and many gold-toothed smiles toward plump Martha Beck," the *New York Daily News* story said on July 12, 1949, "the dapper figure in tan sports jacket . . . turned on his expert charm" (p. 4).

His testimony took a turn for the worse when Robinson confronted Fernandez with details of his many frauds and the dead bodies that seemed to follow him wherever he went. The defendant explained that he was tricked into confessing because the police had made promises in Michigan. "I didn't know if I was coming or going!" he told the court. He told the court that after he saw Janet Fay bludgeoned on the head and unconscious on the floor, he wrapped a scarf around her neck "to stop the flow of blood." Fernandez also described his sexual relations with Martha in a detailed litany that had spectators squirming in their seats. "The trial produced a torrent of sensational testimony as both defendants, apparently eager to prove their lack of sanity, burned the jurors' ears with lengthy streams of obscenity that described the intensity of their love life" (Knappman, 1994, p. 448). This testimony was considered so lurid for its time that the judge had the courtroom doors secured. The *New York Times* said, "The 'lonely hearts' murder trial in Bronx County Supreme Court was disrupted yesterday afternoon by a near riot of would-be spectators outside the courtroom" (*New York Times*, 1949, July 26, p. 22).

But the real drama took place when Martha Beck took the stand on July 25, 1949. Wearing a gray and white polka dot dress, green wedgies on her feet, and deep red lipstick, she told her story to a rapt jury. Beginning with her childhood, Martha Beck listed the many disappointments and heartaches she had suffered all her life. From a domineering mother and scheming men to bad luck and a persistent weight problem, she described a sad and pathetic existence that had some people in the courtroom in tears. "Life was not worth living," she said. "I'd rather be dead than to continue to argue with my mother each day of my life!" (Dillon and Lee, 1949, July 26). Beck told the court that she had attempted suicide on six occasions and almost succeeded each time (*New York Daily News*, 1949, July 27). Of the Fay murder, she said she blacked out momentarily after Mrs. Fay slapped her. She said that she awoke from a daze and found the dead woman lying on the floor in front of her.

Her attorney, Herbert Rosenberg, tried to explain to the court that Fernandez had a power over her and that his love meant everything to her. When asked to describe her sexual activities, Beck refused. "I consider it absolutely sacred," she said. "I will refuse to answer. You referred to the love-making as abnormal, but for the love I had for Fernandez, nothing is abnormal" (Dillon and Lee, 1949, July 27). Crowds gathered at the court-room doors as Martha Beck cried, laughed, and cajoled her way through four days of often-contentious testimony. "Remember, your Honor," she told Judge Ferdinand Pecora, "it's my life I'm fighting for here, not yours!" (*New York Times*, 1949, July 28). When asked why she hadn't told the victims who married Fernandez that he already had a wife in Spain, she replied, "The judge said 'Speak now or forever hold your peace,' so I held my peace" (*New York Times*, 1949, July 30). Martha Beck repeatedly taunted District Attorney Robinson. He found it difficult to get a straight answer from the hostile witness. "A 200-pound figure of wrathful emotion" is how one New York paper described her (*New York Daily News*, 1949, July 30). "Some 300 persons, many of them who had stayed in line four hours, tried to storm the courtroom," said the *New York Daily News* on July 26. "Reserves had to be called out from the Highbridge police station; . . . the public was ordered out of the corridors until order could be restored."

The case went to the jury on August 17 after forty-three days of trial. Beck and Fernandez were found guilty of first-degree murder in the death of Janet Fay. They displayed no reaction when the verdict was read, though the *New York Daily News* said on August 19, 1949, "Mrs. Beck, as she did so many times during the trial, took on a brazen pose" (p. 3). On August 22, they were back in the same courtroom for sentencing. Judge Pecora, as required by law, sentenced both defendants to death. They were on their way to Sing Sing within the hour.

During the admissions procedure at the prison, Beck was asked the routine question, "To what do you attribute your criminal act?" She replied, "Something I got into, I had no control" (Sing Sing Prison files, 1949). "An accident," replied Fernandez to the same question. Their eighteen-month stay on death row at Sing Sing had to be one of the most tumultuous eras in the history of that institution. From the day they entered the prison until the day they were executed in March 1951, the continuing soap opera of the broken-hearted Martha never ceased. Fueled by elaborate press stories of the oversexed inmate and her increasingly erratic behavior, the public had an insatiable thirst for gossip about America's most peculiar killer couple. Rumors of Martha Beck's sexual liaisons with a male guard kicked into overdrive when Walter Winchell carried the news on his radio broadcast. "For several weeks I have suffered in silence because of the rumors started by Mr. Fernandez," she wrote in a letter to Warden William Denno. "To print or say that I am having an affair with a guard is one of the most asinine and ridiculous statements ever!" (Beck letter, 1950, September 25). Fernandez also had a flair for the dramatic. He filed a petition in court to stop his appeals so that he could be executed immediately. The court papers said, "[T]he triangle subjects him to mental torture beyond endurance" and the defendant wished to be executed forthwith "to end his living death!" (Beck letter, 1950, September 25).

LEGAL ISSUES

But there were still several legal matters to be resolved. Defense attorney Rosenberg appealed the conviction based on two main issues. The first was the extended questioning of the defendants in Michigan on the night of March 1, 1949. The police interrogated Beck and Fernandez for many hours without benefit of counsel and allegedly promised that their statements would not be used against them in the state of New York. The second, and more compelling issue, was the fact that both defendants had shared the same attorney, a condition that obviously worked against each defendant during the forty-three-day trial, especially when Beck and Fernandez testified on the stand.

To the first point, the Court of Appeals noted that this very issue "was the subject of a searching preliminary examination which—by testimony covering more than seven hundred pages of the record from witnesses called by the prosecution and defense—developed in detail the circumstances in which the defendants statements were made" (*People v. Fernandez et al.*, 1950). That hearing resulted in the admission of the defendants' statements into trial evidence. Also hurting the defendants' chances for a favorable appeals ruling was the fact that Martha Beck had made a follow-up written statement on March 11 in which it was clear that "it was done at her own request after she was advised of her rights by the Michigan attorney assigned to her by the court, in which confession she stated that she knew that it could be used against her in New York (*People v. Fernandez et al.*, 1950). The Court of Appeals affirmed the defendants' convictions on this issue.

On whether Beck and Fernandez were hurt by sharing the same attorney, the court struggled for fair ground. It was pointed out that Fernandez himself asked for Mr. Rosenberg in a letter to the trial court on June 6, 1949, in which he stated, "Mr. Rosenberg, my present lawyer has done a great deal for me here and I am perfectly satisfied and would appreciate that he be assigned to be my lawyer." At the time, he was fully aware that Mr. Rosenberg was also Martha Beck's attorney. In addition, on several occasions and sometimes at length, Judge Ferdinand Pecora inquired to Mr. Rosenberg whether he wanted additional counsel assigned. Repeatedly, Mr. Rosenberg refused. On one instance, he even stated in open court, "If your Honor pleases, for the record may it be noted that both defendants are perfectly satisfied with counsel that is now representing them" (*People v. Fernandez et al.*, 1950).

Although Beck and Fernandez also lost their appeal on this issue, Judge James Conway, who dissented in the opinion, made clear the inadequate legal representation forced upon the defendants. "We think the court should have exercised its own judgment and not been guided by defense counsel nor by the defendants themselves, who were not competent to decide," he wrote. The defense of Martha Beck, whose hope of an acquittal depended on shifting the blame to her co-defendant, took priority in Mr. Rosenberg's actions in court and thereby could not have helped Fernandez's case. "The final complete abandonment of Fernandez by counsel . . . will be found in his [Rosenberg's] summation," wrote Judge Conway. "[T]he circumstances disclosed on this record rendered it impossible for Fernandez to have a fair trial" (*People v. Fernandez et al.*, 1950). The appeals ruling stood, however, and an execution date was set.

TILL DEATH DO US PART: THE CONTINUING PRISON LOVE STORY

The doomed couple carried on a love/hate relationship to the end. Though they never saw each other again, sympathetic guards and matrons passed notes and letters between them. Some days, they swore their love for each other. A day later, they would not speak. In a letter written to her mother, Martha Beck wrote, "Oh yes, he's brave when it comes to talk and hurting others, he can kill without batting an eyelash, but to hurt himself, he'd never do it. It takes a man to kill himself. Not a sniveling low down double crossing, lying rat like him!" (Beck letter, 1950, September 22).

But it was Martha, the betrayed, lovesick romantic, who continued to capture the imagination of legions of women. They could empathize with a sensitive, overweight, young woman who had known nothing but rejection in her life. They could feel for a woman who wound up on death row because she wanted nothing more than to please the man she loved. In March 1951, she wrote her last letter to Fernandez, in which she professed her undying love. He was ecstatic. "The news brought to me that Martha loves me is the best I've had in years!" he said. "Now I'm ready to die!" However, during his entire time at Sing Sing, and probably without Martha's knowledge, Fernandez continued to write his first wife, Encarnacion, who still lived in Spain with his children. "Kisses and hugs for the children and the baby and for you, receive millions of kisses and hugs from the one who will always love you!" (Beck Letter, 1951, February 6).

On the night of March 8, 1951, Martha Beck and Raymond Fernandez were executed in Sing Sing's prolific electric chair, operated by America's most famous executioner, Robert G. Elliot. Prison officials were unusually accommodating to witnesses. Records show that at least fifty-two people attended the execution, including representatives from the *New York Journal American*, the *Detroit News*, the *World Telegram*, New York's *El Diario*, the *Pensacola Daily Times*, the *New York Daily News*, and the *New York Times*. Martha Beck was the last female executed by New York State (Ethel Rosenberg, executed in 1953, was a federal prisoner and prosecuted by the U.S. government). Before she was taken to the death chamber, Martha had one last statement for the press. "What does it matter who is to blame?" she asked. "My story is a love story, but only those tortured by love can understand what I mean. I was pictured as a fat unfeeling woman. . . . I am not unfeeling, stupid or moronic" (Brown, 1952, p. 186).

THE MEDIA

But the vilification of Martha Beck by the New York press was nothing new. The city's tabloids had a long history of demonizing female criminals that began in the early part of the twentieth century. Beginning with the Ruth Snyder case in 1927, which received massive media coverage quite similar to the O. J. Simpson case during the 1990s, the city's ravenous press savaged the reputations of female suspects in a way that few men experienced. Every iota of Snyder's life, no matter how trivial, was uncovered, analyzed, and reported on. Her sexual history was paraded before the public in a fashion that degraded her and certainly affected her defense at the trial.

This trend became part of a larger, national pattern that has spanned generations and goes to the heart of the way females are treated in America's press. "The most common portrayal of women in the visual media is as a sex object," writes Helen Benedict in her book on the subject, *Virgin or Vamp* (1992). The opposite end of that characterization is the "whore" image. That projection "is connected with cruelty, inhumanity, insensitivity and unscrupulousness" (Benedict, 1992, p. 22). There is no doubt that the contemporary media felt that Martha Beck belonged in that category and deserved to die for her crimes. But it is not an easy thing to execute a woman in America, even when she is convicted of murder. For that reason, the press had to prepare society for the execution that was sure to come.

Aside from the natural opposition to the death penalty, which has always existed in America, even in colonial times, society's reluctance to execute females may be a cultural objection as well. Statistics affirm the notion that America has strong reservations about capital punishment against women. As Streib points out in his detailed analysis of female executions, "female offenders are unlikely to be arrested for murder, only very rarely sentenced to death and almost never executed" (Streib, 2001, p. 1). In New York state, which led the nation in executions until the Supreme Court decided the *Furman v. Georgia* case in 1972, execution of males outnumbers that of females by a ratio of over 100 to one (Sing Sing Prison executions, 1989). Most other states show a similar pattern, while sixteen other states have *never* executed a female (Streib, 2001, p. 7). Between 1900 and 1999, there were over 8,000 legal executions in America. Of those, just forty-six, or 0.6 percent, were women (Streib, 2001, p. 7), though females commit almost 15 percent of all homicides. Martha Beck was only the seventh woman to receive the death penalty in New York during the twentieth century. During the same period, 607 men went to their deaths in New York prisons (Sing Sing Prison executions, 1989).

The execution of a woman in American society is a traumatic event. It may be so traumatic that in order to justify it, the defendant must be perceived as a truly evil person, one who is deserving of such a fate. That may help explain the malicious press coverage that female criminals receive. Newspaper accounts of female killers easily support that theory. Ruth Snyder was called "the blonde fiend" (Margolin, 1999, p. 73). Frances Creighton, thirty-eight, convicted of murdering her boyfriend's wife in 1936, was nick-named "Black Eyed Borgia" (Brown, 1958, p. 102). The irrepressible, forty-two-year-old Eva Coo, who murdered for insurance money in 1935, was called a "roadhouse vamp" (Eggleston, 1997, p. 64). It is important to remember that these descriptions were included in "hard news" stories, not opinion columns. All these women were portrayed in a highly unsympathetic fashion that surely contributed to the public's dislike for them and, at the same time, prepared society for the ugly image of a woman on death row. It was as if the defendant's reputation as a woman, and a potential mother, had to be decimated in order for the inevitable execution to follow.

In 1970, a film was made about the Beck-Fernandez case. It was titled *The Honeymoon Killers* and was the only film production directed by Leonard Kastle. The film starred Shirley Stoler as Martha Beck and Tony LoBianco as Raymond Fernandez. Crudely made and produced in grainy black and white, the story line lacked continuity and was difficult to follow. However, *The Honeymoon Killers* has a certain nightmarish quality about it that seems to project a sense of voyeurism to its audience. The poor quality of the film's editing contributes to a strange and disjointed production. *The Honeymoon Killers* was never taken seriously by the general public and was lampooned by critics everywhere. Not surprisingly, it did very poorly at the box office. "It's such a terrible movie," wrote film critic Pauline Kael. "I wouldn't recommend it to anyone" (Peary, 1981, p. 140). Stoler, who went on to a successful career in films, bore an eerie resemblance to Martha. Her performance in *The Honeymoon Killers* was one of its few redeeming factors. Though the film was less than accurate, it has achieved something of a cult status and is listed in Danny Peary's book *Cult Movies*.

As spectacular as the case of Martha Beck and Raymond Fernandez was in its time, it was quickly pushed aside by news of yet another couple whose crimes angered America in a way it had never experienced before. On March 29, 1951, just three weeks after Beck and Fernandez went to the electric chair, Julius and Ethel Rosenberg were found guilty of selling atomic bomb secrets to the Soviet Union.

A new age of anxiety, paranoia, and fear was about to begin.

REFERENCES

Alone with victim, Mrs. Beck asserts. (1949, July 28). *New York Times*, p. 44.

Beck, M. (1950, September 22–24, 26, 28). Personal letters in Sing Sing case files. Albany, NY: New York State Archives.

Beck, M. (1951, March 1). Personal letters in Sing Sing case files. Albany, NY: New York State Archives.

Benedict, H. (1992). *Virgin or vamp*. New York: Oxford University press.

Brown, W. (1952) *Introduction to murder*. London, UK: Andrew Dakers Limited.

Brown, W. (1958). *They died in the chair*. Toronto, Canada: Popular press.

Buck, P. (1970). *The honeymoon killers*. London, UK: Xanadu Publications.

Dillon, E., and Lee, H. (1949, June 28). Link lonely hearts pair with slain widow. *New York Daily News*.

Dillon, E., and Lee, H. (1949, June 29). Reveal lonely hearts blood money dealings. *New York Daily News.*

Dillon, E., and Lee, H. (1949, July 1). Hearts killer explodes at attorney. *New York Daily News.*

Dillon, E., and Lee, H. (1949, July 6). Fernandez to hit own confession. New York Daily News.

Dillon, E., and Lee, H. (1949, July 12). Took killing to aid love, Gallant Fernandez now recants. *New York Daily News*, p. 4.

Dillon, E., and Lee, H. (1949, July 13). Fernandez admits heart killing in Michigan, denies one here. *New York Daily News.*

Dillon, E., and Lee, H. (1949, July 14). Fernandez tells strange love story. *New York Daily News.*

Dillon, E., and Lee, H. (1949, July 19). Prosecution makes blood tell, then rests lonely hearts case. *New York Daily News.*

Dillon, E., and Lee, H. (1949, July 26). Mean mom, bad men my downfall: Martha. *New York Daily News.*

Dillon, E., and Lee. H. (1949, July 27). Martha bemoans self, jeers rivals. *New York Daily News.*

Dillon, E., and Lee, H. (1949, August 2). Fernandez switches to insanity defense. *New York Daily News.*

Dillon, E., and Lee, H. (1949, August 3). Hearts lover balks move to plead insanity. *New York Daily News.*

Eggleston, N. (1997). *Eva Coo murderess.* Utica, NY: North Country Books.

Elliot, R. G. (1940). *Agent of death.* New York: E. P. Dutton and Co.

Frasier, D. K. (1972). *Murder cases of the twentieth century.* Jefferson, NC: McFarland and Company, Inc.

Hearn, D. A. (1997). *Legal executions in New York state 1639–1963.*

Kivel, M. (1951, March 9). Hearts killers calmly face the last mile. *New York Daily News*, p. 5.

Knappman, E. W. (Ed.). (1994). *Great American trials.* Detroit, MI: Visible Ink Press.

Lonely hearts pair resigned to death in chair tonight, March 8, 1951. (1951, March 9). *The Citizen Register.*

Margolin, L. (1999). *Murderess.* New York: Kensington Publishing Corp.

Mrs. Beck defends lies to the police. (1949, July 30). *New York Times*, p. 28.

Nash, J. R. (1981). *Look for the woman.* New York: M. Evans and Company, Inc.

Nash, J. R. (1995). *Bloodletters and badmen.* New York: M. Evans and Company.

Peary, D. (1981). *Cult movies.* New York: Dell Publishing.

People v. Fernandez et al. 301 NY 302, 93 N.E. 2d 859. Court of Appeals of New York, July 11, 1950.

Police bar crowd at Hearts trial. (1949, July 26). *New York Times.*

Seigel, K. (1949, March 2). 3 lonely hearts murders trap pair; Body dug up here. *New York Times*, p. 1.

Sifakis, C. (1970). *The encyclopedia of American crime.* New York: Facts on File, Inc.

Sing Sing Prison: case files of the condemned. Albany, NY: New York State Archives.

Sing Sing prison electrocutions 1891–196 (1972). Ossining, New York: Ossining Historical Society.

Streib, V. L. (2001, March 30). *Assessing sex discrimination issues in death penalty statutes.* Presented at the Moritz College of Law, Ohio State University.

Warden denies bids to see execution. (1949, September 2). *The Citizen Register.*

12

The Barbara Graham Murder Case: The Murderess "Walked to Her Death as if Dressed for a Shopping Trip"

Sheila O'Hare

Barbara Graham (1923–1955) was found guilty of the murder of Mabel Monahan and was executed, along with two codefendants, on June 3, 1955. Graham achieved popular culture immortality via the later Hollywood film *I Want to Live!* (1958), featuring Susan Hayward's Academy Award–winning performance. Based on *San Francisco Examiner* reporter Edward Montgomery's coverage of the case, the film treats Graham's case as an exemplar of partisan and sensational news coverage. The Montgomery character in the film initially characterizes Graham in a manner that summarizes the majority of actual news articles about the crime and trial: "It's Mrs. Graham's tough luck to be young, attractive, belligerent, immoral, and guilty as hell" (Wanger and Wise, 1958). Montgomery later underwent a change of opinion and came to believe Graham's protestations of innocence. Graham's guilt is still debated today along with the legal issues raised by her trial and execution.

THE DEATH OF MABEL MONAHAN

The crime occurred on the evening of March 9, 1953. The victim, Mabel Monahan, was a sixty-four-year-old widow who lived in Burbank, California.

Barbara Graham in courtroom. (Herald Examiner Collection/Los Angeles Public Library)

Monahan's gardener arrived at the house on the morning of March 11. He notified the police when he noticed that the front door was ajar and that the house appeared to have been ransacked. Monahan's body was found in a blood-spattered hallway, partly within a closet, hands bound behind her back. She had been struck repeatedly on the head and strangled with a strip of cloth. While Monahan's purse containing $474 and items of jewelry had been left behind, the intruders had pulled up carpeting, emptied drawers, and thoroughly searched the house.

Monahan was a frail, partially disabled woman, which made the assault seem particularly vicious; newspapers described it as a "fiendish slaying," linked to the gambling underworld via her former son-in-law, Las Vegas gambler Luther B. (Tudor) Scherer (Walker, 1961). Her cause of death, according to the coroner's office, was asphyxiation. Monahan's daughter offered a $5,000 reward for information leading to an arrest. This provided motivation for an informant who led Burbank police a week later to Baxter Shorter, an ex-convict with a record of property crimes.

Shorter made a statement to the police on March 31. The motive for the crime was robbery. Shorter's crime partners had heard that Tudor Scherer had hidden several caches of $100,000 apiece in the Burbank house. Shorter was able to provide the first names of three of his partners (Emmett, John, and Jack) and a physical description of the fourth partner, a woman. Police quickly focused on John Santo (b. 1900) and Emmett Perkins (b. 1908), long-time felons whose known previous offenses included robbery, weapons violations, and kidnapping. Perkins and Santo were also responsible for a quadruple murder in 1952 in Plumas County, though they would be tried for the Monahan murder first.

Known associates of Santo and Perkins included deep-sea diver John True and Barbara Graham, who was then identified as Perkins's girlfriend. True was arrested by police, questioned, and released; he claimed to have no knowledge of the crime or any of the alleged crime partners other than Santo. However, the April 13 edition of the *San Francisco Examiner* reported that a suspect was being held in the Monahan murder, and hinted that other suspects had been identified. The repercussions were immediate. In the first of many instances in which news coverage impacted the course of the case, Shorter was kidnapped at gunpoint from his home on April 14 and, presumably, murdered in retaliation for his confession.

Shorter's kidnapping and disappearance gave True second thoughts, and when he was rearrested by police, he agreed to testify against Santo, Perkins, and Graham in return for an immunity agreement with the Los Angeles district attorney's office. True had no criminal record, which made him preferable to the missing Shorter as a witness. His account of the crime was generally consistent with Shorter's, but he placed the responsibility for Monahan's injuries on Graham.

According to both True and Shorter, Graham was the first person to approach the Monahan house, using a ruse about car trouble to gain entry. Shorter's account was as follows (Walker, 1961): True entered the house after Graham, Perkins, and Santo a few minutes later, and Shorter last of all. Shorter saw True holding Monahan's head down on the rug; she had already been "beaten horribly." The woman (Graham) said, "Go on and knock her out" (p. 25), and Perkins struck Monahan in the temple with a gun. Santo and Perkins tied up Monahan, dragged her to a hall closet, and joined with the others in searching the house for a safe or cache of valuables. They did not locate Scherer's money or anything of value, and left empty-handed.

True's statement (Walker, 1961) added significant and incriminating details. He stated that when he came into the house, he saw Graham striking Monahan on the face and head with a gun. True, shocked and frightened (by his own account), "grabbed her head in my lap" (p. 80). The others tied Monahan's hands, put a pillowcase over her head, and dragged her body away. They then searched the house for fifteen or twenty minutes. True went into another room and heard someone strike Monahan again in his absence. When they left the house, Santo, Perkins, Graham, and True returned to their base at the La Bonita Motel in El Monte, where they cleaned up. True and Santo left for northern California that same night.

Police also interviewed William Upshaw, who had been approached by Santo about the robbery but had backed out of the venture before the evening of the crime. Upshaw would later testify at trial about his meetings with Santo, Perkins, Shorter, and Graham, and a drive they made past Monahan's home in preparation for the robbery.

The district attorney's office, doubtless wishing to avoid another Shorter incident, moved quickly. True told his story to the Los Angeles County grand jury, and it returned indictments against Perkins, Santo, and Graham. Knowing that they were being sought by police, Santo, Perkins, and Graham made several moves after April 10: first from their homes to the Ambassador Motel, then to Seal Beach, and finally to an apartment in a Lynwood machine shop building. (At trial, Graham explained these relocations by a complicated story involving a guano deal, but she also admitted that she was aware of news stories stating that True had identified his crime partners.) The three were arrested there on May 4, 1953, after an undercover police officer followed Graham to the building.

Graham became the center of media attention almost immediately. The *San Francisco Chronicle* identified the three as suspects in both the Monahan and the Plumas County murders, noting that Jack Santo was the "hottest suspect" and Perkins and Graham were believed to be accomplices. However, the reporter specifically noted "the puncture marks on [Graham's] arms, apparently from using narcotics" and that the three suspects were found "in various stages of undress" (*San Francisco Chronicle*, 1953, May 5, p. 11). Other reports described Graham as naked, or as rising from a bed she was sharing with Santo (Walker, 1961). The *Times* and the *Examiner* featured banner headlines on the arrest, with accompanying photos of Graham.

WHO WAS BARBARA GRAHAM?

To a certain extent, Graham had always been a lightning rod for controversy. Born Barbara Elaine Wood on June 26, 1923 in Oakland, California, she had a troubled childhood. She was the eldest of three children of Hortense Wood, a teenaged mother who had spent time in a female reformatory, the Ventura School for Girls. Graham's putative father, Joe Wood, was absent from her life at an early stage; Hortense is listed as the head of household in the 1930 U.S. census, her occupation indicated as "none." Graham's Alameda County Juvenile Court report from 1937 describes her mother's conduct as "questionable," tagging her as a poor moral influence on her daughter. In later life, Graham spoke of her mother with bitterness: "She's never cared whether I lived or died so long as I didn't bother her" (Davis and Hirschberg, 1962).

Graham ran away from home in December 1936. She was located by authorities and made a ward of the court on March 19, 1937, classified as a wayward girl on the grounds of immorality (she admitted to having multiple sex partners) and being a runaway. She was placed first at the Convent of the Good Shepherd, but she promptly escaped again. In July 1937, the court subsequently sent her to the Ventura School for Girls, where Hortense Wood had also been incarcerated some years before. Graham seemed unable even to feign conformity. Staff at Ventura noted that she attempted escape on several occasions, "smirks and struts around," and was frequently "written up," as much for her attitude as her conduct.

She remained at Ventura until April 1939, and was released from parole in January 1942, an officer noting that she was "impossible to supervise." Graham constantly traveled up and down the state, working at various occupations. She later listed several of them: cocktail waitress, dice girl or gambling shill, hotel clerk, and manager of a "call house" (a brothel).

In the slang of the era, she led the life of a "sea gull," a term for women and girls who hung around the navy yards of Oakland, Long Beach, and San Diego to meet sailors on shore leave; and of a "B-girl," a term for bar women who illegally solicited drinks. On some occasions, Graham admitted to working as a prostitute (Davis and Hirschberg, 1962); on others, she flatly denied it (Execution file, B. Graham). In any case, her activities were morally questionable in the 1950s and implied promiscuity and criminality.

She was also, intermittently, a housewife. Graham married four times (in 1940 to Harry Kielhammer; 1944 to Aloyse Puechel; 1947 to Charles Newman; and 1950 to Harry Graham). She had three children. Sole custody of her two older sons was given to Kielhammer, their father; her third son, Tommy Graham (b. 1951), would feature prominently in media coverage of the trial and its aftermath.

In the same time period, Graham also accumulated a record of petty offenses. She was arrested for disorderly conduct in 1940 and 1942 (under the names Barbara Redcliffe and Barbara Kielhammer), and for vagrancy and suspicion of prostitution in 1941, 1943, and 1944. As Barbara Kielhammer, she was charged with perjury in 1947 for supplying a false alibi for Mark Monroe and Thomas Sittler, who had been charged with assault with intent to commit robbery. She spent one year in the San Francisco County Jail for that offense. In 1951, she was arrested on suspicion of a narcotics violation, but was released the next day for lack of evidence. She had no record of violent offenses. She did, however, frequently associate with men who had records of violent crime.

MEDIA COVERAGE

Graham was an ideal subject for media coverage. In the 1950s, Los Angeles' five daily newspapers—the morning *Examiner* and *Times*; and the evening *Mirror, Herald-Express,* and *Daily News*—were all fiercely competing for readers, and crime stories were always popular. As a woman accused of murder in the course of a robbery—a "man's crime"—Graham's case was particularly attention-getting. The *Los Angeles Examiner* and *Los Angeles Herald-Express* were both owned by William Randolph Hearst, who reportedly favored crime stories involving women, especially when embellished by slangy tags. "Bloody Babs," a nickname reputedly derived from prosecutor Adolph Alexander's opening statement at trial, was one example. Graham was also tagged as the "icy blonde," with phrases like "icy-calm" and "stony" attached to descriptions of her courtroom demeanor. Santo and Perkins did not acquire popular nicknames.

Nichols (1990), in a detailed study of newspaper coverage of the Graham case, reviewed reportage in the five Los Angeles daily papers from Graham's arrest through her execution. He noted that all five papers failed to cover the story objectively, and that all tended to disregard legally significant developments in favor of speculative or sensational articles. This was particularly evident in three areas: (1) the constant emphasis on Graham's appearance, (2) the assumption that Graham was guilty, and (3) the focus on tangential, often lurid, aspects of Graham's personal life.

Appearance and Character

Two of the evening dailies, the *Los Angeles Mirror* and the *Los Angeles Herald-Express,* were well known for their sensational stories, bold headlines, and large photos. Graham's youth and attractiveness made her a better subject than the rather unprepossessing Santo and Perkins. This fact was to her disadvantage during the heated media coverage of the pretrial and trial phases.

In much of the trial's media coverage, Graham was portrayed as a true-crime vamp: callous and emotionless, overly concerned about her appearance, unremorseful, and deceitfully seductive. In one example, Graham's fall down a flight of stairs inspired a number of colorful articles. The *Los Angeles Mirror* used the headline "Bloody Babs' Falls; Delay in Monahan Murder Trial" (1953, August 19, p. 4); it also described how Graham "yawned and stretched languorously" during a description of the brutal murder, and how she "studied her lacquered fingernails" in court. In a follow-up, the *Los Angeles Herald-Express* (1953, August 20) reported that she was "resting easily, wisecracking and flippant . . . after falling down a flight of stairs and delaying her death penalty trial" (p. 2). A reader could easily infer that Graham was unremorseful, vain, and hardened; further, both articles imply that Graham staged her fall to delay the trial.

Graham's hair color was a topic of persistent interest, though it was alternately described as blonde, red, or brown. Graham was referred to as "golden-haired," "reddish-blond," a "bottle blonde," a "redhead," and, later, as a prim brunette. Reporters used her hair color, whether dark or light, to suggest Graham's bad character; she was either flashy and dishonest or "prim" and insincere. Her clothing, pallor, shoes, and weight all received media scrutiny. A single article in the *Los Angeles Herald-Express* (1953, September 1) included references to Graham's "strong hands," "shapely thigh," "bronzed [complexion]," and "tight-fitting summerweight suit," along with a comment that a specific plainly dressed female juror would probably not approve of Graham's clothing (pp. 1, 10).

Needless to say, the male co-defendants' hair color and clothing were rarely, if ever, noted. At the very least, the cumulative effect of all the media interest in Graham's physical appearance was to minimize reportage on Santo and Perkins. Further, it was a small step for the reader to assume that Graham was conducting herself with an inappropriate frivolousness, or attempting to use her good looks to sway the jury. The *Los Angeles Mirror* (1953, September 16) suggested exactly that in a headline that read "Babs Makes Goo-Goo Eyes at Jurors, D. A. Charges" (p. 2). The story actually referred to Deputy District Attorney Leavy's caution to the jury that "Mrs. Graham believes she can turn your heads," a statement that was rhetorical rather than literal.

Bias toward Guilt

Nichols (1990) notes that news stories tended to emphasize Graham's role in the crime. One article referred to Graham as the "key defendant" in the case (*The Los Angeles Herald-Express*, 1953, August 19, pp. 1, 4), a characterization never used by the prosecution or police. Headlines used terminology like "Execution of Barbara Graham, 2 Men Set Tomorrow" and "Barbara, Pals in San Quentin Death Cells Still Hope for 11th Hour Stay" (two examples from *The San Francisco Examiner*, 1955, June 3, pp. 1–2).

Preconviction news stories often displayed a bias toward guilt on Graham's part, failing to qualify statements with "allegedly" or other terms designed to reflect the presumption of innocence. In other instances, Graham was described as having "ducked" questions, implying that she was evasive. Some articles included claims that were utterly unsupported by evidence, as when one article described Graham as "standing unconcernedly by" while Monahan was garroted by Santo and Perkins (*Los Angeles Mirror*, 1953, August 19, p. 4).

Graham's Personal Life and "Sordid Past"

Los Angeles Times Reporter Gene Blake, interviewed in 1988 about the Graham case, discussed the constant pressure on reporters to find fresh angles for their stories, even if no new information was available (Nichols, 1990). While both Santo and Perkins had equally sordid pasts, as well as extensive and violent criminal records, Graham's past and personal life received far more attention.

Her life story was used as a cautionary tale. According to a vivid front-page article in the *Los Angeles Herald-Express* (1953, August 28),

[I]n the wreckage of Barbara Graham's past, littered with broken marriages, smashed hopes and three children . . . lay the story of how she faces the gas chamber today with icy composure. . . . [S]he easily slipped from truancy to highpowered crime. From various sources, including the reports of police and probation officers in San Francisco, where she has a considerable police record, the biography of a bawd who stumbled along the primrose path from being "very promiscuous sexually" to association with the "bigtime" crooks she so admired, can be developed in all its sorry detail. (p. 1)

Loaded terms like "highpowered crime," "considerable police record," "bawd," and "bigtime crooks" were statements of opinion, but they served to paint Graham as a thoroughly bad character who was about to receive her just desserts.

Other reportage downplayed fact in favor of opinion. In its trial coverage, the *Los Angeles Daily News* (1955, September 4) described "unfaithful wife Barbara Graham" as she "looked to her husband for forgiveness but blank-faced Henry Graham avoided her eyes" (p. 3). The story focused on the reporter's speculations about the Graham marriage and Barbara's guilty conscience, rather than the substance of Henry Graham's testimony. Graham's visitors also received coverage. She was photographed during visits with her youngest son, Tommy—placing her in a more sympathetic light, but also pointing out how especially reprehensible her conduct was for a young mother. Visitors seen by Santo and Perkins, including Perkins's son, were of no interest to reporters.

Did sensational newspaper coverage of the trial influence the jury? Graham raised the issue on appeal, as discussed below, without success.

IMPRISONMENT AND TRIAL

While awaiting trial in Los Angeles County Jail, Graham, who was bisexual, became involved in an intimate relationship with a fellow prisoner Donna Prow. Prow was serving a short sentence for vehicular manslaughter. Prow was approached by law enforcement with a deal to reduce her jail time in return for helping to obtain a confession from Graham. As instructed, she approached Graham with an offer of a false alibi, which would be provided by a friend of hers in exchange for $500. Graham, faced with True's testimony, felt desperate enough to seize the opportunity. Prow's supposed friend, actually an undercover police officer named Sam Sirianni, visited Graham in jail on three occasions to plan the alibi. Sirianni taped all of their conversations with a hidden recorder. They discussed the details of the alibi—that they had spent the night together in an Encino motel—to make it convincing. Graham made several incriminating statements during these conversations, including references to Shorter ("he's been done away with"), her need for the alibi ("without you as an alibi, I'm doomed to the gas chamber"), the date and time of the murder ("early in the morning of March 10" rather than the evening of March 9), and, most damningly, an admission that she had been with True, Santo, and Perkins "when everything took place." Prow's sentence was reduced to time served, and she was released from prison.

Graham and her codefendants pled not guilty at their joint trial, which began on August 14, 1953, and lasted five weeks. Police acted on reports that the defendants were part of a "crime mob" by taking extraordinary precautions at her trial. Armed guards were stationed in the courtroom to avert gangland reprisals directed at True or Upshaw, and spectators were searched before entering the courtroom.

True was the prosecution's star witness, but Sam Sirianni's testimony proved to be the most explosive. Apparently Sirianni's testimony as a prosecution witness was unexpected by Graham and her defense attorney Jack Hardy; Hardy moved to withdraw as Graham's attorney, but the court denied the motion. Sirianni testified to his conversations with Graham, reading from a transcription, and the tape recording of one of their exchanges was played in court. The impact of the tape recording was enormous; as attorney Hardy certainly knew, the damage to Graham's credibility was irreparable. In the closing argument, both Hardy and the attorney for Santo and Perkins, Ward Sullivan, denounced the "utterly ruthless" and "deceptive" manipulation of Graham.

Neither Santo nor Perkins took the stand during the trial. Graham, however, elected to testify. She admitted to knowing Santo and Perkins, but stated that she did not know Shorter or Upshaw. Moreover, she said that she had not been with any of them on March 9 and that she had gone along with Prow's plan out of desperation. The prosecution introduced some of the amorous notes exchanged by Graham and Prow, something Graham found particularly distressing. She now testified that she had been home with her husband and son on the night in question. However, the testimony of Henry Graham, a heroin addict, was both vague and contradictory.

The jury deliberated for less than five hours and returned guilty verdicts against all three defendants.

APPEALS AND EXECUTION

After Graham, Santo, and Perkins had been sentenced to death in the gas chamber, Graham met the press "with all the aplomb of a movie queen starring in a colossal production" (*Los Angeles Times*, 1953, September 25, p. 1). Her confidence would be badly shaken during her time leading up to her execution, and reporters began to refer frequently to her "frail" appearance. Graham also suffered from tooth and jaw pain, for which she was prescribed Demerol. Prison psychiatrists found Graham verbally facile, well oriented, of above-average intelligence, and thoroughly sane, though she was "not forthcoming" with them.

Graham was initially held at the State Institution for Women at Corona. She was moved from Corona to San Quentin on November 11, 1953, out of concern that attempts might be made on her life; a memorandum in her file also indicates that officials had received reports that someone might try to free her or even impregnate her via artificial insemination to delay her execution (Execution file, B. Graham). The expense of housing Graham at San Quentin and providing security for her became another hot topic for the media. Her cell was inaccurately described as "luxurious"; it was actually a small, improvised space in the prison hospital. She was returned to Corona on June 23, 1954, with the imminent threat deemed to have passed.

Santo, Perkins, and Graham appealed the trial court judgment and petitioned for a new trial on several grounds: that principal witness True's testimony was insufficiently corroborated, that prejudicial news coverage denied them a fair trial, and that the armed guards and searching of spectators were grounds for a mistrial or change of venue. In its August 11, 1954, opinion in *People v. Santo*, 43 Cal. 2d 319, the California Supreme Court held that the defendants' contentions were without merit. As to True's account, the court found that the testimony of Upshaw and Sirianni, and the evidence of flight on the part of the defendants—the moves that ended in Lynwood— corroborated True.

Further, the court rejected defendants' allegations regarding the effect of prejudicial news coverage. The court noted that (1) the parties had stipulated that no member of the district attorney's office had any part in the adverse publicity, (2) there was no evidence that the adverse news was given to the jury, and (3) the jury, having been admonished to disregard news reports on the case, was presumed to have heeded the court's directive. As to the other contentions, spectators were not searched in front of the jury, and the security precautions were within the trial judge's discretion. Graham alone contended that she should have received a separate trial, particularly because testimony was introduced at trial that was admissible against Santo or Perkins but inadmissible against her. Again, the California Supreme Court held that the trial judge had acted appropriately in admitting the testimony along with an instruction to the jury. The California Supreme Court affirmed the conviction and sentence of the defendants, and a petition for rehearing was denied on September 8, 1954.

Graham's case made its way through the federal courts as well. The United States Supreme Court denied the defendants' petition for *certiorari* (a writ of review) on March 7, 1955, without opinion. Her application for a writ of *habeas corpus* was denied on May 31, 1955, by the U.S. District Court for the Southern District of California.

The legal maneuvering continued until the last hours of Graham's life. On June 3, 1955, the U.S. Court of Appeals for the Ninth Circuit issued its opinion in *Graham v. Teets*, 223 F. 2d 680. Graham's appellate attorney, Al Matthews, argued that constitutional questions raised by the case had not been considered by the California Supreme Court, and thus the judicial remedies open to Graham had not been exhausted (a prerequisite to execution). However, the court noted that Matthews could have filed for a writ of *habeas corpus* in the California Supreme Court as early as March 7, 1955, the day the U.S. Supreme Court denied Graham's petition for *certiorari*. Instead, he waited until May 31 to file his application for the writ in the U.S. district court, where it was promptly denied. He petitioned the Ninth Circuit Court for a stay only on the afternoon of June 2, the day before the executions were scheduled. The Ninth Circuit chided Matthews, stating that "[b]y this purposeful device there is thrown on such federal judges as the writer the strain of hasty consideration of the contentions presented. . . . This I regard a gross misuse of the functions of an officer of the court." Nonetheless, the petition was denied.

Graham was returned to San Quentin on June 2, 1955, the day before her scheduled execution in the gas chamber. She was scheduled to die at 10 a.m. on June 3, but Governor Goodwin J. Knight's office stayed her execution twice, first setting the time back to 10:45 and then to 11:30. In the end he found no basis for executive clemency. Graham was quoted as saying, "Why do they torture me? I was ready to go at 10 o'clock." She wore a blindfold at her own request and thus did not make eye contact with spectators.

At least sixteen reporters were present at Graham's execution, and they again depicted her physical appearance in detail. "The brashly attractive 32-year-old convicted murderess, her bleached blond hair turned to its natural brown . . . walked to her death as if dressed for a shopping trip" (*Los Angeles Times*, 1955, June 5, p. 1). Even the blindfold Graham requested was treated as a fashion accessory in some accounts: "Her face was an ivory cameo accented by the mask [blindfold] and her rouged crimson lips" (*San Francisco Examiner*, 1955, June 4, p. 1); "the mask hid her tired eyes and she looked pretty in her beige suit" (*The San Francisco Chronicle*, 1955, June 4, p. 1). Her hands trembled, and "her small pendant earrings quivered nervously" (*The San Francisco Chronicle*, 1955, June 4, p. 1), but she retained her composure.

The pellets dropped at 11:34 a.m. Gene Blake of the *Los Angeles Times* reported that "it seemed an interminable time before death came. . . . She gasped and drew her head up twice. Then came another gasp. Then her head tipped far back, her mouth agape. Again and again she gasped until her head pitched forward for the last time at 11:37. Her gasps came slowly and fainter. And finally stopped" (*Los Angeles Times*, 1955, June 5, p. 1). Al Martinez, another journalist present at the event, wrote that Graham "gasped and strained against the straps that bound her . . . [f]oam bubbled at her mouth" (*Los Angeles Times*, 1990, March 31, p. 2). She died at 11:42 a.m. Graham's body was claimed by her husband Henry, and she was buried in the Roman Catholic cemetery in San Rafael.

Perkins and Santo were executed at 2:30 p.m. on the same day. They slept soundly, ate heartily, and joked irreverently as they went to the gas chamber (*San Francisco Examiner*, 1955, June 4).

CONSEQUENCES AND IMPLICATIONS

Graham's case raised several significant legal issues. Some newspapers described the reprieves and delays as uncivilized, products of a sadistic legal system that dangled last-minute hopes in front of the condemned woman, only to snatch them away. California Attorney General Edmund G. Brown, later governor, commented on what he called the "cat and mouse" game with Graham's life in her final days. According to Brown, "[t]he way the death penalty has been administered in California in the last two years is a disgrace to the administration of justice. The way the Graham woman was executed was a sad commentary on legal killing in California" (*San*

Francisco Examiner, 1955, June 5). Brown urged the abolition of the death penalty, or, barring that, a provision to reduce the time for disposition of appeals.

Graham's trial occurred well before the U.S. Supreme Court decisions on criminal procedure that protected suspects from coercive police tactics; for example, *Miranda v. Arizona*, 384 U.S. 436, was not decided until 1966. Coerced confessions—including those elicited by abuse, manipulation, or in violation of the accused's right to counsel—would be inadmissible by the mid-1960s. The use of the Sirianni testimony would probably have fallen into this category (Foster, 1997).

In March 1960, then-Governor Brown called the legislature into special session to consider a bill to suspend the death penalty. The next-to-last speaker was Deputy District Attorney J. Miller Leavy, who opposed the bill. In the course of his testimony, Leavy stated that he learned in 1959 that Barbara Graham had orally confessed to the murder of Mabel Monahan during a private conversation with San Quentin Warden Harley Teets. Leavy's bombshell served its intended purpose; the bill failed to pass by one vote. But was the confession story credible?

California Senate subcommittee hearings in 1960 were held to determine whether Graham had been deprived of due process by the prosecution's failure to turn over the transcript of True's original interrogation to the defense. The transcript apparently revealed variations from True's trial testimony, and could have been used to impeach him. Though it seemed hardly relevant, the hearings also included testimony related to the alleged Graham confession. According to Marin County District Attorney William Weissich, Teets (who died of a heart attack in 1957) made the statement as he and Weissich drove to San Quentin on August 30, 1957. Weissich did not reveal this information until 1959, when he was contacted by prosecutor Leavy in connection with a proposed book (later published as *The Case of Barbara Graham* in 1962). As the reporter's transcript of the 1960 hearings reveals, much effort was expended on determining when Graham could have spoken to Teets privately. The hearing's findings on this issue were inconclusive.

Was Graham, in fact, guilty? *San Francisco Chronicle* reporter Bernice Freeman Davis interviewed both Graham and True, and noted that "Barbara had been convicted largely on John True's testimony, and from my own experience I knew that he was careless with the truth." Davis believed that Graham was innocent of the attack on Monahan, but that she had been present during the crime. Graham was short, slender, and did not have a record of violent offenses; it seemed more likely that Santo or Perkins would have physically subdued Monahan (Davis and Hirschberg, 1962). Nonetheless, Graham was almost certainly a participant in planning and carrying out the robbery.

Edward Montgomery, reporter for the *San Francisco Examiner* and later proponent of Graham's innocence, first raised the argument that the left-handed Graham would not have pistol-whipped Monahan with her right hand, as described by True (Sub-committee hearing, 1960). On the same occasion, Montgomery recounted a conversation he had had with Emmett Perkins in prison. According to Montgomery, Perkins stated that Monahan was beaten with her own cane, rather than a gun. Moreover, he allegedly said that Santo had told him "we got to keep the girl out front," presumably because a jury would have difficulty sentencing a young mother to death and her codefendants would benefit by association.

LEGAL AND POPULAR SIGNIFICANCE

As noted above, Graham's trial and execution occurred at the beginning of an era of anti-death penalty activism. Both pro- and anti-capital punishment advocates used the case as an illustration, and its thirty-two-year-old female defendant continued to have media appeal.

Executions of women have tended to give rise to strong sentiments. The "chivalry thesis," which attributes a protective motive and a disbelief in female violence to society in general, is one explanation for the cultural reluctance to execute women. However, a corollary to the thesis is that when women are condemned, they are portrayed as inherently pathological, cunning, and unwomanly—a process of "othering" that allows society to make an exception (Keitner, 2002). This "evil woman" theory places the female defendant outside the definition of appropriately feminine conduct (Shapiro, 2000). Thus, executed women tend to display dominant personalities, seen both in their active participation in the crime and other evidence of aggressive and willful character traits (Carroll, 1997). Graham initiated the violent attack on Monahan and pistol-whipped the victim. Further, she used a ruse to enter Monahan's home and had a record of perjury. Graham's conduct was not simply brutal, but also deceitful. She was attractive and feminine, even demure, but she was revealed to be promiscuous and bisexual. She had a record of perjury and had attempted to buy an alibi. All of these factors made her an aberration, a member of the "unholy trio" (according to the prosecution's closing argument) and utterly unlike the rest of womankind.

Those who felt that Graham had been treated unfairly by the media and the criminal justice system found a vigorous advocate in reporter Edward Montgomery. He continued to be Graham's champion after her execution and successfully lobbied producer Walter Wanger to make a film version of Graham's case, resulting in the 1958 motion picture *I Want to Live!*

I Want to Live!, based on Montgomery's reportage, presents Graham as a streetwise woman who was also a caring mother and loyal friend. Her refusal to "finger" Santo and Perkins as the Monahan killers, while consistent with her personal code of honor, makes her a dupe for the self-serving True, police, and press. Critical reaction to the film was generally positive, and reviewers were impressed by the film's chilling depiction of the execution process and its indictment of capital punishment (*New York Times*, November 19 and 23, 1958). A paperback novelization of the film (Rawson, 1958) included stills from the movie and closely followed its script. It was advertised and promoted as the "true story" of the case.

The movie, in fact, fictionalized or omitted elements of Graham's life in its first half. She was portrayed as a devoted mother to her son Tommy, but her two other sons were not even mentioned. Nor were her first three marriages and her own narcotics use. Her movie arrest took place at night, with Graham stepping alone into the police spotlights; while the depiction had some allegorical truth to it, Graham was actually arrested along with her codefendants at 4 p.m. Edward Montgomery is shown working on the case before Graham's arrest, when he actually did not begin to report on it until the latter part of the trial. On the other hand, the second half of the movie, which concerns the time leading up to Graham's execution, was substantially accurate. Producer Wanger, a death penalty opponent, deliberately set out to show the bleak horror of the death chamber, and also chose to portray Graham sympathetically for maximum effectiveness (Nichols, 1990).

Not surprisingly, some viewers saw the film as propaganda cloaked in a pseudo-documentary style. To *Los Angeles Times* reporter Gene Blake, the film was neither "true" nor "factual" nor a "documentary" (*Los Angeles Times*, 1958, November 28). Bill Walker, a reporter for the *Los Angeles Herald-Express*, also remained convinced of Graham's guilt. In part as a rebuttal to the *I Want to Live!* movie and book, Walker collaborated with prosecutor J. Miller Leavy on *The Case of Barbara Graham*, a retelling that amasses the evidence against Graham. Leavy believed that there was no ambiguity in the case whatsoever. As he stated in 1990, "I didn't prosecute to deter. I prosecuted to punish. Sending her [Graham] to the gas chamber didn't bother me at all" (*Los Angeles Times*, 1990, March 31, p. 2). *The Case of Barbara Graham* provides an excellent chronology of events in the case and large portions of testimony, but it neglects any evidence that would cast doubt on the jury verdict. Since it was intended as a corrective to *I Want to Live!*, the authors are, unfortunately, equally partisan. Graham's case still awaits an objective full-length treatment. Many of the key figures in the case have died, including defense attorney Matthews in 1986, reporter Montgomery in 1992, Burbank police chief Rex Andrews in 1993, and prosecutor Leavy in 1995. The Graham case was referenced in each of their obituaries.

Barbara Graham has remained an intriguing figure in popular culture, though on a more modest scale. In the 1960s and 1970s, her case was included in true crime anthologies, where she again made for colorful and politically incorrect copy. For example, Miriam De Ford wrote, "weak, malleable, self-indulgent, and foolish she always was, but by the ordinary criteria she was as sane as the next stupid little girl with bad heredity and worse upbringing." A 1983 television movie, also called *I Want to Live* (sans exclamation point), retold her story sympathetically, but far less effectively than the original did. Death penalty studies continue to refer to her case and its procedural irregularities (e.g., Bedau and Radelet, 1987; Shipman, 2002). However, Graham's story is, first and foremost, a case study in the influential role of mass media in the criminal justice setting. Newspapers and reporters created the streetwise, loyal, and innocent Graham and the cold-hearted, duplicitous murderess; they were her biggest supporters and harshest accusers. They also ensured that Graham's case—and her elusive character—would retain a place in popular culture.

REFERENCES

Bedau, H. A., and Radelet, M. L. (1987). Miscarriages of justice in potentially capital cases. *Stanford Law Review, 40,* 21–173.

California Department of Corrections. (n.d.). Execution files [Barbara Graham, Emmett Perkins, John Santo]. Manuscript, California State Archives.

California Legislature, Assembly Interim Committee on Criminal Procedure. (1960). Sub-committee hearing re alleged discrepancies and suppression of evidence re Barbara Graham confession: Reporter's transcript of testimony and proceedings, March 21, 1960, Sacramento, California. Sacramento, CA: The Assembly.

Carroll, J. E. (1997, May). Images of women and capital sentencing among female offenders: Exploring the outer limits of the Eighth Amendment and articulated theories of justice. *Texas Law Review, 75,* 1413–1452.

Davis, B. F., and Hirschberg, A. (1962). *Assignment San Quentin.* London: Peter Davies.

De Ford, M. A. (1965). *Murderers sane and mad: Case histories in the motivation and rationale of murder.* New York: Abelard-Schuman.

Foster, T. E. (1997). I want to live! Federal judicial values in death penalty cases: Preservation of rights or punctuality of execution? *Oklahoma City University Law Review, 22*(1), 63–87.

Keitner, C. L. (2002). Victim or vamp? Images of violent women in the criminal justice system. *Columbia Journal of Gender and Law, 11,* 38–86.

Nichols, R. C. (1990). *Los Angeles newspaper coverage and dramatization of the Barbara Graham case.* Unpublished doctoral dissertation, California State University, Northridge.

Parrish, M. (2001). *For the people: Inside the Los Angeles County district attorney's office, 1850–2000.* Santa Monica, CA: Angel City Press.

Rawson, T. (1958). *I want to live!: The analysis of a murder.* New York: New American Library.

Shapiro, A. (2000). Unequal before the law: Men, women and the death penalty. *American University Journal of Gender, Social Policy and the Law, 8,* 427–470.

Shipman, M. (2002). *The penalty is death: U.S. newspaper coverage of women's executions.* Columbia, MO: University of Missouri Press.

Walker, B. (1961). *The case of Barbara Graham.* In collaboration with J. Miller Leavy. New York: Ballantine Books.

Wanger, W. (Producer), and Wise, R. (Director). (1958). *I want to live!* [Motion picture]. United States: MGM.

13

The Sam Sheppard Case:
Do Three Trials Equal Justice?

Kathy Warnes

My God, Spen, get over here quick! I think they've killed Marilyn!
(Neff, 2001, p. 7)

In the early morning hours of Sunday, July 4, 1954, someone stole into the bedroom of Marilyn Reese Sheppard, the pregnant wife of Dr. Samuel Holmes Sheppard, and beat her to death in her bed. In their lakeside home in Bay Village, a wealthy suburb of Cleveland, Ohio, her seven-year-old son Sam Reese Sheppard slept soundly in his bedroom next door, and her husband Sam slept on a couch in the living room. Dr. Sheppard wove together the events of the evening and early morning for the officials who answered his frantic call for help. He and his wife Marilyn had entertained their friends Don and Nancy Ahern at their home the previous evening. After dinner they watched television in the living room. Later that night, Dr. Sheppard fell asleep on the couch in the living room. For the next sixteen years, he told his story countless times of what happened when he woke up, never substantially changing it.

According to Dr. Samuel Sheppard, this is what happened on the morning of July 4, 1954: he was sleeping soundly on the couch when a noise on the second floor awakened him. He was not certain how much time had elapsed from the time he dozed off until he heard the noises upstairs, but he awoke when he heard Marilyn screaming and calling for him to help her, then loud moans and noises. He thought that Marilyn might be having the same painful convulsions that she had experienced during her first pregnancy.

Still half asleep, Sheppard jumped off the couch and rushed upstairs. All the lights were out except a forty-watt bulb in the upstairs dressing room, but as he entered the bedroom he saw a "white form" standing next to the bed where his wife slept. He could not tell whether the shadowy figure was a man or woman, and he did not know how many people were in the room. He started to wrestle with the form, but suddenly someone hit him from behind on the back of his neck and skull and he lost consciousness. He did not know how long he was unconscious.

Dr. Sheppard woke up on the floor beside Marilyn's bed, injured and groggy. He inched himself into a sitting position facing the bedroom door. He saw his wife lying in a pool of blood on her twin bed, beaten and battered on the head and face. She had no pulse and showed no signs of life when he examined her. The doctor ran into their son's bedroom next door and assured himself that his son was sound asleep and unharmed. Then he heard a noise on the first floor and ran down the stairs. He chased what he described as "a large, powerfully built man with a good sized head and bushy hair" through the screen door and down the thirty-six steps to the beach. He attacked the man, but the man caught him in a stranglehold and choked, hit, and knocked him unconscious for a second time, again for an uncertain amount of time.

The next thing Sam Sheppard remembered was regaining consciousness at the water's edge, his head on the shore, legs in the water and his body swaying back and forth in the waves. Staggering back to the house, he went upstairs to re-examine the body of his murdered wife. In his dazed state he thought that this might be some horrible nightmare. Then he went downstairs and called his neighbor and friend, Bay Village Mayor Spencer Houk. He shouted, "My God, Spen get over here quick. I think they've killed Marilyn!" (Neff, 2001, p. 7).

Mayor Houk and his wife, Esther, found Dr. Sheppard hunched in an easy chair in the first floor den. He implored them to do something for Marilyn. Esther Houk went upstairs to the northwest bedroom where she discovered the battered body of Marilyn Sheppard. Marilyn lay face up on the bed, her legs hanging over the foot of the bed, bent at the knees and her feet dangling a few inches above the rug. Blood outlined her body, and blood from her head darkened the quilt, the sheets, and the pillow. Blotches of blood sprinkled the wall, and drops of blood trailed across the carpet and out the door. Her face was turned slightly toward the door and was coated with stringy, clotting blood. About two dozen deep, crescent-shaped gashes scoured her face, forehead, and scalp.

Someone had pushed up Marilyn's three-button pajama top to her neck, leaving her breasts bare. A blanket covered her middle. Her thin pajama bottoms had been removed from one leg and were bunched below the knee of her other leg, exposing her lower body. Esther Houk checked Marilyn's pulse. She didn't feel one.

Mayor Houk called the Bay Village police, Sheppard's brother, Dr. Richard Sheppard, and Don and Nancy Ahern. The local police, including Bay Village patrolman Fred Drenkham, arrived at the Sheppard home. Police officers, relatives, the press, and neighbors trooped through the house. Local police notified Cuyahoga County Coroner Dr. Samuel Gerber and the Cleveland police. Then, Dr. Richard Sheppard arrived, examined Marilyn, and declared that she was dead. He assessed his brother's injuries and took him to Bay View Hospital, which was operated by his family of osteopathic doctors. Conflicting medical reports about Dr. Samuel Sheppard's injuries exacerbated the tensions between osteopathic and medical doctors that existed in the 1950s. Dr. Samuel Gerber and other medical doctors were incensed that osteopaths like the Sheppards performed surgery, prescribed drugs, and competed with allopathic, or traditional, physicians. Gerber felt that osteopaths were bone twisters, a species of inferior doctors, a position that the powerful American Medical Association echoed. The American Medical Association under its bylaws refused to let its member doctors teach at osteopathic medical schools, consult for an osteopath on a patient's care, or even share a common waiting room, and as a result the two branches of medicine did not trust each other. Dr. Gerber mistrusted the Sheppards, their osteopathic training, and their osteopathic hospital; but at this point, Dr. Richard Sheppard managed to care for his injured brother. He also drove his nephew, seven-year-old Sam Reese Sheppard, to his house.

Sam Reese Sheppard remembered that morning. "It's kind of a frozen moment in time. I remember being kind of pushed awake by Uncle Richard, and I was told I didn't have time to get dressed—I was in my pajamas" (Taylor, 1996). A policeman blocked his view into his parents' bedroom. Around him swarmed police officers, coroner's deputies, and jittery relatives. Reporters shouted questions and flashbulbs popped. Sam Reese Sheppard said, "I walked out the back door and down toward the road. There was a clutch of curiosity-seekers and also the press. The flashbulbs started going off in my face. I remember it to this day—the curious murmur of the crowd" (Taylor, 1996).

The crowd still milled around the Sheppard house as Coroner Gerber, the Cleveland police, and other officials arrived. They thoroughly searched the house and surrounding area, taking note of the ransacked living room, the empty medical bag with contents strewn over the floor, and the open desk drawers. They photographed the rooms of the house and interrogated several people, including the Houks and the Aherns. The police sealed the Sheppard home and closed it off to Dr. Sheppard and his family.

From the first moment the police answered the call to the Sheppard home, they suspected Dr. Sam Sheppard of being the murderer. They investigated the case on the theory that Dr. Sheppard had bludgeoned his wife to death, washed the blood off his clothing in the lake, faked his injuries, staged a burglary attempt to deflect suspicion from himself, and delayed calling the authorities to gain time to conceal the evidence. As far as they were concerned, Dr. Sheppard's story of fighting with a bushy-haired intruder was an attempt to cover his guilt. This was the official theory that the Cleveland authorities leaked to the press and the official version of the crime that the state presented at the trial. The authorities did not produce any concrete proof to support this theory.

On the morning of the murder after searching the Sheppard house and premises, the coroner, Dr. Sam Gerber, is reported to have told his men, "Well, it is evident the doctor did this, so let's go get the confession out of him." The coroner never denied saying this to his staff. Dr. Gerber questioned and examined Sam Sheppard while he was under sedation in his hospital room. During the interrogation, the police gave Coroner Gerber the clothes that Sheppard wore the night of the murder, including the personal items found in them (Pollack, 1972, p. 11).

Dr. E. H. Hexter, a Bay Village medical doctor, examined Sam Sheppard that evening at the hospital. Dr. Hexter reported that Sheppard had missing reflexes on his left side, but did not give his finding much weight. He told Dr. Gerber and the detectives that "the only outward injury" he could find was "swelling around the right eye and cheek." The police used his diagnosis to discount Sheppard's story of a "bushy haired intruder." The police also had Dr. Charles Elkins, a noted neurologist, examine Dr. Sheppard. Dr. Elkins found "serious damage to the spinal cord in the neck region, bruises on the right side of his face and lacerations to the mouth." The extent of his injuries and whether or not they could have been self-inflicted were to play an important part in Dr. Sheppard's trial (Pollack, 1972, p. 28).

On July 7, 1954, Marilyn Sheppard was buried in a private ceremony at the Saxton Funeral Home in the suburb of Lakewood. About 250 of Sam and Marilyn Sheppard's friends and family attended the service. The doctor came in a wheelchair, his neck wrapped in a stiff orthopedic collar. He walked in, wearing a suit with no tie, his eyes shaded with dark sunglasses. Their son, Sam Reese, or Chip, did not attend the funeral because of extensive media coverage, but he had picked some pansies for his mother. Weeping, Dr. Sheppard placed the pansies inside the casket.

The police searched the Sheppard house again during the funeral. Bay View Mayor Spencer Houk had officially turned the investigation over to Coroner Gerber and the county sheriff, and detectives had found some additional pieces of physical evidence during this search of the Sheppard house. Near Marilyn Sheppard's bed they found a small piece of leather and a chip of red paint or enamel. The front pages of the newspapers shouted, "Search Murder Home Again" and "Dr. Sheppard Weeps Beside Coffin of Wife" (*Cleveland News*, 1954, July 16).

A July 7 story in another newspaper featured assistant Cuyahoga County attorney John Mahon sharply criticizing the Sheppard family's refusal to permit the doctor's immediate questioning. From the day of Marilyn Sheppard's funeral on, headline stories, especially in the *Cleveland Press*, repeatedly hammered Sheppard's lack of cooperation with the police and other officials. The newspapers also played up Sheppard's refusal to take a lie detector test and decried "the protective ring" thrown up by his family. Front-page newspaper headlines announced that "Doctor Balks at Lie Test; Retells Story" (*Cleveland Press*, 1954, August 1).

On July 20, 1954, the "editorial front" of the campaign against Dr. Sam Sheppard fired its first salvo with the front-page charge that somebody was "getting away with murder." The editorial charged that the investigation into Marilyn Sheppard's death had been inept because of "friendships, relationships, hired lawyers, a husband who ought to have been subjected instantly to the same third degree to which any other person under similar circumstances is subjected." On July 21, another page one editorial demanded, "Why No Inquest? Do It Now, Dr. Gerber" (*Cleveland Press*, 1954).

The coroner announced on that same day that an inquest would be convened and subpoenaed Dr. Sheppard. The inquest was held the next day in a school gymnasium with Dr. Gerber presiding, and the county prosecutor as his advisor and two detectives as bailiffs. Reporters, television and radio personnel, and broadcasting equipment occupied a long table in the front of the room. The hearing was broadcast live with microphones at the coroner's seat and the witness stand. Police brought Dr. Sheppard into the room and searched him in full view of several hundred people. His counsel was present during the three-day inquest, but was not permitted to participate. When Dr. Sheppard's chief counsel tried to put some documents in the record, the coroner threw him out of the room to the accompaniment of cheers, hugs, and kisses from ladies in the audience. Various officials questioned Dr. Sheppard for five and a half hours about his actions on the night of the murder, his married life, and an affair with a laboratory technician, Susan Hayes.

The newspapers continued to stress the evidence that incriminated Dr. Sheppard and touted discrepancies in his statements to authorities. During the inquest on July 26, a large-type headline in the *Cleveland Press* blared: "Kerr [Captain of the Cleveland Police] Urges Sheppard's Arrest." The story said that Detective James McArthur "disclosed that scientific tests at the Sheppard home have definitely established that the killer washed off a trail of blood from the murder bedroom to the downstairs section," a circumstance casting doubt on Sheppard's accounts of the murder. This evidence was not presented at the trial (*Cleveland Press*, 1954, July 25).

The *Cleveland Press* and the *Cleveland Plain Dealer* also spotlighted Dr. Sheppard's personal life, citing his extramarital affairs as a motive for killing his wife. A July 28 editorial in the *Cleveland Press* asked, "Why Don't Police Quiz Top Suspect?" and demanded that Dr. Sheppard be taken to police headquarters. It described Dr. Sheppard in this way:

Now proved under oath to be a liar, still free to go about his business, shielded by his family, protected by a smart lawyer who has made monkeys of the police and authorities, carrying a gun part of the time, left free to do whatever he pleases. (*Cleveland Press*, 1954)

On July 30, 1954, a front-page editorial wondered "Why Isn't Sam Sheppard in Jail?" After calling Dr. Sheppard "the most unusual murder suspect ever seen around these parts," the editorial said that "except for some superficial questioning during Coroner Sam Gerber's inquest he has been scot-free of any official grilling." It concluded by charging that Dr. Sheppard was surrounded "by an iron curtain of protection and concealment" (*Cleveland Press*, 1954).

On the night of July 30, 1954, the Cleveland police arrested Dr. Sam Sheppard at his father's home and charged him with murder. They took him to the Bay Village City Hall where hundreds of people, newscasters, photographers, and reporters awaited his arrival. They immediately arraigned him and bound him over to the grand jury.

Publicity continued to escalate until Dr. Sheppard's indictment on August 17, 1954. Typical headlines during this period included "Dr. Sam: I Wish There Was Something I Could Get off My Chest—But There Isn't," "Corrigan Tactics Stall Quizzing," "Sheppard 'Gay Set' Is Revealed by Houk," "Blood Is Found in Garage," "New Murder Evidence Is Found, Police Claim" and "Dr. Sam Faces Quiz at Jail on Marilyn's Fear of Him." There are five volumes filled with similar clippings from each of the three

Cleveland newspapers, the *Cleveland Press*, the *Cleveland Plain Dealer*, and the *Cleveland News*, covering the period from the murder until Dr. Sheppard's conviction in December 1954 ("Findings of U.S. Supreme Court").

One of the few stories favorable to Dr. Sheppard appeared on August 18 under the headline "Dr. Sam Writes His Own Story." A portion of the typed statement signed by Dr. Sheppard was reproduced across the entire front page. It read in part, "I am not guilty of the murder of my wife, Marilyn. How could I, who have been trained to help people and devoted my life to saving life, commit such a terrible and revolting crime?" (*Cleveland Press*, 1954).

It seemed that most local law enforcement officials and many ordinary citizens felt that Dr. Sheppard could commit "such a terrible and revolting crime," because on August 17, 1954, he was indicted for murder. He would not enjoy another day of freedom for nearly ten years.

THE FIRST TRIAL

From August 17, 1954, the day of his indictment, to October 28, 1954, the first day of his trial, the print and broadcast media of Cleveland tried and convicted Dr. Sam Sheppard many times over. On October 9, 1954, a newspaper editorial criticized defense counsel William Joseph Corrigan's poll of the public to show local bias for a change of venue motion.

Twenty-five days before the trial began, seventy-five people were called as prospective jurors. Jury selection began on October 18, 1954. All three Cleveland newspapers published the names and addresses of the prospective jurors, and many of them received anonymous letters and telephone calls about the prosecution of Dr. Sheppard. Jurors were not sequestered during the trial, and the newspapers printed their names and photos more than forty times. Jurors were not queried about the media accounts they had heard, and trial transcripts were printed regularly. Police, prosecutors, witnesses, and the families of the judge and jurors gave interviews and appeared on camera.

The news media had constant access to the jurors. Every juror except one admitted to reading about the case in the Cleveland papers or having heard broadcasts about it. Seven of the twelve jurors rendering the verdict had one or more Cleveland papers delivered to their homes.

A radio debate broadcast live over WHK on October 19 featured reporters accusing Dr. Sheppard of trying to block the prosecution and asserting that he conceded his guilt by hiring a prominent criminal lawyer. Dr. Sheppard's counsel objected to this broadcast and requested a continuance, but the judge denied the motion. When counsel asked the court to give some protection from such happenings, Judge Edward Blythin replied, "WHK doesn't have much coverage. After all, we are not trying this case by radio or in newspapers or any other means. We confine ourselves seriously to it in this courtroom and do the very best we can" ("Findings of U.S. Supreme Court").

A newspaper headline on October 23, 1954, plaintively asked, "But Who Will Speak for Marilyn?" and called for "Justice to Sam Sheppard." The front-page story focused on the family of the accused. The two brothers of Dr. Sheppard were described as "prosperous and poised." His two sisters-in-law were characterized as smart, chic, and well groomed; his elderly father as courtly and reserved. The newspaper report then noted that Marilyn Sheppard's mother had died when she was very young and that her father had no interest in her murder case. Through quotes from Detective Chief James McArthur, the reporter assured readers that the exhibits of the prosecution would speak for Marilyn. McArthur stated, "[H]er story will come into this courtroom through our witnesses." The story concludes, "Then you realize how what and who is missing from the perfect setting will be supplied. How in the Big Case justice will be done. Justice to Sam Sheppard. And to Marilyn Sheppard" (*Cleveland Press*, 1954).

The intense publicity surrounding the Sheppard case continued into the trial. The trial of Dr. Samuel Holmes Sheppard began on October 28, 1954. Assistant County Prosecutor John Mahon sat on one side of the trial table, along with his assistants Saul Danaceau and Thomas Parrino. Assistant Prosecutor Mahon faced an election for a judgeship in three weeks. His two assistants later would use their public renown from the trial to win their own judgeships. The defense side of the table included Fred Garmone; Arthur Petersilge, the Sheppard family lawyer; and William J. Corrigan Jr. Judge Edward J. Blythin had a reputation as a cautious and patient judge, but he, too, faced voters for re-election in three weeks.

On this first day of the trial, the jury visited the Sheppard home. Hundreds of reporters, cameramen, and onlookers went along with them. The time of the jury's visit was revealed so far in advance that one of the newspapers had time to rent a helicopter and fly over the house, taking pictures of the jury tour.

The newspapers had access to a daily record of the court proceedings, and the testimony of each witness was printed verbatim in the local editions of the newspapers, along with objections of counsel and rulings by the judge. Pictures of Dr. Sheppard, Judge Blythin, counsel, pertinent witnesses, and the jury accompanied the newspaper and television accounts.

Trial testimony proved to be as damaging and controversial to the Sheppard case as the media coverage. Deputy Coroner Lester Adelson described Marilyn Sheppard's autopsy and showed pictures of her death scene and battered face. Defense Attorney Corrigan forced Adelson to admit that he had not analyzed her stomach contents, had made no microscopic study of the wounds, and did not test for possible rape.

Don and Nancy Ahern, and Spencer and Esther Houk, testified that the Sheppards had been having marital difficulties. Dr. Lester Hoverston, a college classmate of Sam and Marilyn who had been their houseguest in early July but was in Akron the night of the murder, testified that Dr. Sheppard had told him that he was considering divorcing Marilyn.

Appearing as an uncontested expert, Cuyahoga County Coroner Dr. Sam Gerber decried what he termed the Sheppard family's lack of cooperation, and described the bloody pillowcase from the murder bed in graphic detail. Dr. Gerber said that he could make out the impression of a surgical instrument in the bloodstain. He did not go into detail about the type of surgical instrument or produce it, but he insisted that the murder weapon could only be a surgical instrument.

Detective Michael Grabowski of the Scientific Investigation Unit and Mary Cowan, the coroner's chief medical technologist, testified about the physical evidence, describing their scientific tests in detail. The prosecution did not dwell on the fact that Mary Cowan testified that she had found seven human blood spots in the downstairs and basement of the Sheppard house but could not type them as Sam or Marilyn's blood. The prosecution argued that the seven spots were Dr. Sheppard's blood trail.

Mary Cowan conceded that her findings of the blood types on the wristwatches of Sam and Marilyn were not definitive. On Marilyn's wristwatch she had found Marilyn and Sam's blood and also a third, unidentified blood factor. The card recording these findings mysteriously disappeared during the trial and did not surface until the Ohio Supreme Court reviewed the case a year later. She also admitted that the bloodstains on Sam Sheppard's trousers were inconclusive. The entire body of blood evidence seemed to confuse everyone involved in the trial, including the judge, jury, prosecution, and defense.

But laboratory technician Susan Hayes, not blood evidence or Coroner Gerber, turned out to be the star witness at the trial. Ms. Hayes testified that she and Dr. Sam Sheppard had engaged in a long-term affair, directly contradicting his denials of their relationship and seriously undermining his credibility.

Outside of the courtroom, the media onslaught continued. On November 21, 1954, in a radio broadcast on station WHK in Cleveland, nationally known commentator Robert Considine labeled Dr. Sam Sheppard a perjurer. Dr. Sheppard's defense counsel asked Judge Blythin to question the jury to find out how many of them may have heard the broadcast, but Judge Blythin did not do so. He also overruled the motion for continuance based on the same ground, saying, "We are not going to harass the jury every morning. . . . I have confidence in this jury" ("Findings of U.S. Supreme Court").

On November 24, 1954, a Cleveland Press newspaper headline announced, "Sam Called a 'Jekyll-Hyde' by Marilyn, Cousin to Testify." The story said that Marilyn Sheppard had recently told friends that Sheppard was a "Dr. Jekyll and Mr. Hyde" character and the prosecution had a witness in the wings to testify to Dr. Sheppard's fiery temper, countering the defense claim that the defendant was a gentle physician with an even disposition. William Joseph Corrigan, the defense counsel, made motions for change of venue, continuance, and mistrial, but they were denied. Judge Blythin took no action, and no such testimony was ever presented.

In November 1954, when the trial was in its seventh week, Walter Winchell, a national broadcaster, reported over WXEL television and WJW radio that a woman named Carole Beasley, who was under arrest in New York City for robbery, claimed that she was Dr. Sheppard's mistress and had an illegitimate child by him. Two jurors admitted that they had heard the broadcast, but Judge Blythin took no action.

On December 9, 1954, Dr. Sam Sheppard testified that Cleveland detectives had mistreated him after his arrest. Although he was not at the trial, Captain David Kerr of the homicide bureau issued a press statement denying Sheppard's charges. The statement appeared under a headline calling Dr. Sheppard a "barefaced liar" ("Findings of U.S. Supreme Court").

Testimony at the trial ended on December 16, 1954, and the jury was sequestered for the first time on December 17. The jury deliberated from December 17–21, for five days and four nights. On December 21, the jury returned with a verdict of murder in the second degree. After the verdict was announced, defense counsel William J. Corrigan discovered that the jurors had been allowed to make telephone calls to their homes every day while they were sequestered in their hotel rooms. The judge had not instructed the bailiffs to prevent such calls. Defense counsel Corrigan moved that this ground alone warranted a new trial, but the judge overruled the motion and took no evidence on the question. Although Corrigan objected, Judge Blythin passed immediate sentence upon Dr. Sam Sheppard: life in prison.

The local and national media had obviously overstepped any bounds of objectivity and tried and convicted Dr. Sheppard before the jury did. Law enforcement officials contributed much to this conviction by contaminating the crime scene and handling the evidence incompetently. Many of the people who believed Dr. Samuel Holmes Sheppard guilty of murdering his wife Marilyn considered him a spoiled rich kid and a womanizer. He had conducted at least one adulterous affair with a laboratory technician at Bay

View Hospital and slept with her at the home of a colleague, as the prosecution proved without a doubt at his trial. A few witnesses had come forward suggesting that Marilyn Sheppard, in her turn, had at least one affair and that an outraged wife had murdered her. But the officials pressing for Dr. Sheppard's conviction prevailed.

As the U.S. Supreme Court was to point out a decade later, the prosecution errors were glaringly obvious, but the defense also made some serious mistakes that helped convict Dr. Sheppard. One of the most serious defense errors was not obtaining its own expert to examine the Sheppard house. Even though Sheppard family members charged that the police refused to turn over the keys, the defense never asked to conduct an examination. The defense also did not vigorously challenge Dr. Sam Gerber's claim that the bloody imprint on Marilyn's pillow came from a surgical instrument, and the defense could have denounced the trial as a circus, as the U.S. Supreme Court would later do, and advised Dr. Sheppard to claim his Fifth Amendment right to be silent.

Dr. Stephen Sheppard kept his brother from the press and alienated reporters, making the theory of a Sheppard family conspiracy to get away with murder appear plausible. The defense did not use the media in its favor as F. Lee Bailey, the lawyer who would ultimately free Sam Sheppard, did.

But Dr. Sam Sheppard delivered the most damaging blow to his defense himself. He lied at the inquest, denying his affair with Susan Hayes. One newspaperman accurately summarized the trial when he said that Dr. Sheppard was tried for murder and convicted by adultery.

INTERLUDE AND THE SECOND TRIAL

The next twelve years brought great tragedy, great hope, and finally, freedom to Dr. Sam Sheppard. After he spent Christmas of 1954 in the county jail, he got the news that on January 7, 1955, his mother, Ethel Sheppard, had committed suicide. Eleven days later, Dr. Richard Sheppard, his father, died of a hemorrhaging ulcer and stomach cancer. In the meantime, William Corrigan presented a brief petition for a new trial, the first in a dozen unsuccessful tries to overturn the Sheppard conviction.

In March 1955, in preparation for the appeal, the defense hired Dr. Paul Leland Kirk, a criminalist. He visited the Sheppard home and submitted a fifty-six-page report to William Corrigan in which he demonstrated that the blood evidence at the scene of Marilyn Sheppard's murder proved the presence of a third person at the scene, and the pattern of blood spatters proved that Dr. Sheppard could not have been the murderer because he was right-handed and a left-handed person had killed Marilyn.

On July 13, 1955, the state court of appeals rejected Dr. Sheppard's appeal, and that summer he was moved from jail in Cleveland to a maximum-security prison near Columbus, Ohio. William Corrigan continued to file appeals, including one to the Ohio Supreme Court in 1956. In November 1956, the U.S. Supreme Court refused to hear the Sheppard case. William Corrigan continued to appeal the case unsuccessfully.

In the meantime, books about the Sheppard case began to appear. In 1956, Louis B. Seltzer, editor of the *Cleveland Press*, published his autobiography, *The Years Were Good*. In his book, he devoted chapter 26 to discussing the Sheppard murder case and why he wrote a series of front-page editorials alleging that the Sheppard family was engaged in a conspiracy to get away with murder. Seltzer wrote,

I was convinced that a conspiracy existed to defeat the ends of justice, and that it would affect adversely the whole law-enforcement machinery of the county if it were permitted to succeed. Because I did not want anyone else on the press staff to take the risk, I wrote the editorial myself. (Seltzer, 1956)

In 1961, Paul Holmes, a reporter and lawyer who had covered the trial for the *Chicago Tribune*, wrote the pioneer book about the case, *The Sheppard Murder Case*. In the first two-thirds of the book, he wrote a balanced account of the trial; and in the last third, he theorized what had really happened the morning of July 4, 1954. After covering the trial and after reading Dr. Kirk's report, Paul Holmes concluded that Dr. Sheppard did not and could not have killed his wife, but was the victim of a propaganda war. He theorized that a man and a woman were the perpetrators and said, "I think the whole business robbed luster from American jurisprudence, and is, in its more literal and reverent sense, a God-damned shame" (Holmes, 1961, p. 78).

Dr. Stephen Sheppard wrote his account of the ordeal in 1964 with the help of Paul Holmes. He called his book *My Brother's Keeper* and included a three-page epilogue about Judge Carl Wienman's district court ruling. In 1966, Paul Holmes wrote a sequel to *The Sheppard Murder Case*, which he called *Retrial: Murder and Dr. Sam Sheppard*. The sequel was rushed into print within weeks of the verdict, and only eighty-eight of the 240 pages were devoted to the second trial. At least fifty pages were the transcripts of testimony by Mary Cowan and Dr. Kirk.

The name of a possible suspect in the murder surfaced in November 1959, when a window washer named Richard Eberling was arrested for stealing from customers. The stolen items he had in his possession included Marilyn Sheppard's ring. He had stolen the ring from Marilyn's sister-in-law, who had received it after her death. When police questioned him, Eberling told them that he had washed Sam and Marilyn Sheppard's windows days before the murder. While he did this, he had cut his finger and dripped blood down the stairs to the basement, where he washed the cut.

The Bay Village police took his statement to John T. Corrigan, the county prosecutor (no relation to William J. Corrigan, the defense lawyer), but John Corrigan displayed little interest in the information. The police relayed the information to Cuyahoga County Coroner Sam Gerber, who said he would have Richard Eberling take a lie detector test, but then he changed his mind. The information lay dormant for thirty years.

Deaths of the some of the key players in the Sheppard murder case continued throughout the years that Sam Sheppard spent in prison. In 1958, Judge Edward Blythin died; and on February 13, 1963, Thomas Reese, father of Marilyn Sheppard, committed suicide. In July 1961, William Corrigan, the original defense attorney for Dr. Sheppard, died, paving the way for F. Lee Bailey to take over the defense. On April 13, 1963, F. Lee Bailey filed a new *habeas corpus* petition in U.S. district court. On July 16, 1964, federal district court Judge Carl Weinman ruled that Dr. Sheppard had been denied a fair trial, and he was released from prison. In May 1965, an appeals court voted two to one to reverse Judge Weinman's decision, but on June 6, 1966, the U.S. Supreme Court agreed with Judge Weinman, ruling that the Sheppard trial had been a "carnival" and that Sheppard was denied a fair trial because the judge failed to control the courtroom atmosphere and prevent jury bias from excessive media coverage.

Dr. Sam Sheppard's second trial began on October 24, 1966, and the new judge immediately sequestered the jury. He also severely limited media access to the courtroom. F. Lee Bailey had intended to introduce evidence to support his belief that Dr. Sheppard's neighbors, Spencer and Esther Houk, were the real murderers, but his attempts to introduce this evidence were suppressed. But, Bailey proved to be an effective cross-examiner. He got Coroner Gerber to admit that he could not describe which "surgical instrument" had made a blood imprint on Marilyn Sheppard's pillowcase. He also forced Coroner Gerber to acknowledge that he had never found the surgical instrument. This admission negated the effect of his impressive testimony during the first trial. Some of the mistakes that the police had made during the original investigation came out in this trial, including missing evidence. A cigarette butt found on the scene had disappeared, and there had been no exam for evidence of rape. The defense rested without calling Sam Sheppard to testify on his own behalf. All the prosecution could do was make the rest of its case against Dr. Sheppard by the strength of its closing arguments. The strategy did not work.

Verdict and Aftermath

On November 16, 1966, the jury found Dr. Sheppard not guilty "beyond a reasonable doubt." After spending ten years in prison and two years undergoing a second trial, Dr. Sam Sheppard attempted to pick up the strands of his life and forge ahead, but the ghosts of the past haunted him for the rest of his life. He married Ariane Tebbenjohanns in July 1964, when he was released from prison, but they divorced in December 1968. He drank heavily, and his attempts to resume his medical career resulted in malpractice suits. In 1969, after trying to return to medicine, Sheppard took up team wrestling and married Colleen Strickland. Four years after being declared not guilty in his second malpractice trial, Sam Sheppard died on April 6, 1970, of liver failure at the age of forty-six.

Two more books about the Sheppard murder case appeared in the 1970s. F. Lee Bailey published *The Defense Never Rests* in 1971, in which he admitted that he had not allowed Dr. Sheppard to testify during his second trial because the doctor was often incoherent from alcohol and drugs. Jack Harrison Pollack published *Dr. Sam: An American Tragedy* in 1972. Pollack became interested in the Sheppard case after he wrote a sympathetic article about Dr. Sheppard before he was freed. His book is a straightforward, objective account of the story, with sixteen pages of photographs and an index.

The 1980s marked the deaths of four more principals in the Sheppard murder case. Spencer and Esther Houk, who were divorced in 1962, died in 1981 and 1982, respectively; and Dr. Sam Gerber, Cuyahoga County coroner, died in 1987.

In 1989, Richard Eberling was convicted of aggravated murder in the death of Ethel May Durkin, an elderly widow, who died on January 3, 1984, after being hospitalized six weeks from a fall in her home. In October 1989, Sam Reese Sheppard began his attempts to solve the murder of his mother, Marilyn Sheppard, and to speak out publicly about his family's ordeal. Not content to have his father declared merely "not guilty," he wanted him to be declared innocent, a legal distinction in Ohio that would forever clear his father's name and possibly open the way for Sam Reese to sue the state of Ohio for damages.

THIRD TRIAL

In March 1990, Sam Reese Sheppard met Richard Eberling at the Lebanon Correctional Institution in Ohio. In 1991, John Corrigan retired as county prosecutor and Stephanie Tubbs replaced him, and in 1992 police records and evidence from the Marilyn Sheppard murder were released. Ironically, the focus of Dr. Sam Sheppard's third trial again rested on blood evidence.

Blood samples taken at the crime scene forty years earlier still existed, and some of the blood did not belong to either Sam or Marilyn Sheppard. Sam Reese decided to use modern DNA technology to find the third blood factor.

In October 1995, Sheppard and his attorney, Terry Gilbert, filed a wrongful imprisonment action asking the Cuyahoga County Common Pleas Court to formally declare Dr. Sheppard innocent. In February 1996, Terry Gilbert won a court order for Richard Eberling to provide blood samples for DNA testing, and in February 1997, DNA tests performed by Dr. Mohammad Tahir revealed that Eberling could not be ruled out as a match for bloodstains from Dr. Sheppard's pants, the wardrobe door, a wood chip from a basement stair, and a stain on the back porch. Dr. Tahir said that Eberling also could not be ruled out as the source of DNA found on two vaginal swabs taken during Marilyn Sheppard's autopsy. He could not say for certain that Eberling was there, only that there was a consistent pattern similar to Eberling's DNA.

In March 1998, Cleveland prosecutors refused to reopen the investigation into the slaying of Marilyn Sheppard despite new DNA tests that her son's defense lawyers said would clear Dr. Sheppard of the 1954 murder. Cuyahoga County Prosecutor Stephanie Tubbs Jones said that the DNA evidence would be inadmissible in court because the tests had been run on contaminated, forty-four-year-old samples. On July 25, 1998, Richard Eberling died in prison at the age of sixty-eight.

Sam Reese Sheppard's civil suit opened on February 14, 2000. Sam Reese Sheppard and Sheppard estate lawyer Terry Gilbert sued the state of Ohio for $2 million dollars in damages and to clear Dr. Sam Sheppard's name. The defendant, the state of Ohio, presented expert witnesses who argued that the blood samples were too old and contaminated. They insisted that the state could not be sure who had handled the blood samples over the years and whether or not they had been handled correctly. William Mason, the prosecutor in the third Sheppard trial, charged that Dr. Sam Sheppard had killed his wife as their marriage fell apart.

Eight jurors deliberated the case for wrongful imprisonment for three hours. The new jury agreed with the state of Ohio that the case was not proven. On Thursday, April 13, 2000, the jury reported the verdict in the third trial of Dr. Samuel H. Sheppard. It found for the defendant, the state of Ohio, declaring Dr. Sheppard "not innocent" in the murder of his wife Marilyn.

WHO KILLED MARILYN SHEPPARD?

Books continued to be published about the Sheppard murder case as Sam Reese fought to clear his father's name. In 1995, Cynthia L. Cooper and

Sam published *Mockery of Justice: The True Story of the Sheppard Murder Case*. It is written from the family's viewpoint, but comprehensively summarizes the case, with 328 pages of text, twenty-one illustrations, forty pages of endnotes, and a fifteen-page index. In 1996, *Endure and Conquer: My 12-Year Fight for Vindication*, by Dr. Sam Sheppard, was published. Dr. Sam Sheppard's story was written, according to his son, by a ghostwriter with the doctor's notes. It narrated his prison experiences, but did not include endnotes or an index. In April 2000, Bernard F. Conners published *Tailspin: The Strange Case of Major Call*, in which he pinned the Sheppard murder on James Call, an Air Force pilot who in 1954 deserted and launched a nationwide burglary spree. Conners suggested that Call could have murdered Marilyn Sheppard while he was visiting his sister in Ohio.

In 2001, James Neff published his book about the Sheppard case, called *The Wrong Man: The Final Verdict on the Dr. Sam Sheppard Murder Case*. A former *Plain Dealer* reporter, Neff worked on the book for years. In it he pointed out the weaknesses in the case against Sheppard, dismissed the Houks as suspects, and suggested that Eberling was the killer. Neff also identified the key thread in all three trials when he said,

[S]ome of the most compelling evidence in the Sheppard case—DNA test results on blood and semen from the crime scene—had not registered with the jury. Dr. Tahir's lab work showed that sperm from a man other than Dr. Sheppard was in his wife's vagina when she died. But Tahir's heavily accented testimony was "hard to follow," as Judge Suster put it. Furthermore, Terry Gilbert's direct examination of Tahir failed to give the jurors a solid understanding of how DNA worked, said Assistant prosecutor Steve Dever, who was grateful. (p. 281)

Just as in the first trial, confusion and misunderstanding about blood and semen evidence worked in favor of the prosecution, and Dever dismissed Tahir's results as junk science. His position revealed a great irony, since he, as a criminal prosecutor, routinely used DNA test results produced by coroner's office technicians trained by Dr. Tahir to get convictions. The jury in this trial simply dismissed the DNA evidence. Just as in the first trial, the jury ignored forensic evidence that could possibly exonerate Dr. Sheppard.

Eliminating Dr. Sam Sheppard and James Call as possibilities, the writers and scholars of the Sheppard murder case have suggested three strong suspects in Marilyn Sheppard's murder. Despite the civil jury's finding, Richard Eberling remains a strong suspect because of the long string of suspicious deaths connected to him and his conviction for the 1984 murder of Ethel May Durkin. Eberling knew the Sheppard house well, including the basement entrance, which often was left unlocked. The trail of blood down the steps is almost certainly Eberling's. He stole repeatedly over decades and may also have burglarized homes that he knew.

On the other hand, there is no evidence to place Eberling in the house on the morning of the murder, although he did fit the general description of the "bushy haired intruder" that Dr. Sheppard wrestled. There is no evidence that Eberling was ever involved in a sex crime, and he was believed to be homosexual. Dr. Leland Kirk in his extensive analysis of the blood evidence said that the killer was left-handed, while Eberling was right-handed.

James Neff, in his book *The Wrong Man*, concluded that Eberling was the killer. He based his opinion on the same evidence that Pollack uses in *Dr. Sam: An American Tragedy* and on a final interview with a dying and possibly delirious Eberling.

F. Lee Bailey favored the theory that Spencer and Esther Houk separately or together killed their neighbor Marilyn Sheppard, although on superficial examination it seems far-fetched. But suspicion of Mayor Houk goes back to August 1966 when police unceremoniously brought him to the central police station for questioning as a result of a lead that Dr. Steve Sheppard had given the police. Before the second trial, F. Lee Bailey had hinted to reporters that the killer was a left-handed woman and the Houks were his suspects at the second trial. During cross-examination, Bailey brought out that the Houks were famil- iar with the Sheppard home and could get between their house and the Sheppard's house by walking on the beach. He brought out that they had set a fire in their fireplace on a July night when the overnight low was sixty-four degrees. If he had been allowed, Bailey would have called a bakery driver who had seen Houk kissing Marilyn Sheppard to testify.

After Dr. Sheppard's acquittal, Bailey convinced Bay Village police to investigate the evidence against the Houks, but after hearing the evidence the grand jury did not act. Grand jurors doubted that Houk, who walked with a limp, could have been the man who ran from Dr. Sheppard.

In 1982, the owners of the property that had formerly belonged to the Houks found a pair of fireplace tongs buried four to five inches under their back yard. The tongs were nearly two feet long and weighed one and three-quarters pounds. They appeared to match some but not all of the wounds in Marilyn's head, but a metallurgist said that the absence of corrosion indicated that they could not have been buried for twenty-eight years.

Sam Reese Sheppard said that he had a tape of an interview with Spencer Houk made shortly before he died in 1980 that appeared incriminating. He took the accusations seriously enough to lay out two scenarios, one in which Spencer Houk was the killer and one in which it was Esther. He stopped his inquiry into the Houks only when the evidence against Eberling began to mount.

Paul Holmes avoided speculation through most of *The Sheppard Murder Case*, but in the end he suggested a "hypothesis" in which Marilyn was killed with a flashlight by a woman whose husband faked a burglary to cover up for her and inadvertently set up Dr. Sheppard as a suspect. Holmes wrote that no one ever checked their car for bloodstains or tested the ashes in their grate.

Jack Harrison Pollack titled the final chapter of his 1972 book, *Dr. Sam: An American Tragedy*, "The Guilty." In this chapter, he reported that Harold Bretnall, a private detective who worked for the Sheppards, had planned before he died to write a book about the Sheppard murder. In his notes, Bretnall had written, "Marilyn Sheppard was murdered by someone who was a frequent visitor to the Sheppard home." Pollack said, "After carefully ruling out all other possibilities, Bretnall concluded that Marilyn's killers were a woman and a bushy-haired man living in bondage with their awful secret" (Pollack, 1972, pp. 225–235).

Pollack was impressed with Bretnall's findings, and he also concluded that the finger of suspicion still pointed most stubbornly to a couple, a woman and a man. According to Pollack, the gossip of Bay Village seemed to support this theory, especially the word that a tooth chip belonging to neither Marilyn nor Sam was found in the bedroom after the murder and the tooth of one Bay Village resident was reportedly extracted immediately after the crime. Pollack did not document or give a source to these statements.

When the accusations resurfaced in the 1990s, the Houks were both dead, but their grandchildren insisted that their grandparents could never have committed such a horrible crime. They said that Esther was not left-handed as had been often reported, and they said that as Esther lay dying in 1982, she called her daughter to her bedside and asked her to defend her if they accused her of the Sheppard murder (McGunagle, *Crime Library*).

Marilyn Sheppard was the first victim in this fifty-year-old murder case, but her murder irrevocably changed and claimed other lives as well. Other victims included her husband, her mother and father-in-law, her father, and her son. But perhaps the most tragic victim of all is the belief of ordinary citizens in the impartiality of the American judicial system.

REFERENCES

Cleveland News. (1954, July 7).
Cleveland Press. (1954, July 20, 21, 24, 26, 29, 30; August 18; October 9, 23).
Findings of the U.S. Supreme Court: *Sheppard v. Maxwell.* Retrieved from http://www.samreesesheppard.org/shepvsmax.html [The transcript is also available at FindLaw as *Sheppard v. Maxwell* 384 U.S. 333 (1966) http://caselaw.lp.findlaw.com/scripts/getcase.pl?court=us&vol=384&invol=333]

Holmes, P. (1961). *The Sheppard murder case.* New York: McKay.

McGunagle, F. Dr. Sam Sheppard. *Court TV's Crime Library.* Retrieved from http://www.crimelibrary.com/notorious_murders/famous/sheppard/marilyn_18.html?sect=1

Neff, J. (2001). *The wrong man: The final verdict on the Dr. Sam Sheppard murder case.* New York: Random House.

Pollack, J. H. (1972). *Dr. Sam: An American tragedy.* Chicago: Henry Regnery Co.

Seltzer, L. B. (1956). *The years were good.* Cleveland, OH: The World Publishing Co.

Taylor, M. (1996, April 7). *San Francisco Chronicle.*

14

The Emmett Till Murder: The Civil Rights Movement Begins

Marcella Glodek Bush

In the early hours of a Saturday morning in August 1955, two men kidnapped fourteen-year-old Emmett Till from his great-uncle's house near Money, Mississippi. Three days later, Till's tortured, swollen, and decomposing body was found snagged on some tree branches in the Tallahatchie River—one eye gouged out, one side of his forehead crushed, a bullet in his skull, and a seventy-five-pound cotton gin fan tied around his neck. His body was so badly bloated and disfigured that his great-uncle Mose Wright could only identify Till by the initial ring, once his father's, that he wore.

Till was a black adolescent from Chicago, Illinois, the only son of Louis Till and Mamie Carthan. He had suffered from non-paralytic polio since age three, and the effects of the disease left him with a slight stutter. His mother taught him to whistle to aid his fluency. His speech impediment did not make him shy, however. His family and friends described him as an outgoing boy who liked to tell jokes. Till's father was killed while serving in the army in World War II. When the army returned his father's personal effects, the ring bearing the initials LT was included. Emmett Till's mother later married, and divorced, Gene Bradley.

Mrs. Mamie Till-Bradley, Till's mother, was born in Mississippi but moved to Chicago with her parents when she was two years old. Many aunts and uncles still lived in Mississippi, and Emmett and his cousin Curtis Jones planned to visit relatives for two weeks in August 1955. The boys would stay with their great-uncle, Wright, a preacher and a sharecropper who grew cotton. Till was looking forward to seeing his Mississippi cousins again, and his mother was happy that her son could enjoy the countryside after a hot city summer.

On August 20, Mrs. Till took her son to the 63rd Street railroad station in Chicago. Knowing that her son was unskilled in the differences between segregation in the North and segregation in the South, and aware of his impulsive nature and penchant for jokes, she warned him about his behavior while in the South. She advised him not to speak to white people or risk trouble with them, and to be humble if necessary.

MONEY, MISSISSIPPI

In 1955, only fifty-five residents lived in Money, Mississippi, a cotton gin town with a gas station and three stores. On the evening of August 24, Jones and Till drove with several cousins to Bryant's Grocery and Meat Market, which was owned by Roy and Carolyn Bryant. The Bryants had two small sons and eked out their living selling basic necessities to poor black sharecroppers. Poor themselves, the Bryants lived in a room behind the store. The Bryant-Milam family owned a chain of such stores in the Mississippi delta (Huie, 1956).

Till and Jones joined several other black youths who were listening to music and talking on the front porch of Bryant's store. While Jones played checkers with an elderly black man, Till boasted about life in the North, particularly his friendships with white people. When he showed the others a photograph of a white girl that he kept in his wallet, and bragged that she was his girlfriend, the Mississippi youths dared Till to go into the store and flirt with Mrs. Bryant. Till took the dare. Accounts differ about what Till did after he entered the store. After Mrs. Bryant testified at the trial, various newspapers reported that Till said, "Bye baby," "What's the matter baby? Can't you take it?" "You needn't be afraid of me," and "I've been with white women before" (Metress, 2002). Some mentioned that he gave a "wolf whistle" as he was leaving the store, but that was not mentioned in Mrs. Bryant's testimony. If he did whistle, however, he may have been using the whistle to overcome his stuttering. Till's actions shocked the crowd outside the store. The old man playing checkers warned Till about the consequences of his actions and urged him to leave the area. When Mrs. Bryant came outside to get a gun from her brother-in-law's car, Jones, Till, and the cousins jumped into the truck and fled the scene.

Bryant was not alone in the store that evening. When her husband was out-of-town, her sister-in-law Juanita Milam came to the store with her children in the afternoon and stayed until closing: 9 p.m. on weekdays and 11 p.m. on Saturdays. Milam then drove Bryant and her children to the Milam home. In the morning, either Milam or his wife would drive Mrs. Bryant back to the store. Bryant's husband carried a .38 Colt automatic, and Milam kept a .45—a souvenir from World War II. Mississippi law permitted its citizens to carry guns whenever they thought they were in imminent danger. Mrs. Bryant was afraid that evening. She knew that Till was not from the area, and she claimed later that she thought he was a man. Till was five feet, five inches in height and weighed about 160 pounds. Bryant was twenty-one years old and stood five feet tall and weighed 103 pounds.

REPRISAL

Initially, the adolescents kept the incident secret from their great-uncle, but news of Till's actions quickly spread throughout the black community. Till wanted to go back to Chicago and his cousin, Jones, agreed, but the Wright family thought that if he stayed away from Bryant's store, he would be safe. No one in Wright's family thought that Mr. Bryant would come looking for Till—he was only a boy and he was from the North. Three days later, however, when Mr. Bryant returned from a trucking job in Texas, delivering shrimp, he heard about Till's action from the black community. He could not ignore the situation or he would be labeled a fool. He asked his half-brother Milam to meet him early Sunday morning.

In his *Look* magazine article, Huie (1956) detailed the events of Till's kidnapping. Bryant and Milam drove out to Wright's cabin sometime after midnight, demanding to see the boy from Chicago. Wright tried to bargain with the two men in an effort to minimize their anger, and Wright's wife Elizabeth offered to pay them for any trouble that her nephew caused. Wright begged them to just give Till a whipping and pleaded that they not take Till with them. The two men, however, ordered Till to dress and to get into the back of their pickup truck. They ordered Wright not to cause any trouble, and they drove off. Associated Press correspondent Sam Johnson and Global News Network editor Olive Arnold Adams (1956) both state that Wright testified to this kidnapping sequence of events at the trial (Metress, 2002, p. 222).

THE ARRESTS

Wright did not call the police, but Jones informed the Leflore County Sheriff George Smith the next morning that Till was missing. The sheriff questioned Milam and Bryant, who both admitted abducting the adolescent, but reported that they had turned him loose, unharmed, that same night. They were arrested and charged with kidnapping. When Till's body was found three days later, the indictment changed to murder. Because the body was found in Tallahatchie County, that county was ascribed jurisdiction. The two defendants remained, however, in Sheriff Smith's custody until the grand jury convened the following Monday, September 5.

The sheriff wanted to bury the body immediately, stating that because the body was so badly decomposed, identification could not be made. Jones called Mrs. Till to tell her about her son's death and his forthcoming burial in Mississippi. Till's mother wanted her son's body and insisted that it be shipped back to Chicago. The sheriff directed the mortician in Mississippi, however, to sign an order for the coffin to remain unopened.

Initially, no local lawyers agreed to defend Milam and Bryant. Therefore, the state appointed a special prosecutor but gave him no budget or personnel to conduct a probe. The sheriff did not investigate the murder, nor did he help the prosecution prepare its case.

THE MEDIA

When Milam and Bryant were arrested, several Mississippi newspapers reported the story, but when Till's mother's insisted on an open-casket funeral, she brought national attention to her son's murder. During the four days of the viewing at the Rainer Funeral Home in Chicago, thousands of people saw Till's body. Till's photograph gained national attention in newspapers and magazines and mobilized the National Association for the Advancement of Colored People (NAACP). According to media reports, the photograph inflamed both northern and southern audiences, who subsequently denounced the barbarity of segregation in the South and demanded justice in Mississippi in the Till case. When the case became a national event, five prominent Mississippi delta attorneys signed on to the case; they raised $10,000 for the defense fund. *Jet* magazine published an unedited photograph in its September 15 issue of Emmett as he lay in his coffin.

MOUNTING THE TRIAL

In Mississippi, the severe censure from northern press editorials and civil rights groups solidified white public opinion in defense of their society. Influential African American weeklies such as the *Chicago Defender*, the *Baltimore Afro-American*, the *New York Amsterdam News*, and the *Cleveland*

Call and Post denounced southern injustice and promised reprisal if Mississippi failed to provide a fair trial. The National Association of Colored People labeled the crime a "lynching" and, in doing so, received recrimination from southern newspapers. Tom Ethridge, a writer for the *Jackson Daily News,* explained that "lynching" was defined by militant Negro zealots as "any killing involving a colored victim and a white killer" (Metress, 2002). Mississippi Governor Hugh White and others stated that the crime was not a "lynching" but a murder. More than seventy newspapers and magazines sent reporters—including the black press—to the trial. Medgar Evers, the first field secretary for the NAACP, was also present.

Indicted for murder by the grand jury on September 6, Bryant and Milam were taken to Tallahatchie County for arraignment; the sheriff's office held no inquest prior to the trial. Again the accused admitted to kidnapping Till, but insisted that they released Till unharmed. At the time of the trial, Mississippi preserved transcripts of appealed cases only; consequently, no transcript exists of the Bryant and Milam trial. Information, therefore, about court proceedings depends on newspaper and other media accounts as well as personal recollections and interviews.

Circuit Judge Curtis M. Swango presided over the trial and determined that the case would be tried in open court; he ruled that no photographs, sketches, recordings, or broadcasts would be allowed in the courtroom. District Attorney Gerald Chatham served as the prosecuting attorney and was assisted by former FBI Agent Robert B. Smith; five defense attorneys included senior defense attorney J. J. Breland, C. Sidney Carleton, J. W. Kellum, John C. Whitten, and Harvey Henderson. All officers of the court were white.

Jury Selection

Jury selection began on September 19, and it took a day and a half to appoint an all-male, all-white jury from the defendants' county. According to an article published in the African American newspaper the *Chicago Defender,* prospective jurors were dismissed if they had contributed to the defense fund of the defendants, were related to the attorneys or defendants, had formed any definite opinions about the defendants' guilt or innocence, or if they lived in the county where the killing took place (Metress, 2002).

Accounts differ about court attendees, but men outnumbered women and whites outnumbered blacks; the courtroom was segregated with blacks sitting in a corner in the back of the hot, crowded courtroom, and the white press near the judge and jury. The press included local, national, and foreign representatives, and the three existing national television networks also covered the trial, but did not broadcast from the courtroom. The defendants faced the judge with their wives and children (four boys, ages two to four years) next to them each day. Till's mother arrived on the second day of the trial with her father, a cousin from Chicago, and Congressman Charles Diggs from Michigan; both Mrs. Till and Diggs sat at the black press table. Sheriff Strider placed the two defendants under guard and called out the National Guard to support city police because he had received anonymous letters and telephone calls that threatened mob violence. In coverage by the *Jackson Daily News* on September 5, 1955, Strider is quoted as reporting that most of the letters were postmarked from Chicago.

Testimony

The state based its case on identification: the jury would find that both defendants could be identified as Till's assailants, and the identification of the body pulled from the river could be identified as Till's *beyond a reasonable doubt*. The state called six witnesses: Wright; Till's mother; Mrs. Bryant; Chester Miller the undertaker; Levy ("Two-Tight") Collins (a black who allegedly accompanied Bryant and Milam in the kidnapping and murder); Sheriff Strider (who stated that a bullet caused the hole in the deceased's head); and Robert Hodges, the boy who found the body. Mrs. Till testified that she positively identified her son's body and her late husband's ring, and had warned her son about his behavior with white people while visiting his Mississippi relatives. When defense counselor J. J. Breland began questioning her about the newspapers that she read in Chicago, prosecutor Smith objected to that line of questioning, fearing that the photo of Till might be introduced. Judge Swango removed the jury to determine whether the defense's line of questioning was relevant or diversionary. He subsequently deemed it not relevant to the case, and excluded every question and allowed no references to the questions. As a result of the ruling, the defense had to drop Till's mother as a witness.

Prosecutor Chatham's opening statement promised to put the defendants together with Till and in the area where Till's body was found. The NAACP undertook the responsibility to provide a safe place for the trial witnesses that Chatham had ferreted out from their hiding places. Chatham well understood how dangerous it was for blacks to testify against whites in a court of law in Mississippi.

Chatham opened with the prosecution's first witness: Mose Wright, who testified that Milam and Bryant were the two men who had taken his nephew Emmett that night. Chatham's other witnesses, also blacks, testified that they had seen Bryant and Milam at a plantation and had heard screams and cries coming from a shed in the back. They testified also that they unloaded a tarpaulin from that shed and then cleaned the truck used to transport the tarpaulin. After their testimonies, the NAACP secured hiding places for them outside Mississippi.

Cross-Examination

On cross-examination, defense attorney Carlton challenged Wright's identification of Bryant and Milam as the two men who came to his house in the early morning hour of August 28. Wright insisted that he could identify the two accused even though the only light available was a flashlight allegedly held by Milam. Then the judge ruled out Smith's testimony about a conversation with Bryant that placed Bryant at Wright's home and later with Till at his store; the jury was out of the room, however, for that testimony. According to Associated Press correspondent Sam Johnson, the judge ruled that the state must first prove that Till was murdered before an identification of the murderers could be allowed.

The defense next raised the issue about the identification of the body. Leflore County Deputy Sheriff Cothran's testimony suggested that the cotton gin fan might have caused the damage to the body's head. Sheriff Strider testified that the decomposition of the body was more like that of a body that had been in the river ten days, not three, and a Greenwood physician concurred. Strider also testified that a photograph of Till did not match that of the body pulled from the river. Neither defendant took the stand in the trial.

Closing Remarks and the Verdict

The defense attorneys argued that there was no motive for the crime, no positive identification, no reasonable theory, no identification by Bryant of Till, and no positive identification of the body from the river. Defense attorney Kellum appealed to the jury as white men that they should not convict other white men in a black man's killing. Defense attorney Carlton argued that the theory of the crime offered by the prosecution was unreasonable: if the men who came to Wright's house planned to murder Till, why would they identify themselves?

The prosecution appealed to moral and legal issues. District attorney Chatham—a southerner—argued that a whipping, not a killing, would have been the moral thing to do if Till had insulted Bryant. He stressed that Wright, Willie Reed—a black field hand whose testimony placed J. W. Milam and Till together on the morning after the kidnapping—and the others were telling the truth, and he urged the jury to consider the case on its merits—Till's mother identified the body as her son's; several people on the river scene identified the body as a black male.

On the fifth day of the trial, in sixty-seven minutes, the jury returned a verdict of not guilty. One jury member later told a reporter, "It would have been even shorter, but we stopped to drink some pop" (Gado, 2003). Bryant and Milam were free men who, under double jeopardy, could not be tried again for the murder.

THE OUTCOME OF THE TRIAL

The outcome of the trial caused controversy in the media. In the months following the trial, northern white daily newspapers and black weeklies condemned Mississippi for its inability to bring justice in a particularly brutal murder of a youth; some called for federal intervention (Metress, 2002). Others raised questions about what truly happened in the case. Few, if any, focused on the effects that the murder and its subsequent trial had on citizens in the hamlet of Money, Mississippi. Most white southern newspapers tempered their censure of Mississippi and focused blame on the sheriff's lack of investigation in the case, and on the prosecutors who went to trial with flimsy evidence (Metress, 2002). Mississippi media blamed organizations like the NAACP for agitating the situation or decried it as a communist plot to destroy the South's way of life and to display America's racial inequality to the world. Individuals expressed their opinions in letters to newspaper editors, and radio announcers stated their views in on-the-air editorials and on-the-spot coverage of the trial (Metress, 2002; Smith, 2003). Some northerners expressed moral outrage about the verdict as a miscarriage of justice, while others wrote about equal justice out of religious convictions; still others demanded equality for blacks. Some southerners defended southern mores, insisting that white women deserved protection from black men in the South. Individual expressions of feelings included impotence, frustration, revenge, and retaliation. Black commentators expressed anger, but not surprise about the verdict (Metress, 2002).

LOOK MAGAZINE INTERVIEW

In the months following the trial, theories of conspiracy surfaced in the press. In 1956, the two defendants told their story to William Bradford Huie, a *Look* magazine journalist and author, and were paid $4,000—not for their interview, but for a release for their movie rights. During the interview, Milam confessed to the killing and rationalized his reasons for doing so. Milam revealed that at first they planned to scare Till. When they failed, Milam rationalized that "as long as I live and I can do anything about it, niggers are going to stay in their place . . . and when a nigger even gets close to mentioning sex with a white woman, he's tired of livin'" (Metress, 2002). Milam interpreted Till's bravado as arrogance. Till was a troublemaker. He came from the North with money to spend and nicer clothing than his cousins living in the South. He gave blacks in the South ideas about racial equality. Milam decided to make an example of Till. He and Bryant and two black men drove for several hours trying to find a cliff that Milam had discovered when he was duck hunting the year before—a bluff with an impressive 100-foot drop to a canyon below. Milam intended to scare Till by pistol-whipping him, during which he would then shine a flashlight into the canyon with the implication that he would push Till over the cliff. After Milam's failure to locate the cliff in the dark, Milam took him to a shed in back of his house. There, Milam pistol-whipped the boy, and when Emmett still would not humble himself to Bryant and Milam, they wrapped him in a tarpaulin, put him back in the truck, and drove to the Tallahatchie River. At the river, Milam gave Till one last chance to humble himself. When Till did not, Milam ordered him to remove his clothes, made him carry the seventy-five-pound cotton gin fan to the river's edge, and shot Till in the head with his .45 Colt revolver.

Milam and Bryant felt that they had nothing to hide when telling their story. They never thought that they were in legal jeopardy. They assumed that the white community knew what they did and later sanctioned their act by contributing money to their defense fund. In the rural South in 1955, the plantation system still existed. Because blacks were not well educated in the South, they were tied to low-paying jobs, and most were sharecroppers. Milam rented Negro-driven mechanical cotton pickers to plantation owners. He was considered a bully who kept blacks working hard and in their place. In an interview with Milam and Bryant's defense attorney, John C. Whitten, Huie quotes Whitten as saying "that Milam was the killer and Bryant a coat-holder. Milam is older; he won a battlefield commission; he looks like the family leader. . . . He's the overseer type; he works Negroes, lives among them" (Metress, 2002).

The blacks who helped Milam and Bryant on the night of Till's murder did so because their lives and livelihood depended on their support. Neither Milam nor Bryant regretted killing Till, but they understood why the black community shunned them after the trial. They could not understand, though, why the white community shunned them. Journalist Huie wrote in his *Look* magazine article that a Tallahatchie citizen explained the situation to him: "[Y]ou know there's just one thing wrong with encouraging one o' these peckerwoods to kill a nigger. He don't know when to stop—and the rascal may wind up killing you" (Metress, 2002).

AFTER THE TRIAL

The NAACP's field secretary Medgar Evers attended the Till trial and continued to investigate the murder after the trial to ferret out issues not raised at the trial. Other black organizations staged major rallies in the northern cities and in the Midwest. They promoted black marches to both protest the verdict in the Till case and to engender their cause for equality. Looking ahead to an indictment and trial of Bryant and Milam for kidnapping, and the need for black witnesses to testify, black organizations requested defense funds for these witnesses' safety. Bryant and Milam were never indicted on charges of kidnapping, however, even though they had publicly confessed. The state of Mississippi never explained why.

In fear for their lives, Wright's family left Money after the night Bryant and Milam appeared at their home; Wright returned for the trial, but his wife did not. Other blacks who testified include Willie Reed, who placed Bryant and Milam at the plantation shed; and Amanda Bradley, who testified to the beating in the shed. They, too, needed and received assistance to relocate away from Mississippi and the South.

Wright and his family moved to Chicago and never returned to Mississippi. Blacks boycotted Bryant's store, it closed, and the family moved to Texas. Eventually, all the stores that the Bryant-Milam family owned closed also. The Bryants divorced in 1979. Milam tried farming, but blacks refused to work for him, and whites demanded a salary that he could not afford to pay. Eventually, he, too, moved to Texas. Both brothers died of cancer.

Emmett Till's mother became a teacher in Chicago. Sponsored by the NAACP, she lectured throughout the United States about segregation and her son's death. She retired in 1978 and died in 2002 at the age of eighty-one. Her death once again brought Emmett's memory to the public forum. Nearly complete at the time of her death, Mamie Till-Bradley's memoir *Death of Innocence: The Story of the Hate Crime That Changed America* (written with Christopher Benson) has been subsequently published by Random House. Public Broadcasting Service (PBS) aired *The Murder of Emmett Till* on January 20, 2003. Till's death continues to raise issues about racial inequality in America and the lack of federal investigation into the murder.

SOCIAL, POLITICAL, AND LEGAL ISSUES

The U.S. Supreme Court's school decision in *Brown v. Board of Education* on May 17, 1954, opened to the world the social fabric of the southern way of life—a society in which racial segregation permeated all spheres of life. In response to the court ruling, southern states each began a movement of resistance. Mississippi formed the Mississippi Sovereign Committee to prevent federal and judicial interference in the powers of the state government. A new group, the Citizen's Council, formed to control blacks economically by threatening their jobs, credit, and mortgage renewal if they participated in desegregation.

Public Remarks about Segregation in Mississippi

Mississippi Senator James Eastland advised his constituency that "[o]n May 17, 1954, the Constitution of the United States was destroyed because of the Supreme Court's decision" in *Brown v. Board of Education* and admonished them to "not be obliged to obey the decisions of any court which are plainly fraudulent [and based on] sociological considerations" (Williams, 1987, p. 38). Lew Sadler, a white Mississippi radio announcer covering the trial, defended the South's way of life and stressed that blacks and whites mingled daily without ramifications in Mississippi. He said, "the only line we draw is at the door of our schools" (Metress, 2002).

Election Year Efforts for Voting Registration

In contrast, while blacks in the North also faced discrimination and segregation, they had access to the voting ballot and entry-level jobs in the city government. In the summer of 1955, the executive secretary of the NAACP, Roy Wilkins, addressed an audience on the city of Chicago's "Salute to Negroes in Government" day. In the North, blacks were moving against the apartheid of American history.

The South feared and subdued any efforts to mobilize the black vote—by lynching if necessary. Just prior to Till's arrival, two black men were killed in Mississippi: Lamar Smith, an NAACP activist, and the Reverend George W. Lee, both solicitors of black voting registration. In Tallahatchie County in 1955, more than half of the residents were blacks, but none were registered voters. Therefore, none of them could serve on the Bryant-Milam trial jury. Milam, in his interview with Huie, asserted, "Niggers ain't gonna vote where I live! If they did, they'd control the government" (Metress, 2002).

Political and Social Overtones at the Trial

The media crush that descended on Tallahatchie County soon recognized the political and social scene of the South. Sheriff Strider had segregated black and white reporters and photographers, and audibly announced to the assembled courtroom audience, "We haven't mixed so far down here and we don't intend to" (Metress, 2002). He acknowledged black reporters by saying, "Hello, niggers" (Metress, 2002). Another deputy sheriff also audibly expressed his opinion in the courtroom about the political position of Charles C. Diggs, a U.S. congressman, when Diggs requested seating in the courtroom. "What?" he asked. "A nigger Congressman?" (Williams, 2002, p. 51).

In his closing remarks, District Attorney Smith moved for a justice that protected the rights of both black and whites. He stated that "Emmett Till down here in Mississippi was a citizen of the United States; he was entitled to his life and his liberty" (Metress, 2002). Defense attorney Kellum, however, used his summation to continue prevailing southern tradition. He declared, "I want you to tell me where under God's shining sun, is the land of the free and the home of the brave if you don't turn these boys loose; your forefathers will absolutely turn over in their graves" (Williams, 2002, p. 52).

National-Level Observations

Both Mississippi writer William Faulkner and former first lady Eleanor Roosevelt mirrored Smith's concern for justice, especially since as a nation, American democracy must uphold justice. But President Eisenhower made no official statement about the Till murder and subsequent trial outcome. In a letter to Attorney General Herbert Brownell and FBI Director J. Edgar Hoover, James L. Hicks drew a blueprint for justice in the Till case. Hicks, an investigative reporter, had the credentials to warrant their interest. He served as bureau chief for the NAACP and, in 1955, became the executive director of the *New York Amsterdam News*. He was the first black member of the state department's correspondence association and the first black reporter to cover the United Nations. Newspapers throughout the United States ran his coverage of the trial.

In the letter to Brownell and Hoover, Hicks appealed for a federal investigation of the trial based on his charge of witness tampering. In minute detail, Hicks described how the sheriff's office prevented witnesses from testifying, named witnesses who knew details of the case not brought out at trial, and named accomplices to the murder, along with their locations. Neither the attorney general nor the FBI offices responded.

Social Effects of the Trial in Mississippi

A small group of Mississippi citizens pulled Emmett Till's body from the Tallahatchie River and tried to bury it, both literally and figuratively, in Mississippi's consciousness and soil. Till's mother, however, determined that the world would be witness to the fate that her only son, fourteen years old, endured in a South that alienated, segregated, and discriminated against blacks. While the world saw the injustice of the South, the black citizens of the delta saw black witnesses testifying against white citizens—the beginning of the mobilization of the black response to their lack of basic legal, social, and political rights. The civil rights movement, sparked by the death of Till, would bring political, legal, and social upheaval in a time of unprecedented economic prosperity in America. Television would be the new medium to bring these events into the American living room.

Although television shows in the 1950s emphasized traditional white family roles and society's conformity, young people were becoming aware of the increasing integration of black and white cultures in America, especially in music. While conformity and complacency defined Americans in the 1950s, Americans were socially challenged by a rebellious youth culture, the Beat Generation, and the decisive civil rights struggle.

THE TRIAL IN LEGAL AND POPULAR CULTURE

The train traveling to Mississippi on August 20 conveyed Till and Jones to a society that had developed a Jim Crow legal system after the Civil War—a system that treated blacks as inferior to whites. Jim Crow laws violated blacks' civil rights despite the 1868 constitution of Mississippi, which guaranteed in its bill of rights that "[a]ll persons resident in this State, citizens of the United States, are hereby declared citizens of the State of Mississippi" (1868 Constitution of the State of Mississippi, p. 1). Under the U.S. Supreme Court ruling of the 1896 *Plessy v. Ferguson* "separate but equal" doctrine, blacks could be legally segregated as long as equal accommodations were provided for them; thus, blacks were segregated from public parks, buildings, and classrooms. Blacks could vote but had to pass a literacy test in order to do so. Most could not pass the literacy test because they were segregated from the white school system. Blacks were also fixed to a limited economic position that reduced them to segregated, inferior public accommodations and low-quality housing. Blacks drank from separate water fountains and could not use public toilets. They could not enter a white person's house through the front door, and they had to step aside when a white person passed them on the street. A black man had to remove his hat and bow his head when spoken to by a white person. Businesses and restaurants refused to serve blacks or provided separate counters away from white customers. Blacks could not rent or purchase homes in white neighborhoods. Whites in Mississippi, therefore, did not fear public opinion or punishment when white supremacists felt it necessary to punish black transgressions, because white supremacists controlled the court system and legislature.

Till violated the most sacrosanct category of black behavior toward whites: he did not show respect to a white woman. In the *Look* magazine interview, Milam claimed that he and Bryant only wanted to scare Till, but Till refused to acknowledge his transgression against Bryant's wife, and he would not even beg for mercy. Operating within a supremacist mindset, the men felt that they had no other choice but to kill Till. An all-male, all-white-supremacist court of law justified their action when they voiced the words *not guilty.*

Southern Violence, National Involvement

Emmett Till returned to Chicago by train—not as the young man returning home from a visit to relatives in the South—but as a body in a wooden casket bearing an order to remain sealed. His mother's insistence to open that casket at the railroad station in Chicago sparked the civil rights movement, and when *Jet* magazine released the photograph of Till's body, it spotlighted the violence that blacks in the South suffered. Till's death focused national attention on American racial inequality that ultimately led to the passage of the Civil Rights Act in 1964 and the Voting Rights Act in 1965. The civil rights movement also elevated black consciousness and racial pride.

Popular Culture

Till's murder inspired numerous songs, poems, essays, and novels by both famous artists and amateurs, who submitted their entries to local newspapers. Popular songwriters Bob Dylan and Pete Seeger, poet Langston Hughes, authors Toni Morrison and Lewis Nordan, and actors and producers Ossie Davis and Ruby Dee are among the famous artists who memorialized Emmett Till. Amateur writers and poets submitted their works primarily to local newspapers. The realities of the case may have been misconstrued in some works, but their primary focus portrays injustice. We do not know exactly what Till said or exactly how he reacted to Milam and Bryant during his ordeal, but the literary response was "bravery," and his bravery helped raise black consciousness. Some contend that Till was a murder victim and should not be called the sacrificial lamb of the civil rights movement. Till's mother, however, made the nation look at her son and face how he was killed. The media's coverage of Till's murder increased civil rights organizations' membership, and the civil rights movement attracted young people who began to peacefully boycott buses and march for equality. According to Christopher Metress (2002), editor of *The Lynching of Emmett Till*, the lack of a trial transcript and the proliferation of materials about Till enables the reader to appreciate how people grappled with the issues of the murder and trial in 1955, and allows us to continue the process today.

REFERENCES

Bolden, T. (2002). *Tell all the children our story: Memories and mementoes of being young and black in America.* New York: Henry A. Abrams.

Crow, C. (2003, Summer). The lynching of Emmett Till. *The History of Jim Crow.* Retrieved September 3, 2003, from http://www.jimcrowhistory.org/resources/lessonplans/hs_es_emmett_till.htm

Crowe, C. (2002). *Mississippi trial, 1955.* New York: Phyllis Fogelman Books.

Gado, M. (2003). Mississippi madness: The story of Emmett Till. *Court TV's Crime Library.* Retrieved September 10, 2003, from http://www.crimelibrary.com/notorious_murders/famous/emmett_till/index.html?sect=7

Henry, H. (Director). (1987). *Eyes on the prize: Awakenings (1954–1956)* (Videocassette). Blackside.

Huie, W. B. (1956, January). The shocking story of approved killing in Mississippi. *Look.* Retrieved September 10, 2003, from http://www.pbs.org/wgbh/amex/till/sfeature/sf_look.html

Johnson, S. (1955, September 21). Wright's testimony. Greenwood Commonwealth. 1868 constitution of the state of Mississippi. (2002–2003). *Mississippi History Now.* Retrieved September 3, 2003, from http://mshistory.k12.ms.us/features/feature8/1868_state_constitution.html

Metress, C., (Ed.). (2002). *The lynching of Emmett Till: A documentary narrative.* Charlottesville, VA: University of Virginia Press. Retrieved September 10, 2003, from http://archipelago.org/vol6-1/hicks.htm

Smith, M. A. (2003). The murder of Emmett Till: The film and more. WGBH Foundation: Public Broadcasting Service. Retrieved September 3, 2003, from http://www.pbs.org/wgbh/amex/till/sfeature/sf_look_letters.html

Tuttle, K. (2003). Jim Crow. *Encarta Africana.* Retrieved September 3, 2003, from http://www.africana.com/research/encarta/tt_026.asp

Williams, J. (1987). *Eyes on the prize: America's civil rights years, 1954–1965.* New York: Viking.

Index

About the Editors and
the Contributors

FRANKIE Y. BAILEY is Associate Professor at the State University of New York, Albany. With Steven Chermak, she is co-editor of *Media Representations of September 11* (Praeger, 2003) and *Popular Culture, Crime, and Justice* (1998). She is author of *Out of the Woodpile: Black Characters in Crime and Detective Fiction* (Greenwood, 1991), which was nominated for the Mystery Writers of America 1992 Edgar Award for Criticism and Biography, and *"Law Never Here": A Social History of African American Responses to Issues of Crime and Justice* (Praeger, 1999).

STEVEN CHERMAK is Associate Professor and Director of Graduate Affairs in the Department of Criminal Justice at Indiana University. He is the author of *Searching for a Demon: The Media Construction of the Militia Movement* (2002) and *Victims in the News: Crime and the American News Media* (1995).

JAMES R. ACKER is Professor at the School of Criminal Justice, University at Albany (SUNY). Acker has authored numerous scholarly articles and is co-author or co-editor of several books including *Two Voices on the Legal Rights of America's Youth*; *Criminal Procedure: A Contemporary Perspective*, 2nd ed.; and *America's Experiment with Capital Punishment: Reflections on the Past, Present, and Future of the Ultimate Penal Sanction*, 2nd ed.

SEAN E. ANDERSON is Assistant Professor of Criminal Justice at Monmouth University. He is the co-founder, with Gregory J. Howard, of the *Journal of Criminal Justice and Popular Culture.*

LEANA ALLEN BOUFFARD is Assistant Professor at the Department of Criminal Justice and Political Science, North Dakota State University. She is the author of several scholarly articles including "The Military as a 'Bridging Environment': Differential Outcomes of the Military Experience" (*Armed Forces & Society*, 2004); and "Examining the Relationship between Military Service and Criminal Behavior during the Vietnam-Era" (*Criminology*, 2003).

ELIZABETH K. BROWN is a Ph.D. student at the School of Criminal Justice, University at Albany (SUNY).

MARCELLA GLODEK BUSH is Research Associate at the Research Initiative for Teaching Effectiveness, University of Central Florida.

BRENDAN J. BUTTIMER is a Ph.D. candidate of History, Mississippi State University.

CHRISTINE M. ENGLEBRECHT is a Ph.D. student at the School of Criminal Justice, University at Albany (SUNY).

MARK GADO is a Police Detective in New Rochelle, NY, and has worked as a federal agent with the DEA. He is a writer for *Court TV's Crime Library* and an author of many criminal justice and historical crime articles in *Law Enforcement Journal*; and he has written several cover stories for *Strange Days* magazine, *Cobblestone, A History Magazine for Young People,* and *Crimemagazine.com.*

ERNEST L. NICKELS is a Ph.D. student and Instructor at the Department of Criminal Justice, Indiana University–Bloomington.

SHEILA O'HARE is Social Sciences Bibliographer at the University of California, Santa Cruz. She is the author of the forthcoming book *Legal Executions in California, 1851–Present: A Comprehensive Reference.*

MATTHEW PATE is a graduate of the Department of Criminal Justice, University of Arkansas at Little Rock.

DIANA PROPER is a Ph.D. student at the School of Criminal Justice, University at Albany (SUNY).

LISA N. SACCO is a Ph.D. student at the School of Criminal Justice, University at Albany (SUNY) and Assistant Editor at the *Sourcebook of Criminal Justice Statistics.*

JOE WALKER is President of the Southern California Crime and Intelligence Analysts Association.

KATHY WARNES is a journalist/historian and a Ph.D. candidate at the University of Toledo. Publications include local history books, journal articles, and fiction.

KELLY WOLF is a Ph.D. student at the Department of Criminal Justice and Political Science, North Dakota State University.